Roman Architecture

Oxford History of Art

Titles in the *Oxford History of Art* series are up-to-date, fully illustrated introductions to a wide variety of subjects written by leading experts in their field. They will appear regularly, building into an interlocking and comprehensive series. In the list below, published titles appear in bold.

Oxford History of Art

Roman Architecture

Janet DeLaine

OXFORD
UNIVERSITY PRESS

Great Clarendon Street, Oxford, OX2 6DP,
United Kingdom

Oxford University Press is a department of the University of Oxford.
It furthers the University's objective of excellence in research, scholarship,
and education by publishing worldwide. Oxford is a registered trade mark of
Oxford University Press in the UK and in certain other countries

Published in the United States of America by Oxford University Press
198 Madison Avenue, New York, NY 10016, United States of America

British Library Cataloguing in Publication Data
Data available

Library of Congress Control Number: 2022952000

ISBN 978–0–19–284212–1

Printed in the UK by
Bell & Bain Ltd., Glasgow

In memory of Amanda Claridge
1949–2022

Acknowledgements

The ideas expressed in this book have developed over many years, during which I have taught at two institutions—the University of Reading and the University of Oxford—and spent much (but never enough) time at my third intellectual home, the British School at Rome. I am indebted to all three institutions, in particular to the Fell Fund of the University of Oxford which allowed me to be released from teaching at a critical moment, and to Valerie Scott and her team in the library at the BSR, which has provided me with both the calm space and the material resources to carry out my research. Above all I owe much to the many students at all levels on whom I have tried out my ideas and who have given me fresh insights, and in particular my Masters students in the City of Rome at Reading and in Roman Architecture at Oxford, who together with my doctoral students have been crucial in taking me out of my comfort zone and making me think about topics that, left to myself, I might not have ever addressed.

Over the years many friends and colleagues have provided me with information and images, shown me their sites, or shared ideas which have contributed to the writing of this book. In particular I would like to thank Carla Amici, James Andrews, Evelyne Bukowiecki, the late Amanda Claridge, Stefano Camporeale, Giuseppe Ceraudo, the late Jim Coulton, Serafino Cuomo, Penny Davies, Francesco de Angelis, Hazel Dodge, Nathan Elkins, Clayton Fant, the late Sheila Gibson, Kathy Gleason, Kutalmış Görkay, Fred Hirt, John Hopkins, John Humphrey, Mark Wilson Jones, Lynne Lancaster, Ray Laurence, the late Judith McKenzie, Giangiacomo Martines, Dominik Maschek, Maura Medri, Antonio Pizzo, Bettina Reitz, Ben Russell, Natascha Sojc, Phil Stinson, Monica Trümper, Paolo Vitti, Rita Volpe, Susan Walker, Kate Welch, and the late Ulrike Wulf-Rheidt. I owe a particular debt of gratitude to Katherine Dunbabin, Niccolò Mugnai, and Charlotte Potts for their meticulous reading of the whole manuscript, saving me from numerous errors and greatly improving the overall structure. I am equally grateful to Jo Berry, Dirk Booms, Beth Munro, Leah Bernardo-Ciddio, and Konogan Beaufay who acted as research assistants at key times, and to the latter and Luka Pajovic for preparing some of the illustrations.

My gratitude is also due to my editors at OUP, who kept faith with me over the many delays. Finally, my thanks are due above all to my partner David Wilkinson, whose unfailing belief in the project gave me the confidence finally to complete it.

Dorchester on Thames

June 2020

Contents

Abbreviations

AGRW	R.S. Ascough, P.A. Harland, and J.S. Kloppenborg, *Associations in the Greco-Roman World: A Sourcebook* (Berlin and Waco, 2012).
AJA	*American Journal of Archaeology*
ARID	*Analecta Romana Instituti Danici*
AntAfr	*Antiquitiés africaines*
ArchCl	*Archeologia classica*
BABesch	*Bulletin antieke beschaving. Annual Papers on Classical Archaeology*
BollArch	*Bollettino di Archeologia*
BullCom	*Bullettino della Commissione Archeologica Comunale di Roma*
CIL	*Corpus Inscriptionum Latinarum, Consilio et Auctoritate Academiae Litterarum Regiae Borussicae Editum* (Berlin, 1863–1974).
CuadArquitRom	*Cuadernos de arquitectura romana*
GRA	J.S. Kloppenborg, P.A. Harland, and R.S. Ascough, *Greco-Roman Associations: Texts, Translations, and Commentary* (Berlin and New York, 2011–20).
ILS	H. Dessau, *Inscriptiones latinae selectae*, 3 vols (Berlin, 1892–1916).
IMilet	Th. Wiegend, G. Kawerau, A.Rehm, and P. Herrmann, *Milet: Ergebnisse der Ausgrabungen und Untersuchungen seit dem Jahre 1899* (Berlin, 1889–1997).
JDAI	*Jahrbuch des Deutschen Archäologischen Instituts*
JRA	*Journal of Roman Archaeology*
JRS	*Journal of Roman Studies*
JSAH	*Journal of the Society of Architectural Historians*
Latomus	*Latomus. Revue d'études latines*
LTUR	E.M. Steinby (ed.) *Lexicon topographicum urbis Roma* (Rome, 1993–99).
MAAR	*Memoirs of the American Academy in Rome*
MEFRA	*Mélanges de l'École française de Rome. Antiquité*
Omni	*Revista Numismática OMNI*
Pallas	*Pallas. Revue d'études antiques*
PBSR	*Papers of the British School at Rome*

PHI   *Packard Humanities Institute numbers for Greek inscriptions*
       <http://epigraphy.packhum.org/inscriptions/>
RM   *Mitteilungen des Deutschen Archäologischen Instituts, Römische*
       Abteilung
ScA   *Scienze dell'Antichita: Storia, archeologia, antropologia*
WA   *World Archaeology*
ZPE   *Zeitschrift für Papyrologie und Epigraphik*

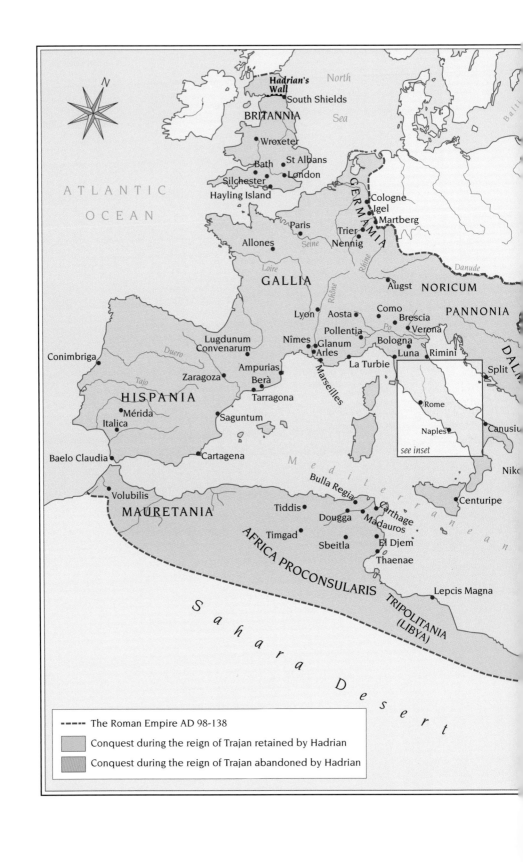

N

North
Sea

Hadrian's
Wall
South Shields
BRITANNIA

Wroxeter

Bath St Albans
Silchester London
Hayling Island

ATLANTIC

OCEAN

Cologne
Igel
Martberg
Trier
Paris
Allones Seine Nennig

GERMANIA

Loire

GALLIA
Augst NORICUM

Rhône

Lyon Aosta Como
Brescia
Pollentia Verona
Lugdunum Nîmes Glanum Bologna
Convenarum Arles Luna Rimini
Conimbriga Duero Ampurias La Turbie
Berà
Zaragoza Tarragona
HISPANIA
Mérida Saguntum
Italica
Baelo Claudia Cartagena

PANNONIA

Po

DAL

Split

Rome

Naples Canusiu

see inset

M e d i t e r r a n e a n

Niko

Bulla Regia
Carthage Centuripe
Tiddis Dougga
Madauros
MAURETANIA
Volubilis Timgad
Sbeitla El Djem
Thaenae

AFRICA PROCONSULARIS TRIPOLITANIA (LIBYA)

Lepcis Magna

S a h a r a   D e s e r t

- - - - The Roman Empire AD 98–138

Conquest during the reign of Trajan retained by Hadrian

Conquest during the reign of Trajan abandoned by Hadrian

Rhine
Danube
Marseilles
Tajo

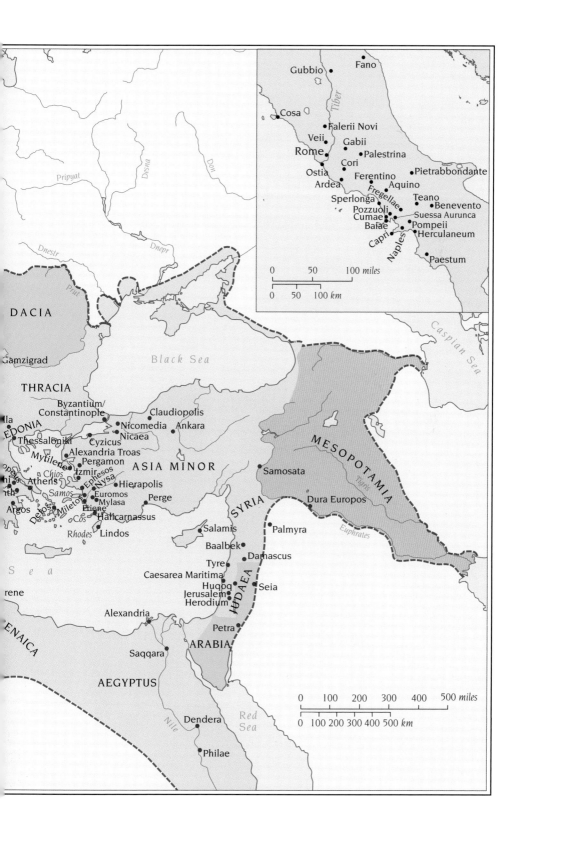

Gubbio
Fano
Cosa
Tiber
Falerii Novi
Veii
Gabii
Rome
Palestrina
Cori
Ostia
Ferentino
Pietrabbondante
Ardea
Aquino
Fregellae
Teano
Sperlonga
Benevento
Pozzuoli
Suessa Aurunca
Cumae
Bafae
Pompeii
Capri
Herculaneum
Naples
Paestum

0   50   100 miles
0   50   100 km

DACIA

Pripyat
Desna
Don
Dnestr
Dnepr
Prut

Gamzigrad
Black Sea
Caspian Sea

THRACIA
Byzantium/
Constantinople
Claudiopolis
EDONIA
Nicomedia
Ankara
Thessaloniki
Cyzicus
Nicaea
Mytilene
Alexandria Troas
Pergamon
MESOPOTAMIA
Izmir
ASIA MINOR
Chios
Ephesos
Nysa
Samosata
Athens
Samos
Euromos
Hierapolis
Miletos
Mylasa
Perge
Tigris
Argos
Delos
Piiene
Dura Europos
Cos
Halicarnassus
SYRIA
Rhodes
Lindos
Salamis
Palmyra
Euphrates
Baalbek
Sea
Tyre
Damascus
Caesarea Maritima
Huqoq
rene
Jerusalem
Seia
Herodium
JUDAEA
Alexandria
Petra
ENAICA
ARABIA
Saqqara
AEGYPTUS

0   100   200   300   400   500 miles
0   100 200 300 400 500 km

Nile
Dendera
Red
Sea
Philae

Introduction

Architecture was fundamental to Roman culture—a culture which was essentially urban in nature, a culture of cities which found expression in, and was structured by, the built environment. The act of building was almost entirely the privilege of the political and economic elites, either as individuals or collectively, and much architecture was specifically a political creation. But while building was the prerogative of a dominant class, the resultant structures shaped the experiences and perceptions of all who used them, or only saw them from afar. The Roman world was highly visual, and its buildings provided the framework for all of life. Nowhere is this clearer than the way in which orators relied on memorized spatial relationships, connected in the mind's eye to specific places in a house, in order to establish order and recall content by journeying through them. The Roman advocate Quintilian, writing in the later first century CE, gives the most detailed account, basing his explanation on 'a spacious house divided into a number of rooms', but also adds, 'what I have spoken of as being done in a house, can equally well be done in connection with public buildings, a long journey, the ramparts of a city…'.[1] In this book, as in the Roman world, the built environment will provide the experiential context for understanding Roman society.

So important are the physical remains of Roman buildings that even today, some 2,000 years later, many still condition the way we experience our own environment, both urban and rural, from the Pantheon or the Flavian Amphitheatre (the Colosseum) in Rome to Hadrian's Wall or the aqueduct bridge of the Pont du Gard. These four structures are as symbolic of the world of Rome as they are in their different ways representative of Roman architecture. Yet none are without ambiguity, and they serve also to remind us of the difficulty of finding any simple definition of 'Roman'. The Pantheon, as both temple and imperial audience hall, reflects the fundamental role of religion in Roman life, and the intimate relationship between religion and politics. The form of the Pantheon, however, is ambivalent, the entrance porch with its tall columns and triangular gable [2] owing much to Greek temple forms, like that of the Parthenon in Athens, while the circular domed interior [3] is a thoroughly Roman creation relying on the skill of Roman engineers working in concrete.

On the other hand, the giant ellipse of the Flavian Amphitheatre [4], with its tiered arcades, is a uniquely Roman architectural form for a uniquely Roman function; yet here too the Roman arches are dressed up with Greek-style columns [1].

Fig. 1

The Flavian Amphitheatre (Colosseum), Rome, c. 70–80 CE. The exterior shows the typical Roman combination of arch and column.

I

Fig. 2

The Pantheon, Rome,
c. 110–125 CE. The exterior
combines a typical temple
façade of columns and
triangular pediment, while
the circular domed rotunda
can only be experienced
from the inside.

The shape and organization of the amphitheatre and its function as a focus of secular entertainment for the people of Rome encourage us to think of it as a football stadium, its nearest modern equivalent; but this is to fail completely to recognize the otherness of the Roman world, in which the afternoon's entertainment was enjoyed amid the blood and smell of death.

If the Pantheon and Flavian Amphitheatre represent the heart and core of the Roman empire, then Hadrian's Wall embodies the extent and might of that empire [5]. On one level the Wall had a simple military function: to defend Roman territory against threats from those outside. Yet the Wall was also the boundary of that territory, set almost at one end of the known world and manned in part by Syrian archers brought from the other. As such, it was also a symbolic gesture, an alien intruder set into a cleared agricultural landscape, its visibility a large part of its power.

The Pont du Gard, the great bridge carrying the 50-kilometre aqueduct serving the Roman city of Nemausus (modern Nîmes) over the river Gardon, also represents Roman power, but power over nature [6]. For many, the Romans' fame as builders rests with their great engineering works such as the aqueducts, roads, and sewers, utilitarian structures devised for the benefit of the people. The bridges and the long substructures which carry the aqueduct channels over the countryside invariably used that most quint-essentially Roman form, the arch, technically sophisticated but also strongly symbolic, the form of city gates and triumphal monuments recording Roman military power [7].

By these great engineering works, nature itself was transformed: hills levelled and valleys raised, land carried across water, and water made to run high above land. No wonder that Dionysius of Halicarnassus, a Greek scholar writing at the end of the first century BCE, believed that 'the three most magnificent works of Rome, in which the greatness of empire is best seen, are the aqueducts, the paved roads and the construction of sewers'.[2]

All these four structures belong to the high watermark of the Roman empire, which is defined chronologically as the period which starts with the rule of Augustus, its first emperor. Geographically, however, the Roman empire was the area under the hegemony of Rome. Until the middle of the third century BCE this was confined to Italy, yet, by the time the Pont du Gard was built 250 years later, it had grown to encompass the whole Mediterranean basin and beyond, reaching finally to the Rhine and the Danube, the Euphrates, the Sahara, and northern Britain. The ambiguity of the expression 'the Roman empire' is symptomatic of the problems we have in defining 'Roman'. The Roman world was not a static, fixed entity; nor was it uniform. While in a narrow legal sense a 'Roman' was a citizen of Rome, and at its most fundamental 'Roman' architecture can be defined as the architecture of the city of Rome, these two definitions do not in any way encompass all the individuals who might have thought of themselves as Roman or all the buildings in the Roman empire which might be classified as Roman. As early as the middle of the second century BCE there were Romans from Italy settled in Spain alongside Greeks, Punic colonists from Carthage in North Africa, and the native Iberians, all of whom within a century or two could be classed as 'Roman'. Likewise, much of the architecture

took its inspiration from the city of Rome, but used local materials and drew on local traditions of craftsmanship; other buildings, however, had a predominantly local heritage. These dichotomies of city and empire, familiarity and otherness, Roman and native, global and local cultures, and the way in which architecture helped to define being 'Roman' at different times and in different places of the empire, will be a recurrent theme of this book.[3]

It is almost impossible for us to imagine the amount of building which was carried out in the long years of Roman power, a period equal to that from the early Middle Ages to the present day, and over the whole of an empire almost the size of the USA. Although only a very small proportion of what once existed remains in the archaeological record, we still count the amphitheatres in their hundreds and the baths in their thousands. There were more types of building fulfilling more different functions than at any time before the mid-nineteenth century, bringing with them the kind of endless variation we normally associate with the Victorian period. Given the scale and range of the phenomenon, is not possible to write a comprehensive overview which does justice to all the evidence in the small span of this book. Nor is this its purpose. It is not intended to be a manual or a handbook, but rather explores the relationship between architecture and Roman society: the who and why, not just the what and when. To do this, we need to look not only at what was built but also at how architecture was

Fig. 5

Hadrian's Wall, near
Housesteads,
Northumberland,
c. 122–126 CE. The wall,
originally partly of stone
and partly of turf, was 80
Roman miles (c. 117 km)
long and more than
4 metres high, incorporating
80 milecastles (fortlets)
and 158 turrets, supported
by 16 forts.

represented in text and image. The treatment is therefore deliberately select-
ive and personal. Although the approach is generally thematic, in the chapters dealing with building types an attempt has been made to give a
chronological structure to some of the material. While some mention will
be made of buildings beyond the third century CE, particularly where continuity is clear, no attempt will be made to deal with the changing conditions
and new building types of what we call late antiquity.

It is important to understand the limitations of the evidence for understanding Roman architecture. Most Roman architectural remains come
from urban sites, but none of them survive intact—even Pompeii was not in
fact 'frozen in time'. Rather, as we see it today, Pompeii is the result of a
series of intrusive actions, starting with the earthquakes leading up to the
eruption of 79 CE and including Roman salvage, the treasure-hunting of the
eighteenth century, and changing practices in conservation and restoration.
In the rest of the empire, the geo-political histories of Roman sites in the
western European provinces have meant that many continue to be important urban centres, so that only isolated and random fragments of Roman
buildings survive in view or have been recovered from deep excavations.
Rather more remains in the eastern empire and North Africa, although
many abandoned urban sites were robbed for their valuable building materials. The degree of excavation and publication has often depended on
regional political histories and on attitudes to the Roman past; until quite
recently, many European regimes privileged the Roman period as a legitimation of their own empires, giving preference to public buildings or grand
houses and country villas as representative of 'the grandeur that was Rome'

and the ones most likely to provide portable works of art to fill European museums, ignoring the local and the everyday.

The city of Rome presents a particular problem. Not only has it a continuous history of urban settlement over some 1,400 years since the end of antiquity, its buildings being constantly cannibalized to source the next phase of development, but it had almost as long a history in antiquity where similar processes were at work. The early history of Roman architecture is therefore very deeply buried, fragmentary and poorly preserved, destroyed through fire and flood or demolished to make way for grander structures in more permanent materials. This is particularly critical for understanding the third and second centuries BCE, when many of what we recognize as the key Roman building types developed. Most of what we know about them comes from the written sources, themselves not earlier than the end of the third century BCE and most Augustan or later in date. These give us the names of buildings, often their dates of construction, sometimes the political circumstances, and occasionally a glimpse of how they functioned—but almost never any details of their actual architecture. Rather, we rely on the relatively better-preserved structures in mid-Republican cities in Roman Italy to piece together the development of these key buildings, an exercise which has its own problems, since it is not at all clear that these were in fact the replicas of buildings in Rome they have often been assumed to be.

In addition, complete and intact buildings are extremely rare, even the Pantheon having been subject to restoration; nor is it always easy to detect what is original and what reconstruction. Understandably, large monumental

Fig. 7

Arch of Septimius Severus, Roman Forum, dedicated 203 CE. This triumphal monument erected by the Senate of Rome celebrates the emperor's victory over the Parthians. The pedestals under the columns are decorated with relief sculpture of conquered barbarians, while the main panels show narrative scenes from the campaigns.

structures such as amphitheatres tend to survive better than small buildings, but even then only ever partially, and very few Roman structures did not go through some kind of modifications during the course of what were generally very long lives. This makes much of the physical evidence for Roman architecture less accessible to non-specialists than its ubiquity would suppose. Quite often, we can deal only with plans reconstructed on partial and uncertain evidence, or with isolated blocks of architectural ornament from which whole orders have to be reconstituted. Almost never does the surface decoration, which was an essential element of the Roman architectural aesthetic, survive intact and *in situ*. Reconstructions, traditionally as architectural exercises on paper and increasingly as three-dimensional computer graphics, are invaluable for helping reconstitute the fragments but bring with them the danger of becoming fixed as somehow true, despite the fact that they inevitably involve some degree of educated guesswork. The reader is therefore advised to take the reconstructions employed here as, at best, indicative.

An Empire of Cities

1

You have made a city from what was once the world.
Rutilius Namatianus, *On His Return*, l. 66 (c. 416 CE)

In the autumn of 416 CE, Rutilius Namatianus, urban prefect in charge of the city of Rome just two years previously, left the city for his native Gaul. At the start of the long poem he wrote about the voyage, he eulogized the city of Rome, counting among its glories its temples and aqueducts, baths and gardens. By then, the Pantheon [2, 3] and the Flavian Amphitheatre [1, 4], already as much tourist attractions in the ancient world as they are now, had come to symbolize the greatness of the city; the Pantheon was described by one awestruck visitor of the time as being 'round as a whole city district', the Flavian Amphitheatre as towering 'so high that human sight could scarcely see the top'.[1]

Their enormous size made them wonders in a city of wonders, reflecting the power the idea of Rome had even after it had ceased to be the capital of the Roman world. Yet for Rutilius, 'Rome' was also an empire and a whole civilization, one of the few that took its name from a city rather than a race or a larger geographical unit, echoing the oration in praise of Rome by Aelius Aristides nearly two centuries earlier.[2] The aqueducts Rutilius admired in Rome, while essentially urban structures, also represent the tentacular extension of the city into the countryside, a highly visible demonstration of control over territory. Even Hadrian's Wall [5], with its gates and towers and once covered in gleaming white plaster to imitate stone,[3] is essentially an urban form, like the city walls which defined the formal boundaries of so many Roman towns, separating civilization and the rule of law within from the wildness of nature without. The city was the heart of empire.

The City of Rome

As far as we can tell, Rome began to emerge as a cohesive settlement by the river Tiber sometime in the eighth century BCE, part of a dramatic trend towards a common urban culture which involved many of the diverse peoples of the Mediterranean littoral and in which the peoples of Greece and the Levant played a crucial role. The basic model, which appeared simultaneously in centres such as Rome, Athens, and Carthage, was that of an urban centre providing the focus of political, religious, and social activity, and a land-based territory around it. Many of the myths and legends of early Rome, such as the story of Romulus and Remus, are concerned with its foundations as a city under divine patronage, and with its evolution from

Fig. 8

Timgad, Algeria, aerial view showing Arch of Trajan as symbolic gateway to the city, with the theatre and forum behind.

the rule of kings to the rule of the people, the Roman Republic. These stories, closely tied to the physical topography of the city, gave the inhabitants of Rome a strong sense of place which lasted throughout the city's long history.

The formation of the Republic, traditionally dated to 509 BCE, marked the beginning of an evolving state structure which continued until the middle of the first century BCE. Individual identity and collective power were both dependent on the possession of citizenship, based on ownership of land in the territory but exercised politically by voting in person in the city itself. In return, the citizens provided the army, at first a seasonal militia which was called on to defend the state and to protect their own land in times of danger, but which also could and did act as aggressor against neighbouring powers. The state therefore demanded an allegiance above any looser ties of common language or culture; citizenship defined the Roman.

The possession of Roman citizenship was also the key to political control, which during the Republic was in the hands of a deliberating body (the Senate), its members elected by the citizens as a whole. Election depended largely on birth and wealth, which in turn was based predominantly on land ownership, so that real power was generally concentrated in the hands of a few families or individuals, with rivalry between them often intense. Magistrates were elected from this same group; among them were the pair of consuls who held executive power for a single year, junior magistrates called aediles responsible for the day-to-day running of the city, and the censors, also elected in pairs but only every five years, who kept the list of citizens, maintained public morals, and increasingly oversaw public finances, including the contracts for public buildings.

Roman expansion brought considerable advantages for members of the ruling elite, since the consuls acted also as Rome's generals, and then as the governors of the new territories. Conquered territory meant increased wealth, for the individual as war booty and for the state as extra lands for new settlement, or, worked by the original inhabitants, as a source of tribute and taxes. Not surprisingly, the major political figures were often also the major military figures, men such as Scipio Africanus, Pompey the Great, and Julius Caesar, all of whom annexed vast territories on behalf of the Roman state. Political and military power brought the possibility of leaving a permanent mark on the face of the city, in the form of public buildings paid for out of family wealth or war booty and bearing the name of the donor to mark the holding of high office or celebrate a victory in war, such as Rome's first permanent theatre built by Pompey the Great in the Campus Martius. This area outside the walls of Republican Rome was particularly connected with the citizen body in its military guise, and was the starting point of the Roman triumph, a procession to celebrate the success of a Roman general, normally against a foreign foe. The triumph, which included captives and booty, the Senate and magistrates, and the triumphant general and his army, passed into the city through one of the city gates, the Porta Triumphalis, along the Circus Maximus and on into the Forum Romanum, ending with sacrifices at the Capitoline Temple [53]. This was the highest honour the state could pay to its military commanders and was only granted after due deliberation by the Senate.

From the power struggles of the first century BCE, Octavian, great-nephew and heir of Julius Caesar, emerged victorious, and under the title of Augustus (meaning 'revered') took all real power into his own hands while ostensibly restoring it to the Senate. The new system of absolute rule by Roman emperors bearing the title Augustus lasted in Rome, with some modifications, for over 400 years. In addition, the emperor was at least nominally the head of the Roman armed forces, so that political and military power gradually passed out of the hands of the old Roman nobility. Senatorial status was still, however, highly prized, as it continued to give access to military and civil command. New senators increasingly came from the provinces, initially from the western Mediterranean and North Africa and later also from the eastern empire. Like Roman citizens in the early Republic, senators could only exercise their prerogatives at Rome, unless absent on state business, and were required to own property in Italy.

The origins of the emperors also began to change. While Caesar and Augustus had belonged to the old Roman nobility, a century later Trajan became the first emperor to be born outside of Italy, at Italica, an early Roman settlement in Spain. The end of the second century CE saw the first North African emperor, Septimius Severus, a highly capable military commander whose arch in Rome commemorates his campaigns against the Parthians in the East [7]. Given that Septimius Severus took as his second wife a Syrian priestess, it is perhaps not surprising that it was their son Caracalla who finally granted universal Roman citizenship to the rest of the empire. Thereafter the empire, not Rome, regularly provided its emperors, and they came increasingly from among its military commanders rather than from the Senate. Traditionally the reign of the last Severan emperor, Severus Alexander, is held to mark the beginning of the 'third-century crisis' in which, over fifty years, twenty-two recognized emperors and countless usurpers rose briefly to power, mainly from the army.

Under this rapid succession of rulers, most of whom spent much of their time fighting on the frontiers, the city of Rome gradually ceased to play such an important role as the seat of empire. Few major buildings were constructed in Rome during this 'third-century crisis', apart from the new city walls put up in great haste by the emperor Aurelian under the threat of barbarian invasion. The court and the administration were most often where the emperor was, and this was rarely in Rome. Towards the end of the third century CE the emperor Diocletian, a native of the Balkans, reorganized the empire by dividing it into West and East and sharing power with a colleague, as well as creating two junior emperors to succeed them. Each of these emperors had his own imperial base, but none of these was Rome; instead they were located nearer the unstable borders of the empire, for example at Trier in Germany [9] or Nicomedia in Asia Minor, which saw substantial building programmes to raise their status as suitable seats of empire. When, twenty years later, the empire returned to the absolute rule of one man, Constantine the Great, he was able to complete the move away from Rome by founding a new capital of his own at the ancient Greek site of Byzantium, renamed Constantinople.

Fig. 9

Imperial baths
(Kaiserthermen), Trier
(Germany), late third to
early fourth century CE.
Previously the provincial
capital of Gallia Belgica,
Trier was made the imperial
capital of all the Gauls
under Diocletian. The form
and the construction
techniques recall those of
the city of Rome.

The sack of Rome by Alaric and the Goths in 410 CE struck dismay into the hearts of Romans everywhere. St Jerome, one of the early Christian scholars but trained in the Graeco-Roman classics, heard of the disaster at Bethlehem in Israel and lamented: 'who could believe that after being raised up by victories over the whole world Rome should come crashing down, and become at once the mother and the grave of her peoples?'[4] The city of Rome was last under direct control of the emperor in Constantinople in the sixth century CE, although already in 476 CE it was ruled by its first barbarian king. Thereafter, except in legend, history, and sentiment, the Roman empire generally ceased to have anything to do with Rome.

The Empire of Rome

From the start, the Roman empire incorporated a large number of different ethnic groups, diverse in language, religion, customs, and social organization. The transformation from city-state to empire began in Italy, a varied mosaic of native peoples including the Etruscans together with settlers from the wider Mediterranean, particularly the Greeks of southern Italy.[5] Rome made close alliances with some pre-existing political units, but in other areas had to impose control. One key strategy was the establishment of new settlements—the colonies (*coloniae*). While some, those closest to Rome or accessible by sea, were small garrisons of Roman citizens who exercised their political rights at Rome itself, the larger, more distant colonies were self-governing city-states in their own right with their own citizenship, but owing military obligations to Rome. Their religious and political organization, however, was based on that of Rome, and many of their public buildings were inspired by those at Rome, such as the forum basilicas which proliferated in the second century BCE following the building of the first examples in Rome [85]. Likewise, the settlers, whatever their origins, had certain legal rights at Rome, as did some older independent city-states in Italy (the *municipia*) allied to Rome. All non-citizen residents in Rome, whether slaves or citizens of other states, were in different degrees politically and legally disadvantaged, not least in the fact that, however wealthy, they were debarred from any serious participation in the political process.

The next dramatic step, only achieved after a painful period of civil war, was to extend Roman citizenship to the rest of Italy. Direct exercise of political rights at Rome itself was no longer expected of all but was limited to the few with sufficient wealth, talent, and ambition to make it at the top, irrespective of their place of birth; active participation in the duties of Roman citizenship was otherwise restricted to volunteer service in the now professional Roman army. At the same time, full Roman citizenship was not incompatible with residence in and loyalty to a local community, and local politics rather than the politics of Rome were the focus of interest for those with no wider ambitions. At the same time, Roman society assimilated the Hellenistic practice of euergetism, the voluntary gift-giving by individual members of the wealthy elite classes for the benefit of the wider urban community, both at Rome and in the towns of Roman Italy. While some of the expenditure was on ephemeral benefits such as feasting and games, building had a more lasting impact; the returns for the benefactor were social prestige and advantage in competitive local politics, displayed to the public by their names inscribed on buildings and by portrait statues of them dedicated in the most public of places, above all the forum, by a suitably grateful community.

As Rome expanded further into the Mediterranean, it came into contact and conflict with a wider variety of indigenous peoples, and with the major powers of the Mediterranean where some kind of cultural as well as political hegemony was exercised by the leading city-states or urban-based monarchies. From the third century BCE the major gains were from the former territories of Punic Carthage in Sicily, Spain, and North Africa, and from the Greek-speaking Hellenistic kingdoms in the East including Syria and Egypt, founded by the Macedonian generals who were the successors to the empire of Alexander the Great, and sometimes from the Greek city-states of the western Mediterranean such as Massilia (Marseilles). These large units had themselves been acquired by conquest and were already culturally mixed; the urban-based powers generally controlled ethnically different and sometimes largely rural indigenous populations by means of polyglot mercenary armies.

Not even the urban centres, however, were uniform in origin or nature. The ancient Greek city-states might be totally autonomous, or under the control of a non-Greek power such as Persia, or dominated by one of the Hellenistic kings. These existed in tandem with new cities of mixed populations such as Alexandria in Egypt, founded by Alexander the Great, and with even older cities of non-Greek origin including Jerusalem and Tyre with their very different languages, cultures, and religious beliefs. Being cities was what they had in common, and it is here, especially among the higher levels of society, that cultural assimilation—often in both directions— worked best. In taking over these areas of the Mediterranean littoral, Rome was entering a world which was culturally complex but already committed to one essential premise: that cities were the prime focus of political power, of local administration and the exercise of law, of religion, and of social organization. Specific building types such as basilicas were developed to serve these various functions, and cities were the driving force behind the creation of a Roman architecture.

Beyond the coastal fringe, the local populations tended to be organized on a tribal basis, either settled in small villages and dispersed farmsteads or leading a more nomadic pastoral existence. Spring and mountain cave, rural sanctuary and defensible hill-fort all provided regional focal points, but cities on the Mediterranean model were rare. Even in parts of Asia Minor and in the hinterland of Carthage, where Greek and Phoenician rule had been in place for many centuries, the rural populations long preserved at least part of their traditional indigenous cultures into the Roman empire. This is also the situation Rome met with in northern Europe, although here it applied to whole populations. The key difficulties lay not purely in language or religious practices but in the absence of a civic structure. When the Roman statesman and historian Tacitus says of the Germans—Rome's classic barbarians—that 'they never live in cities and…their villages are not laid out in our way, with buildings adjacent and connected', he could have been writing of many of the indigenous populations of mainland Europe from Spain to Romania before their absorption into the Roman empire.[6]

One solution for the Roman conquerors was to encourage an urban way of life on the Roman Mediterranean model. Tacitus again presents a picture of how his father-in-law Agricola, as governor of Britain, set about taming the scattered and uncivilized Britons. First place was given to encouraging them to build temples, civic centres, and houses; this was followed by education for the sons of the chiefs, the learning of Latin, and the wearing of Roman national dress, the toga; finally came the private enjoyment of leisure, in conversation, at baths, and at dinner parties.[7] Although Tacitus in this passage is trying to make a point about the decay of Roman society while vaunting the moral qualities of his father-in-law, he identified a pattern which can be traced archaeologically all over the western empire: with the encouragement of Rome, the elites of native communities apparently built towns on a Roman pattern, adopted Latin as an official language, and embraced Mediterranean social habits. That the process is less clear in the eastern Mediterranean is largely due to the existence of already well-established forms of urban civilization which the Romans found comprehensible and within which they could operate political control. Not all the peoples incorporated into the Roman empire were equally foreign.

The establishment of new urban communities on the Mediterranean model was not just a way of civilizing the barbarians. Although the Roman empire was gained largely through military conquest, and maintained against outside attack and internal rebellion by the army, on the whole Rome depended on the cities in the empire to administer the territory on a day-to-day basis. This in turn required the cooperation of local elites with a dual loyalty both to Rome and to their local communities. The bait was Roman citizenship, which provided the opportunity for these local potentates to enter the wider framework of Roman politics and power. But for this to work, the meaning and nature of Roman citizenship had to grow beyond a simple one-to-one relationship with the city-state.

The process by which all of Italy was admitted to Roman citizenship provided a model for this wider empire. The new form of citizenship, radical in its definition of the relationship between citizen and state, was the master-card for the incorporation of vast areas of new territory. Colonies of Roman citizens, often army veterans, were established overseas in newly acquired territory to act as outposts of Rome, as the earlier colonies in Italy had been. Roman citizenship was also held out to individuals, communities, or whole peoples anywhere in the empire as a privilege to be sought after, in return for proven loyalty to Rome and the increased adoption of Roman political and cultural models. Often the politically active elites with which the central Roman government had most dealings were one step ahead of the rest of their people, full citizenship being one of the rewards for holding local magistracies. This can be seen in operation at Lepcis Magna in Libya, a wealthy town of Punic origin which remained nominally independent until the later first century CE. Its leading families energetically embraced Roman hegemony under Augustus, instigating a veritable building boom at the end of the first century BCE. Most of the buildings were of Roman type, including a theatre [10].

Augustus promoted the theatre at Rome and in the colonies as both a symbol of Roman cultural supremacy and a visible manifestation of his renewed principles of social order, so that its appearance in Lepcis Magna may reflect a strong desire on the part of its elite to conform to current Roman norms. The dedication, however, reveals just how complex was the cultural situation [11]. The text is bilingual, in both the Latin of the Roman

Fig. 10

Theatre, Lepcis Magna, Libya, dedicated 1–2 CE, stage building (*scaenae frons*) replaced 146/7 CE. The solid outer wall may reflect the use of solid ashlar construction instead of the mortared rubble vaulting used in contemporary theatres in Rome and central Italy.

masters and the neo-Punic of the local community, while the name of the dedicator, Annobal Tapapius Rufus, shows him to have been ethnically Punic but to have adopted a Latin surname;[8] his titles reveal him as a high-ranking magistrate of the town and a holder of both native and Roman priesthoods. His family continued to play an important role in local politics until the later part of the first century CE, when they seem finally to have been granted Roman citizenship. In the theatre and other buildings of Lepcis Magna, architecture, language, and name were all put on public display as claims to a Romanness which had very little to do with ethnicity or place of birth or domicile.

A Graeco-Roman Culture

Among all the varied cultures which Rome absorbed from the peoples with whom it came into contact, none had a more profound effect than that of the Greeks. Imported Greek objects appear in Rome from the seventh century BCE, while the early western Greek colonies of Neapolis (Naples) and Cumae lay only 200 km to the south. Although Greek city-states were scattered throughout the Mediterranean, the games held at the all-Greek sanctuaries of Delphi and Olympia in the old Greek homeland provided a common meeting point for the exchange of information and the reinforcement of their common Greek culture. Following the conquests of Alexander the Great, Greek culture provided a common bond between the urban-based elites of the Mediterranean, even if they were politically at odds. Greek was the language of literature, philosophy, art, science, and rhetoric—in short, of all learning; and Athens, Alexandria, and Pergamon were the universities of the civilized world. From at least the third century BCE, educated Romans learnt the Greek language, imported Greek scholars, artists, and architects, and adopted many aspects of Greek culture; so too did educated Carthaginians such as Hannibal.

At the same time, Roman attitudes to Greek culture were often ambivalent. Even among those who benefited from a Greek education were some who decried the loss of old Roman virtues and habits on moral grounds and denounced the pursuit of Hellenistic Greek luxuries as un-Roman.[9] Through the second and first centuries BCE, as Rome became increasingly embroiled in the affairs of the East, these two responses to Greek culture—fascination and fear, absorption and resistance—became ever more complex and ever more tied to political expediency. Mainland Greece, with Athens as its cultural capital and the seat of Greek philosophy, being politically of little account, could be maintained in a position of cultural and moral superiority, while the newer and infinitely more dangerous Hellenistic kingdoms of the East such as Syria, where Greek was contaminated with the outlandish foreign cultures of Persia and Egypt, could be castigated as the source of debilitating luxury and moral decay.

The ambivalence was nowhere more clearly exploited for political ends than by Octavian (later Augustus) in his battle against Mark Antony and Cleopatra, who were portrayed as representing the worst of the decadent and immoral East, while he himself stood for the old Roman Republican virtues. As well as reviving ancient Roman religious ceremonies, Augustus encouraged the wearing of the distinctive toga by citizens and passed laws regulating social behaviour at all levels of society. In his Forum, he was portrayed as the descendant of the two legendary founders of Rome, the Trojan Aeneas whose mother was the goddess Venus and the Latin Romulus whose father was the god Mars; but he was also shown as the successor to a long line of famous Roman generals and statesmen whose achievements were listed below their portrait statues [12]. The two greatest contemporary works of literature, Virgil's epic poem *The Aeneid* and Livy's monumental prose history of Rome *From the Foundation of the City*, provided a written counterpart to the Forum of Augustus.

Fig. 12

Forum of Augustus, Rome, vowed 42 BCE, dedicated c. 2 BCE. Statues of the Julian line descended from the legendary founder Aeneas, together with Roman Republican generals and statesmen (the *summi viri*), lined the porticoes.

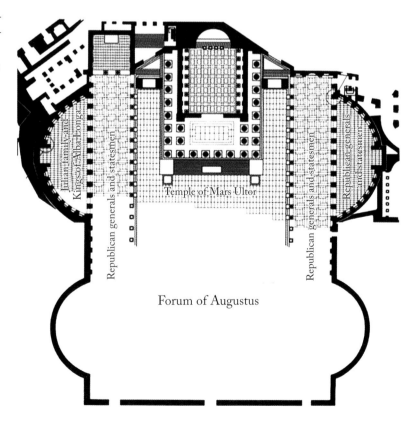

Julian family and Kings of Alba Longa

Republican generals and statesmen

Temple of Mars Ultor

Republican generals and statesmen

Republican generals and statesmen

Republican generals and statesmen

Forum of Augustus

This does not mean that Augustus rejected all Greek influences. Rather, he championed the culture of old Greece, and particularly that of classical Athens, which had flourished after its defeat of the Persians, a triumph of democratic city-state over despotic empire. This was the Greek equivalent of Rome's own early Republican past, a fitting model for the Augustan present. Augustus' patron deity was Apollo, guardian of the paramount oracle of the early Greek world at Delphi. In places the artistic styles and architectural forms of the Athenian fifth century BCE, like the caryatids in the Forum of Augustus, were employed in preference to more contemporary styles from the Hellenistic East [13]. These distinctive elements, readily recognizable to the educated and cultured elite, transformed the older Roman models to which they were applied. In many ways it can be argued that Augustus reinvented Roman culture as the heritage of all Roman citizens, not just the residents of Rome, and gave it new visual expression which acknowledged the Greek contribution while denying any major role to the non-Greek elements of the Hellenistic East. This is the culture which numerous Roman citizens, of Italian origin but settled in Augustan colonies, took west.

Such fine distinctions and deliberate archaisms were difficult to sustain. At some levels, particularly among the elite of Rome itself, Greek remained the antithesis of Roman. The senatorial order read the increasingly autocratic behaviour, the love of Greek games, and the adoption of Greek ways by the emperors Caligula and Nero as equally symptomatic of their old enemy, Hellenistic despotism. Yet this could not last, since it was equally Greek language and culture that linked elites of all origins in the Mediterranean through their education. Participation in Roman military and civil service carried elements of this common culture to the farthest reaches of the empire. The early career of the emperor Hadrian was typical: born probably in Spain, he gained his main military experience in central Europe

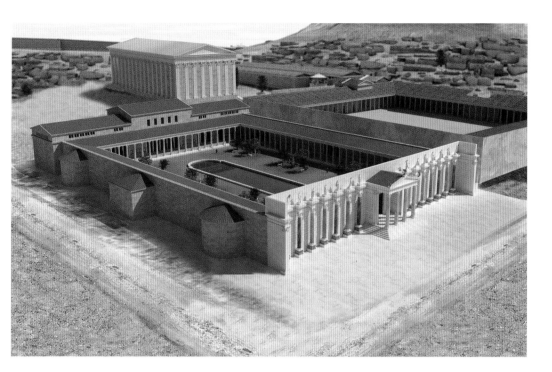

Fig. 14

Library of Hadrian, Athens, 132 CE. Pausanias (1.18.9) calls this Hadrian's 'most famous structure'; measuring 87 × 125 metres, it had 100 columns of Phrygian marble in the interior court, a gift of the emperor.

and Germany, was honoured by Athens, and was acting as governor of Syria at the time of Trajan's death. As emperor he toured the whole Roman world from Britain to Egypt, encouraging and occasionally financing a veritable building boom, giving particular attention to Greece and the Greek East [14].[10] Hadrian represents an emerging new cultural climate, called by modern scholars 'the Second Sophistic', in which this Greek basis of elite learning (*paideia*) merged with Roman ways to create a more unified Graeco-Roman culture.

It would be a mistake, however, to imagine that the Second Sophistic removed all differences. Geographical and social divides continued to matter. Latin was still the language of politics and administration in the West, but only rarely in the East. The old Hellenistic cities retained at least some civic autonomy, with their own distinctively Greek magistracies and political structure, giving them a rather different social and physical character to the cities of the West whose organization was largely based on that of Rome. Roman civic cults, especially those of Jupiter Optimus Maximus or the Capitoline triad of Jupiter, Juno, and Minerva, were commoner in the West than in the cities of the East, which retained their original patron deities; but the worship of the emperor drew the two together, as did the similarities between Roman and Greek deities, particularly Jupiter and Zeus, the protective deities of the emperor and the Roman state. On the whole, it was on the public level that Rome mattered most, where Greek ways were largely an admittedly privileged provincial variant. On the private level, however, Greek culture was a matter of class. The verbal and visual reinterpretation of Greek myth, the subtleties of Greek literature, and the intricacies of Greek moral philosophy were the cornerstones of social intercourse discussed at elegant dinner parties between the educated upper classes, even when the language used was Latin, not Greek. Late Latin and Greek poetry and the mythological floor mosaics of late Roman houses from Britain to Syria show that this common elite culture survived even the growing power of Christianity and was still strong in the fifth and sixth centuries CE, long after traditional Roman religion had been banned.

The physical mobility of the early imperial period, in no small part the result of an unprecedented phase of exceptionally settled conditions and vast improvements in communications, also encouraged the spread of a common culture even at lower levels of society. Within the army, native troops from one region were sent off to distant parts of the empire and served alongside contingents of other origins, with Latin as the common language, while retired soldiers sometimes returned home, bringing their new language and culture with them, or were resettled in veteran colonies. Merchants and traders travelled widely, many being freed slaves working on behalf of members of the Roman upper classes. The cities attracted workers from the countryside, with Rome the greatest draw-card of them all. Graeco-Roman culture penetrated the lower classes least in rural areas, and in some areas was barely skin deep. Only in Greece itself, and the Greek territories in Asia Minor, was Greek culture widely spread—after all, it was part of their own particular local heritage. The gap, however, remained between the geographically mobile upper classes of Roman society, sharing

Fig. 15

Temple of Mars Mullo, Allones, France, second century CE. The temple combines the tall central *cella* of the Romano-Gallic temple form with the pedimented portico of traditional Roman type.

a common urban Graeco-Roman culture and knowledge of either—or preferably both—Latin or Greek, and the ethnically and culturally more diverse but geographically more localized natives, whose bilingualism encompassed at best either Greek or Latin plus their native language. While written documents are few, the buildings created by the people on the periphery of Graeco-Roman society reflect their responses to the dominant cultural forms which shaped their wider environment [15].

The infinite variety within the corpus of Roman architecture is thus the result of a whole series of individual human choices made within the framework of different geographical circumstances and in the context of different attitudes to society and different expectations of the role played by architecture within it. The sheer volume of building in the Roman world also encouraged an unprecedented degree of experimentation; despite the vast number of surviving buildings from the Roman empire, virtually no two are precisely identical, the minute number of 'twins' being very close in space and time and normally part of the same development. At the same time, it is usually easy to identify a building as being in some sense Roman. The similarities reflect a common concept—or set of concepts—about what buildings should look like; the differences, the desire of the individual for a unique creation to fit a unique set of circumstances which include function, time, and place. The development of architectural expression in the pluralistic society which was the Roman empire is the main theme of this book.

Architects and Roman Society

> I do not believe that any can with justice suddenly profess to be architects unless, faced from an early age with the need to climb the steps of the discipline, they have reached the highest temple of architecture, nurtured in the knowledge of most of the letters and arts.
>
> Vitruvius, *On architecture*, I.I.II (c. 25 BCE)

Roman architecture may have been largely in the control of the political and economic elite, but the creation of fine buildings did not often happen without the direct intervention of architects. By the time the first monumental buildings were erected in Rome in the sixth century BCE, the practice of architecture already had a long history in the Mediterranean world, and the architect as the learned inventor or conceiver of complex buildings, designed to the special requirements of specific clients, had a history which stretched back to the almost legendary Egyptian Imhotep, who designed the very first of the pyramids at Saqqara for King Zoser in the middle of the third millennium.

What differed within the ancient world was the position of architects in society, and the relationship of architects with their patrons. Both these things are specific to culture, time, and place. In Egypt architects belonged to the priestly class and architecture was a secret art. The Roman world was closer to ours, with architecture as one of the recognized professions and architectural discourse the common property of the educated. At the same time, only a tiny number of Roman architects are known by name, and even fewer can be associated with specific buildings in the city of Rome or elsewhere. If anything, we know more about the architects of fifth-century Greece than those of Rome in any period. The explanation for this lies in the overwhelming importance of the individual patron, whose elite views are perpetuated in the written sources. Because of the political significance of building, it is the name of the patron which is usually associated with a given structure; we may think of Sir Christopher Wren's church of St Paul's in London, but for the Romans the Pantheon was built by Agrippa, Augustus' lieutenant. Even after its reconstruction by Trajan,[1] it was still Agrippa's name which was written large on the front of the building [2], and his name which was associated with it in the literature of the time.

There are exceptions, but they are few. Equally, most of the references to architecture in the ancient literature were written by patrons and from their point of view; the architect is largely silent.

Vitruvius, *On architecture*

The one exception is Vitruvius, whose book *On architecture* is the only complete architectural treatise to survive from antiquity, covering everything from the role and training of the architect and architectural theory to town planning, hydraulic engineering, and even sundials and siege weapons. As well as providing technical information, Vitruvius also gives us the clearest expression of what elite Romans considered important about architecture. In his first book, he gives pride of place to public buildings in their urban setting, to city walls, to the temples of the gods, and to urban amenities, while private buildings in town and country do not appear until book 6; and he insists that all building needs to be structurally sound, to be suited to its purpose, and to be pleasing to the eye.[2] Throughout he also gives specific rules of proportions in design, recommends specific types of construction, and prescribes specific forms for specific functions.

The uniqueness of *On architecture* has led it to be exalted as a privileged text.[3] Putting it in perspective is made doubly difficult because of the pre-eminent position Vitruvius held during the Renaissance, which has influenced the whole concept of architecture in the west ever since. Because the Renaissance gave the written word precedence over material evidence, the rules and precepts of Vitruvius were held as canonical even when it was clear that they were at odds with the remains of classical antiquity. Modern archaeologists have not been immune to this canonization either, using Vitruvius as a touchstone both of the correctness of any reconstruction of ancient buildings and of the 'Romanness' of any example of provincial architecture from anywhere in the empire. Yet Vitruvius was very much an individual, writing at that critical period in Roman history which saw the transition from Republic to empire, and his writing can only be understood in the light of his specific time and place.

On architecture was the work of Vitruvius' old age, completed at the end of a long career. It is likely that he was born no later than the 70s BCE, so that most of his working life coincided with the most turbulent period of civil war in Rome's history. After a broad-based education in the liberal arts, he came to the attention of Julius Caesar when working on public buildings, although the only public building we know he designed was a basilica for the town of Fanum Fortunae. Augustus employed him as a military engineer in charge of the construction and repair of heavy artillery, and afterwards advanced Vitruvius in his career, perhaps in connection with the urban water supply of Rome, where his name was associated with the introduction of a new standard of measuring water rates. He also had the support of Augustus' sister Octavia. While he may have only begun his actual writing in the last years before the defeat of Antony and Cleopatra, the final version being dedicated to Augustus not long after 27 BCE, it is clear that he had been collecting material over the course of his long working life.

Vitruvius' career places him within the orbit of the most important political figures of his day at Rome. Augustus portrayed himself as the restorer of the Republic; renewal was the catch-cry, and this included urban renewal expressed in major public building works. Although Vitruvius was not himself the architect of any of them, his writing was equally a response to the age in which he lived and the men who shaped it. In the preface to *On architecture*, addressed to Augustus, he wrote:

For I perceived that you have built and are now building many things, and will also in time to come take in hand both public and private buildings, so suited to the grandeur of our history that their memory will be handed down to posterity. I have written a detailed treatise so that, by reference to it, you might inform yourself about works made previously and about what kind of works might be done in future. For in these volumes I have laid open all the rules of the discipline.[4]

Such a claim comes as a surprise when Vitruvius' precepts are compared with actual surviving examples of Augustan architecture. For example, his rules for temple design belong more to the world of Greek than to Roman practice, and he makes no reference to the extensive use of coloured marbles, to the specifically Roman development of the Corinthian order, or to the advances in the use of mortared rubble construction which are typical of the Augustan period. These discrepancies have brought Vitruvius his detractors, who have seen him as conservative and/or second-rate and therefore dismiss his work as having no relevance for understanding Roman architecture of the imperial period.

This is as much a mistake as considering him the only true authority on the subject. Vitruvius was, after all, a pioneer. In attempting to compile a definitive account of the discipline of architecture, he was breaking new ground among Latin authors; in fact, he only recognizes three Roman writers on architecture, none of them professional architects. Instead, he cites numerous Greek commentaries on individual buildings or on specific aspects of the discipline which provided most of his material on theory, temple design, water sources, time-keeping, and mechanics.[5] This means that Vitruvius had to some extent to assemble his own data for the specifically Roman building traditions of central Italy, largely from personal experience and observation, and from what he himself was taught as a student of architecture, now many years past. It is not clear if and when Vitruvius ceased to practice as an architect, but he admits that his fame was small, which may imply that his major building commissions were few. Is it any wonder he sought safety in the precepts and practices of his youth?

It could also be argued that Vitruvius was responding to Augustus' own twin programme of reforming society ostensibly on traditional Republican lines and of reshaping what was best in Greek culture in Roman guise. The chapters on public buildings (book 5) are particularly significant. As well as giving a—to us—disproportionate amount of space to the theatre, an important instrument in Augustus' attempts to restructure Roman society, Vitruvius also carefully distinguished between Italian and Greek practices, reflecting Augustan interest in recreating a common Roman culture for the cities of Italy.[6] Over the same period, Vitruvius could have watched the erection of two major Augustan monuments inspired in part by Greek taste, made of marble in the Greek tradition, and using Greek workmen to carve it: the temple dedicated to Apollo—the archetypal Greek deity—on the Palatine Hill, adorned with ancient Greek sculpture; and the Forum of Augustus with its Temple of Mars Ultor and its Caryatid decoration **[12, 13, 63, 64]**. Basing the discussion of temples on Greek sources must have seemed only right and proper in the circumstances. In addition, Greek learning and culture were the mark of the educated man and essential to give status to the new genre of the architectural treatise.

This last aspect was vital for ensuring Vitruvius the fame he hoped for from the publication of his treatise. Although the ostensible recipient of *On architecture* was Augustus, there are numerous allusions throughout the work to a wider audience. Despite the technical detail, for example on methods of construction or the weight of lead waterpipes, he was not aiming primarily at other architects or builders but at those members of the elite who commissioned buildings as patrons and/or who had to supervise their erection as civic magistrates. These and other well-to-do citizens formed another kind of potential audience, those who, confident in their own education, chose to build for themselves without the help of an architect.[7] Like the manuals of builders' work and prices which began to appear with the building boom in eighteenth-century England, the treatise of Vitruvius would assist a patron to keep a check on his contractors and not be cheated on quality.

At the start of the section on public building Vitruvius discusses the difficulties raised by the use of technical language, but promises to keep the text short in the interests of the reader with little time to spare from the pressure of public and private business.[8] Translating terms from the Greek must have been one problem, the specialized nature of jargon another. It is perhaps not surprising that some architectural terms appear here for the first—and occasionally for the only—time in Latin literature. Vitruvius provided sufficient knowledge and vocabulary for the non-specialist to communicate effectively with either architect or contractor on their own terms. At the same time, the strong basis in Greek natural philosophy and architectural writing allowed him to take a high moral and educational stance and to lay down the law on matters of aesthetics, thus raising the status of architectural discourse within the corpus of Latin literature. While his treatise is mentioned by only a very few later writers, its success and continued relevance can be judged by the way that even in the fifth century the learned and high-flying Sidonius Apollinaris, a native of Roman Gaul, prefect of Rome and later Bishop of Auvergne, held Vitruvius up as the model of a first-rate architect.[9]

On architecture was therefore a novel creation, albeit within the Roman tradition of encyclopaedic scientific and technical writing for an educated audience. Not only was it a product of its time and place and of Vitruvius' personal circumstances but it also gave form to the idea of Roman architecture at the very time that Roman culture as a whole was being redefined. Vitruvius was not alone in his day in seeing architecture as a matter of vital concern. That it was in fact fundamental to the formulation of the Augustan regime is shown above all in the *Res Gestae*, Augustus' own account of his achievements, where three of the thirty-five sections are devoted to his building programmes. There are even verbal resonances between the two which suggest a common language of debate about the role of building in the shaping of society. The moral tales which adorn the introductory prefaces to many of the books of *On architecture* and the emphasis on *decor* or appropriateness as a vital element of architectural design had their counterpart in contemporary poetry, where the hubris and moral corruption of society were portrayed in architectural metaphors.[10] Not everyone in Augustan Rome would have agreed with Vitruvius in detail, but few would have contested his principles.

Seeing Vitruvius as one voice in a broader, ongoing debate about the nature and value of architecture may be the most valid way of assessing his real significance for our understanding of Roman architecture. While his specific rules and opinions are expressions of largely personal preferences, his choices of subject matter and the broader philosophical context reflect common concerns. Indeed, it has been argued that the more abstract the topic, the more chance there is of finding echoes of Vitruvius' rules in actual practice, as this area above all reflects the theoretical principles which were at the basis of ancient architectural training.[11]

The Roman Architect

The seriousness of architecture as a profession was reflected by its position among the Roman canon of liberal arts. Vitruvius gives us a vivid picture of the ideal education of an architect, expecting him to be:

literate, a skilled draughtsman, and good at geometry; to be well-versed in history, a diligent student of philosophy, with a knowledge of music, and not ignorant of medicine; to know law and have experience in astronomy and astronomical calculations.[12]

Acquiring such a broad-based education was by necessity a slow business, and Vitruvius pleads for the title of 'architect' to be reserved for those who had undergone rigorous training. Not that Vitruvius anticipated the architect excelling in all these manifold fields, but he expected him to have at least a moderate knowledge of all of them.

We have no idea how common this ideal broad-based education was in practice, but anecdotal evidence suggests that well-trained architects were not unusual and had sufficient standing to argue the toss with their clients. The lawyer and politician Cicero, Vitruvius' older contemporary, had to endure a detailed lecture on optics in Greek from the architect Cyrus when Cicero dared to criticize the narrowness of some windows in one of his villas.[13] Almost 500 years later, an edict of the emperor Constantine encouraging the recruitment of potential architecture students to fill a dearth in the African provinces suggests that the ideal education at least had hardly changed; the edict was aimed at young men, eighteen years in age, with a taste in the liberal arts.[14] Given that the edict also promised a salary for the trainee and exemption from taxes for him and his family, it would seem that there were economic implications for such an arduous training scheme. State assistance apart, this would have only been feasible for the relatively well to do, like Vitruvius' parents whom he thanks for providing his education; such an education could also be supplied to a promising slave by a wealthy owner. But it comes as no surprise to find that not all who professed to be architects were so well educated. Vitruvius himself complains bitterly that the discipline is practised by persons without training or experience even in construction, let alone architecture.[15] In the high demand for architects during the building boom of the Augustan peace following years of civil war, this may be more than just sour grapes.

The nature and extent of an architect's training and education also had implications for his social standing. A knowledge of architecture, according to Vitruvius, had to include both theory and practice, head-work and hand-work. It is an important distinction, as theory was based in Greek philosophy and thus shared with every educated person, while practice was craftsmanship, normally the preserve of those who specialized in specific fields such as medicine or music. According to Cicero, these were the honourable professions, along with architecture and teaching—but not for the upper classes.[16] After all, they were still only professions, and other crafts within the remit of an architect, such as skill in drawing or knowledge of the working of stone, were too closely allied to manual work to be considered suitable for members of the elite.

Other factors affected social standing. Although Vitruvius argued that all architects should be men of good birth, the legal and social status of architects appear in practice to have been very mixed; not surprisingly, few if any are known to have been even of the equestrian class.[17] Many architects were engaged by a form of contract called a mandate, in which they were paid an honorarium and had their expenses reimbursed, rather than being paid a daily wage like a workman; the distinction was based on their higher level of expertise and the fact that the employer was paying for technical skill and/or advice rather than actual manual labour. At the same time, there are numerous slaves mentioned in the literary sources working as architects for the water board in Rome or for powerful men like Crassus on speculative development. In the complex world of Roman social relations, some of these slaves could eventually earn their freedom and practise architecture for themselves. Nevertheless, the example of Cyrus, who in his will divided his estate between Cicero and another—rival—politician of the day, reminds us that the top architects were independent men of means.

The Origins of Architects

It is likely that Cyrus was Greek, possibly from Asia Minor and perhaps even of distant Persian origins. The Greek world certainly had a long tradition of highly skilled architects, whose talents were exercised originally for the benefit of the city-state, and later for influential individuals in the Hellenistic kingdoms. In the sixth and fifth centuries BCE commissions for the few types of monumental buildings—mainly temples and stoas—were scarce, and the architect was consequently a relatively rare figure. Architecture as a separate profession barely existed, and indeed the term 'architecture' is unknown before the second century; an 'architect' was originally just a master craftsman, especially a carpenter or shipwright. The change came with the new circumstances of the Hellenistic age. The growth of urbanism and the proliferation of new building types led to an increased need for trained architects, now working as often for individual clients as for a community and on a wide range of commissions, including the very necessary field of military defences. Some that we know of, like Deinocrates who designed Alexandria for Alexander the Great,[18] worked for the most powerful political figures of the day. The growing importance of Rome in the second century BCE, and Rome's involvement with the Greek East, attracted some of these men to work for Roman patrons. Indeed, it has been argued that from this point on, most of Rome's architects were Greek. The situation, however, is more complex.

Nowhere is this clearer than with the first two architects known to be associated with Rome, Hermodorus of Salamis and Decimus Cossutius, both of whom worked for powerful clients on major temple commissions. They are an interesting pair, in many ways representative of the mixing-pot world of the Mediterranean in the mid-second century BCE. Hermodorus was the architect responsible for the first marble temple built in Rome, the Temple of Jupiter Stator, and the first Greek architect known to have worked there.[19] His patron in this project was a Roman consul and general, the Hellenophile Quintus Caecilius Metellus Macedonicus, who had gained his last name from his victories in Greece. Cossutius, on the other hand, was a Roman citizen who redesigned the giant unfinished Temple of Olympian Zeus in Athens [17] for the Romanophile Seleucid king Antiochus IV of Syria, who had spent time in his youth as a political hostage at Rome.[20] Other individuals with the name Cossutius are known from Puteoli and Pompeii on the Bay of Naples, and from a number of Italian trading centres in the eastern Mediterranean, where some at least were involved in the marble trade. If these two men can be considered typical of the exchange of individuals and ideas between East and West in the later Hellenistic period, it is not surprising that this period saw the creation or development of many building types and styles, like the basilica and the Corinthian order, which were to be fundamental to the canon of Roman architecture. Hermodorus may, however, have been an exception; there were certainly highly capable Roman—or at least Italian—architects working in

Fig. 17
Temple of Olympian Zeus, Athens. Begun in the sixth century BCE but abandoned before completion, the project was restarted, on even more colossal lines, in local Pentelic marble and the Corinthian order, by the Seleucid king Antiochus IV Epiphanes (175–164 BCE), employing the Roman architect Cossutius. Complete, this would have rivalled in size and splendour the fourth-century Ionic Temple of Artemis at Ephesus, one of the wonders of the Hellenistic world, but it was abandoned unfinished on Antiochus' death. It was finally completed and rededicated by the emperor Hadrian in 132 CE.

Rome in the late Republic whose presence is attested in literary or epigraphic sources, men like Lucius Cornelius, who most likely worked for Lutatius Catulus on the early first-century rebuilding of the Capitoline temple.[21]

If we look for the counterparts to architects such as Hermodorus and Cossutius in the imperial period, men working on major commissions for the men of power, we find the same mix of Roman and Greek. Of the three figures working at Rome who can be associated with surviving remains, the engineers Severus and Celer, associated with the Golden House of Nero, and the architect Rabirius who designed some of the imperial palace on the Palatine for the emperor Domitian, appear from their names to have been Roman citizens and possibly of free birth. The third, Trajan's architect Apollodorus of Damascus, was clearly Greek, but from the Levant.[22] Apart from the fact that Severus, Celer, and Rabirius worked on what were basically private commissions, building palaces for the emperor, and Apollodorus worked on public buildings, including the Forum and Baths of Trajan, there is no easy stylistic division to argue that they were working in completely separate Greek and Roman traditions. All their projects were founded in building types which already had a long tradition in Rome and central Italy, but drew much inspiration originally from the Hellenistic East; all combined that fundamentally Roman medium of brick-faced concrete with a use of marble and the columnar orders which had its origins in the Greek world, but had long since become naturalized in Rome. What mattered most was that these were clearly men of outstanding ability, whose talents commended them to the emperors themselves and who therefore were given the opportunity of changing the face of Roman architecture.

These men were clearly exceptional. While some architects, including those at the top of their profession, were highly mobile, many appear content to have remained in their local region and served their local communities. Architects were to be found everywhere, as the emperor Trajan pointed out to his conscientious governor of northern Asia Minor, Pliny the Younger. In a fascinating correspondence which gives a real insight into the functioning of imperial administration, Pliny reports to the emperor on a whole series of over-ambitious public building projects by different cities in his area, and asks the emperor to send him an architect to sort them out. Trajan's terse reply concludes:

As for the baths at Claudiopolis, which you say have been started on an unsuitable site, you must decide yourself what advice to give. You cannot lack architects—every province has skilled men trained for this work. It is a mistake to think they can be sent out more quickly from Rome when they usually come to us from Greece.[23]

This last statement is hardly borne out by funerary inscriptions and other dedications, which show a natural preponderance of Greek-speaking architects in the eastern empire and Latin-speaking architects in the West.[24] The very small number of individuals with Greek names from Rome and Italy are all either slaves or ex-slaves, and their names may not necessarily reflect their ethnic origin. Only in the two examples where father and son who are Roman citizens both bear Greek surnames does a Greek origin seem fairly secure. On the other hand, there are a handful of architects with purely Roman names in the East among the Greeks, one of whom bears the surname 'Romanus', surely an indication of place of origin. While the sample is statistically very small, what it does suggest is that there were far more architects in Greece and particularly Asia Minor than in any other part of the Roman empire apart from central Italy. This may just reflect a higher degree of commemoration, due to the superior wealth or social status of the eastern architects and those of Italy, but it may also correlate to the extremely high density of wealthy and well-established urban centres in these areas with their consequent demands for the services of architects. The relative dearth of such centres in the European provinces may be equally significant for the distribution of architects. In the West the Roman army accounts for a third of the named architects in the survey, all but one of whom are Roman citizens. Many of these, like Vitruvius, were no doubt concerned more with machines than buildings, but some must have designed and overseen the erection of fortifications and permanent military camps. A move from military to civic architecture has been argued for architects in the northwestern provinces like Britain,[25] and even Apollodorus of Damascus was well known for his military works.

Trajan's offhand comment, frequently quoted, is therefore misleading; not all architects in the Roman world were Greek, not even in the East. But Trajan may have been repeating a common misapprehension which reflected a deeper truth. Greek architectural writing and Greek natural philosophy provided the textual basis for Vitruvius' *On architecture*, to be set alongside local Roman practice. The very recognition of the architect as a respectable individual with valuable skills to offer may itself have entered Roman consciousness from Greece; there is no hint of a pre-existing Roman tradition along these lines, no whisper from the early Republic of a Roman equivalent to Iktinos or Kallikrates, the architects of the Parthenon in Athens. In other words, it was the Greek idea of architecture and of the position of architects in society, developed in the city-states of the eastern Mediterranean and given a new focus by the conditions of the Hellenistic age, which helped formulate the Roman concept of architecture and of the role of architects in society.

It may be no coincidence that the largest concentration of inscriptions on public buildings in the west which record the names of architects comes from Campania in the later first century BCE. Not only did Campania, particularly the Bay of Naples, have a long history of Greek settlement, but it was also the chosen leisure resort of that part of the Roman nobility most sympathetic to Greek culture. Cossutius may originally have come from this region, and we have record of an architect of the Augustan period, probably a freedman of the high-ranking senator Lucius Cocceius Nerva, who also was engaged in large-scale building operations as well as being an architect.[26] Other recorded names have no apparent connection to powerful men. At Pompeii, for example, the freed slave Marcus Artorius Primus had his name publicly recorded as the architect for the refurbishment of the theatre on a marble plaque at one of the entrances to the building [18].

We have no surviving examples of such a public recognition of an architect's contribution from Rome, although that does not necessarily mean they did not exist. However, in most of the few cases where the architect's name does appear on a building, it very much takes second place

Fig. 18

Inscription of the freed slave Marcus Artorius Primus, architect, from the theatre at Pompeii, Augustan. He may have been responsible for the rebuilding of the *scaenae frons*.

to that of the patron at whose expense the work was done. Architecture in the Roman world was always a collaborative affair.

Beauty—The Responsibility of the Architect

In book 6 of *On architecture*, Vitruvius assigns responsibility for a successful building to the three groups who are involved in its creation: the patron, the builders, and the architect:

> For when a building has grandeur, the expenditure of the patron is praised; when it is well made, the management of the workforce is approved; but when it is the grace of its design which gives it authority, then the glory belongs to the architect.[27]

As Vitruvius makes quite clear, the crucial role of the Roman architect, like the modern one, was in design. Unfortunately, it is precisely on the question of how Roman architects went about this that Vitruvius appears at his most confused, and his text has understandably been interpreted in a number of ways. Much of the problem lies in the fact that Vitruvius was trying to translate from the theoretical Greek of his sources into Latin, which is notoriously ill-adapted to the expression of abstract thought. The result is, if anything, even more difficult to translate into English or any other modern language, a problem which troubled Renaissance translators as well. Mark Wilson Jones has shown, however, that it is possible to reduce his system to three progressive stages in the design process, and the three attributes which result from them. In brief, these three stages are: deciding on the theoretical basis of the design (*ordinatio*), which produces an abstract mathematical harmony (*symmetria*); working out the detailed composition (*dispositio*), which creates the visual harmony (*eurythmia*); and evaluating the finished design within its physical and social context (*distributio*), in order to ensure its appropriateness (*decor*).[28]

Of these three stages in the design process, Vitruvius returns most frequently to *symmetria*. This is a concept deeply rooted in Greek philosophical and artistic thought, and Vitruvius is able to cite several Greek treatises that he has consulted on the subject.[29] It has little to do with our concept of symmetry, but is concerned with the properties of numbers and pure geometric forms, and with mathematical relationships between the parts and the whole, in part what we call proportion. For the Greeks, mathematics was an essential part of natural philosophy, a way of understanding the cosmic order. For various mathematical reasons the numbers 10 and 6 (the basis of our decimal and duodecimal systems) were believed to be 'perfect' numbers; but they also were thought to be reflected in nature in the form of a man's body, while the body itself formed the basis of all systems of measurement. The shape of the perfect man was also defined within two primary shapes, the circle and the square. Mathematical investigations had also shown that the surface areas and volumes of perfect solids like cylinders, cones, and spheres, if of the same diameter, were related by simple ratios such as 1:1, 2:1, 3:2, 4:3, and so on. Furthermore, these same kinds of simple numerical ratios also created musical harmonies; for example, the ratio 2:1 gives the octave, 3:2 the perfect fifth, 4:3 the perfect fourth. Greek philosophers were thus able to embrace all of nature and the cosmic order in a system of numbers which produced both perfect forms and perfect harmonies.

In Vitruvius' system, the three major elements of this world order—perfect numbers, perfect forms, and musical harmonies—also provided architecture with its abstract beauty. The defining form for the basilica he designed at Fanum Fortunae (modern Fano) was a central nave 120 Roman feet long × 60 feet wide. Its dimensions thus combined the two perfect numbers of 6 and 10, while its shape was a perfect square doubled and its proportions of length to breadth reproduced the harmony of the octave. The columns of the nave were 50 feet tall, with a diameter of 5 feet, giving a proportion of 1:10; size and proportion are thus related to the perfect number of 10. This is not just a piece of academic pedantry on Vitruvius' part. As more metrological analyses are done on Roman buildings, it is becoming increasingly clear that whole number multiples of 6 and 10 units (usually feet or cubits) and simple proportions based on musical harmonies lie at the heart of many designs.

Sometimes more complex geometrical relationships replace the simple proportions as a way of ensuring a relationship between the whole and the parts. The most common ones are based on the diagonal of a square, which is related to its sides in the ratio of 1 to the square root of 2 ($1:\sqrt{2}$). Like the circular function pi (π), which relates the diameter to the circumference or area of a circle, the square root of 2 cannot be written in simple digits but is easy to construct geometrically with ruler and compass; its use thus gives further insight into the physical processes of design. The basic figure underlying the Pantheon design is a simple example of this construction [19].

The rotunda is developed from a circle 150 Roman feet or 100 cubits in diameter, measured through the centres of the columns, while the size of the projecting porch is determined by doubling a square which is inscribed exactly within this circle. The *symmetria* of the scheme is completed by making the height of the rotunda equal to its diameter, adding the sphere to the circle and square of its underlying forms.

What is perhaps surprising is that *symmetria* is the aspect of design which is the least immediately visible in a finished building. This is particularly the case with regard to ground plans; few people can distinguish between, say, a room 12 metres wide and one 13 metres wide, or one whose proportions are 1:2 rather than 13:24. *Symmetria* therefore had largely a conceptual significance, and was the element above all which placed architecture within the rarefied world of Greek philosophy and thus could reveal its function and status within the whole cosmic order. Without *symmetria*,

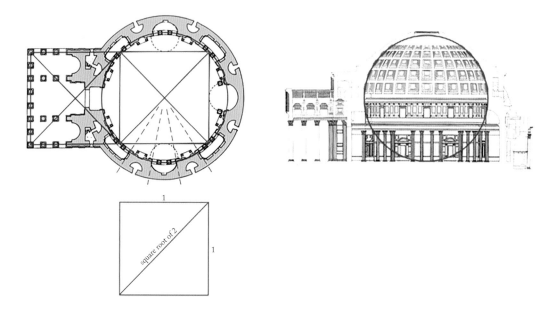

Fig. 19

Reconstructed design
scheme of the Pantheon,
Rome, c. 110–125 CE.

a building was not architecture, and without the education which taught its rules, no designer of buildings could claim to be an architect.

The purely theoretical nature of *symmetria*, however, is made clear by Vitruvius' discussion of *distributio*, and the resulting *eurythmia*. This was the really crucial stage of architectural composition at which the abstract concept was turned into a working design and the numerical proportions into a physical reality; here too questions of form and considerations of function intersected. At a basic level, this meant simply making sure that height and breadth and length were suitably related to each other, and that all was done in accord with *symmetria*. But this is not enough; indeed, it is only the start. Now, at this point in the design process, the search for visual beauty and elegance of effect took precedence over purely abstract considerations, as Vitruvius says:

> When the scheme of the *symmetria* has been decided and the dimensions calculated, [the architect] must apply his critical judgement to the site, taking account of its particular use or appearance in order to show what is to be adjusted by additions or subtractions from the *symmetria*, so that it may appear to be planned correctly and its elevation may leave nothing to be desired.[30]

This is where the inherent individual skills of the architect took over from the discipline he had learnt; imagination and invention, not theory, were the real source of *eurythmia*.

The Corinthian order, with its highly distinctive acanthus-leaf capitals, demonstrates the process. For the major temples of imperial Rome, an underlying set of design rules has been identified based firmly within the general principles of mathematical harmony described above.[31] The fundamental rule is that the height of the column shaft is 5/6 of the total height of the column including capital and base, giving a simple proportional relationship which is also founded on the two perfect numbers. From there on a number of alternatives are possible—for example, the lower diameter of the column can be either 1/10 of the total height of the column or 1/8 the height of the column shaft—but all involve simple relationships with either the height or the lower diameter of the column. This means that all these major Corinthian columns do not look alike simply because of the distinctive appearance of the capitals with their rows of acanthus leaves and curved volutes, but because of an underlying similarity in their proportions. At the same time, they are all subtly different not just because of differences in overall size or materials or style of carving but also because of the effects of the variation allowable within the basic rules.

Invention and imagination were not, however, allowed to have completely free rein within the framework of *symmetria*; the architect was also expected to exercise his individuality within the constraints of *decor*. For Vitruvius this is a very broad concept which encompasses conforming to convention or precedent in making style suit the subject; or ensuring consistency within an established style; or working with nature by taking account of purely physical circumstances, like using local materials or siting a building to make the best use of natural light. The primary meaning of *decor* is visual grace or beauty, but Vitruvius combines this with its more metaphysical meaning of appropriateness or seemliness, one of the essential Roman virtues for those living in the public eye.

Cicero's great moral essay, *On Duties*, which was widely read and may have inspired Vitruvius, shows how closely the two are related. For Cicero, *decor* is the application of limit and order to all aspects of life, the restraint of reason on impulse. The guide to *decor* is nature, both universal nature common to all and, within that, the nature of the individual, provided it is honourable; the specific external context and one's own status provide the key. Consistency—being true to one's nature—is also an essential part of *decor*. Because *decor* involves visibility as well as fittingness, it is not surprising that Cicero includes a discussion of the kind of house suitable for a man of rank and political weight, admitting the need for the house to match the standing of the owner and allow the reception of many guests, while advocating moderation in expense and luxury; 'one's standing', Cicero writes, 'ought to be enhanced by one's house, but not won entirely because of it; the master should not be made honourable by the house, but the house by the master'.[32] If the equivalent passages in Vitruvius put more emphasis on the house than the man, that is only to be expected in a work devoted to architecture rather than to moral virtue. What is more important is that, as with *symmetria*, *decor* too exalts the architectural discourse into the world of philosophy, this time the practical ethics of one of Rome's leading statesmen. In the immediate context of Augustan Rome, it is *decor* which, mediating between the universal truths of the cosmos and the individual inspiration of the architect, validates the importance attached to architecture in the reshaping of Roman society.

There is no simple way to identify the operation of *decor* in the archaeological record in the way that we can detect the perfect numbers and simple proportions of *symmetria*. One rather curious text, however, suggests that it was still current in the second century CE. The author, Lucian, was a typically cosmopolitan Roman of the Second Sophistic; born in Samosata on the

Euphrates at the eastern edge of the Roman empire, widely travelled from Gaul to Athens and Egypt, he wrote in Greek, although his native language was probably Aramaic. The work purports to be a eulogy of the engineer/architect Hippias through the description of one of his minor works, a set of public baths.[33] Hippias is praised for his wisdom in music, harmony, engineering, geometry, and astronomy—he clearly had a Vitruvian education—and his building is praised for its Vitruvian virtues of being fitted to the nature of the site, in accordance with the general idea of a bath, and suitably lit, while the rooms are of the appropriate height, with the breadth in the right proportion to the width; needless to say, the whole is seen as an exercise in beauty. The closing lines, praising the water clock which bellows like a bull and the two toilets, remind us that this is the world of satire, but satire must be based in experience to strike a chord in the audience. The educated elite who formed the audience were clearly expected to recognize both the figure of the architect and the language of architectural discourse, virtually unchanged over the two centuries since Vitruvius wrote.

Exploring Diversity—Type and Variation

The interplay between *symmetria*, *eurythmia*, and *decor* was not just an academic discourse but lay at the heart of that diversity within conformity which is one of the hallmarks of Roman architecture. The doctrine of *decor* reflects a common expectation of what a building of a given functional type, or a column of a given architectural order, should look like. This seems to be particularly true for ceremonial public buildings like temples and amphitheatres, where the function was closely bounded by the strictures of society as a whole. Here familiarity of appearance comforted the user with a sense of belonging, an essential commodity in a world as mobile as that of Rome. This translates into the existence of widely shared rules of design, of common families of *symmetria*. The major amphitheatres of the imperial period provide just one example where the formal similarities are not just coincidental but reflect the application of the same kind of rules of proportion or geometry; that is, they share the same *symmetria*.[34] It was the variation on these accepted patterns introduced by the architect, however, which satisfied the desire of the patron to be associated with something that would be as unique as well as a lasting memorial to their name.

This is only part of the story. Not all buildings were as circumscribed as temples and amphitheatres; baths and houses in particular, which catered for the needs and pleasures of the individual rather than of society as a whole, gave an altogether vaster scope for the exercise of diversity. This is obvious even from Vitruvius' rules for the design of the Roman house, which give three basic schemes and allow for a wide variation of proportion according to size.[35] The larger number of separate elements—rooms and courts—alone allows for more possible variation and therefore greater individuality. Here it is similarity in design process which is surprising, rather than the diversity, as it suggests a deliberate imitation to a specific end.

The most intriguing example is that of the imperial *thermae* of Rome, the Baths of Trajan, Caracalla, Severus Alexander, and Diocletian.[36] These all share a similar axially symmetrical design, focused on a central sequence of swimming pool (*natatio*), triple cross-vaulted cold hall (*frigidarium*), warm

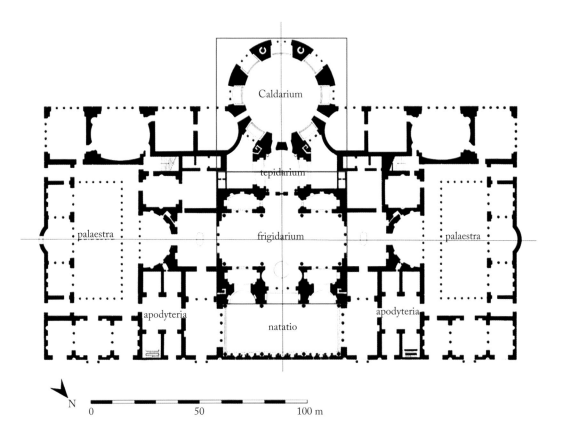

Fig. 20

Reconstructed 'double-square' design scheme (marked in red) for the Baths of Caracalla, Rome, 211–217 CE. The first 200 Roman feet (59 metres) square is centred on the intersection of the two main axes at the *frigidarium*, while the second gives the outer edge of the *caldarium*.

passage (*tepidarium*), and hall with hot bathing tubs (*caldarium*), with lateral exercise courts (*palaestrae*) and rows of hot rooms flanking the *caldarium*. Rather than the similarities being simply a response to the same functional requirements, these buildings share a complex geometric design process, based on an initial 200 Roman feet square, with the *frigidarium* at the centre and defined by the diagonals of opposing 100 feet square [20].

At the same time, the buildings are all clearly different. The architect of the Baths of Diocletian, for example, was clearly aiming for a larger building overall than the Baths of Caracalla, yet could achieve it while adopting the same kind of design process.[37]

The complexity of the process and the close links between the very small number of examples suggest that descriptive accounts of the individual designs, accompanied by a plan or series of plans, were retained in imperial archives and used as a source by successive architects. The technical and logistical problems of erecting these exceptional buildings, particularly when there had been a long break since the last one, might account for this, but there is also an ideological aspect to be considered. The imperial *thermae* as buildings were identified very closely with their builders, the emperors. Their style was distinctive: on a general level in plan morphology as we have seen; in exotic construction techniques such as the use of iron for ties and in vaulting;[38] in detail of elevation such as the great triple cross-vaulted halls [16]; and in decoration, such as the unnecessary giant granite monoliths which appear to support them.

Earlier imperial baths—those of Agrippa, Titus, and Nero—were rebuilt apparently to conform closer to this evolving imperial model in the second and third centuries. Outside of this narrow group of buildings, provincial imitations exist, but on a smaller scale and without any evidence for the underlying design process. All this suggests that these buildings were designed to an exclusive imperial template, a complex and highly elegant design process which was not available to the average architect and could not easily be guessed at; after all, the outline of the original 200 foot square is all but invisible in the finished buildings. Such a template had an important ideological role in maintaining imperial exclusivity; and exclusivity was one of the major demonstrations of imperial power.

The existence of common design processes, such as that for the imperial Corinthian order, which link orders or buildings widely separated in time and place, suggests a different mode of transmission. One possibility is that each architect simply studied the previous orders or buildings and invented his own process from scratch, and that these processes ended up being similar because all the architects were trained in the same basic principles. The mechanics of this are, however, hard to imagine; it is more likely that some of the design processes became codified and were studied as a normal part of an architect's training. Vitruvius' predilection for providing design rules for particular circumstances no doubt reflects this, a point made clear with the rules of thumb he provides for designing artillery 'in accordance with my own experience and with the instructions of my teachers'.[39] Some of his own rules, for example that the height of the columns in a peristyle should equal the width of the colonnade,[40] seem to have had common currency over a long period; others, like his rules for the Corinthian order, did not. Fashions change, particularly during periods of rapid development and intense building with the concomitant opportunities for experimentation; it is hardly a coincidence that the rules for the Corinthian order settle down at the time of a massive increase in temple building under Augustus. The spread of this rule for the Corinthian order, with its origins in the city of Rome, to examples in the rest of the empire reflects in turn the commonality of knowledge made possible by a universal empire and the mobility of individuals made possible by the Roman peace. But it is worth noting that when change occurs, the *kind* of rules do not change, since their basis was in the unchanging truths of mathematical harmony.

Discussing Design

Although design was the architect's responsibility, it was normally prepared to the client's brief and when completed still had to pass the client's scrutiny. The degree of patron intervention then, as now, must have varied enormously both with the individual and with the nature of the project. Pliny the Younger, for example, in rebuilding a Temple to Ceres on one of his estates, seems to have set out some basic requirements of size (larger) and materials (marble) but left the details of the design to his architect Mustius.[41] Cicero's letters, on the other hand, show him and his brother Quintus taking a more active interest in their private building projects, debating the relative merits of different possibilities, and delighting in the finished effect or deciding on changes where it did not please.[42] An earlier phase in the interaction between architect and client appears in an anecdote set in Rome in the second century CE, at a visit to Cornelius Fronto, tutor and later close friend of the emperor Marcus Aurelius:

> Several builders were present, summoned to construct some new baths, and they were showing Fronto different plans of baths drawn on pieces of parchment. When he had selected one plan and specifications from them, he asked what the cost would be of finishing the whole project.[43]

Here the point of contact is the plan. Even in the modern world, where plans are everywhere, the ability to read them easily and conjure up a mental image of what they represent is by no means universal. It is a problem that Vitruvius understood well, and he makes it a critical difference between architect and layman that 'the layman cannot understand what is in hand unless he sees it already done; but the architect, when once he has formed his plan, has a definite idea how it will turn out in terms of beauty, usefulness and suitability'.[44] Cicero is one example, commenting that he could see the promise in the design of Quintus' townhouse now that the work was underway better than he could from the plan alone.[45]

There were alternatives. Vitruvius makes it clear that in addition to plans, some kinds of elevations and three-dimensional views were also used, as were models.[46] All these may have made architectural designs easier to appreciate, but plans had their own mystique. Few actual architects' drawings on papyrus or canvas survive from the Roman period, but there are several representations of plans in marble and mosaic which were clearly intended for public display and not necessarily as a legal record; they include, for example, several plans of tomb enclosures and the plan of a bath building in mosaic, with written dimensions but not necessarily to scale [21].[47]

This is an interesting, and indeed an exceptional, phenomenon. It assumes a remarkably widespread ability to recognize what a plan was and what it stood for, even if the observer had difficulty, as Cicero did, in trying to imagine the three-dimensional reality it represented.

In part, such an expectation can be related to the official role of maps and plans in Rome and in colonial settlements. From at least the middle of the second century BCE, maps showing the division of Roman territory had been inscribed in bronze and displayed publicly in the capital, and sufficient examples in bronze and on marble survive to show that their equivalents were set up in the local administrative centres—that is, in the associated colonies—as well, together with the laws governing the colony.[48] Following the total reorganization of the city of Rome under Augustus, it is likely that an equivalent map was made of the city itself for public display; what survives are a very few fragments of its first replacement, under Vespasian, and considerably more of the last version dating to the reign of Septimius Severus.[49] The plan was engraved on marble slabs at a scale of 1:240 [22], but presupposes a working version on more manageable materials which formed part of the state archives and was used for administrative purposes.

Archive plans have a history which goes back to the third millennium, but the public display of the plan in permanent form is as far as we know a

Fig. 21

Measured drawing of a mosaic plan showing baths, found in Via di Porta San Lorenzo, Rome, probably from a second- to third-century CE suburban villa. The Roman numerals appear to give the dimensions of the rooms, while the pairs of parallel lines passing through the walls seem to indicate windows, and the green areas pools.

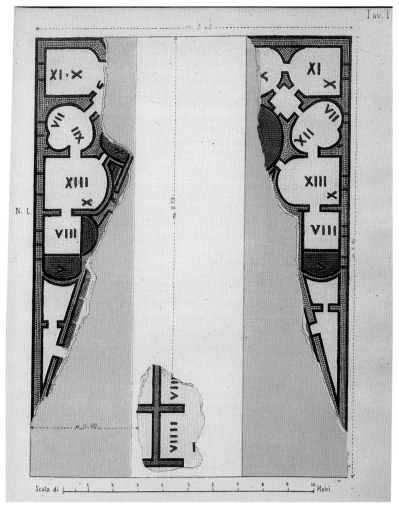

particularly Roman phenomenon. It goes hand in hand with the whole epigraphic habit of the Roman world, with the public display of laws and the monumentalization of building inscriptions, as a way of making permanent and visible the ordering of Roman society. Tomb plans are perhaps wider reflections of this way of thinking.

A rather different attitude to plans is represented by the floor mosaic of the baths. Here the context is domestic, and the plan a talking point, perhaps representing the building in which the mosaic was found or one built for the owner. In any case, it strongly suggests that plans had taken on a life of their own and could be treated as artefacts in their own right. This is an extraordinarily sophisticated way of thinking, and is yet another pointer towards the intrinsic role that architectural discourse played in elite society. Understanding a plan as the distillation of a building also implies accepting an abstract pattern as a reasonable representation of three-dimensional reality; that is, of the built environment as experienced. This in turn has implications for the nature of spatial perception in Roman society which have not yet been fully explored.

The use of the plan as an artefact is perhaps just one manifestation of a much wider phenomenon. One of the changes which can be observed in Roman architecture during the late Republic and early empire is the growing importance of buildings of complex design, composed of varied, interlocking, and often curvilinear shapes, which can only really be appreciated precisely as plans. The earliest hint of this is in the mountain fortress of Herod the Great, a great lover of Rome and things Roman, at Herodium, south of Jerusalem. The near-contemporary written description of a fancy aviary-cum-dining-room on the country estate of Varro, a Roman scholar and contemporary of Cicero whose works included the earliest known account of architecture as a liberal art, may reflect the same trend.[50] The largest concentration of such buildings, as well as the most varied and innovative, are to be found among the pavilions and baths of Hadrian's Villa at Tivoli [23, 133],[51] although there are elements in the imperial palace on the Palatine and in several bath buildings in Italy and North Africa, such as the Baths at Thaenae [24].

The same fascination with two-dimensional representations of complex geometries appears in the design of numerous mosaic and marble floors of the period, and the interest may have developed out of the same kind of late Hellenistic advances in geometry which allowed the development of the amphitheatre. On the other hand, many of the more sinuous designs are based on a grid of squares with inscribed circles, and the trick was to create an entirely curvilinear shape or space out of the basic grid. The extent to which this type of planning was developed in response to a different view of nature is unclear, but the possibilities are intriguing. If the simple ratios and pure forms of circle, square, and sphere relate to musical harmonies and the universal order of the cosmos, these complicated geometric puzzles relate

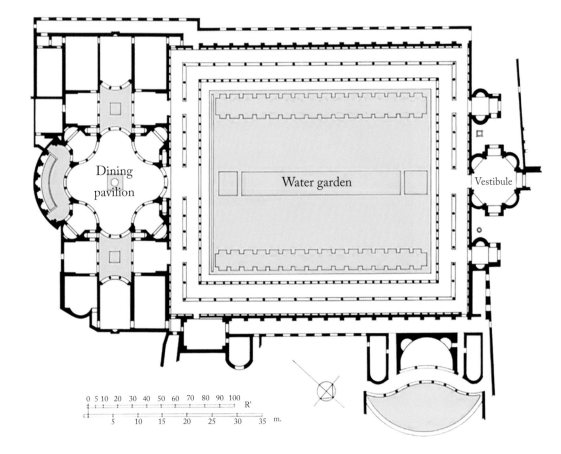

Dining pavilion

Water garden

Vestibule

0 5 10 20 30 40 50 60 70 80 90 100 R'

5 10 15 20 25 30 35 m.

Fig. 23

Plan of the so-called 'Piazza d'Oro', a dining pavilion and water garden at Hadrian's Villa, Tivoli, c. 130 CE. The blue areas are water features and the green open spaces. The undulating curves of the main pavilion were developed from circles set in a grid of nine squares.

more to the kind of forms produced by living nature like the intricate patterns of shells or flowers.

Many of the later buildings, with their sinuous reverse curves, are particularly confusing for the observer, full of surprise and constantly foiling expectation in a way we normally associate with the Italian Baroque. In fact, there is a direct link, as the buildings of Hadrian's Villa were a key source of inspiration for such Baroque masterpieces as Borromini's S. Ivo alla Sapienza and S. Carlo alle Quattro Fontane in Rome. Plans of this kind appear to be restricted to private residences and baths, the two categories where, as we have seen, the imagination of the architect was least under the constraints of *decor* and most at the service of the patron's desire for novelty. It is not surprising to find so many of the examples associated with Hadrian, who is argued to have had an active interest in architectural design; close consultation between emperor and architect is at least feasible. These plans are complex geometric puzzles, architectural conceits which may have remained a private joke between architect and patron or, like the mosaic plan, may have provided a dinner-party conversation piece among an educated elite. After all, most of the plans are of dining halls, garden pavilions, or baths, the focus of elite entertaining. These buildings are intended to impress and delight, even amuse, a cultivated audience, and here, more than

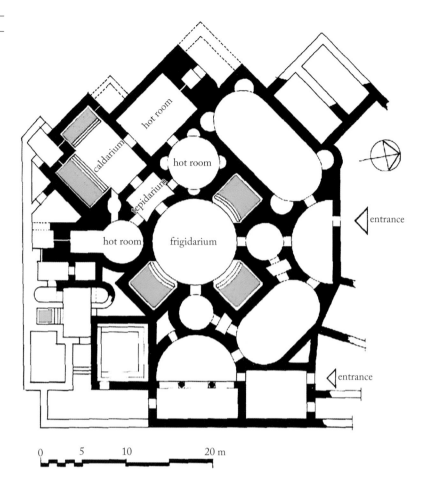

Fig. 24

Reconstructed plan of the
Large Baths, Thaenae,
Tunisia, probably later
second or third century CE.
The complex plan was
based on a square centred
on the *frigidarium*, rotated
through 90 degrees

caldarium

hot room

hot room

tepidarium

hot room

frigidarium

entrance

entrance

0   5   10   20 m

anywhere, we can see the training of the architect and the education of the patron meet over the drawing board.

The importance of architects in creating the built environment of the Roman world is clear. In the chapters which follow, it is essential to remember that few if any of the public or private buildings in whatever part of the empire were the result of some kind of natural evolution. Rather, they were the result of the choices made by individual patrons, whose desire for originality could only be met by the imagination and invention of individual architects working within but rising above the established conventions.

Construction: The Civilizing Art

3

...then indeed from the construction of buildings [men] progressed step by step to other crafts and sciences, and led the way from a wild and uncultivated life to a tamed and educated one.

Vitruvius, *de architectura* 2.1.6

The Romans have a long-standing reputation as builders and engineers. Renowned for their monumental utilitarian works, especially roads and aqueducts which inspired, among others, the early Victorian railway engineers, they were also masters of creating vast interior spaces such as the Pantheon, the clear span of its concrete dome unsurpassed until the nineteenth century [3]. As Vitruvius was well aware, the great achievements of Roman structural engineers required a thorough understanding of the available materials, the techniques of construction most suited to them, and the kinds of structural systems in which they could be employed.[1]

Vitruvius' chapter on construction is one of the few where his own observations and practical experience shine through, as when he describes the precise sound that good pit-sand makes when rubbed between the fingers, a test still used by builders today.[2] It was also the one where he was possibly in greatest danger of losing his audience. While the Roman upper classes might appreciate the intellectual skills of architectural design, they scorned all manual work. Yet developments in construction techniques do not appear in isolation but are generally a response to the demands of architects and their patrons for larger, more complex and novel structures, built more quickly and economically, often requiring innovative approaches and original solutions [25]. As one of Vitruvius' fundamental principles of architecture, *distributio* or economy includes the judicious selection of materials as a prime factor in managing the cost of construction,[3] something that would have been of considerable interest to his audience. It was to their advantage to understand the recommendations of their architects and builders when it came to building materials, and to be able to detect poor materials and shoddy workmanship.

To begin with, however, Vitruvius sought to engage his audience on a far more elevated level, by presenting construction as the first of all human crafts, the keystone of civilized life which allowed the emergence of man from his wild and rustic state.[4] Here Vitruvius again reflects Greek philosophy and contemporary thought, which emphasized the theory that man did not invent but discovered what already existed in nature.[5] His account of how man learnt to construct shelter from natural materials by observing and imitating the birds and animals of the field and forest strikes a surprisingly

Detail of Fig. 50

Wall painting showing a construction scene, from the Tomb of Trebius Justus, Rome, probably fourth century CE. This is the only known depiction which clearly shows Roman builders laying brick-faced mortared rubble walls.

45

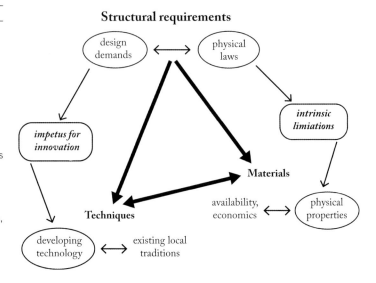

Fig. 25

The parameters of construction. There is a constant tension and interaction between the intrinsic physical limitations created by the inherent properties of building materials (on the right) and the impetus for innovation which grows out of the design demands of architects and patrons (on the left). At each point of the triangle, the architects and builders have to balance the desired effect against the limitations, including cost and availability of materials, and the conservative impulse of local building traditions versus the need for innovation.

Structural requirements

design demands ⟷ physical laws

impetus for innovation

intrinsic limiations

Materials

Techniques

availability, economics ⟷ physical properties

developing technology ⟷ existing local traditions

modern, evolutionary note. Significantly, he says that the ancient building on the Areopagus in Athens roofed with mud and the 'Hut of Romulus' in Rome [26] call to mind the customs (*mores*) of the distant past. Thus Athens and Rome, the twin homes of civilization and culture recognized by the Augustan age, stand at the start of the further development of construction as a precursor to all other arts and sciences, based no longer on direct imitation of nature but on human ingenuity reinforced by careful observation of cause and effect.[6]

The Building Blocks of Rome

The primitive structures described by Vitruvius used very common basic materials and simple techniques already widely employed throughout the Mediterranean region by the eighth century BCE: timber frames, mud-brick, pisé or wattle-and-daub walls, thatched roofs, wooden shingles. The first reported bridge across the Tiber, the seventh-century Pons Sublicius, was said to have been built in timber without the use of iron.[7] These types of materials, however, are short-lived, and both the 'Hut of Romulus' and the Pons Sublicius only survived into the empire by being constantly rebuilt in the traditional fashion, in response to religious strictures.[8]

Starting in the late seventh century BCE there was a remarkable and widespread—although not universal—shift to stone as the material of choice for higher-status structures, a phenomenon which encompassed the Greek world as well as central Italy, representing an ongoing cultural transformation that scholars have associated with the emergence of the *polis*.[9] Stone has the great advantage of permanence but, especially when used in large squared blocks (ashlar), requires special tools and highly skilled workers, and involves large and heavy individual elements, beyond what one or two men could easily handle without recourse to some form of machine,

Fig. 26

Reconstruction of an eighth-century BCE timber-framed hut, based on excavations on the Palatine Hill, Rome.

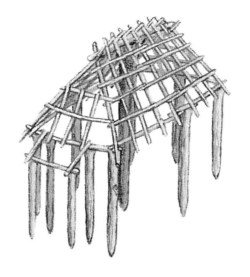

and hence more infrastructure for transport and lifting into place. While in some ways these extra requirements could be seen as a disadvantage, making building far more expensive and requiring access to and control of much greater resources, this in itself added to the status of the structures. Only the wealthiest individuals, or the whole of the community together, could afford such outlay. If Rome's first bridge was made of timber, its first walls were made of stone.[10]

Rome is exceptional in the largely limestone Mediterranean in that it lies at the intersection of two ancient volcanic systems, the Alban Hills to the south and the Sabatine Hills to the north [27]. These provided various grades of tuff, a rock formed from consolidated volcanic ash,[11] which has the advantage of being soft, easily cut, and relatively lightweight, reducing manpower requirements; unfortunately, these tuffs are also relatively weak, with little resistance to weathering. As the varieties found in the centre of Rome are fairly poor in quality, more suitable material eventually was sought

Fig. 27

Simplified geological map indicating the main building materials of Rome and its hinterland.

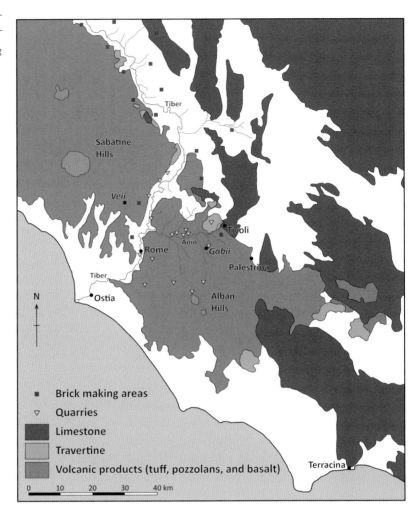

further afield. In the early fourth century, a yellow tuff from just north of Rome was used for the c. 11-kilometre circuit of the city walls [28].

Although only marginally stronger than that of Rome, it was easily and economically transported down the river, and had an extra symbolic value, reflecting Rome's conquest of the Etruscan city of Veii. From then on, the introduction of new and better types of stone often went hand in hand with Rome's territorial expansion. The quarries of the famous travertine, a form of limestone which is resistant to weathering, relatively easy to work, and occurs in horizontal beds from which regular blocks can be obtained, were controlled by the independent but allied city of Tibur (modern Tivoli), which did not become formally part of the Roman state until the first century BCE. Thus to begin with at Rome it was only used sparingly, at points of particular stress such as architraves, or column capitals and bases, or the foundations under columns, with the softer and weaker tuff used for the remaining bulk of the structure. By the Augustan period, however,

Strabo was able to consider Rome well supplied with travertine along with two types of tuff,[12] all of which could be transported economically by water along the River Anio to the Tiber just above Rome.

The other important advance was the development of 'concrete', or mortared rubble, another response to the accident of Rome's volcanic geology which was to have a profound impact on the development of Roman—and indeed much subsequent—architecture. Plaster and mortar made from a mixture of lime and ordinary quartz sand had a very long history, and were widely employed in the ancient Mediterranean. Vitruvius was well aware of the drawbacks: it dries slowly, he says of lime mortar, and a wall cannot be built up without interruption but needs regular pauses in construction, and cannot support a vault.[13] As it happens, Rome does not have many good supplies of ordinary sand; what it has instead are pit-sands (*harenae fossiciae*), ashy volcanic deposits, usually black, red, or grey in colour, which react with lime in a completely different way to sand to produce a strong and quick-setting mortar.[14] In modern terminology the pit-sands are pozzolans, named after the volcanic *pulvis Puteolanis* from near ancient Puteoli (modern Pozzuoli) on the Bay of Naples, which Vitruvius praises for its ability to set underwater and thus its value in harbour works. Presumably because this light-brownish pozzolan looks very different from the red-black pit-sands of Rome, Vitruvius treats them as different materials, yet they have a similar basic reaction with lime and similar virtues in construction.

The properties of these abundant local pit-sands when used in mortared rubble gradually became apparent to Roman builders. Initially it was used like ordinary lime-mortared rubble, as a substitute for solid stone construction in foundations or as the rubble fill of thick walls with faces of carefully cut ashlar. The major step to using it as a building material in its own right for free-standing walls seems to have been taken around the middle of the second century BCE.[15] In foundations the rubble and mortar could be laid in wooden formwork or thrown into a trench, but for most walls above ground some kind of permanent facing was needed to provide a regular surface and to make the shaping of elements such as corners, doors, or windows simpler. In the earliest examples at Rome the facing, like the rubble of the core, was normally of tuff, in fist-sized irregular pieces fitted fairly close together and with a smooth outer face, a technique Vitruvius called *incertum* [29a].[16] The corners and edges were either made in ashlar [35] or from blocks roughly the size and shape of modern house bricks [34].

Over time the basic technique was refined, as better qualities of pit-sand were identified and different materials and techniques used for the facing. By the middle of the first century BCE a distinctive form had evolved, Vitruvius' *reticulatum* [29b], where each facing block was a tall pyramid with a square face, the point interlocking with the rubble of the core to form a strong bond, and the face set on the diagonal to form the net pattern which gave it its name. Although Vitruvius was very dismissive of this technique, which he thought was too prone to crack along the diagonals,[17] it continued in use in Rome into the second century CE, when it was gradually overtaken by the material which we most associate with imperial Rome: brick [29c]. Fired brick had been used as a construction material in the Mediterranean since at least the third century BCE, but rarely in Rome until the first century BCE, when pieces of broken rooftile began to be used for facing walls. By the middle of the first century CE specially made bricks had become common, often made in standard sizes—two-thirds (*bessales*), one-and-a-half (*sesquipedales*), and two (*bipedales*) Roman feet square but only an inch and a half thick—some of which had perhaps evolved specifically for the modular construction of hypocaust floors in bath buildings, although small tiles were also used.[18] The majority of the clay sources and production centres lay along the middle Tiber valley north of Rome, taking advantage of easy river

Fig. 29

Facing techniques for mortared rubble construction, examples from Ostia. (a) *incertum*, mid-second to end first centuries BCE; (b) *reticulatum*, first century BCE to second century CE; (c) brick, first century BCE to fourth century CE. Stone blocks ((a), mainly second century BCE to early first century CE), broken rooftile ((b), mainly first century BCE to first CE), and brick (first to second century CE) were used at openings and points of stress.

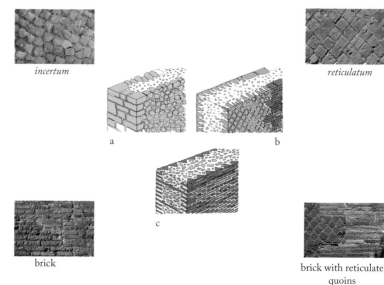

incertum

reticulatum

a

b

brick

c

brick with reticulate quoins

transport. In wall facings the bricks were broken along the diagonal into rough triangles, trimmed as required, and set with their longest edges on the face.[19] Whole *sesquipedales* or *bipedales* were used in arches or as levelling courses, originally at the base of walls but later in so-called 'bonding courses' which generally went through the whole thickness of the wall at regular intervals and helped keep the walls vertical, as well as providing a way of tracking the progress of construction in complex structures. The increasing distinction between facing and core, in terms of the shape of the elements and sometimes the actual materials, is a peculiarly Roman development and one of the keys to its success.

By the middle of the second century CE brick had become the dominant facing material for mortared rubble walls in Rome, often in combination with *reticulatum*, and a whole new aesthetic developed especially for utilitarian structures, taking advantage of contrasting colours and travertine insets [30, 123]. Although it is easy to assume that this was the normal form of construction for the Roman empire, it was actually a distinctive and exceptional technique which was not widely replicated outside of the large cities of central Italy, except in certain types of buildings. The status of the brick and reticulate technique lingered on into the fourth century CE, when it was exactly replicated in prestigious marble veneer [31] for the interior of a fine reception room in a seaside *domus* at Ostia.[20]

Covering Space

Building walls is one thing, but bridging openings and covering space is another. Here timber has distinct advantages over stone, which is liable to

Fig. 30

Hemicycle of Trajan's Market, Rome, c. 106–113 CE. The arched openings on the first-floor level are framed by low-relief pilasters in brick with travertine capitals and bases.

Fig. 31

Reconstructed wall veneer from the Edificio della Porta Marina, Ostia, fourth century CE. The imitation reticulate is made from Egyptian red porphyry, green porphyry from Sparta, yellow Numidian from Tunisia, and purple-veined white Phrygian marble from central Turkey, while the 'bricks' are in Numidian marble, with white palombino limestone, probably from Italy, used to represent the mortar joints.

crack if used as a simple beam over all but modest spans; the weak tuff presents a particular problem. Vitruvius notes that where the spacing between temple columns is equal to three column diameters there is danger that the stone lintels across them might break, whereas any spacing greater than this cannot use stone but requires wooden beams.[21] Architects sometimes used the two in combination, as in the Doric Forum porticoes at Pompeii where the tuff lintels were supported on timber beams and the whole originally stuccoed over to imitate an entirely stone structure.[22] Covering large spaces required the use of the truss [32a], a fixed triangle of beams in which all the loads generated by the roof covering and any environmental forces such as wind were absorbed without creating outward thrusts on the walls.[23] While the origins of the roof truss are obscure, it was already in use in Rome and central Italy as early as the sixth century BCE,[24] and it was essential in the development of basilicas (see Chapter 5). By the late first century BCE there were some very large halls, including the Diribitorium (where votes were counted in elections) which must have used a truss for its 100-Roman-foot (29.5-metre) span.[25]

The other solution to spanning openings was to use an arch [32b], which relies on setting wedge-shaped blocks (voussoirs) radially, so that the downward forces across the opening created by the loads are gradually transferred sideways to the supports. Here the softness of tuff and its ease of working could be an advantage as it simplified the accurate cutting of the voussoirs, something that required much more labour and skill for the harder limestone. Even tuff arches, however, generated outward forces, and the stability of the structure depended on the resistance of their supports. Thus the earliest surviving examples are as gateways in city walls [143] and covering cisterns and drains such as the great *Cloaca Maxima*. Semi-circular arches and

Fig. 32

Roman devices for covering space: (a) triangular roof truss; (b) voussoir (cut-stone) arch.

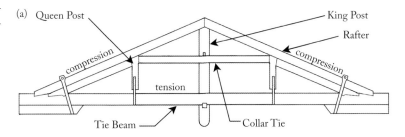

(a) Queen Post King Post Rafter compression compression tension Tie Beam Collar Tie

Parts of a truss

(b)

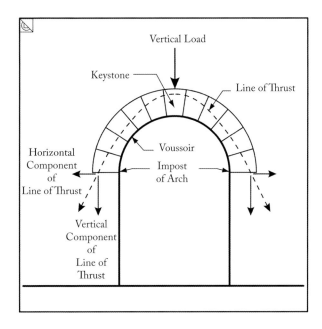

Vertical Load

Keystone

Line of Thrust

Horizontal Component of Line of Thrust

Voussoir

Impost of Arch

Vertical Component of Line of Thrust

barrel-vaults were the norm, providing one of the key visual elements which make Roman architecture so easily identifiable. The 24.5-metre central span of the aqueduct bridge of the Pont du Gard [6] demonstrates the extent to which Roman builders could take this technology.

By the early first century BCE at the latest, Roman builders had also developed the flat or lintel arch, which can be thought of as a pre-cracked lintel where the 'cracks' are designed to produce wedge-shaped pieces which cannot collapse unless the supports give way. This ingenious device could be used in temples and porticoes, as in the forum at Pompeii [33], where the constraints of *decor* demanded a traditional flat architrave but the design span posed problems of stability.

The most significant Roman innovation in terms of covering space was, however, the substitution of mortared rubble for cut stone, particularly given the demands on skill, labour, and time required for cutting and laying voussoirs. By the later part of the second century BCE vaulted mortared rubble was being used for very large structures inconceivable in cut stone, most

Fig. 33

Forum portico, Pompeii,
c. 62–79 CE, limestone.
The architrave and frieze of
the Doric lower order are
combined and treated as
wedge-shaped lintel (flat)
arches.

notably the so-called 'Porticus Aemilia', possibly shipsheds (*navalia*), in the docks area south of the Aventine [34].[26] While the actual vaults do not survive, the arches which cover the doors and windows linking the bays provide a clue to the evolution of vaulting in mortared rubble. The blocks of tuff which form the arches appear as small voussoirs on the face of the wall, but with a layer of mortar between them which would not have been there in true ashlar construction. In other early vaulted structures the irregular pieces of core are also set radially, as if the builders imagined the structure to be acting like a traditional vault even though it was the mortar which ultimately provided the strength. By the mid-first century CE, builders seem to have realized that vaults worked just as well with the rubble laid horizontally, and this continued to be normal practice. While for a long time these rubble vaults could not reach the spans of timber roof trusses, they had the inestimable advantage of being largely resistant to the deleterious effects of moisture and above all to fire.

The development of this completely new and in its day experimental material and technique can be seen as response to the new political and economic conditions of the second century BCE, with the expansion of Roman hegemony into the Hellenistic East and the great wealth that came with it. The scale of public building increased greatly, to the point that, according to Polybius, it became the chief expense for the Roman treasury.[27] The basilicas and porticoes that were such a feature of the period certainly all required a substantial workforce of masons and carpenters trained in the traditional skills, and this was also the period of the earliest marble temples in Rome, which required material, and almost certainly skilled workmen,

Fig. 34

'Porticus Aemilia'/? *navalia*, Rome, later second century BCE, mortared rubble faced in tuff *incertum* and blocks. This enormous structure, the largest known from this early period, was nearly 500 metres long and 90 metres wide, divided into fifty bays covered by parallel barrel-vaults, each with a span of over 8 metres.

imported from Attica.[28] It was, however, the large-scale infrastructure works—roads, bridges, aqueducts, and sewers—which formed the bulk of public construction; the 'Porticus Aemilia'/*navalia* presumably came into this category.

Such structures may have formed one of the testing grounds for the new material, together with the substructures used to enlarge elite housing, helped by the sheer volume of construction which allowed for rapid experimentation in what is traditionally the most conservative of trades. The impetus arguably came from the highest levels of Roman society who had ultimate control over valuable state contracts, and the political need to have them completed as quickly and economically as possible. Roman architects and builders of the period quickly came to appreciate the value of parallel barrel-vaulted cells of uniform height for creating terraces, as for the monumental sanctuary at Palestrina [62], or for luxury villas [125].

On their own or in combination with long barrel-vaults running parallel to a hill, parallel barrel-vaults had the structural strength of solid masonry terracing walls but required far less material while providing versatile usable spaces. The continuous, mutually self-supporting arcades of the Flavian Amphitheatre [1] are the ultimate example of this basic concept, which became an important leitmotif of Roman architecture. Another important combination was to buttress the sides of the main barrel vault with a series of smaller barrel-vaulted rooms at right angles to it. This was especially useful where a free-standing hall with a large span was required, the buttressing rooms providing extra functional spaces visually subsidiary to the main one, creating a clear spatial hierarchy [35].

Further experimentation with intersecting barrel-vaults of the same height at the crown led to the development of cross-vaults, the most successful and versatile form of vaulting in the imperial period [16].[29] Capable in theory of unlimited expansion in either direction, they had the advantage of allowing much more movement between contiguous spaces than barrel-vaults did, and provided the possibility of inserting large windows in the vaults on all sides. All the forces generated by the vault had, however, to rest on piers at the corners of the vault, requiring thicker walls or even more buttressing, so that it is not surprising that cross-vaults only appear regularly in Rome from the mid-first century CE onwards, as Roman architects developed more confidence in their material. The advantages of the cross-vault can be seen in the different systems used in the annular passages of the Augustan Theatre of Marcellus [36] and the Flavian Amphitheatre [37], less than a hundred years apart. The difficulty lay in creating the connections between the passages which ran just behind the first-floor arcades on the façades, and the radial passages which led towards the stage or arena. In the Theatre of Marcellus, the upper radial passages are covered with barrel-vaults which extend across the annular passage on stone lintels, many of which are now cracked, while in the Flavian Amphitheatre both radial and annular passages are covered with barrel-vaults which intersect to form cross-vaults, an altogether more visually elegant and structurally efficient system.

For rooms with a circular or octagonal plan the natural solution for roofing was a dome or related form. Vitruvius mentions domes only in relation to the circular sweating rooms (*laconica*) of bath buildings,[30] and our earliest surviving examples are in fact those of the early first-century BCE Stabian

Fig. 35

'Market building' at Ferentinum (Italy), late second to early first century BCE, mortared rubble faced in *incertum*, with limestone door jambs and voussoir arches. Parallel rooms open off the central vaulted space at right angles, buttressing the vault.

Fig. 36

and Forum Baths at Pompeii. These were on a modest scale with spans of only 6 metres, but by the Augustan period Roman builders were experimenting with quite substantial domes. The so-called 'Temple of Mercury' at Baiae on the Bay of Naples [38], in reality the cold room of a bath building, has a span of 73 Roman feet (21.6 metres), with both a central circular opening (oculus) and four large windows cut into the sides of the dome, but the builders were clearly concerned about its stability. Externally, the supporting drum rises vertically almost a third beyond the springing of the dome, and is almost surrounded by other rooms which act to prevent the structure moving outwards.[31] Over time, Roman builders developed a number of ways of reducing the natural tendency for the domes to spring apart at their base, including reducing the weight of the rubble in the top of the dome and adding extra material in steps to the outside of the curve; nevertheless, many of them, including the Pantheon, show signs of vertical cracks at the springing.

The Economics of Mortared Rubble Construction

While stone ashlar remained the technique of choice for the outward face of prestige buildings, by the early imperial period mortared rubble provided most of the supporting structure. Its success as a building material was due to its combination of cheapness and flexibility, allowing the builder to choose the most appropriate components for the specific task in hand and to meet the specific budget of the patron. The cost differentials could be

Fig. 37

Flavian Amphitheatre (Colosseum), Rome, c. 70–80 CE. Roofing of the upper ambulatory, using continuous cross-vaults.

substantial. Mortared rubble required less skilled labour as well as less man-power overall than ashlar, so that even a plain wall in tuff ashlar has been estimated to have cost perhaps three to four times as much as the equivalent in *incertum* or *reticulatum*, and a travertine one more than twice that again.[32] The rapidity with which mortar made with pit-sand gained strength was another economic advantage, since it allowed buildings to be put up quickly without compromising on strength. This has been confirmed by the dates painted on the brick face of the 'library' in the early second-century Baths of Trajan **[39]**, which indicate that the 15-metre-high complex walls of the semi-circular building were erected in only two months.[33]

A different kind of economic advantage came from the fact that mortared rubble walls did not require freshly quarried or prime quality material. Since the strength is mainly in the mortar, the material of the core could include quarry waste, damaged or unwanted ashlar blocks, or indeed any durable redundant materials such as fragments of large terracotta pots, broken rooftiles, smashed-up pieces of flooring, or thick wall plaster. The speed of construction and ability to absorb waste materials made mortared rubble an ideal material for rapid reconstruction after natural disasters such as fire or earthquake, something that can be seen following the great fire of Nero in 64 CE. Reticulate facing could also be made from second-hand materials, in this case redundant ashlar blocks, which would save on quarrying and transport costs, as evidenced by the random mixture of different coloured

Fig. 38

'Temple of Mercury' (part of a bath building), Baiae, late first century BCE. Drawing by Giovanni Battista Natali (d. 1765), showing the central oculus and two of the four rectangular windows in the dome. The water is well above the Roman ground level because of a geological process (bradyseism) caused by volcanic action.

and textured tuffs seen in much reticulate. While it has been argued that the introduction of *reticulatum* marks a spatial division of labour between those who made the reticulate blocks at the quarry and the builders on site,[34] recent finds of the debris and waste from making the reticulate blocks on the site where they were used strongly suggest that (re)processing was an urban industry, which bought up unwanted ashlars from demolition sites and reworked them into reticulate pieces.

Use was also made of redundant amphorae, the ubiquitous transport containers of the Mediterranean. Whole amphorae have been found used in land drainage, in foundations, and, especially in the area around the emporium area of Rome, set vertically as the main structural elements of enclosure walls.[35] Olive oil amphorae posed a particular disposal problem, since, unlike wine amphorae, they could not be cleaned for reuse, leaving a 35-metre-high hill of 'empties' (the Monte Testaccio) in the *emporium* district. Sporadically from the second century and more frequently in the late third to fourth centuries CE, for example in the Circus of Maxentius just outside of Rome, they were used in mortared rubble vaults. Usually set in the haunches of the

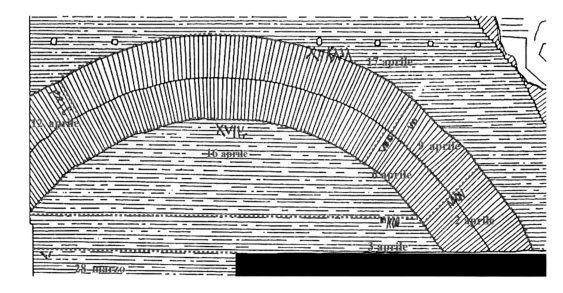

Fig. 39

Baths of Trajan, Rome, 104–109 CE. The sequence of dates, in Roman numerals and using standard abbreviations for the months, was painted in red on the bare surface of the wall and indicates the order of construction.

vaults, for a long time these were thought to have helped in their stability, but Lancaster's analysis shows convincingly that, in this position, they would if anything be more likely to destabilize by reducing the weight at the critical location.[36] What they did save was materials and labour.

Purpose-made brick shows us the other side of the picture. It was not an intrinsically economical material, unlike recycled rooftile fragments, requiring kilns, fuel, and skilled operators to produce. Tuff—as reticulate or in rectangular blocks shaped like modern house bricks—must always have been a viable alternative, although diminishing supplies of recyclable ashlar may have tipped the balance in terms of cost. The widespread adoption of brick does, however, coincide with the greatly increased demand for building materials as Rome expanded upwards and outwards, or had to rebuild itself after a succession of fires and floods. The practice of stamping bricks with complex texts [40], increasingly common in Rome from the middle of the first century CE, shows they were largely produced on land owned by members of Rome's senatorial elite, while the actual production was operated by their slaves or freedmen, or contracted out to others. The development of brick as a material produced on an almost industrial scale specifically to face mortared rubble may, therefore, result from the entrepreneurship of a relatively few well-placed families exploiting the natural resources of their estates under the impetus of large-scale imperial building projects.[37] Not surprisingly, in the uncertain conditions of the third century CE, recycled brick from demolished buildings, identifiable by short lengths, damaged edges, and uneven thicknesses, became increasingly common, while in the late empire alternating courses of blocks and bricks, both employing reused materials, replaced solid brick as facing in all but the most prestigious structures.

Structural Innovation and the Problem of Scale

The development of a vaulted architecture in mortared rubble was in itself a major innovation, which, as long ago pointed out by John Ward-Perkins, led

Drawing of a brickstamp (*CIL* XV 1018), mid-second century CE. The text reads: 'From the estate of Domitia Lucilla, brick of Fortunatus, slave of Domitia Lucilla'.

to a revolution in the treatment of interior space.[38] It was its application to large-scale buildings in particular that produced some of the most enduring symbols of ancient Rome while providing the greatest challenges. Roofing wide-span structures poses serious difficulties whatever the construction technique, and structures such as the Pantheon are testament to the exceptional levels of skill and applied knowledge of Roman builders.

For certain buildings, particularly traditional temples and basilicas, the roof truss was the standard solution, including for the Trajanic Basilica Ulpia [94], the largest traditional basilica ever built, and for the main state rooms in the imperial palace on the Palatine with spans close to 100 Roman feet (29.5 metres) [130].[39] One of the advantage of using a timber roof like this even after it was possible to cover such spans in concrete was that it did not require such a massive supporting structure; the disadvantages included the risk of fire (the Diribitorium burnt down in 80 CE) and the increasing difficulty of obtaining the long beams needed for the main horizontal elements which had to span the full width of the structure. Drawings made before the roof of the Pantheon porch was replaced in the early seventeenth century provide evidence of bronze roof trusses, suggesting further experimentation with the established form.[40]

The carpentry skills and expertise in building trusses which were needed for the traditional basilicas also contributed to the creation of the large span vaults which are the most famous achievements of Roman architecture. All vaulted structures made of mortared rubble under the Roman system needed some form of rigid temporary support (centering) to give the vault its shape until the mortar gained sufficient strength for the vault to be self-supporting. While this was a simple matter in small-span structures, it became perhaps the most crucial element in the construction of wide-span ones such as the Pantheon. If anything, this was a more difficult task than building the roof of a basilica, because it also had to able to be dismantled in a controlled fashion once the mortared rubble of the vault had cured.

Setting up temporary military camps with timber walls, towers, and buildings, and the erection of temporary theatres and amphitheatres that were demolished after a short period of use at specific festivals, presumably contributed to the development of the carpentry skills needed for formwork and centering systems in large-scale projects. It is perhaps no coincidence that the architect of the earliest of the really wide-span cross-vaults in the Baths of Trajan and the largest of all Roman domes in the Pantheon was most probably Apollodorus of Damascus, a man known in antiquity for his largely timber bridge over the river Danube.

From the time of Trajan onwards, wide-span cross-vaults were used in series to cover some of the largest clear spaces the Romans ever attempted. The tall and imposing triple cross-vaults of the giant *frigidaria* of the imperial *thermae* [16] were over 70 Roman feet wide and nearly 200 Roman feet long (c. 22 × 60 metres), but appeared to be resting only on eight giant columns; the real supporting structures would have been barely visible to anyone in the central space. They owed their stability to the buttressing effects of parallel barrel-vaulted spaces set perpendicular to the long axis, a device in use since the late Republic but here enhanced by extra masonry above their supporting walls, invisible from the interior. The free-standing triple cross-vault of the Basilica Nova, built at the beginning of the fourth century, exceeded even these, with a clear span of just over 85 Roman feet (25 metres), and even its supporting barrel-vaults—all that now survive—are the widest known from Rome [41]. This was an extraordinary achievement, to be compared only with the Pantheon in terms of large-scale vaulting.

Trajan's Pantheon in many ways epitomizes the way that Roman builders developed and exploited the potential of concrete construction through careful observation and experimentation. The mortar in the Pantheon was of the highest quality, using well-sieved and clean pit-sand from the deepest strata, mixed in accurate proportions with thoroughly burnt and slaked lime from the whitest limestone, which had the fewest impurities and produced the best mortar. Adjusting the weight and size of the rubble in different parts of the structure produced a continuous but variable building fabric, with each part designed to be as structurally effective as possible [42]. The pieces were smallest in the walls, and larger in the foundations and dome, in

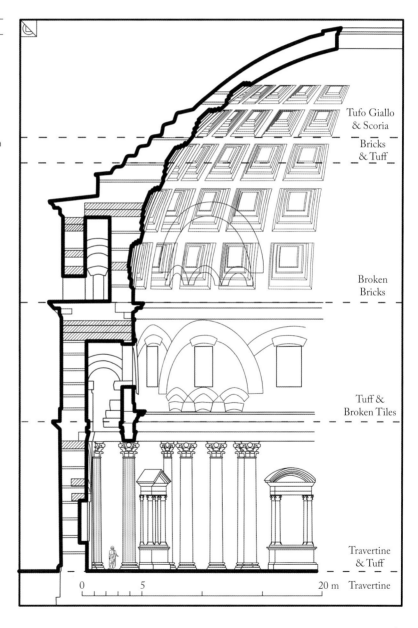

Fig. 42

Pantheon, Rome, c. 110–125 CE. Section showing grading of materials from heavy travertine in the foundations, through travertine mixed with tuff, tuff mixed with brick, just brick, and alternating courses of scoria (aerated lava) from the Bay of Naples and the most lightweight of tuffs for the crown of the dome.

Tufo Giallo & Scoria

Bricks & Tuff

Broken Bricks

Tuff & Broken Tiles

Travertine & Tuff

0   5   20 m   Travertine

order to exploit the weight differential in the materials, and to create the lightest possible crown which would exert the smallest possible thrust on the supporting drum, itself made of heavier and more resistant material. The drum itself is a complex structure [43]. At ground level the 6-metre-thick circular wall is divided by eight major recesses into piers, which in turn are hollowed out by a series of invisible cavities. Two sets of solid brick vaults, appearing on the outside as a series of blind (or relieving) arches, run all or partway through the structure, connecting the piers and carrying the thrusts from the dome over the voids. The under faces of these brick vaults were lined with *bipedales* over *bessales*, a common device which helped simplify the removal of the formwork which supported the 9-metre-wide vaults during construction. Attention was also paid to other areas of potential structural stresses. Over the colonnades screening the recesses on the inner face of the drum, small brick arches spring from wedge-shaped travertine impost blocks set directly over each column, relieving the 3-metre spans of the entablatures from most of the load from the wall above. The drum was extended on the outside for about a third of the total height of the dome and a series of seven stepped rings added to the outer profile of the dome

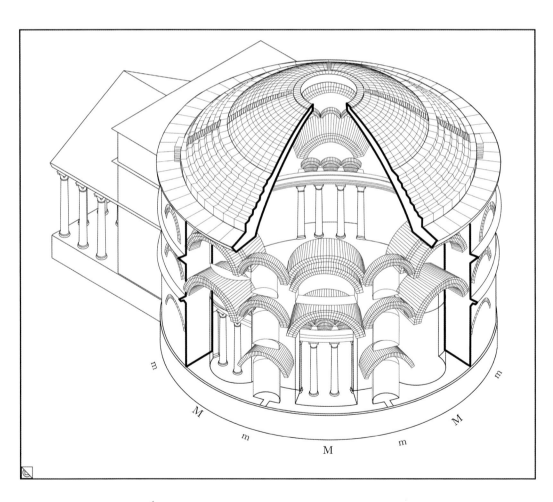

above that, all to add volume and weight at the most vulnerable part of the dome where stresses were greatest and the dome most likely to fail.

Although they lacked the scientific and mathematical advances which lie at the heart of modern construction engineering, the builders of the Pantheon clearly had a sophisticated empirical understanding of their materials and techniques. The adaptability and flexibility of mortared rubble construction encouraged experimentation in a way that was not possible with ashlar. Some of the resulting innovations were designed to facilitate the construction process, some responded to concerns with structural stability, while others were answers to specific design requirements. Most were concerned with aspects of vaulting, and many with problems caused by increased scale to fulfil the different ambitions and requirements patrons had for their buildings. For the Pantheon, the driving need was the emperor's desire and his architect's ambition to amaze by rebuilding the old Pantheon to the same basic size and shape as the previous version, but covering this vast circular space with a dome.[41] Imperial resources made the experiment economically feasible, and the mixture of tradition—in maintaining more or less the earlier plan—and spectacular innovation in the great dome ensured that the display of imperial power to impress and over-awe was culturally acceptable. Although no other temple at Rome itself (as far as we know) even attempted to repeat the model created in the Pantheon at the same scale, the success and acceptability of the design, and its potential for application to other types of building, can be seen in the circular domed *caldarium* of the Baths of Caracalla a hundred years later, only three-quarters the diameter of the Pantheon but just as high, the dome resting entirely on eight piers linked only by solid brick arches.

Constructing Illusions

Solving problems of scale for public buildings was only one side of the experimentation and innovation that is the hallmark of Roman construction. The other lies equally in responding to the demands of exceptionally wealthy patrons, but in terms of their private property where questions of *decor* were less important than the opportunity to impress, amaze, and amuse. One early use of vaults to create interior spaces was for grottoes in elite villas.[42] Often decorated with pumice and shells and with the addition of running water, these *nymphaea* were meant to evoke the caves that were traditionally thought of as the homes of the nymphs. To what extent caves originally inspired Roman architects to experiment with vaulting can no longer be recovered, but it would fit Vitruvius' ideas of imitating nature. A real cave with spectacular views out across the bay was utilized for the seaside dining room of the imperial villa at Sperlonga, its decoration including a sculptural reconstruction of Odysseus blinding the cave-dwelling cyclops Polyphemus, creating a different kind of mythical ambience.[43] These *nymphaea* were architectural conceits, evoking a mythologized nature which was knowingly artificial, an illusion meant not to deceive but to elicit applause.

Not all the illusions that Roman architects created in mortared rubble can be read so easily. At a distance of 2,000 years, at most we see only the solid but ruined mass of walls with just the start of the vaulting, and none of the interior decoration which was an integral part of the architect's design:

the scaffolding of the stage set and not the set itself. With vaulted concrete, the architect was no longer confined to a bipartite orthogonal structure, dependent on a clear distinction between vertical wall and horizontal ceiling. In cross-vaulted rooms, the area between the springing and the crown of the vault was an ambiguous surface, part of the wall or part of the vault depending on how the architect chose to decorate it. In the Baths of Caracalla, the division between marble veneer and glass mosaic or stucco is often the line of the springing of the vault, but sometimes lower than this, making what is really wall appear like vault, while in other spaces the lunettes are taken up with windows, making the vault appear just lightly pinned down at its corners.[44]

This illusionistic manipulation of interior space through a combination of vaulted mortared rubble and applied decoration can already be found in the famous octagonal room of Nero's Golden House [44]. Here the wide and shallow dome with its large oculus rises from eight piers at the corners of the octagon, linked only by exceptionally wide flat arches. Clad in marble veneer, the piers would have appeared even less substantial, merely a sub-dued background to the eight slender columns in the angles which would have appeared to support the dome almost on their own. If the dome itself was covered in glass mosaic, as the limited evidence indicates, or even draped with coloured silk as some scholars have suggested,[45] the immediate appearance would have been that of a tent, giving the illusion of an ephem-eral structure which completely denies the corporeality of the unprepossess-ing medium from which it is actually made. Light was another important element in creating the illusion; while that from the oculus filled the central

Fig. 44

Octagonal room, Esquiline Wing, Nero's Golden House (Domus Aurea), Rome, 64–68 CE. The natural light in the side rooms comes from skylights above the dome, adding to the elusive quality of the space.

space, that from the five main side chambers, achieved by clerestory windows above the haunches of the dome, suggests a series of open pavilions beyond the central space. The inspiration seems to have been the fabulous tents of the Persian and Hellenistic kings, such as that of the third-century BCE Ptolemy Philadelphus, whose extravagant dining pavilion, hung with embroidered scarlet and white silk and decorated with gold and precious works of art, was still a topic of learned conversation in the early third century CE.[46] The choice of dark blue and gold for some Roman vault mosaics may be imitating the actual fabrics used in the courts of these eastern potentates, woven in gold thread on deep-purple cloth, while others represent ivy or vines on light or dark backgrounds, suggesting a different type of ephemeral structure such as a pergola.

This kind of architecture also led to the creation of novel variations on the dome, the so-called 'umbrella' or 'segmental' domes where the inner surface is divided into flat or concave segments, or even alternating segments of both. Structurally these are little different to true domes, but would have required much more elaborate formwork. Such vaults are admittedly not common, the most varied and sophisticated collection known being the pavilions of Hadrian's Villa at Tivoli, in the so-called 'Serapeum' [133] and the vestibule of the so-called 'Piazza d'Oro', where the undulating surface of the vault appears to spring from the narrowest of projections once supported by impossibly slender columns. In the 'Piazza d'Oro' vestibule the illusion of a lightweight structure was further emphasized by the real paring away of the supporting walls, leaving the curves of the semi-circular recesses visible on the outside.

Hadrian's Villa provides another demonstration of the ingenuity of Roman architects and builders when it came to concealed methods of providing structural stability where vaults were supported on colonnades.[47] The problem lay in the outward thrust that a vault exerted on the architraves of a portico, particularly where the supports were widely spaced, leading Roman builders to add iron reinforcing bars anchored in stone blocks in order to absorb the unwanted thrusts [45], a development perhaps of the

Fig. 45

Island Villa ('Teatro Marittimo'), Hadrian's Villa, Tivoli, c. 118–138 CE: (a) Ionic outer colonnade, with wedge-shaped travertine blocks and brick lintel arches originally covered in marble veneer; (b) schematic reconstruction of the iron tie bars supporting the brick lintel arches.

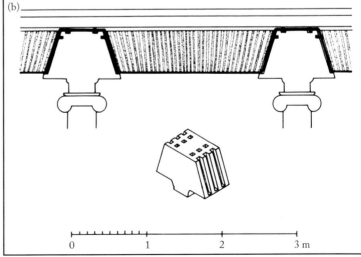

use of metal clamps to hold adjacent blocks in place in traditional ashlar construction. In several buildings parallel iron bars were anchored in mushroom-shaped stone imposts seated on columns to support brick lintel arches over spans upwards of 3.5 metres. Marble veneer gave the impression of stone lintels, but ones beyond the normal possible span—another illusion of lightness and fragility of structure. This is just one of two systems already in use by the Augustan period and well established by the time of Hadrian.

The other, used in the Augustan Basilica Aemilia, the Trajanic Basilica Ulpia, and the imperial *thermae*, had iron ties embedded within the mortared rubble of colonnade vaults, again to resist the outward thrust, but this time at right angles to the vault, not parallel to it. The combination of iron and mortared rubble is based on the same principle as modern reinforced concrete, but, compared to the late nineteenth century, the production of iron in the Roman period was very much more costly, and the manufacture of continuous steel rods by extrusion unknown. Not surprisingly, then, this innovative use of iron in combination with concrete seems to have been largely restricted to achieving particular effects in the most prestigious structures, when considerations of cost were not paramount. For normal Roman building requirements, therefore, good mortared rubble using vaulted and arched shapes could answer most needs simply because they avoided excessive tension in built forms.

Local Means to Imperial Ends

Given the overwhelming importance of the building materials and techniques of the city of Rome in the development of Roman architecture, it is easy to forget how exceptional those were. The particular coincidence of the volcanic and limestone geologies which conditioned the construction practices of Rome was met in very few other places in the Roman world, and local building materials and traditions were often very different. Even in Republican Italy, the construction techniques for city walls varied between the regular ashlar blocks of Rome's fourth-century BCE walls in volcanic tuff [28], the massive polygonal masonry with heavy stone lintels found in the limestone areas to the east and south, and mud-brick. Greece and the Hellenistic world had a long-standing history of trabeated ashlar construction, mainly in limestone or in marble for the most prestigious structures, but with some limited use of structural brick and rubble.[48] In general, the bulk of construction needed to employ locally available materials for the cost of transport not to be prohibitive. Vitruvius' older contemporary Cicero is said to have replied to the people of Chios (Turkey), when they showed off their city walls built of the local marble, that he would have been much more impressed if they had been built of the travertine from near Rome.[49]

Elsewhere, quite different forms of construction were used. By the second century BCE a distinctive technique using a framework of vertical and horizontal stone blocks [52], for which the misleading term '*opus africanum*' has been coined, had started to be used in a zone which ran from Carthage in the south to Pompeii in the north, perhaps originating in the Greek part of Sicily but then spreading under Punic influence to southern France and Spain.[50] In the northwestern provinces stone construction was unknown, and timber, straw, and earth conditioned indigenous building techniques which reminded Vitruvius of the primitive huts of the early Romans.[51] While these local techniques on the whole continued under Roman rule, the increase in scale and volume of construction which went with the growth of urbanism in the early to mid-empire, and the desire to reproduce Roman-style buildings, provided a major impetus for change in building technologies in many Roman provinces, especially those on the periphery of the empire. Direct imitations of the techniques of the capital were rare; instead, we find adaptations of Roman techniques or quite frequently new and innovative systems designed to give a Roman effect using quite different means.

The most significant introduction was the extensive use of lime mortar, sometimes in conjunction with pre-existing traditions of dry-stone walling without much further change, as in Mauritania Tingitana (modern Morocco),[52] but most often in association with a facing of small roughly square to rectangular blocks laid in courses. In many examples across the empire the influence of Roman construction is clear in the distinction between facing and core, and in the bands of brick or tile which imitate those in *reticulatum* in Rome and Italy [109]. The thin bricks of Rome, developed as a facing for mortared rubble or as elements in standard hypocaust construction for bath buildings, were also largely an introduced material, used in a very different way from the thick bricks of the Hellenistic world and northern Italy which acted as building elements in their own right.[53] Outside of the particular conditions of the city of Rome, however, the large-scale use of brick as general walling only appears in special applications, particularly in baths, or in the late empire in imperial cities such as Thessaloniki and Trier [9], presumably in imitation of Rome itself.[54] Only in a small number of areas such as the eastern part of Cilicia (Turkey) where there was no good building stone but ample clay did brick become a major building material.[55] In fact, some areas, notably North Africa, actually imported products of the urban brick-makers of Rome and from the area of Campania, arguably as cash cargoes rather than simply saleable ballast.[56]

In some cases, choices reflected specific political and personal circumstances which tied the commissioner or the community to Rome. Reticulate is a case in point. Despite only being visible during construction, its unique and distinctive facing would have been immediately recognizable to anyone who had seen the architecture of the capital, and seems to have retained its cachet through the second century CE, when it is found in a limited number of examples from Greece, Asia Minor, North Africa, and the Levant.[57] It was *de rigueur* in Augustus' prized city foundation of Nikopolis in western Greece, built to celebrate his crucial victory at Actium, and appears in many of the projects of Herod the Great of Judea, who had close ties to Augustus' circle and had spent time in Rome; he seems even to have imported *pulvis Puteolanus* from the Bay of Naples to build his harbour at Caesarea.[58] Herod's projects are a prime example of materials and construction techniques used as a demonstration of the power to command exceptional resources and of close ties with the centre of the empire.

Outside of the volcanic areas of central Italy which supplied the soft tuffs suited to the creation of regular reticulate blocks, reticulate would have been difficult and expensive to produce, yet to no structural advantage; the

Fig. 46

'Basilica', Bulla Regia
(Tunisia), probably second
century CE. The stone
uprights reflect the common
local technique ('opus
africanum'), but combined
here with limestone
reticulate imitating the
Italian technique.

benefits were entirely those of prestige. In several provincial examples of the later first to mid-second centuries CE, reticulate was combined with brick bands and quoins, in imitation of changing modes of use in central Italy. The so-called 'basilica' in the Numidian city of Bulla Regia (Tunisia) [46] translated this into a unique scheme where *reticulatum* in hard limestone was used as fill in the local *opus africanum* technique, a telling mix of Italian and local building traditions. The interior of the finished building still has traces of its marble veneer, so that the choice must have been symbolic, a visual claim by the commissioner to ties with the centre of empire that was only effective during the period of construction. While this is an exceptional case, it is hard to imagine the more standard examples of *reticulatum* being other than the products of Italian workmen.

The only other situation where brick was used extensively in the eastern empire was in vaulting, which was one of the principal challenges facing builders in the provinces.[59] In the absence of the pozzolans which made Roman mortared rubble so suitable for large-scale vaulted construction, much ingenuity was applied to developing alternative solutions particularly in new types of buildings imported from Rome, such as baths, where vaulting was very much an essential part of the style. While small pieces of rubble set voussoir fashion in lime mortar were often used, one of the most successful and long-lived alternatives was to use solid brick with a supercargo of rubble. Two systems were used, sometimes in combination. Square or rectangular bricks could be set radially as voussoirs, with the length of the brick parallel to the direction of the vault, or they could be set alongside each other in rows (the so-called 'pitched-brick') with the thickness of the brick parallel to the vault. The latter technique, widely used in Roman Asia Minor, already had a very long history in the east in mud-brick construction, and became fundamental to Byzantine architecture. Both, especially the 'pitched-brick' technique, used brick for vaulting in a very non-Italian way, yet still can be seen as saving on labour compared with the stone alternatives. These latter required the time-consuming and highly skilled dressing of individual blocks of complex shape in a precise geometry to function effectively, and

Fig. 47

Baths of Julia Memmia,
Bulla Regia (Tunisia),
c. 230 CE. Cross-vault using
terracotta vaulting tubes.

a much higher quantity of skilled labour as well as lifting machinery to put them into place.

A very different technique, developed and employed sporadically in parts of Italy, Sicily, central North Africa, Syria, and Britain, was the use of vaulting tubes [47].[60] In small and medium spans, a strong permanent centering could be made of interlocking tubes bound together with fast-setting gypsum on which the vault could be laid in a weaker mortar with a longer curing period. In modern construction parlance these were rudimentary thin-shell structures, their strength dependent on their curved forms. They had the added attraction of requiring no separate wooden formwork, but this was not necessarily their primary or only advantage. After all, these tubes were a specialized non-reusable product which became an integral part of the structure, required in large numbers (the vaults of some baths needed around 200,000 tubes), and their manufacture consumed substantial amounts of fuel and considerable skilled labour. Although a rudimentary form had been used in Hellenistic Sicily, their most widespread use in third-century CE Tunisia has been associated with the increase in specialized ceramic workshops producing amphorae to serve the burgeoning olive oil industry. The fact that there is no evidence surviving before the early Byzantine period for their use in spans wider than 12 metres suggests, however, that there were limits either to their intrinsic stability over greater distances or—more likely—to their ability to support the extra weight of the larger vaults while the mortar in them slowly gained strength.

For the less traditional vaulted structures, particularly baths, new and original solutions sometimes had to be found which moved far away from the traditions of Rome. New forms of large stone vaulting emerged on occasion, for example for the so-called 'Temple of Diana' at Nîmes [48], while others experimented with brick elements, such as the unique double-shell vaults of the Large Baths at Argos in Greece, or the hollow voussoirs used over the great pool at Aquae Sulis in Britannia.[61] The impetus behind these

Fig. 48

'Temple of Diana', Nîmes
(France), early first or
second century CE (the date
is disputed). Barrel-vaulted
roof built of stone armchair
voussoirs supporting stone
slabs between.

technical innovations appears to have been the desire for emulation, for achieving a Roman appearance, rather than for any savings on labour per se. Historically, innovation and experimentation in construction techniques is expensive, especially in the early stages, with failure always a possibility. The use of imported technology, requiring the acquisition or production of special materials, or the development of substitute technologies, often for one-off building projects, in order to serve what are basically ideological ends must have placed a financial burden on cities and their benefactors across the Roman empire.

While there is little epigraphic and literary evidence about the mobility of builders compared with architects and marble workers, this is the simplest explanation for how details of construction practices were transferred across the empire. On the periphery, from the provinces of Britannia and Mauritania Tingitana in the West to Cilicia in the East, the use of mortar and other new techniques including brick production and vaulting tubes came with the army,[62] while in the central Mediterranean regions with existing urban structures and building traditions it was the patrons, many with direct connections to the imperial capital, who would have been the driving force. In both cases, however, the evidence of the buildings suggests that imported techniques were selectively assimilated into existing traditions, presumably through local builders working initially alongside the incomers.

The Roman Building Industry and the Organization of Construction

The process of experimentation and innovation in construction which was one of the hallmarks of Roman architecture presupposes a large and dedicated workforce with a high level and variety of relevant skills, plus some degree of structured organization which would allow those skills to be transferred and improved beyond the life of an individual, and a commercial operation beyond the scope of the household: in other words, a Roman building industry. This existed even before the building boom of the second century BCE, as public building works were from an early date let out to contract, which assumes that there were contractors (*redemptores*) to tender for them and skilled workers to provide the labour.[63] It is really only from the first century BCE, however, that the shape of the industry begins to become clear.[64] According to Strabo, Augustan Rome was a constant building site, driving major developments in building technology.[65] Hand in hand with this went organizational changes which affected the industry, including the creation of the *curatores operum publicorum*, magistrates in charge of public buildings and temples. These officials oversaw construction either using their permanent workforce, particularly for day-to-day maintenance, or let the work out to contract. All this suggests a flourishing, active, and innovative construction industry, which continued largely unchanged for the next two centuries.

Contracts and contractors are key to understanding the building industry at Rome. Only one copy of an actual contract survives, the *Lex parieti faciundo Puteolana* of 105 BCE which records the terms for creating a new formal gateway in the Roman colony of Puteoli.[66] It stipulates the precise location, design, dimensions, materials, construction details, and decoration of the project. A completion date is given as well as a payment schedule, involving sureties to safeguard the public investment. The last instalment was only to be paid on completion, subject to approval by a committee of town councillors. Although the specifications may have been provided by an architect, those approving the work needed to understand the language and nature of construction, one context where Vitruvius' *On architecture* would have been invaluable. The contractor himself had to be experienced in the building trades and good at organization, with access to sufficient funds. Contracting for large-scale imperial projects would have required exceptional wealth and often patronage at the highest level, to provide not only recommendations but also the necessary securities.[67] Thus we find Tiberius Claudius Onesimus, contractor for the emperor's building works (*redemptor operum Caesaris*) under the Flavians, who was a freed slave of Claudius or Nero.[68]

One particular area in which some *redemptores* specialized was the provision of heavy lifting equipment.[69] The Augustan poet Horace provides a cameo portrait of a *redemptor* hurrying along with his mules and porters, in charge of a large crane for hoisting blocks of stone and large timbers.[70] Just such a crane appears in a relief from the elaborate, richly decorated, and clearly expensive funerary monument of the Haterii **[49]**, which arguably belonged to the *redemptor* Q. Haterius Tychicus, probably a freed slave of an important senatorial family.[71] The prominence of the crane in the image suggests that it had a strong symbolic importance for the owner. While simple lifting devices were essential on most building projects, complex structures employing large columns, ashlar blocks, or roof trusses required larger and more specialized machines and components, representing a significant investment and a particular expertise beyond that of the ordinary builder.

Fig. 49

Marble funerary relief
showing a treadmill crane
operated by nine men, from
the Tomb of the Haterii,
Rome, c. 100 CE.

Similarly, expertise in the complex carpentry needed for the formwork and centering of large vaults and experience in laying and decentering them successfully must have recommended certain contractors for public works.

Most *redemptores* presumably began as military engineers, or in the civil building trade, like Onesimus who held office as one of the chief magistrates of the *collegium* of the *fabri tignarii* (the association of builders). Although the association was said to go back to the regal period, when their function was as military engineers,[72] little is known of it under the Republic, but in the Augustan period it was (re?)organized, adopting a hierarchical and quasi-military structure. Thereafter there are records of both the *collegium* as a body and its individual members until the beginning of the fourth century CE.[73] This is the largest known *collegium* in Rome, with over 1,380 members, divided into at least 60 cohorts (*decuriae*) of 22 men, each with its own officials (*decuriones*), all under the control of six senior magistrates (*magistri quinquennales*) elected for a five-year period. Rather than representing all those actively engaged in building including common labourers, the members of the *collegium* were most likely to have been master builders or contractors who had their own 'firms', as they had to pay a membership fee. Some of the senior members of the *collegium* were men of considerable wealth, as demonstrated by their funerary monuments, such as that of Lucius Cincius Martialis, *quinquennalis* and head of the tenth cohort, who provided a *columbarium* with thirty-two places for members of his cohort, including his son and heir.[74]

Many of the recorded *fabri tignarii* appear to have been the freed slaves, or the descendants of freed slaves, of important families including those of the emperors, as was common in the *collegia* of Rome. They may have owed their success to the financial support of their former owners, or even been trained in the households of their senatorial patrons, like the supposed 500 slave architects and builders in the household of the wealthy Crassus.[75] While this may have been exceptional, there is epigraphic evidence for builders in the funerary monuments of other senatorial families, particularly that of Statilius Taurus, Augustus' close ally and the builder of the first permanent amphitheatre in Rome. One freedman, T. Statilius Antiochus, went into successful business himself, and had his own funerary plot complete with marble plaque.[76] The training of skilled builders through the aristocratic household was not the only possibility; one legal case records a builder who bought and trained a slave acting on the express instructions of a friend, in a form of apprenticeship.[77] Quite a few of the known *fabri tignarii*, on the other hand, have names which suggest they came from elsewhere in Italy, such as nearby Praeneste, or from the provinces, men who perhaps had come to seek their fortunes in the capital.

Apart from Crassus' 500 architects and builders, most of the sources suggest that the units which made up the construction industry tended to be small and flexible. The heads of these building 'firms' presumably had a core of skilled workers who could cover all aspects of ordinary construction, carpentry being one of the essentials. Although good masons and bricklayers were needed for the fine facing in reticulate or brick of many buildings, this was by no means as difficult a skill to acquire as those needed to work in squared stone, and could be learnt on site. Much of the work was simple labouring: fetching and carrying, mixing mortar, filling in the core, and keeping the masons supplied with materials. Most of the tasks were repetitive, and materials came in small units, or like mortar could be subdivided into man-loads, so that little heavy equipment like cranes was needed. A scene from the fourth-century Tomb of Trebius Iustus in Rome is surprisingly familiar [50]. The five workmen wear the short one-shouldered tunic of the slave or labourer: two bricklayers stand on scaffolding on either side of a brick-faced wall, while one labourer brings up a load of mortar in half an amphora, another carries a load of bricks or rubble in a basket, and a third mixes mortar or slakes lime, using a long-handled hoe. Such a group might have made up the basic unit of the workforce under the direction of a *faber tignuarius*, with some of the unskilled tasks taken on by day labourers. Not surprisingly, the ordinary free poor working as day labourers on building sites are rarely mentioned in the ancient sources, but the legal texts suggest that their employment was common practice.[78]

Fig. 50

Wall painting showing a construction scene, from the Tomb of Trebius Justus, Rome, probably fourth century CE. This is the only known depiction which clearly shows Roman builders laying brick-faced mortared rubble walls.

Even with the help of casual labour, it is unlikely that any single individual member of the *fabri tignarii* had a sufficiently large body of workers, whether slave, freed, or freeborn, to take on major imperial building projects himself. Estimates suggest that the Pantheon required something in the order of 200 masons and labourers over seven to eight years, while the Baths of Caracalla needed at least 4,000–7,000 workers on site over four to five years.[79] The skilled labour was presumably provided by a number of these building 'firms' working together, either hired independently for piece work, as has been suggested for the Markets of Trajan,[80] or working as a consortium. One source of such collaborative ventures could have been the *collegium* of the *fabri tignarii*. Although scholars cannot agree on the extent to which *collegia* functioned in relation to actual work practices, the inevitable social ties between members, particularly within the closer-knit groupings of the cohorts, must have made the forming of consortia easier. If each of the twenty-two members of a cohort represented a 'firm' of only four to five skilled workmen, they could, with an equal number of day labourers, have furnished the basic workforce required for the Pantheon. As the heads of the cohorts appear to have held the position for life, they would have provided both continuity and a fount of experience, which would have facilitated cooperative ventures. This is one possible source of the uniformity of building practice which is especially surprising given the sheer amount of building in imperial Rome, as individual 'firms' might have worked together in different combinations on projects of different sizes. Large projects with hundreds, or even thousands, of workers on site every day also required high-level organizational skills, not only in terms of overall coordination, which was presumably the task of the architect(s) and/or contractors, but also in relation to individual tasks or areas of construction. Historically, the rate of supervision for work-gangs is one in ten, but a large site would require further levels of organization above this. The military-like hierarchy of the *fabri tignarii* may not only reflect their supposed origins as military engineers but also the way that building sites themselves must have been organized. A late Roman mosaic of a building site from a synagogue in Israel, thought to represent the legendary building of the Tower of Babel [51],[81] depicts the wide variety of tasks and occupations on a complex building site. It also shows some of the hazards faced by the workers, from a fight between different tradesmen to from a fall from scaffolding—still today a main cause of death on building sites.

One important aspect of site organization was the supply of building materials, which could be the responsibility of either the patron or, more commonly, the builder. By the early empire, stone quarries and clay-pits for brickmaking were recognized as potentially profitable resources on large rural estates, along with lime production and stands of timber, provided that the products could be transported to Rome economically.[82] Brickstamps allow us to see that this involvement went to the highest levels of society, starting with the Augustan senators Asinius Pollio and Domitius Afer; the latter, from the south of France, was consul in 39 CE and on good terms with Tiberius, the emperor responsible for the first large-scale use of brick in Rome, in the camp of the Praetorian Guard on the outskirts of the city.[83] From then on, the main market for facing brick, and the most likely stimulus to its development, were the emperors, who needed a reliable supply of first-class material for their vast building projects. Several of the *curatores operum publicorum* also owned brickfields, where their public position could have given them a market advantage, and not just in Rome.[84] Domitius Afer's bricks are also found at the Roman colony of Carthage, a key Augustan project; with two of his heirs being governors of Africa in the late first century CE, the family developed specific ties of patronage and further access to the North African market. Other major players include M. Rutilius Lupus, prefect of Egypt under Trajan, and Hadrian's urban prefect,

Fig. 51

Floor mosaic showing a construction scene, probably depicting the building of the Tower of Babel, from the synagogue at Huqoq, Israel, c. early fifth century CE. As well as the fight between two workmen (left of centre) and the man falling from the tower (upper right), there are scenes of stone transport, stone-working, woodworking, and a large crane operated by a capstan.

M. Annius Verus, whose son married Domitia Lucilla [40], the heir of Afer's brickfields, becoming the parents of the emperor Marcus Aurelius.

Thus over the course of the second century, the brickfields supplying Rome increasingly came into the private possession of the emperor and his family, until Caracalla owned virtually all of them; the emperor was clearly acting in a well-established elite tradition, rather than being actively interested in controlling the market.[85] The actual brick production was operated through agents or let out on contract, the stamps providing evidence for complex relationships between individual landowners, owners of production units (some 7 per cent of whom were women), and even occasionally individual brick-makers.[86] Stone quarrying presumably operated in much the same way, although here too it is possible that the large tuff quarries along the Anio belonged to the Roman state, as the travertine ones appear to have belonged to Tibur in the Republican period.

Specialized materials often came from much further away, such as the lightweight scoria from Vesuvius on the Bay of Naples used in vault construction.[87] By the mid-imperial period long timbers for important constructions were brought from as far away as the Alps, the home of the larch, and possibly even Lebanon, where there are records relating to the marking of trees, including cedars, belonging to the emperor Hadrian.[88] Just as important, but much more visible in the archaeological record, is marble, which became the signature material of the emperors. The nearest sources, developed under Julius Caesar and Augustus, came from above Luna (Carrara) in the Apuan Alps, but the coloured marbles most closely associated with empire travelled very long distances from Greece and the islands, Asia Minor, North Africa, and Egypt [65]. Large timbers and column shafts also created problems in terms of transport through the city,[89] which must have been yet another area of specialism within the construction industry.

Overall, the quantities involved are impressive. The Romans quarried something like 5.5 million cubic metres of travertine over four centuries, 100,000 cubic metres of which were needed just for the Flavian Amphitheatre. While we have no way of estimating how much tuff or pit-sand or brick or lime was needed altogether over the centuries to feed the building industry at Rome, even allowing for recycling, various calculations for specific buildings suggest that the extraction and production of the basic building materials, without including transport, needed as much as a third of the manpower required to put them in place. Given the quantities of materials required for construction, the exploitation was likely to have been highly profitable. At least part of that profit went to landowners, most often members of the senatorial elites of Rome, and these were also the people best placed to supply the large numbers of river craft and draft animals required to transport the materials to Rome.

If we put together the manpower and materials consumed by the city of Rome in the imperial period, the overall economic impact—and therefore potential political power—of the Roman building industry is startling. A broad estimate for the Severan period suggest that perhaps 5–6 per cent of the total population of the city and its immediate hinterland was involved in construction and the production and transport of building materials, some 15–25 per cent of the adult males.[90] The employment of such a large section of society on cash terms, as seems to have been the case with most building workers, would also have had considerable knock-on effects among the urban populace who provided them with services—food, accommodation, clothing, tools, luxuries. The large continuous investment in construction by the emperors and the elites of Rome over a considerable period of time provided exceptional economic stability for the main players in the building industry, in which they could refine and experiment with their materials and techniques in order to meet the expectations of these demanding patrons.

While the picture for Rome and for Ostia, which had its own equivalent of Rome's *collegium* of the *fabri tignuarii*, is fairly clear, we are much less well informed about the organization of construction in the provinces. With a few exceptions, *fabri tignuarii* are relatively rare, their place apparently taken by undifferentiated *fabri* (workmen).[91] At Lyon they are connected with *artifices tectorum* (roofers), while at Mediolanum (modern Saintes) there were *lapidarii* (stone workers) and *structores* (wall builders).[92] In general, associations of *fabri* or *fabri tignuarii* are found particularly in Italy, the south of Gaul, and the central European provinces, but not really in Britannia or any of the African provinces, except in two instances where they are almost certainly military rather than civil. Where they do occur, they seem to be modelled on the *fabri tignuarii* of Rome, divided into cohorts and run by their own magistrates, with patrons from among the local dignitaries. Some were wealthy enough to build their own temples and headquarters, and to set up statues to benefactors. A couple of inscriptions from northern Italy cast an interesting light on the actual workings of the *collegia*. They record verbatim the procedure for co-opting new patrons, giving the date and place of the meeting, and the setting up of statues in the headquarters to the new patrons, who in one case were husband and wife.[93] Rarely, however, is light thrown on the builders themselves. One *faber tignuarius* from the Italian Alps was clearly a local of Celtic extraction (his family name was Cunopennus), while another from Arles was lauded on his sarcophagus as a hydraulics expert.[94] Associations of construction workers also appear in the eastern empire, as do the equivalents of *redemptores*.[95] While it is possible to iden-tify some different areas of expertise, such as the *xylikarioi* (carpenters), or levels of skill, such as the *oikodomoi* who seem to have been master builders, on the whole the terminology in the epigraphic evidence is as vague in the east as it is in the west.

Asia Minor does, however, provide us with the best direct evidence that builders there could and did act in concert over conditions of work. An association of builders (*ergepistatoi*) in Hadrianic Pergamon started a strike that it took the governor of the province to resolve, docking the pay of the striking workers, while at Miletos it took the oracle of Apollo to persuade the protesting *oikodomoi* and *ergolaboi* on the theatre site back to work.[96] This raises the question of the supply and status of building labour. The army appear to have built mainly for themselves or in civic centres con-nected to military bases, but they did provide expertise, especially in the supply of materials, in logistics, and in engineering, bringing new building technologies to recently conquered parts of the empire. While corvée labour is attested, there is no indication in the surviving evidence that large numbers of workers on civil building sites across the empire were constrained, as shackled slaves or condemned criminals, although the latter did labour in the mines and—possibly—quarries. But even in the imperial granite and porphyry quarries of the eastern Egyptian desert, run by imperial procurators with military personnel in support, the labour was either slaves and freedmen attached to the quarry, or locals employed on a waged basis. The survival of thousands of temporary documents from the quarries, written on pottery sherds (*ostraca*), gives a unique insight into working conditions, from rates of pay to sick-lists, and throws light on the plethora of other personnel at the site, including doctors and barbers, doorkeepers and water-carriers.[97]

On the whole, it would seem that material production and construction in and for the cities of the Roman world was largely the preserve of private enterprise, working under contract for a city or for a wealthy private patron. Despite the small scale of the building units, the *collegia* provided opportunities both for the exchange of ideas and for collaboration, while the generally peaceful conditions of the empire, combined with the military expansion of the frontiers, the demand for skilled workers, and the global interests of patrons, produced a specialized and mobile workforce which could provide the impetus to new ways of building across the Roman world. Without this, neither the urban ideal which lay at the heart of Rome's idea of empire nor the elaborate and luxurious residences which emphasized the power of its ruling classes to amaze would have been possible. The frequency with which the process of building construction appears in Latin literature is a strong indication of both the pervasive reality of living with building sites in the Roman world and the eternal fascination that the creation of permanent monuments from raw materials has for those uninitiated in the ways of building.[98]

Building for the Gods

…the temple fills every vista, and at the same time reveals the city and the magnanimity of its inhabitants.

Aelius Aristides, *Orationes* 27.17

Introduction

Religion lies at the heart of Roman culture and society, and the temples to the gods were their most cherished and significant buildings. From the start of the Republic, temples were the dominant buildings on the hilltops of Rome and in the main public gathering places, the Forum Romanum and the Campus Martius. Cult was fundamental to the idea of Roman statehood, none more so than that of Jupiter Optimus Maximus, Juno, and Minerva (the Capitoline temple) on the Capitoline Hill [53]. Although the ancient sources said it was largely the work of the last king of Rome, Tarquinius Superbus, the temple was believed to have been finally and, significantly, dedicated only in 509 BCE, the first year of the Republic.[1] It quickly became the setting for sanctifying Roman power, 'a pledge of empire', as Tacitus called it. The new consuls sacrificed at its altar at the beginning of their term in office, as did successful generals celebrating their triumphs, while Republican governors took vows there before leaving for their provinces.

The Traditions of the Republic

Temples and houses account for all the earliest known buildings in Rome, and it is not always possible to decide whether an archaic structure was domestic or sacred. The ambiguity remains in the Latin; Vitruvius calls a temple an *aedes*, or sometimes *aedes sacrae*—sacred building—using the Latin word for a building which was also, if less commonly, used for a house.[2] Over the sixth century BCE, however, temples were gradually differentiated from other types of buildings, acquiring a general form which was to remain the basis of all Roman temples to come. Vitruvius describes a particular 'Tuscan' (i.e. Etruscan) style of temple to which many of the early temples of Rome and central Italy, including Etruria, belonged; the Capitoline temple was of this form.[3] The basic concept—a rectangular room (*cella*) for the statue of the god, with a colonnaded porch and a pitched tiled roof with gable end—has close parallels with the Greek temples which appeared in increased numbers at just this time. Tuscan-type temples, however, had almost square *cellae*, sometimes divided into two or three parts longitudinally, and/or flanked by two wings (*alae*), and preceded by a colonnaded porch as deep as the *cella*. The widely spaced (*areostyle*) columns, with simple capitals consisting of a flat square plate (*abacus*) above a circular

Fig. 52

Capitolium, Dougga (Tunisia), 167–169 CE. The tetrastyle façade is in a standard form of Roman Corinthian, but the walls of the *cella* are made in the local '*opus africanum*' technique.

Fig. 53

Temple of Jupiter Optimus Maximus, Juno, and Minerva (Capitoline temple), Capitoline Hill, Rome, said to have been dedicated c. 509 BCE. Plan and elevation (a) and computer reconstruction (b). The surviving foundations suggest a temple measuring 62 × 54 metres. Note the human scale.

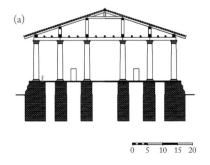

(a)

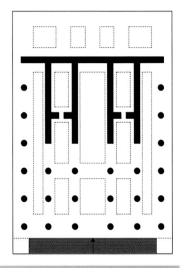

0   5   10   15   20

(b)

rounded cushion (*echinus*), supported wooden architraves, above which was an open triangular gable end (the pediment), decorated with terracotta plaques [54] and sculpture. But it was the elevated straight-sided podium with frontal steps, very different to the low all-round stepped platform (*crepis*) of Greek temples, which was to become the most distinguishing feature of Roman temples. While these structures would have been recognizable to Greek (and other) visitors to Rome as temples, the differences in plan and elevation marked this as a distinctly local conception.

The Capitolium was set apart by its unprecedented scale. Although the precise reconstruction is much debated, the fragmentary remains of the foundations and podium suggest a huge rectangular structure (c. 54 × 62 metres), with three *cellae* and most probably colonnaded *alae* as well, and three rows of six columns across its porch, making it the largest of its type known to have been built.[4] Several technical and decorative details show the influence of the earliest colossal Greek temples such as the Temple of Artemis at Ephesus and the Temple of Hera at Samos, but it was also their

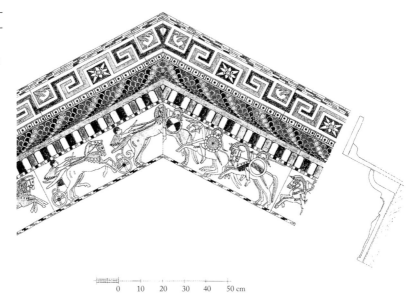

Fig. 54

Reconstruction of the
terracotta pediment
decoration of an unidentified
Etrusco-Italic temple,
c. 530 BCE.

0   10   20   30   40   50 cm

rival, making both a claim to and a demonstration of power through monumentality. Although further embellished in the course of the Republic, the Capitolium appears to have survived fundamentally unchanged until damaged by fire in 83 BCE.[5] Its long life and great religious as well as political importance appear to have given sanctity to its form, and in the eyes of ancient writers the low-roofed structures with their wide eaves, terracotta statues and decorations, and open-fronted pediments, represented the very soul of the ancient Republic and the heart of Roman religious traditions.[6] Although none approached the Capitolium in size, many temples of this 'Tuscan' type continued to be built at least into the early first century BCE, in both Rome and central Italy, including the temple on the Arx at the colony of Cosa (c. 150 BCE) **[56]**.[7] Even communities not under direct Roman control, such as the great Samnite rural sanctuary at Pietrabbondante (late second century BCE), used the same basic temple form,[8] while the earliest known 'Tuscan'-style temple with a triple cella found outside of Italy is at the allied Iberian city of Saguntum in eastern Spain, and not—as might have been expected—in a Roman colony.[9]

In the highly competitive arena of Republican politics, temple building was a major opportunity for self-presentation among the senatorial elite. Temples were built by the consuls or other magistrates either as thanksgivings or to propitiate the gods in times of trouble, as was the Temple of Apollo Medicus in the Campus Martius which was promised to the healing deity after a plague in 433 BCE.[10] As Rome expanded, manubial temples became popular, vowed by generals in return for divine aid in battle and paid for by war booty; they had particular connotations of triumph and remained a charge on the family of the victorious general. With the proliferation of temples in Rome, it appears that ways were sought to distinguish one from another and to enhance the prestige of the founder **[55]**. Specific Greek elements were assimilated into the traditional Roman pattern, although by

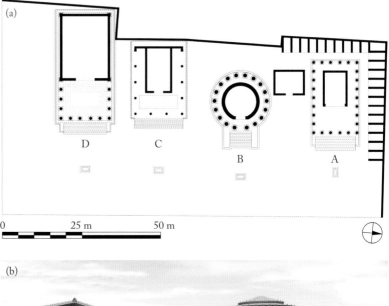

Fig. 55

Plan (a) and computer reconstruction (b) of the Republican victory temples in Largo Argentina, Rome. Identifications and dates are disputed, but the following are generally accepted (from right to left): A: Temple of Juturna, hexastyle peripteral, 241 BCE, rebuilt first century BCE; B: Temple of Fortuna Huiusce Dei (Fortune of this day), circular peripteral, c. 100 BCE; C: Temple of Feronia, tetrastyle Tuscan *sine postico*, early third century BCE; D: possibly Temple of the Nymphs, hexastyle prostyle, c. later second century BCE.

Fig. 56

The Roman orders. From left to right: reconstructed Tuscan order, Cosa, so-called 'Capitolium', c. 150 BCE; Doric order, Cori, Temple of Hercules, c. 100 BCE; Ionic order, Rome, Temple of Portunus, c. 100 BCE; Corinthian, Temple of Castor and Pollux, Rome, 6–7 CE, all drawn as if for a column of the same height. Each order has its own distinctive form of column, especially the capitals, and arrangement of the entablature, which consist of the architrave above the columns, the frieze, and the cornice. The Renaissance architects included the Composite, but as this followed all the rules of Roman Corinthian order apart from the type of capital, it should not be classed as an order in its own right.

no means in a linear, developmental way. The key changes, notable already in the third century BCE, were the use of closely spaced columns, reflecting a change to stone entablatures and presumably the closed pediments typical of Greek temples,[11] and the replacement of the wide *alae* with narrow side colonnades (which Vitruvius calls peripteral *sine postico*), on the model of Greek peripteral temples but without the rear colonnade. Occasionally there are also fully peripteral versions, but often with a narrower colonnade (*peristasis*) than in a truly Greek temple, and without the rear porch.

Irrespective of these features, the high podium, frontal steps, and deep porch remained as the hallmarks of the Roman temple, reflecting the different cult practices and other functions of Roman temples compared with Greek. While both provided shelter for participants as well as houses for the gods, the continuous *peristasis* of the Greek temple was ideally suited to processions, but the deep porch of the Roman temple speaks more of static gatherings or meetings, and the high podium and frontal aspect provided a platform from which to see and be seen, particularly in the taking of *auspices*, signs from the gods seen in the flights of birds or thunder and lightning, which was a fundamental element in Roman religious practice, particularly in relation to political activities.

If the needs of ritual meant that Roman temples largely retained the functional elements of their form, the same constraints did not apply to their decoration. By the end of the second century BCE, when our evidence is clearer, western Hellenistic forms of the Greek Doric and Ionic orders [56] were being widely used for Roman temples, as in the early first-century BCE Ionic Temple of Portunus in the Forum Boarium in Rome [57].[12] These small temples usually had a single *cella* and a deep *pronaos* (porch), four columns across (tetrastyle) and two deep, but the outer walls of the *cella* were decorated by engaged pilasters or semi-columns, in a visual reference either to the real colonnades of Greek peripteral temples or to the flanking columns of the Capitolium, creating a long-lived and distinctively Roman format, often referred to as pseudo-peripteral. While Ionic dominated Hellenistic temple architecture in the East, and was the preferred order for Hermogenes of Priene, the late third-century architect much admired by Vitruvius,[13] the particular form of Ionic capital used frequently in Rome and central Italy, with the volute corkscrewing out

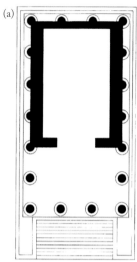

towards the eye and often with four equal faces, suggests a rather different local aesthetic which arguably developed in Greek southern Italy and Sicily rather than in the Greek East.[14]

If we really want to see the dynamics of cultural interaction in Rome and Italy in the third to first centuries BCE, however, we need to turn to the final—and ultimately the most important—columnar element introduced from the Hellenistic Greek world into Roman architecture: the Corinthian capital [58].[15] This was widely used in the Greek East as a variant of Ionic, originally for decorative effect on the inside of temples and then on the outside of minor monuments, but Corinthian capitals do not appear to have been used for the main external order of temples in central Italy before the second century BCE. The variety of components which make up Corinthian capitals—the ring(s) of acanthus, the vertically curving volutes, the abacus, and the triangular decorative zone between them—allowed for much variation, which crystallized into recognizable types in different parts of the Hellenistic world.

The versions of Corinthian particularly favoured in central Italy, which again appears to have originated in Sicily and Greek south Italy, had the standard two rows of acanthus typical of the old Greek heartlands, but with relaxed, almost shaggy acanthus leaves;[16] a further variant had large corkscrew volutes, and outsized six-petalled flowers on the abacus [58a]. Alongside this appears a more unusual form, characterized by a broad shape with a single row of acanthus and massive outer volutes with a large bust of a deity between them [58b]. The shape is associated particularly with Ptolemaic Alexandria, but the detail reflects a western taste for large three-dimensional and often figural ornament, visible also in the pottery of places such as Hellenistic Centuripe in Sicily and Canusium in Apulia. The appearance of this from Rome down through Italy, Sicily, and into Punic Carthage reflects the close connections which existed between these areas from at least the third century.[17] To find this type of capital used as the main temple order at the Roman Republican colony of Paestum should not

therefore be surprising; its mixed Ionic and Doric entablature may have the same hybrid origins.[18] In contrast, the tall and slender capitals of the Round Temple by the Tiber [58c], with their taut double ring of acanthus, small volutes, and delicate acanthus flower on the abacus, suggest the importation of a contemporary Greek form. While it was the latter that gradually became the most common form of Corinthian capital in late Republican Rome, in places including Cora, Pompeii, and Praeneste two, three, or even all four of these variants could co-exist.

By the second century BCE, Republican consuls, generals, censors, and provincial governors therefore had a wide choice of possible forms and styles from which to choose when commissioning new temples or rebuilding existing ones [55]. The choice of style was not simply a question of personal taste or fashion but could be symbolic of class, wealth, allegiance, and the nature of the gesture being made. The introduction of marble for temple building in Rome at this precise moment made it a key symbol of the ongoing tension between those conservative members of the Roman elite who preferred the old ways (the *mos maiorum*), exemplified by the timber entablatures and terracottas of the venerable Capitoline temple, and the progressive elements who embraced the riches and fashions of the newly conquered Hellenistic East.[19] According to the written sources, the first marble temple in Rome was that of Jupiter Stator (c. 146–143 BCE), designed in Greek fashion as peripteral and probably Ionic by the Cypriot architect Hermodorus of Salamis, for the Roman general Metellus, conqueror of Macedonia.[20] Nothing of this remains, but the later circular Round Temple by the Tiber, in Pentelic marble imported from Attica and on a low stepped base (*crepis*) typical of Greek temples, gives us a hint of its impact [59].[21]

Creating the Setting

Metellus' Temple of Jupiter Stator was not a stand-alone structure, but was built alongside an existing temple to Juno Regina, and surrounded by a four-sided colonnaded portico (*quadriporticus*) [60].[22] Temples as buildings had been relative late-comers to the sacred landscape of Rome, ritual activity originally taking place at natural features such as springs or groves, or at altars set up in the open air within consecrated spaces delimited by boundary markers (*templa*). The elaboration and monumentalization of sacred space was therefore a logical development, distantly inspired by the sanctuaries of Greece, where the linear stoa had originally developed to provide shelter for visitors.[23] The use of the columnar orders, borrowed from the visual language

of temples, imbued stoas and porticoes with a dignity appropriate to their context [61]. Not surprisingly, they were popular gifts by communities and, in the Hellenistic period, by autocrats like Antigonas Gonatas, king of Macedon, who financed a stoa in the Sanctuary of Apollo on Delos.

From at least the fifth century BCE, some stoas in important Greek sanctuaries were also victory monuments, including the Stoa of the Athenians at Delphi used for displaying the booty from naval victories against the Persians, and that added to the sanctuary of Athena at Pergamon by Eumenes II (c. 190 BCE), dedicated to Athena Nikephoros ('Bringer of Victory').[24] Both arguably may have influenced Cn. Octavius, consul in 165 BCE, to build the first known monumental *quadriporticus* in Rome, which commemorated his naval victory over the Macedonian king Perseus,[25] just as the Porticus of Metellus [60] was built to display works of Greek art acquired as spoils of war a few decades later. The most recent reconstruction of the Portico of Metellus gives it some 180 columns, in itself a display of conspicuous consumption, compared to only 70 columns in the near-contemporary stoa of the Pergamene king Attalos II at Athens. Small wonder that their introduction at Rome was later associated with the start of public extravagance and private luxury.[26]

Similar orthogonal arrangements had become more common in the Hellenistic period, but the sites which provide the closest possible parallels—Pergamon, Rhodes, Delos, Kos—were at the time firmly in the Roman sphere of influence, with a high level of diplomatic contact which facilitated the

Fig. 60

Restored original plan of the Porticus of Metellus in the Campus Martius, Rome, post-146 BCE. It enclosed the Temple of Juno Regina (on the right), founded in 179 BCE, to which was added the Temple of Jupiter Stator, reputedly the earliest marble temple in Rome (c. 146–143 BCE).

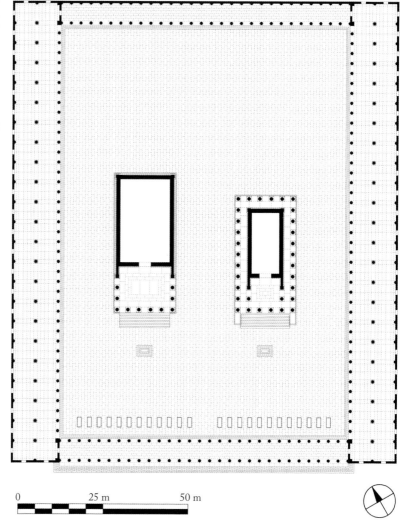

0   25 m   50 m

exchange of ideas and personnel on a cultural as well as political level, as we have seen with the architects Cossutius and Hermodorus. The introduction of the *quadriporticus* thus appears as a specific choice from an international *koine* of a particular form, one especially suited to Roman requirements and taste. The rigidly rectangular format reinforced the augurally bounded shape of the sacred *templum*, in contrast to the more organic siting of many stoas in Greek sanctuaries.

More specifically Roman and Italian features appear in a number of important sanctuaries of the mid-second to first century BCE in central Italy where porticoes frame the main temple. Two particular elements which distinguish several of these sanctuaries are the addition of a stepped theatre-shaped area on axis in front of the temple and the use of vaulted concrete to create dramatic terraces; the best known and one of the earliest (c. 120 BCE) is the Sanctuary of Fortuna Primigenia at Praeneste (modern Palestrina), east of Rome [62].[27] The setting of major temples on high places was common

Fig. 61

Terracotta Campana plaque, first century CE, representing a portico set on an arcaded substructure, with statues and fountains in the intercolumniations, and decorative garlands strung between the columns.

in the Greek world, and in the Hellenistic period some of these were further elaborated into a series of distinct terraces enhanced by stoas and linked by monumental staircases. The flexibility of vaulted concrete as a medium, however, compared with the Greek tradition of building solid structures, opened up greater possibilities of orchestrating processional routes designed to serve ideological and spiritual needs, and of separating these from routes serving the more mundane and material needs created by the large numbers of visitors, something that is clearest at the Sanctuary of Hercules Victor at Tibur (modern Tivoli).[28]

The theatre-shaped areas may also have served rather different cultic needs than their Greek equivalents, and not always the same one. While true theatres were not uncommon in Greek sanctuaries, for example at Delphi, they were usually independent structures with no direct topographical relationship to the main temple. In the sanctuaries of Latium and central Italy, on the other hand, the theatre-shaped area was set on axis and in front of the temple as part of an integrated whole. While some of these appear to have been standard Roman-type theatres with a small orchestra and integral stage building (e.g. at Tibur), others were simply a set of concentric tiered steps, with a non-standard 'orchestra' and without a permanent stage building. At the Sanctuary of Juno at Gabii (c. 150 BCE), where the theatral area is cut off from the temple and its porticoed precinct by a wall with a single door, the 'orchestra' is very wide and the 'cavea' very shallow. By contrast, the theatral area at Praeneste is set on its own terrace with a very small 'orchestra' reached by a steep axial stair and no obvious place for a stage. Because of the steepness of the site, the large terrace below is almost invisible from the 'cavea', virtually excluding the theatral area from any normal use as a space for dramatic performances. At the same time, the relative insignificance of the actual temple to Fortuna and the lack of an obvious

space for an altar in front of it suggest that this theatral area did fulfil an important cultic or ceremonial function, the nature of which is not recoverable but may be related to the famous oracle which attracted the many visitors to the sanctuary.

The architecture of both the porticoes and the terraced sanctuaries made extensive use of the columnar orders. The sanctuary at Praeneste employed all three in a vertical hierarchy of Doric, Italic-Ionic, and both Italic and Greek forms of Corinthian,[29] an extension of a usage also found in double-storey porticoes and stoas, which seems to have crystallized in the Hellenistic East. While the structures at a basic level served the needs of large audiences, the orders enhanced the prestige of the sanctuaries, while adding considerably to the cost of construction. Interestingly, the exceptional terraced structure at Praeneste was not a royal commission or the gift of a particularly wealthy single benefactor but was funded by local businessmen, whose wealth derived from the lucrative markets of the Hellenistic East, and whose idea for the sanctuary and its communal funding may have been inspired by the examples they saw there, but reinterpreted very much in a local idiom.

A New World Order

By the end of the second century BCE when the sanctuary at Praeneste was being built, the Corinthian order was well established not just for important porticoes but also for major temples in Rome,[30] including the rebuilding of the prominent and ancient Temple of Castor and Pollux facing onto the prestige space of the forum.[31] Irrespective of the materials, Corinthian, particularly when used with an Ionic entablature, had the virtue of giving the greatest possible opportunity for both elaboration and variety, and hence the creation of a unique structure as the signature of its patron and his position in politics and society. It was also inherently the most expensive choice, as Corinthian capitals required at least three to four times the amount of highly skilled labour to produce as Ionic capitals for the same-sized columns and same material. A large Corinthian temple with many columns was thus a clear demonstration of the ability to commit great resources even without the use of marble.

Nevertheless, even in the late Republic, it was not the only choice. Vitruvius, in a discussion of the key concept of *decor* or appropriateness,[32] considered Corinthian only suitable for delicate and feminine deities (Venus, Flora, Nymphs), while assigning Doric to the war-like and strong (Minerva, Mars, Hercules), and Ionic for the rest. It is certainly possible to point to examples which fit Vitruvius' prescriptions, beginning with the maintenance of the 'Tuscan' form of the Capitoline temple at least until 83 BCE when it was destroyed by fire, and possibly as late as 41 BCE when it still appears this way on coins, if not later.[33] In his day the ancient Temple of Quirinus, the deified Romulus, was rebuilt in the Doric order, while somewhat earlier Pompey the Great had chosen the Tuscan form for his temple to the rustic and virile Hercules.[34] The known Ionic temples are mainly to very local Roman deities, including Vesta, Saturn (rebuilt in the mid-first century BCE), and Janus, or to the personifications of manly virtues Honos and Virtus. Corinthian presents more difficulties, as scholars have often pointed out. Yet, if not exactly in line with Vitruvius' prescriptions, there is an interesting pattern in the temples at Rome which we are reasonably certain used Corinthian capitals in the second and first centuries BCE. As well as Venus and Flora, they include 'peaceful' female personifications such as Fides (Faith) and Fortuna, and above all Greek or foreign deities including Apollo and Magna Mater. The Temple of Castor and Pollux (the Greek *Dioscuri*) fits this pattern.

By the time that Augustus commissioned his first temple projects, while Corinthian was a likely choice, it was not the only one, nor was it necessarily self-evident that one specific form of Corinthian was about to be transformed into the pre-eminent order for the new regime. The earliest example we can be sure of is the Temple of Apollo on the Palatine, begun probably in 36 BCE, an appropriate choice for this very Greek deity, often portrayed as a slender youthful figure.[35] It is perhaps more surprising that Augustus chose the Corinthian order for the Temple of Mars Ultor [63, 64], the Roman god of war and divine father of Romulus and Remus.[36]

In accordance with *decor*, and given his claims to be restoring the Republic and reviving traditional religion at Rome, Augustus might have been expected to use the ancient Tuscan order, or the Doric, looking back to classical Athens, the Greek equivalent of Rome's own early Republican past, as a fitting model for the Augustan present. Rather than emulating the Doric Parthenon, however, Augustus appears to have chosen another Athenian temple as his model, both in its 60-foot order and in the basic form of Corinthian capital used: the giant Temple of Olympian Zeus, the Greek equivalent of Jupiter [17]. Vitruvius reveals a contemporary appreciation

Fig. 63
Forum of Augustus and
Temple of Mars Ultor,
Rome, dedicated 2 BCE.

of the temple's size, refinement, and magnificence,[37] and some of Augustus'
allies are said to have thought of completing the temple in his honour;[38]
indeed, it is possible that work was being carried out there at the same
time as Mars Ultor was being built. All of these elements together—its
location in Athens and origins in the late sixth century BCE, the deity it
honoured, and the involvement of a Roman architect in the Hellenistic

Fig. 64
Temple of Mars Ultor,
Forum of Augustus, Rome,
dedicated 2 BCE. Detail of
the Corinthian order.

reconstruction—provided the Temple of Mars Ultor with a compelling precedent which was such an important aspect of *decor*.

For the order truly to fulfil the requirements of *decor*, however, it needed its own distinctive entablature. According to Vitruvius, mixed and hybrid orders were to be avoided because it was not appropriate to transfer elements of one order to another, yet Corinthian capitals in Italy were used with Ionic or Doric entablatures, or even a mixture of the two.[39] The solution was again based strongly in precedent, but developed in a specifically Roman way. Above a standard Ionic architrave and frieze, a strongly projecting cornice— subtly recalling perhaps the wide overhanging eaves of the traditional Tuscan temples—was ostensibly supported by scrolling brackets (modillions); those of the Temple of Mars Ultor were closely modelled after examples on the door of the fifth-century BCE Erechtheion at Athens. Rectangular and curved brackets had already found their way into entablatures by the first century BCE, but mainly on minor monuments or domestic interiors. Only in the mid-first century did they begin to appear on major buildings in Rome.[40] The addition of an acanthus leaf to the underside of the modillion, first seen in the late first-century Temple of Apollo Medicus,[41] strongly suggests an attempt to achieve harmony between the formal appearance of the cornice and the Corinthian capital.[42]

The final element which conferred prestige and authority on Augustus' signature temples was the use of marble. By Vitruvius' day, marble was firmly established as the main contributor along with large size to the achievement of *magnificentia* (grandeur/magnificence), a positive virtue when applied to public buildings and one which reflected glory on the patron,[43] being the result of great outlay. It also conferred *auctoritas* (authority/dignity) on a building,[44] as befitted the temples to the gods, and could be further embellished by painting and gilding, as on the capitals and entablature of Augustus' Temple of Apollo on the Palatine.[45] The specific marble chosen was highly significant. Augustan temples were made of marble from the Apuan Alps at Carrara, high above the Roman colony of Luna, which had caught the attention of Julius Caesar as a potential substitute for the customary architectural marbles imported from Athens. It is debatable whether in the early days of its exploitation Luna marble would have been necessarily much easier or cheaper to acquire, but its ideological significance as a specifically Italian and Roman material should not be underestimated. For the first time, it naturalized the use of marble, removing all taint of eastern luxury and putting Rome on a par with Athens. To the Roman mind, the association of specific marbles and decorative stones with particular places went beyond the simple labelling of a stone after its place of origin [65]. The coloured marbles used for the interior decoration of Augustan temples thus arguably carried a message beyond that merely of *magnificentia*. Coloured marbles—the tawny yellow Numidian, the purple-veined Phrygian, the red granite of Egypt—represented a new geography of power and empire,[46] in much the same way as the statues personifying all the nations in Augustus' *Porticus ad Nationes*, or Agrippa's world map in the *Porticus Vipsania*.

There was a long history of highly decorated temple interiors in the Greek world, including the first known example of a Corinthian capital in the fifth-century BCE Temple of Apollo at Bassae, and Corinthian was often

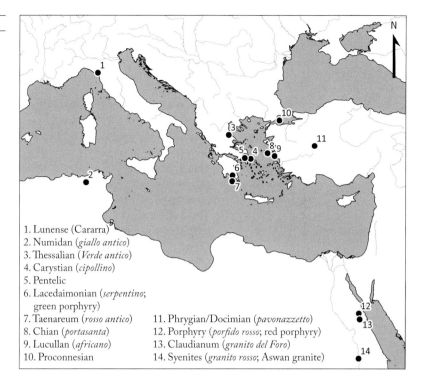

Fig. 65

Distribution map of the main sources of marble used in the Roman empire.

N

1. Lunense (Cararra)
2. Numidan (*giallo antico*)
3. Thessalian (*Verde antico*)
4. Carystian (*cipollino*)
5. Pentelic
6. Lacedaimonian (*serpentino*;
   green porphyry)
7. Taenareum (*rosso antico*)
8. Chian (*portasanta*)
9. Lucullan (*africano*)
10. Proconnesian
11. Phrygian/Docimian (*pavonazzetto*)
12. Porphyry (*porfido rosso*; red porphyry)
13. Claudianum (*granito del Foro*)
14. Syenites (*granito rosso*; Aswan granite)

used even with a severe Doric exterior. Once Corinthian was moved to the exterior to become the main order of the temple, however, other modes of embellishment were sought to maintain the dignity and magnificence of the abodes of the gods. From the literary sources it appears that the various kinds of coloured marble started to be imported to Rome in any quantity for architectural use only in the first century BCE,[47] so were still something of a novelty when the Temple of Mars Ultor was being built. The double interior colonnade adorning the side walls of its interior [66] had shafts of Phrygian marble, which was used again in some of the rich veneers of walls and floors. These coloured marble shafts were combined with figured capitals, where the volutes of the standard Corinthian were replaced by the foreparts of the winged horse Pegasus [67], which appears to have featured on the helmet of the great statue of Athena Parthenos at Athens, and possibly also on the helmet of Mars Ultor in Augustus' temple. Figured capitals, too, although known from the Hellenistic period and earlier, only seem to have appeared in Rome at about the time Vitruvius was writing, notably in temple interiors including that of Apollo Medicus, where the capitals demonstrate their appropriateness by including snakes wrapped around a tripod with gorgons, symbolic of Apollo's oracle at Delphi.

By the time of its inauguration in 2 BCE, the Temple of Mars Ultor had few rivals in Rome for size save the Capitoline temple, and none for splendour. Like Caesar's Temple of Venus Genetrix, it was octastyle and peripteral *sine postico*, making twenty-six columns in all, set closely together (pycnostyle) to emphasize the exceptional height of the façade and to fit in as many columns as possible [12, 63]. At 60 Roman feet high, these were the

© altair4multimedia.it

Fig. 66

Computer reconstruction of
the interior of the Temple
of Mars Ultor, Rome,
dedicated 2 BCE. Unlike the
white marble exterior, this
was richly decorated with
coloured marbles from
around the empire.

Fig. 67

Figured pilaster capital with
Pegasus volutes from the
interior decoration of the
Temple of Mars Ultor,
Rome, dedicated 2 BCE.

tallest in the city, one-fifth larger than those of Apollo Palatinus, and almost two-fifths larger than those of the Temple of Venus Genetrix. But its significance did not lie just in its *magnificentia*. Augustus also conferred on it a major role in state rituals relating to war and empire. According to Suetonius, he decreed that the Senate should meet there to consider wars and claims for triumphs, military commanders should set out for their spheres of action from it, and victorious generals should bring the tokens of their triumphs there on their return.[48] It was also the place where boys formally celebrated their passage to manhood by taking on the *toga virilis*,[49] and it is perhaps no coincidence that the year of its inauguration was also when Lucius Caesar, Augustus' younger grandson and co-heir, passed this important milestone. Just as the Capitoline temple because of its political importance had set an architectural model for Rome and the Republic, so the Temple of Mars Ultor became the architectural model for the new empire of the Principate.

The language of Mars Ultor was reinforced and developed in the final reconstruction of the Temple of Castor in the Roman Forum **[68]**. According to the ancient sources, it was dedicated by Augustus' step-son and ultimate heir, Tiberius, in 6 CE, following the recent deaths of Augustus' grandsons Gaius and Lucius Caesar, who were heroized as the new Castor and Pollux. Even more lavish than the Temple of Mars Ultor, it had thirty-eight columns in all, towering 50 Roman feet tall on a podium some 24 Roman feet above the forum. The whole order is richly detailed, from the intertwining

Fig. 68

Temple of Castor, Rome, rebuilt and rededicated c. 6 CE. This final version was in Luna marble, and in a Corinthian order with fully developed acanthus and scroll modillions. This is the fourth temple on the site, replacing a smaller Corinthian temple in travertine dedicated in 117 BCE, itself a rebuilding of a temple of the early second century BCE; the much smaller original temple dedicated in 484 BCE was in the Tuscan order.

helices and decorated abacus of the capitals to the scroll and acanthus modillions, the first known example of what was to become the standard imperial form. The exquisite and refined workmanship of the fragments now lying around the temple strongly suggest that the same sculptors were employed as worked on the Temple of Mars Ultor; in both, many of the fine details, such as the veins on the leaves of the acanthus, would not have been visible at all once the capitals were in place. Such detail takes us beyond *magnificentia* as simply conspicuous expenditure for the public good to *decor* and *pietas*, where only the very best that could be acquired by imperial power and resources was appropriate for the gods. Yet it is worth remembering that not all Augustan temples were so richly treated. The Temple of Magna Mater, the Idean mother goddess tied by her Trojan origins to the legend of Aeneas, although restored by Augustus and sufficiently important to be named in his *Res Gestae*, the public document of his achievements, was only of stuccoed tuff. The full force of Augustan *magnificentia* was reserved for those temples of particular import for the emperor himself or his close family.

The Temples of Imperial Rome

The *auctoritas* conferred on the Corinthian order by its use in the major Augustan temples, particularly those closely connected with the emperor and his family, established it as the order of choice for all subsequent major temple constructions in the city of Rome, irrespective of their size, plan, or function. Corinthian was used for all the known temples at Rome dedicated to the deified emperors, and for temples to emperors' personal deities such as Domitian's Temple of Minerva or Septimius Severus' colossal Temple of Hercules and Bacchus on the Quirinal. Even the venerable Capitoline temple was eventually rebuilt using the Corinthian order, probably following a fire in the Flavian period, when, according to Plutarch, Pentelic columns from Athens were used in Domitian's rebuilding.[50] What is clear from all the ancient evidence, however, is that the original layout of the Capitoline temple was maintained because of religious scruples, as it had been through all earlier rebuildings, with only the height being increased to give it greater visual prominence.[51]

As far as we can tell from the surviving evidence, most of the imperial temples were of conventional form, sometimes free-standing and sometimes with the rear wall engaged with the surrounding architecture, as had been the Temple of Mars Ultor.

A new aesthetic comes with Vespasian's Temple of Peace, which Pliny the Elder included among the three most beautiful buildings in the city of Rome [69, 93].[52] Built out of booty from the Jewish Wars and designed to display its spoils, the emphasis was on the precinct, reminiscent of the victory porticoes in the Campus Martius; the temple proper was integrated into the U-shaped porticus, its pedimented porch aligned with the rear portico and its *cella* flanked by rectangular rooms. The house of the goddess Pax (Peace) stood out only because of its axial position and the use of a giant Corinthian order lifting its pediment above the lower sloping roofs of the flanking colonnades. The effect was to place exceptional emphasis on the open space, laid out as a formal garden with walks between rose-beds and water features, interrupted only by the altar at the far end in front of the temple.

Fig. 69

Artist's reconstruction of the
Temple of Peace, Rome,
dedicated 75 CE, paid for by
the spoils of the Jewish War
(70–71 CE). Two versions
have been given here for the
portico and the temple
proper, that on the right
with taller columns for the
temple porch and an attic
above the colonnade of the
portico. While there is
ample evidence for water
features and rose-beds, the
actual design shown here is
overly influenced by
modern ideas.

Two other exceptional temples were among the wonders of Rome marvelled at by Constantius II in his notable visit of 357 CE: the Temple of Roma and Venus and the Pantheon.[53] Hadrian's Temple of Roma Aeterna and Venus Felix, its feast day celebrated on the traditional birthday of Rome and in late sources simply called the Temple of the City, was the last of the three great state temples of imperial Rome [70].[54] If the Capitoline temple represented the Rome of the Republic, and the Temple of Mars Ultor the military might of conquering Rome, Hadrian's new creation exalted the golden age of Rome's universal empire, prosperous and eternal, encompassing East and West. Decastyle and dipteral, with 128 60-foot Corinthian columns of Proconnesian marble, two *cellae* back to back, and on a *crepis* of seven steps, this could not have been more different in design. Instead, it was far more directly influenced by the Temple of Olympian Zeus at Athens, which—by no coincidence—was completed by Hadrian. The importance of the Temple of Roma and Venus is easy to underestimate, partly because it is not well preserved and partly because of its Hellenistic Greek layout, which has been assumed to be part of the criticism of the temple by Trajan's architect Apollodorus of Damascus recorded in one ancient source.[55] Nothing in the source, however, mentions the Greek style, only the need for it to be on a higher platform to give it more prominence, and that the statues of the goddesses were too tall for the *cellae*; the latter simply echoes an ancient comment about one of the most famous statues of antiquity, Pheidias' fifth-century BCE chryselephantine statue of Olympian Zeus at Olympia. The extraordinary investment of resources and manpower this temple represents can be seen in the twenty years it took to complete.

Architecturally in direct contrast with Hadrian's Temple of Roma and Venus is the most famous and—to us—most Roman of all the city's temples, Trajan's Pantheon [2-3, 19, 42–43]. Begun in the latter part of Trajan's

Fig. 70

Temple of Roma Aeterna and Venus Felix, Rome, vowed by Hadrian in 121 CE and not finished before 135 CE: (a) the plan (A) shows the original decastyle, dipteral design with a rectangular double *cella* in ashlar construction, alongside that (B) of the octastyle Hellenistic Temple of Olympian Zeus in Athens, to the same scale; (b) the view is what remains of the structure as rebuilt by Maxentius in brick-faced mortared rubble following a fire in 307 CE.

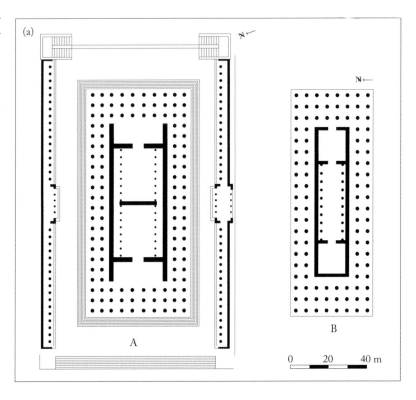

reign, and completed by Hadrian not long after 123 CE, its vast circular domed *cella* has already been discussed as an exemplary exercise in Vitruvian design and one of the prime achievements of Roman construction. The original Pantheon, built by Augustus' close collaborator Agrippa and rebuilt by Domitian, is thought to have been a circular *templum* with a monumental entrance portico;[56] with its Caryatids and bronze capitals, it would have been among the more lavish of Augustan buildings.[57] Much has been written on its original function, but there seems to be no reason to assume it was anything but a temple to all the gods, particularly Mars and Venus, and including the most recent addition to the Roman pantheon, Augustus' adopted father Julius Caesar; that Hadrian transacted public business there merely puts it on a par with other temples in Rome where the Senate was accustomed to meet.[58] Equally, none of the complex modern theories about its cosmic significance can be supported by the available ancient evidence. By the time of the Trajanic building, circular temples had had a long history in Rome, starting perhaps with the one to Vesta, while large domed structures had become familiar elements of bath buildings. Whether, therefore, the dome had any specific significance to most Romans is debatable. Rather than the eventual form of the temple, it may have been the close association with Agrippa and Augustus, whose statues stood in niches at the back of the porch, and with Deified Julius Caesar, which made it an expression of the intimate relationship between the new world order and the powers above.

In its Trajanic form, the Pantheon would have fulfilled all the requirements of *magnificentia*: exceptional size, daring and impressive construction, and the large-scale use of varied marbles inside and out. According to a convincing recent analysis, the monolithic granite columns of the pedimented porch were originally intended to be 60 rather than 48 Roman feet tall, which would have set it alongside such iconic temples as Mars Ultor and the rebuilt Capitolium in terms of sheer scale.[59] While this has been explained by the possible loss of one or more column shafts on the long voyage from the eastern desert of Egypt where they were quarried, one alternative opened up by the redating of the Pantheon is that they were commandeered by Hadrian for his Temple to Deified Trajan, which almost certainly had columns of just this exceptional size and material and was reportedly the only temple on which Hadrian placed his name.[60] If so, it throws light on Hadrian's priorities, and reminds us that our privileging of the Pantheon does not necessarily reflect that of its contemporaries, for whom the design may not have seemed quite as original and radical as it does to us. Compared with the vast projects of Trajan in his forum and baths, or Hadrian in the Temple of Roma and Venus, this was a relatively small building project, just part of a larger programme of reconstruction in the Campus Martius following a fire. By the fourth century, however, it was on Rome's 'must-see' list, notable for its great size—'round as a whole city district'[61]—while its early seventh-century conversion to a church, which ensured its survival, also speaks of its contining importance to the city.

Negotiating Empire

The changed political circumstances of the empire brought a new wave of temple building across the empire for cults relating to the emperor, many owing much architecturally to the temples of Augustan Rome. Existing settlements in the Roman sphere of influence, as well as the new colonies founded by Julius Caesar or Augustus, clamoured to give divine honours to the new regime as a way of expressing loyalty to and recognition of the new realities of power. Over 40 per cent of the new temples to known deities built in Italy under Augustus and his Julio-Claudian successors were for cults in some way connected with the emperor,[62] while the joint cult of Roma and Augustus was particularly widespread in the provinces, from Barcelona in Spain to Caesarea Maritima in Israel. In Asia Minor, the power of Rome and its officials had been recognized by the early second century BCE by the foundation of cults to the goddess Roma (the personification of the power of Rome), and even individual Roman magistrates were honoured in this way.[63] The latter reflected a long tradition of heroizing individuals of particular significance for a city, especially founders, which in the Hellenistic period had transmuted into a ruler cult in recognition of those who had power over the life of the community. Not surprisingly, therefore, temples to Roma and Augustus, to Augustus alone or in conjunction with the tutelary deity of the community, or in the east to the *Theoi Sebastoi*, proliferated, accounting for 95 per cent of known new temples in this period.

On the whole, these cults of the emperor were not directly imposed by or paid for by Rome, but were offerings from cities, from local officials in their capacity as magistrates, and from important individuals, since temples were very much a part of civic identity and could be major players in inter-city rivalries. This was particularly true for the imperial cult temples set up on behalf of provinces rather than individual cities, which required the approval of the emperor and Senate at Rome. The earliest known is the Temple of Rome and Augustus at Pergamon in Asia Minor, represented on the city's coinage as a temple with a probably Corinthian façade but seemingly on a tall stepped *crepis* in the Greek style, with *Rom(ae) et August(o)* on the entablature [71]. Although the ancient sources say that it was intended as a focal point for the Greek residents of the whole province,[64] the language of the coins is the Latin of the deities and presumably of the cult, rather than the Greek of the population. The benefits were not just in terms of enhanced prestige; equally important were the practical advantages to be had from the closer ties to the Senate and the emperor, and the economic advantages provided by the hordes of visitors, especially at the regular sacred games related to the cult. When the province of Asia was subsequently given permission to establish a second provincial cult to Tiberius, Livia, and the Senate, eleven cities competed for the privilege,[65] rather in the way that

Fig. 71

Pergamon, *cistophorus* of Augustus, silver, 20–18 BCE. On the reverse is a representation of the provincial Temple of Rome and Augustus, and the legend COM(munis) ASIAE (the 'community' or province of Asia).

modern cities compete for the right to host the Olympic Games. Provincial cults were equally as important in the western empire, the one dedicated to the Deified Augustus at the Roman colony of Tarraco (modern Tarragona) by the people of Hispania supposedly setting the precedent for the other provinces.[66] A recent study of the fragmentary archaeological evidence indicates that the temple had a 50-Roman-foot Corinthian order, made in imported Luna marble by skilled workers from Rome (or at least Italy), its stylistic details deriving from the great Augustan temples;[67] the replication of this whole architectural language of urban *magnificentia* helped secure the status of the provincial cult.

From the time of Augustus onwards, a Corinthian temple on a high podium with frontal steps and a deep porch became the standard expression of 'becoming Roman' in religious architecture in Italy and the western provinces, a visual expression of political allegiance. Only in Asia Minor did Hellenistic temple forms continue to be built even for temples to Roma and Augustus, most notably the Ionic peripteral temple on a low stepped platform at Ankyra in Asia Minor.[68] Nevertheless, others looked more distinctly Roman; the temple at Mylasa in Asia Minor [72] has the deep porch and frontal steps of a Roman temple, but with Composite capitals and decorative tops and bottoms to the column shafts, while the otherwise Roman-style temple in the Upper agora at Ephesus had a low Greek-style *crepis*.[69] The Roman form of peripteral, combined with a high, straight-sided podium with frontal steps and a Corinthian order, was also used especially for important temples around the empire, including contemporary temples to Deified Trajan in Italica [73],[70] the city of his birth, and to Zeus and Trajan on the acropolis in Pergamon, probably the most important Roman sanctuary in Asia Minor. Both of these were set in colonnaded precincts, in a formulation that had by then become *de rigueur* where space and finances allowed.

Even without the incentive of provincial cult privileges, wealthy communities and individuals still engaged in competitive temple building, especially in the eastern empire. One of the most extraordinary examples is the colossal Temple of 'Hadrian', octastyle and pseudodipteral with Corinthian columns perhaps 70 Roman feet high, built by the city of Cyzicus on the Sea of Marmara, using marble from the nearby island of Proconnesos. We have a rapturous account of its building in Aelius Aristides' panegyric to the city, which says that the temple reveals the magnanimity of the city and its inhabitants and that it could have been the offering of no other city than Cyzicus.[71] The speech focuses on its great size which makes it appear 'beyond the power of man to accomplish', the engineering equipment and transport developed specifically for the project, the expenditure of time and money, and the beauty that exceeds its size.[72]

At the other end of the scale, smaller communities relying on local financing often could only fund more modest projects. In the city of Dougga in North Africa, the Capitoline temple dedicated in the 160s as a votive offering for the safety of the emperor by two members of the local elite, at their own expense, was a simple arrangement using only six Corinthian columns in local stone, albeit of excellent workmanship [52]. Some communities, lacking a wealthy senatorial or local patron, could only finance their temples by subscription. When, under Hadrian, the quiet city of Euromos in Asia

Fig. 72

Temple of Roma and Augustus, Mylasa (Asia Minor), c. 11 BCE–2 CE, drawing by Richard Pococke (1704–65). The frontal access, the podium, and the deep porch are typical Roman elements, but the wider colonnade owes more to Greek temple forms. The additional decorative elements at the top and bottom of the column shafts are typical of late Hellenistic architecture in Asia Minor.

The TEMPLE of AUGUSTUS and ROME at MYLASA.

Minor chose to rebuild a relatively modest peripteral temple to Zeus Lepsynos in the Corinthian order, it relied on prominent members of the local community for funding the expensive fluting of the columns. Only those on the north long side and the rear, the aspects most visible to anyone approaching the sanctuary from a distance, were fluted, however, and these bear inscriptions indicating who paid for them and the specific number donated—six in one case of a magistrate and his daughter. The lack of flut-

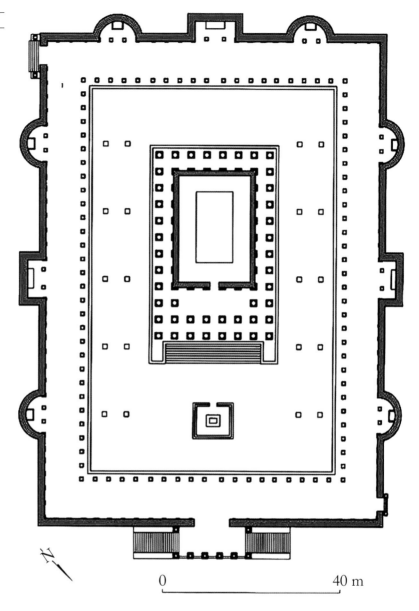

Fig. 73

Reconstructed plan of the
Temple of Deified Trajan,
Italica (Spain), early
Hadrianic. The temple is
octastyle, peripteral, and
with frontal steps, set in
a colonnaded precinct
articulated with alternately
rectangular and semi-
circular recesses.

0   40 m

ing on the columns on the least visible side of the temple suggests that
insufficient donors could be found to put the final decorative touches to the
temple.[73] Contrast the actions of the wealthy senator Pliny the Younger,
who, under religious pressure, had a temple to Ceres rebuilt on one of his
rural estates in Italy both larger and with marble columns, adding a new
porticus to house the 'great gathering from the whole region' attracted to the
sanctuary on its feast day.[74]

Alternative Traditions

The building of new temples and the rebuilding of existing ones on a grander
scale remained an important element of civic munificence throughout the

imperial period. Apart from the great boom in the Augustan period, the pattern is not uniform across the empire, but depended greatly on the degree of urbanism and the relative wealth of communities, so that the floruit of temple building was the first century CE in the western Mediterranean, but the second and third centuries in North Africa, while the under-urbanized northwestern provinces never produced the kind of religious landscapes that were standard in the Mediterranean. Pre-existing traditions also had a significant role to play. Although Greek- and Roman-style temples had been the ultimate symbols of cult in Italy and around the eastern Mediterranean since the sixth century BCE, they did not inevitably become the rule for specific cults which did not share their underlying practices.

Egypt is the extreme case. It retained its own very ancient deities, most of which the Greeks and Romans found very alien, and its own tradition of religious architecture; nevertheless, many of the surviving Egyptian-style temples dedicated to Egyptian deities are in fact Hellenistic and/or Roman in date.[75] Their traditional designs were codified in the 'Book of the Temple', a manual describing how the ideal Egyptian temple should be built; all the forty surviving fragments of the manual are of Roman date but the original goes back to the Ptolemies, who set in train an extensive programme of temple building in the Egyptian manner and to native Egyptian deities as a way of legitimizing their power. The Temple of Hathor at Dendara, begun under Cleopatra's consort Ptolemy XII but completed by Augustus, is a case in point [74]. There was certainly a political agenda, as the date of dedication was 30 August BCE, the first month of Roman rule in Egypt. Indeed, more Egyptian-style temples were initiated under Augustus than under any subsequent emperor, a move which helped present the new Roman ruler as a natural successor to the Ptolemies and thus ultimately the Pharaohs. In contrast, the temple to Augustus at Philae in upper Egypt was recognizably Roman, a tetrastyle Corinthian building on a podium, built by the Roman governor of Egypt in 13/12 BCE; only the use of local materials in a combination

Fig. 74

Egyptian-style Temple of Hathor at Dendara, Egypt, dedicated by Augustus 30 BCE.

of red granite shafts and entablature and black basalt capitals gives the whole an exotic air.[76] Compared with the hundred or more Egyptian-style temples built in the Roman period, classical-style temples, generally dedicated to Graeco-Roman deities, were relatively rare outside of the capital Alexandria, and stood in sharp contrast to those in the local tradition, with little cross-influence or hybridity of form or decoration.[77] Classical orders were, however, used in ancillary buildings in Egyptian sanctuaries, including monumental gateways and thoroughly Egyptian-type buildings such as birthing houses, where the constraints of the priestly manual gave way to the invention of the architect, working in the fashionable Graeco-Roman idiom.

Elsewhere under Roman influence, local arrangements were regularly dressed up in the Graeco-Roman orders, especially Corinthian, or entirely new forms were created inspired by Roman temple traditions. In the Semitic cults which dominated the Phoenician Near East and Punic North Africa, and the Celtic ones of the northwestern provinces, the impact of Rome can be seen as one side of a dialogue with local ritual requirements creating new forms of religious architecture. Parallel patterns of transformations of cult places can be observed in both these cultic regions, with the Graeco-Roman idea of the temple as the house of the god—indicated by the columnar façade with triangular pediment—coming to dominate the exteriors, while the internal dispositions were more directly conditioned by the very different requirements of the specific cult rituals.

While there is evidence for temple structures in the Near East from as early as the Bronze Age, in the Punic world these only begin to appear from the sixth century BCE, as part of the contemporary move towards the monumentalization of cult to be found in the Greek and Italic centres of the Mediterranean, including Rome. In North Africa, this often took the form of regular porticoed enclosures housing altars, votive stele, and small single-room shrines rather than temples in the Graeco-Roman tradition.[78] Despite the fact that Roman influences through conquest and alliance go back to the mid-second century BCE in North Africa, it is only in the Augustan period, in response to the changed political circumstances, that temple building really seems to take off. The result is a series of largely Roman-style temples dedicated to gods which, while ostensibly Roman in name, had close affinities with and sometimes replaced the older Semitic deities, particularly Saturn = Ba'al Hammon (also equated with Jupiter), and Caelestis = Tanit (also equated with Juno Regina). The absence of a podium and the presence of three or more *cellae* located at the rear of a porticoed enclosure have led some scholars to identify a specific Romano-African temple type that they argue developed from the porticoed enclosures of the rural shrines.[79] The multiple *cellae* and overall arrangement but on a common podium can, however, also be found in late Republican sanctuaries in Italy, for example in Ostia and Brescia, both probably early first century BCE. This raises interesting questions about direct or indirect architectural influences, in which direction, and in what particular cultic circumstances; some scholars have even suggested origins in the *principia* of Roman legionary fortresses.[80]

A much stronger argument can be made for the creation of hybrid Roman and Semitic forms in the Roman Near East. While the exteriors of many temples might have passed for Roman or at least Hellenistic, the interior arrangements were very different. Most temples dedicated to Semitic deities had an inner shrine (*adyton*) within the walls of the *cella*, recalling the rear rooms in the pre-Roman Punic temples, and many had substantial staircases between the porch and the *cella*, leading to an area of flat roof, despite the use of pediments on the short sides of the temples which otherwise imply a full gable roof.[81] The most spectacular examples of these hybrid forms originated during the fertile years of the early empire. The colossal Temple of Jupiter Heliopolitanus at Baalbek [75] was begun shortly after the foundation of the colony of Julia Augusta Felix Heliopolitanus in 16 BCE and was still not finished by the time of Nero. Externally, it would have appeared as a fairly standard—if exceptionally

Fig. 75

Temple of Jupiter Heliopolitanus, Baalbek, begun in the early first century CE. The columns are 65 Roman feet tall (c. 19 metres), and in the fourth row of blocks from the top of the platform are the 'Trilithon', three single blocks each c. 20 metres long and weighing 800 tonnes.

large—peripteral Corinthian temple of Hellenistic-Roman type, but it had an inner shrine (*adyton*) in the rear of the *cella*; the form was replicated on a slightly smaller scale in the adjacent and better-preserved 'Temple of Bacchus' [76].[82] In the Temple of Bel at Palmyra [77], on the very eastern fringe of the Roman empire, the local elements also affected the external appearance, with an off-centre entrance along one of the long sides to allow for two *adyta*, and a roof-line decorated with crow-stepped merlons in a tradition than may be traced back to the Assyrians, if not before, and was current in Parthian temple architecture.[83]

These are but two examples of hybrid Near Eastern temple forms, which show a remarkable degree of variation. Other temples in the region are notable for their concentric plans. The Temple of Ba'alshamin at Seia is roughly square [78], with a colonnaded, pedimented entrance which might have set up expectations of a standard Roman-type temple within, but was in fact only a façade flanked by two towers. In common with the less elaborate neighbouring Temple of Dushara, the *cella* was square with four internal columns, supporting some form of roof. Like the temples at Baalbek and Palmyra, these both belong to the early period of Roman influence, when local traditions were strong. The temple erected nearly a century later alongside these two is more immediately recognisable as belonging to a thoroughly Roman tradition, except for its architectural ornament, which is very local in style. Many other later temples do not seem to derive particularly from the Semitic tradition, but some still reflect the exceptional level of architectural experimentation which is the hallmark of this region. The best known is the third-century Temple of 'Venus' at Baalbek [79], which

Fig. 76

Interior of the 'Temple of Bacchus', Baalbek, Lebanon, mid-second century CE. The interior walls are decorated with an engaged giant order framing two rows of niches, while steps at the rear lead to the *adyton*.

Fig. 77

Temple of Bel, Palmyra,
Syria, completed around
32 CE. Despite the
Corinthian colonnade (a),
very little of the layout (b)
owes anything to Graeco-
Roman temple design. The
two *adyta* (D and E) have
flanking staircases leading
to roof-top altars, and the
entrance to the temple
(A) and its *cella* (B) are in
an asymmetrical position on
the long side. The temple
was deliberately destroyed
in 2015 by forces of the
self-styled Islamic State.

(a)

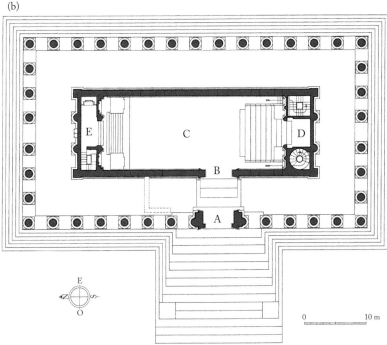

(b)

combines a horseshoe-shaped *cella* with a shallow tetrastyle porch and a
scalloped outer colonnade framing niches set into the exterior wall of the
cella. What is striking in all these eastern temples is the insistent use of the
Graeco-Roman pedimented façade irrespective of the interior arrangements, a strong indication of the symbolic power of this motif within the
cultural milieu of the Roman empire.

Similar phenomena can be seen at the opposite end of the empire in the
shrines to local deities of the northwestern provinces. Temple structures in

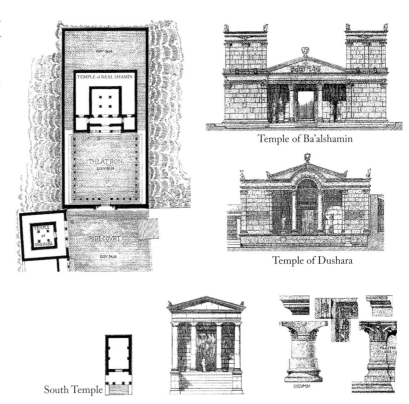

Fig. 78

Temples in the sanctuary at Seia (modern Si', Syria): Temple of Ba'alshamin and Temple of Dushara, end first century BCE South Temple, late first century CE. The plans are to the same scale, as are the elevations. In the first two, traditional Semitic layouts were given a veneer of Graeco-Roman orders; in the South Temple, the standard Roman layout was given a local flavour by the use of a specific capital type (called a Nabatean capital) and associated decorative details.

Temple of Ba'alshamin

Temple of Dushara

South Temple

this area do not seem to have appeared before the middle of the first century BCE, and reflect the ever-increasing interweaving of indigenous and Roman ideas of deity. The earliest appear as post-holes from simple wooden structures, usually reconstructed as a single centrally planned room, square or circular, with either a metalled path or sometimes a covered veranda (ambulatory) around it. There is much debate about the architectural origins of these structures, but while some, such as Hayling Island in southern Britain of the early first century CE, may pre-date formal Roman conquest, none appear to pre-date Roman influence, and scholars tend to see them as predominantly Roman provincial creations merging Roman and vernacular elements.[84] From the early Julio-Claudian period onwards, these are increasingly replaced with stone versions with a tall centralized *cella* lit by high windows, and surrounded by a colonnaded veranda, sometimes still in wood [80].[85] In the later second and third centuries, many underwent further monumentalization in an even more classicizing—or 'Romanizing'—style, with the introduction of podia, pedimented columnar porches, and sometimes full colonnades, while retaining the essential tall centralized *cella*, as in the Temple of Mars Mullo [15].[86]

There are parallels here with developments in the Near East and in other areas, particularly North Africa, where local traditions persisted. In all cases the local elements are strongest in rural or peri-urban sanctuaries, the areas least affected by the influence of core Roman values. These also tend to be distinguished by an agglomeration of many small cultic elements, multiple

Fig. 79

Temple of 'Venus' at Baalbek, Lebanon, third century CE, drawing by Luigi Balugani (1737–70). From the front the scalloped exterior colonnade and the circular domed *cella* would have been largely masked by the more standard pedimented columnar façade.

altars, and votive deposits, as well as small temples and shrines, all within a sacred area focused on a specific site or landscape element which is the inherent source of sanctity. The sites chosen for many new cult places, in contrast, were carved out of the urban landscape and not related to places of pre-existing ritual importance, and these tend to be temples in the Graeco-Roman manner and very often political and civic in function, especially relating to some aspect of imperial cult. There is also a time element; the most variety and experimentation with hybrid forms occurs in the early years of the empire, but by the Severan period far fewer temples were built in non-traditional forms and many existing temples were rebuilt on ever more classicizing lines.

In assessing the Romanness of provincial religious architecture, we also need to keep in mind differing perceptions: what was Roman to a provincial may have appeared provincial or even exotic to a Roman. The introduction of Roman building technology in the West, for example, provided the means to make permanent and monumentalize indigenous ideas of religious space, in the process creating new architectural forms. In the same way, in both the northwestern provinces and the areas with a Semitic heritage, the introduction of Roman surface decoration altered the appearance of, and created new aesthetics for, local sacred space. The use of a familiar common language of decoration and of elements shared with Roman cult places helped in the recognition of this as part of a shared experience, even if the underlying cult practices were different.

Fig. 80

Full-scale reconstruction of the Romano-Celtic Temple of Lenus Mars, from Vicus Cardena (Martberg, Germany). Many small temples of this kind, known mainly from excavated ground plans, have been found in an area from the UK and the Netherlands to Germany and northern France.

The columnar porch with triangular pediment and frontal staircase, together with the Roman Corinthian order, entered the architectural language of the whole empire as a symbolic shorthand for 'temple', irrespective of what precise arrangements lay beyond, whether the domed rotunda of the Pantheon or the concentric structures of Near Eastern or Celtic cult places. This shorthand appears in many different art forms, from putative representations of specific temples as propaganda on coins [71] and narrative reliefs adorning public buildings to generic depictions of idealized cityscapes in decorative painting [82], mosaic, and sculpture. The status and dignity accrued to this iconic image was also transferred to other kinds of public and private buildings and building elements, especially the simple aedicule composed of a pair of columns or pilasters supporting a pediment [30]. Temples were the key Roman expression of *pietas*, but also one of the very few forms of conspicuous consumption and self-presentation which would not attract any negative response from peers; their importance at the core of Roman society and of Roman architectural language should not be underestimated.

Housing the City

5

Panopeus [is] a city of the Phocians, if one can give the name of city to those who have no town hall, no gymnasium, no theatre, no *agora*, no water cascading into a fountain, but live in dwellings no roomier than huts, just like those in the mountains.

Pausanias, *Description of Greece*, 10.4.1 (second century CE)

One of the most extraordinary discoveries among the recent excavations in Rome is a monumental wall painting giving a bird's-eye view of a maritime city **[82]**.[1] This has welcome resonance with Vitruvius: there are the city walls with their towers and gates, temples, a theatre, porticoes, a possible forum, streets.[2] The same vision pervades ancient accounts of the foundation of the city of Rome, most of which were contemporary with Vitruvius, and informs Virgil's description of the legendary building of Carthage in the *Aeneid*,[3] where physical construction is intertwined with allusions to the social and political constitution of the city, in the formulating of law and the selection of magistrates—the necessary elements of a civilized urban life. Without them, as Pausanias makes clear, a settlement has no claim to be a city.

Form Follows Function: The Creation of Public Buildings

Vitruvius is clear about the importance of public spaces designed to fulfil the political and social imperatives of Roman urban culture. The distinctive Roman public building types—forum, basilica, markets, and *tabernae*; Roman circus, theatre, and amphitheatre; and baths—are the physical manifestations of those spaces. Two forces were at work in their evolution: an increased specialization of function which led to dedicated buildings to serve them; and the impact of changing fashions of public building which came with the new models and modalities of the Hellenistic world. Nothing that we know about Roman public architecture, however, leads us to assume that Roman politicians adopted any Hellenistic Greek civic architecture wholesale, any more than they adopted Greek temple forms. Rather, they took inspiration from Hellenistic palaces as much as from Greek civic buildings, and adapted ideas and elements of architectural design to their own purposes.

These buildings were generally secular and civil, and at Rome under the Republic the responsibility for their construction lay generally with the censors and aediles in their civic capacity, acting on behalf of the Senate and usually with public funds, in contrast to many temples and porticoes paid for directly from the spoils of war (*ex manubiis*) under the instigation of the consuls acting in their military capacity. Over time ambitious politicians came to realize the prestige that could accrue by engaging in these kinds of public buildings, especially outside the special conditions of war. The sums could be great: in 179 BCE the Senate set aside the whole state income for the year for public building.[4] Censors left their names on the buildings erected under their care as an important element of self-promotion, and with them often a familial

Fig. 81

Forum of Nerva (Forum Transitorium), Rome, finished c. 96–97 CE. The columns stand only a little way from the boundary wall, to which they are attached by short sections of entablature (*ressauts*), in order to give the impression of a full portico.

117

responsibility for their future maintenance or reconstruction, as happened with the Basilica Aemilia in the Forum Romanum.[5] The same officials were also responsible for infrastructure works including streets, drains, bridges, and aqueducts—the true marvels of Rome—which equally bore their names.[6]

The extraordinary wealth of the great generals of the late Republic led them to emulate the notable euergetism of Hellenistic monarchs, using their war booty and private funds to build major secular monuments in Rome as permanent memorials to military success and political power, but on an unprecedented scale and with an extraordinary degree of richness. The ultimate success of Augustus in establishing an autocratic dynasty was made abundantly clear in the fact that, by the end of his reign, public building in the capital had virtually become the prerogative of the emperor and his family. This transformation of the city, noted by ancient writers and carefully spelled out in Augustus' own account of his life's work (the *Res Gestae*), was a major contribution to legitimizing his new position in Rome. What began as utilitarian structures supplying the needs of public life came over the course of the Republic to represent the glory of the city, in direct relation to the degree of magnificence—*publica magnificentia*—in the size and materials of the buildings.[7] Following Augustus, other founders of dynasties in particular, notably Vespasian, Trajan, Septimius Severus, and eventually the Tetrarchs, tended to seek legitimization for their regimes through lavish new public monuments often built *ex manubiis* in good Republican fashion, or through the restoration and embellishment of established major landmarks built by previous emperors.

Housing the Republic

Central to the development of Roman public buildings was the Forum Romanum; according to one second-century BCE politician, the 'mirror of the *res publica* [the state]', a meeting place where the community discussed the ordering of society, decided its laws, and managed foreign relations [83].[8] From the start it appears to have been a constructed and formally surfaced space, created as early as the seventh century through a massive project of drainage and artificial terracing on an impressive scale, arguably one of the first major communal undertakings of the fledgling city—indeed, its creation has been seen as inseparable from the formation of the city itself.[9] Although renewed several times between the Republican and the Severan periods at progressively higher levels and paved in increasingly permanent materials, the open area of the Forum Romanum remained into the early empire a multi-purpose space accessible to the Roman people as a whole, a place for formal mass meetings and impromptu political rallies, for demonstrations and more than the occasional riot. From an early date the place for state funerals of the political elite, under the empire it continued to host state occasions where the emperor and the people could meet.

Fig. 83

Reconstructed plan of the Forum Romanum at the end of the second century BCE. Key: (1) *Comitium*; (2) *Rostra*; (3) *Curia*; (4) Temple of Vesta; (5) Temple of Saturn; (6) Temple of Castor and Pollux; (7) Temple of Concord; (8) Basilica Porcia; (9) Basilica Fulvia/ Aemilia; (10) *Tabernae Novae*; (11) Basilica Sempronia and *Tabernae Veteres*; (12) Basilica Opimia; (13) *Macellum*.

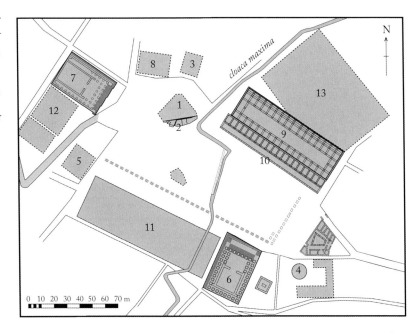

The political heart of the Republican Forum Romanum was the *comitium*, the oldest of the three locations where eligible citizens met to vote, with its integral tribunal (later called the *rostra* from the prows of ships captured in Rome's first naval victory) from which the magistrates addressed the people and dispensed justice. Refashioned over the centuries in response to changing political circumstances, the *comitium* provided a sensitive indicator of both the growth and the changing political role of the Roman people. Sometime in the third to second centuries BCE it may have taken on at least a partly circular form, in imitation of Greek political meeting spaces, but this is disputed.[10] Nothing, however, marks the increasingly autocratic state more than the reduction and then disappearance of the *comitium* space by the time of Augustus. In contrast, despite several rebuildings, the *curia* which rose behind it was the most stable of the political spaces, emblematic of the crucial and long-lasting power of the Senate, which still played an important role under the emperors. Although a third-century CE rebuild, the simple but monumental rectangular hall we see today [84] matches the description in Vitruvius and arguably goes back to the original; as an inaugurated space (a *templum*), it is not surprising that the antiquity of the design and the restrictions of *decor* required this to be maintained throughout the long centuries of Rome.

The Forum Romanum was also a natural meeting place for informal exchanges between individuals and particularly for commerce. In the early Republic the only permanent commercial structures were the *tabernae*, one- or two-roomed units with wide openings to the forum space, which originally formed part of the aristocratic houses facing the forum space. Even by the later fourth century BCE, when the *agorai* of Greek and Hellenistic cities were bounded by elegant colonnaded stoas, Rome's forum was still flanked by *tabernae*, housing everything from bankers to butchers. The creation of a separate market building (the *macellum*) in the third century removed some of the sale of foodstuffs from the Forum, which, together with adding wooden balconies or galleries to the remaining *tabernae*,[11] gave the open square a new dignity.

Written records show that at about the same time the first basilica was created as a covered extension of the Forum. The basilica became one of Rome's main public building types and one of its enduring architectural inventions, of enormous post-antique importance in the development of Christian churches. The basic design comprised a rectangular hall divided by columns into a wider central nave and narrower aisles, usually on all four sides, with the nave lit by a clerestory and covered with a trussed timber roof; this created a multi-functional enclosed space that could be used as a whole, or divided off into discrete areas using temporary barriers. The plans of the few known Republican examples, at Cosa, Ardea, Pompeii, Praeneste, and the reconstructed plan of Basilica Fulvia/Aemilia in the Forum Romanum [85], show considerable variety in overall proportions and in the connection to their adjacent fora, which identifies these as individual designs, variations on a common model to suit the particular sites and circumstances.[12] Some were open to the forum along one long side through a colonnade, in the manner of a Greek stoa, while others had more limited access through doors, as at Pompeii which has its short end on the forum. The key feature that sets all except for Praeneste apart from Greek stoas even of the same period is the clear span of the nave. In the range of 12 to 18 metres, these are roughly twice that of any of the known stoas, and required a different roofing solution, producing a different visual and aural ambience, and creating true interior spaces.

The name 'basilica' is a puzzle. Not only is the word Greek in origin but it also means kingly, an odd idea in stridently anti-monarchical mid-Republican Rome. No particular Greek stoa is likely to have been the direct model, and there is no evidence that the basilica itself existed as a Greek

Fig. 85

Plans of early basilicas to the same scale. Key: (1) Rome, Basilica Fulvia/Aemilia, 179 BCE; (2) Cosa, c. 150 BCE; (3) Praeneste, c. 120 BCE; (4) Pompeii, c. 100 BCE; (5) Ardea, c. 100 BCE.

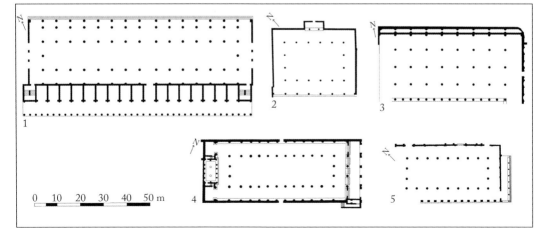

0   10   20   30   40   50 m

public building type. Our best guess at the inspiration for the architectural form is the royal audience and reception rooms of Hellenistic palaces, the type of spaces where from the early third century BCE Roman ambassadors were received by powerful Greek monarchs. The suggestion that the original basilica, perhaps to be equated with the Atrium Regium mentioned in the texts, fulfilled the same function in housing royal embassies from the Hellenistic kingdoms is more controversial, and is not entirely supported by the ancient sources.[13] Whatever the origins of the name and the form, the three basilicas built adjacent to the Forum Romanum in the early second century BCE were clearly buildings of great importance and the focus of competitive elite building. All were publicly funded and contracted for by censors: the Basilica Porcia of 184 by the rigid traditionalist Cato the Elder, which roused controversy in being the first to bear the name of an individual; the Basilica Aemilia, contracted in 179 by the next censors, on a much grander scale and clearly meant to outdo that of Cato, who was on the opposite side politically and culturally; and facing it across the forum, the Basilica Sempronia of 169, built by Tiberius Sempronius Gracchus, son-in-law of Scipio Africanus who was a bitter political enemy of Cato.[14]

The function of these early basilicas is not easy to pin down. At least by the first century BCE, the literary evidence associates basilicas with business, as the home for bankers, moneychangers, and *negotiatores* (those engaged in wholesale transactions), while the nature of the architecture, rich with high-status columns, argues for this to be business very much at the upper end of the market rather than that of everyday shop-keeping; in modern terms, the stock exchange rather than the shopping mall. This interpretation makes sense of the design of the Basilica Aemilia [83, 85]; originally open to the Forum Romanum only through one door between the *tabernae*, its real access seems to have been from the north through a stoa-like colonnade onto the *macellum*, and from the streets on its short sides. We also hear of different groups using basilicas as a base, for example the tribunes of the *plebs* met in the Basilica Porcia, suggesting a political function. More circumstantial is the evidence for their use as law courts. Precisely at the time that the basilica was being developed as a building type, there was a major change in the working of civil law. Previously confined to the patrician priesthoods and applied only to citizens with much of the power vested in the heads of families, law had become secularized, involving specialist lawyers (the jurists), and was extended to foreigners, since much of it was concerned with contracts for sale or lease, and partnerships.[15] Thus the exercise of civil law, like the conduct of other kinds of business, may have moved out of the houses of the senatorial aristocracy and into the new basilicas, which had replaced the houses on the Forum.[16] By the early empire the juridical function of the basilicas in the Forum Romanum and in Rome's colonies was fully established, their interior arrangements making it easy to cordon off different areas for different hearings simultaneously, with some, like the basilica Vitruvius designed for the city of Fanum Fortunae, having separate permanent tribunals for trials.

Performance Spaces

Alongside the Forum Romanum, the Roman Republic's chief locations for celebration and display were two other areas of legendary importance: the

Circus Maximus below the Palatine[17] and the Campus Martius north of the Capitoline. The latter, in origin a marshy plain, was closely connected to the Roman people as a military body and the starting point of the Roman triumph. The Romans believed that the Circus Maximus had been designated as the place for chariot racing already by the king Tarquinius Priscus,[18] at a time when such races were becoming increasingly a part of the various Greek games at Olympia and elsewhere. At Rome they were connected with the Roman Games (the *Ludi Romani*) in honour of Jupiter Optimus Maximus, the protective deity of the Roman state, while theatrical performances appear to have been a later introduction to the games, perhaps in the mid-fourth century BCE; both were also put on to celebrate military victories at triumphs and the dedication of temples. Wild beast shows (*venationes*) came later, possibly as early as the third century BCE, when unusual animals from foreign campaigns began to be exhibited at triumphs; later too were the first recorded displays of Greek athletics in the Circus Maximus. In the later years of the third century there was also a considerable increase in the number of *ludi*, as games were instigated in honour of the fertility goddesses Flora and Ceres and the foreign deities Apollo and Cybele (Magna Mater), together with the *Ludi Plebei*, a public festival aimed at the plebeian populace. The defeat of Hannibal and Rome's further military expansion also meant that games celebrating Roman military success increased in number and splendour over the second century, particularly after the successful annexation of Greece and Asia Minor.[19] Gladiatorial games (known as *munera*) were a different matter. Known in Rome already in the mid-third century BCE, when the written sources connect them with aristocratic funerals, they were only much later included formally in the *ludi*, although the little evidence we have suggests that these too had military and political connotations.[20]

Since the senatorial elite of the Republic provided the priests, the magistrates, and the generals involved in the giving of games, they were also the ones placed to gain favour with the public by putting on a good show and by improving the physical conditions for the spectators. Temporary wooden stands, especially for spectators of high rank, were one important contribution and presumably were all built in much the same way, whether in the Forum Romanum, the Circus Maximus, or beside the temple of whatever deity was being celebrated.[21] The precise arrangement of the stands was related to the shape of the arena of performance, itself determined by the specific needs of the activity or contest involved, and by constraints imposed by the natural topography or the pre-existing built environment. The other way that the games could be enhanced was by improving the staging for the performances, the earliest being the introduction of starting gates for the races in the Circus Maximus in 329 BCE.[22] Competitive building in relation to games and performances really took off in the second century BCE, as it had with the building of basilicas. The censors again played a role; in 179 BCE, the same ones who were responsible for the Basilica Aemilia also provided a temporary theatre near the Temple of Apollo in the Campus Martius for the *Ludi Apollinares*,[23] while the next pair of censors topped it by ordering stages to be built for all games given by aediles and praetors.

It is not surprising, therefore, that one of the projects of the censors of 154 BCE was the building of a permanent theatre. These had already become common in Greek south Italy and Sicily by the fourth century, while in the second century there was something of a boom in Campania and Samnium, including at Pompeii.[24] According to Livy, however, when the theatre at Rome was partially built, Publius Cornelius Scipio Nasica, the leading man of the Senate and from an old patrician family, carried a motion for its demolition, as being 'not only useless, but injurious to the morals of the people'.[25] While this could be seen merely as typical of the conservative and anti-Greek elements in the Roman Senate, a permanent theatre posed two difficulties in the political situation of the mid-second century. Firstly, it could provide a permanent focus for spontaneous political gatherings away from the traditional locale of the Forum Romanum, in the way that Greek theatres did; and secondly, by carrying the names of the censors responsible, the permanent theatre would detract from the prestige accrued to later magistrates through their temporary constructions. The performances themselves were clearly not a moral concern, as expenditure on stage buildings and other luxuries continued to grow. From the start of the first century BCE we hear of sophisticated *trompe l'oeil* painted stage scenery, theatres fitted with awnings (*velaria*) to shade the audience, roofed theatres, stage buildings covered in silver, gold, and ivory, and even a pair of revolving theatres.[26] The ultimate theatre stage was that built in 58 BCE by Aemilius Scaurus, Sulla's phenomenally wealthy stepson, who as aedile created a three-storey structure said to have had 360 columns, the first level of marble 38 Roman feet (over 11 metres) tall, the second of glass (presumably glass mosaic imported from Alexandria), and the third of gilded wood.[27] Pliny's description is certainly exaggerated, calling it the 'greatest of all the works ever made by man', but there is no doubt that this was made to impress; it may also have contributed to Scaurus' money problems, which led him five years later to sell his large house on the Palatine.[28] The temporary nature of these constructions emphasized the element of conspicuous consumption and extravagant waste, and hence the wealth and power to command exceptional resources of their promoters, but dressed up as—at least to some—morally and politically acceptable public magnificence.

Unfortunately, little of this helps directly with understanding the formal architectural development of Roman theatres in this period. These differ from Greek theatres in being free-standing, having a semi-circular rather than a horseshoe-shaped auditorium (*cavea*) with a semi-circular rather than a circular orchestra, and a different stage design with a tall and highly decorated stage backdrop, the *scaenae frons*, joined to the end walls of the *cavea* to make a single, enclosed D-shaped space [86]. Part of the answer to this design lies in the kinds of performances put on in the Roman theatre.[29] Prior to the third century BCE, these were predominantly burlesques and farces, full of music, dancing, slapstick, and obscenities, closer to our idea of pantomime or *commedia dell'arte* than the tragedies and comedies of classical Greece. Depictions of similar performances on painted vases from Greek south Italy show a raised wooden stage with steps down to the orchestra area [87]. The earliest real plays we have come from the Roman playwright Plautus around 200 BCE, when the Greek New Comedy he was drawing on had itself moved away from the traditional use of the circular orchestra. Stage directions in some of Plautus' plays suggest a backdrop with

three doors and a porch over at least the central one, with two further entrances on the side wings (the *paraskenia*) presupposing some lateral space either side. About the same time it seems that some of the orchestra space was already given over to special seats for senators. The stage could therefore be extended sideways without encroaching on the working area of the orchestra, and ultimately could be linked to the extension of the *cavea* towards the stage, creating the familiar D-shape. It is also significant that the stage backdrop had become an element of spectacle in itself, rather than simply providing the setting for the action as in the early Greek theatre.

The evolution of a fixed type of place designated to hold gladiatorial contests—originally called *spectacula* but better known under the later name of amphitheatre—is even more difficult to determine and has led to conflicting theories. Vitruvius noted that the long rectangular shape of Roman fora and their flanking porticoes, with their wide column spacings and balconies, were determined specifically by the custom of giving gladiatorial games in them,[30] first attested in the funeral games of Marcus Aemilius Lepidus in 216 BCE.[31] Although gladiatorial contests were already being held elsewhere in the city, including in temporary theatres and in the Circus Maximus, the fashion for holding them in the Forum seems to have quickly taken hold. This was due at least in part to the importance of the Forum for the elite families whose funerals were an opportunity to remind the people of Rome of the achievements of the deceased and their distinguished ancestors; but it was also the place for ambitious men seeking higher public office to put on shows to curry favour with the populace. As with the theatre, understanding the evolution of the amphitheatre is hampered by the habit

Fig. 87

Red-figured bell-krater,
Puglia, c. 380–370 BCE.
The scene is from a South
Italian comedy. The action
takes place on a simple
raised wooden stage, with
frontal steps and a door
with a projecting porch.

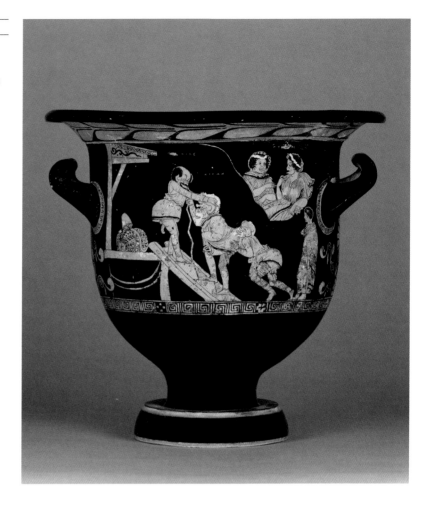

of erecting temporary stands at Rome right until the end of the Republic, despite the fact that permanent amphitheatres had been built elsewhere in Italy since at least the early years of the first century BCE, most famously at Pompeii [88]. Several scholars have argued that the oval or elliptical shape, the most distinctive feature of Roman amphitheatres, developed from the desire to fit temporary stands into the irregular trapezoidal shape between the *tabernae* fronting the two long basilicas of the second-century Forum Romanum, while providing the best possible viewing conditions for the greatest number of spectators to watch the very mobile spectacle of gladiatorial combat.[32] Other theories suggest that the form originated in Campania and Samnium where the earliest examples are found, or that it was connected with gladiatorial exercises becoming part of military training at the end of the second century, and thus with the veterans settled in cities like Pompeii after the end of the Social Wars, by when the form was already well developed.

Although these are likely explanations for the creation and popularity of permanent amphitheatres in the first century BCE, they do not in themselves provide any entirely convincing explanation for its overall shape. While an informal oval may have arisen naturally as crowds gathered to watch the

Fig. 88

Amphitheatre, Pompeii, c. 80–70 BCE. The continuous arcade supports an earth bank on which the seats were installed, while the six arches at the front support one of the staircases leading to the seating in the upper part of the *cavea*. The local magistrates Quinctius Valgus and Marcus Porcius had it built at their own expense.

action at early gladiatorial contests, a slow evolution by trial and error towards a formal elliptical shape to fit the Forum Romanum rather under-estimates the sophistication of the architects of the day, who were quite capable of using complex geometrical design processes for theatres,[33] and presumably could also have done so for amphitheatres. The pair of back-to-back wooden theatres erected in Rome by the tribune Gaius Curio for his father's funeral games in 52 BCE, which rotated to form an amphitheatre for gladiatorial games, suggests a close connection in the mind of the designer.[34] Many early amphitheatres, including that of Pompeii, appear to have been set out as ellipses, one of the sections of a cone, easily drawn—or laid out on the ground—using two fixed focal points and a set length of cord stretched between them.[35] The standard work in antiquity on conic sections was written by Apollonius of Perge at the library of Alexandria around 200 BCE, and its revised version sent to his friend Eudemos of Pergamum. Both Alexandria and Pergamon had great libraries where copies of the *Conics* could presumably be found, and therefore accessible to the architects of the later second to early first century as part of the knowledge exchange which typified this period. It may not be too speculative to imagine the elliptical amphitheatre as designed by a single architect, perhaps a military architect/engineer working for one of the Roman generals where the practice of gladiatorial exercises as military training was being established. The inscription from the amphitheatre at Pompeii makes it clear that it was built specifically by and for the new veteran colony imposed by Sulla on the old Samnite city. The design would have set it apart from the existing theatre as something related, but new and distinctively Roman.

The other contribution to the development of Roman theatres and amphitheatres came from constructional requirements.[36] Even in some Greek-style theatres, there was a problem in supporting the ends of the raked *cavea*, which could only be achieved by a substantial and solid masonry wall to retain the loose earth fill of the embankment. In Roman theatres and amphitheatres, at least part of the superstructure was usually free-standing, increasing the structural problems. By the early first century BCE, mortared rubble had replaced solid ashlar walls, and novel solutions found. In Bononia (modern Bologna), the internal structure of the theatre was divided into compartments by radial and curved walls to distribute the fill, with the external façade designed as a blind arcade which has very close parallels with the amphitheatre at Pompeii, of a similar date.[37] In other theatres in northern Campania, the architects went a step further, using hollow vaulted structures linking radial walls. Both of these systems show the same kind of thinking as seen in the terracing of the great sanctuaries of Latium, or in the so-called 'Porticus Aemilia' (?*navalia*) at Rome [34]. In other words, in this period a flexible solution was developed which could be applied by architects wherever necessary to contain an embankment or create a terrace. Rather than being something specific to a single area of central Italy, the development of the standard Roman theatre and amphitheatre forms should be placed in the context of the building boom of the late second to early first centuries BCE which was fuelled by the extraordinary wealth of central Italy—and not just Rome—in the wake of Rome's imperial expansion in the East, combined with the development of the revolutionary material of vaulted concrete which allowed the ambitious plans of local elites to be brought to fruition.

Catering for the Individual

The last major type of public building that epitomizes Roman society is very different in nature. Baths, like fora, had to cater for individuals with their own particular reasons for being there, but differed in having a very specific practical function relating to the actual physical body of the individual; despite statues of the healing deities Aesculapius and Hygieia being common in Roman baths, these, like the basilica, were fundamentally secular buildings. Baths also had very different design requirements to any other type of Roman public building. Here the personal trajectory, requiring flexibility and choice for the individual, was paramount, with the bather deciding when and how to use the facilities, unlike the more rigid hierarchies imposed by theatres or amphitheatres, or the goal-specific functionality of basilicas, where the individual went to find a specific banker or trial.

Public baths had been a feature of urban life in the Greek world at least from the fifth century BCE, and were relatively common in the larger Hellenistic cities, including those in Sicily and Greek southern Italy. Although there are no surviving remains, they must have existed at Rome by 199 BCE, when one of Cato the Elder's duties as aedile was said to have been testing the temperature of the water in the public baths,[38] and remains of them survive from the mid-Republic at colonies such as Fregellae.[39] Bathing in public was certainly a normal and established part of Roman daily life by the first century, as witnessed by the construction of a set of public baths just behind the forum at Pompeii in the early years of the colony, but, unlike basilicas, baths are not mentioned in the historical sources among the major works of the censors in Rome, and appear to have been considered as purely utilitarian rather than prestige buildings. The epigraphic record of towns in Italy in the early first century BCE suggest that their construction, enlargement, and repair were on the whole publicly funded, and the projects the responsibility of local magistrates rather than individual benefactors.

As with the other Roman public building types which developed during the Republic, there are many theories about the origins of the specific features which mark these out as Roman rather than Greek.[40] The key differences are the use of communal hot pools in the Roman bathing regime rather than the individual hip-tubs of the Hellenistic baths, and a clear sequence of rooms with increasing gradations of heat in contrast to a more amorphous distribution of rooms. Associated with the Roman system is a type of underfloor heating called the hypocaust, where the floor was supported on a series of short pillars (*pilae*) through which hot gasses flowed; while elementary forms of hypocausts are known from the Greek world, they were never used there on the same scale or so systematically. One possible origin for both technology and method of use is the availability of naturally heated springs in the volcanic regions of central Italy, especially Campania, and Sicily (where immersion pools are found alongside hip-baths). Hot baths are certainly associated with Campania anecdotally in the ancient sources, but that tells us nothing about their architecture. The earliest known example of what became the standard 'Republican' form is the Stabian Baths at Pompeii **[89]**, where the series of contiguous rectangular rooms roofed with parallel barrel-vaults have now been identified as the original phase of the baths and securely dated to the later second century BCE,[41] a time when other typical Roman buildings like the basilica and amphitheatre were also being developed.

Whatever the actual process of evolution, these are likely to have been the form of baths familiar to those living in the city of Rome at that time. As well as the differences in the facilities and heating methods, the individual rooms are considerably larger than those found in most Hellenistic baths,

Fig. 89

Stabian Baths, Pompeii, plan of the original construction, later second century BCE. The men's baths at the south and the smaller women's baths on the north each consists of a dressing room (*apodyterium*), slightly heated room (*tepidarium*), and hot room with heated pool (*caldarium*); the two suites are separated by the space for heating water and hypocausts. The original circular dry sweating room (*laconicum*) is attached to the exercise court (*palaestra*), following Greek practice.

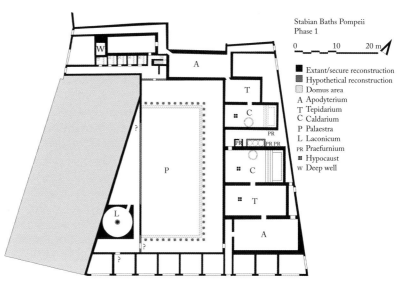

Stabian Baths Pompeii
Phase 1

0   10   20 m

■ Extant/secure reconstruction
▨ Hypothetical reconstruction
☐ Domus area
A Apodyterium
T Tepidarium
C Caldarium
P Palaestra
L Laconicum
PR Praefurnium
⁑ Hypocaust
W Deep well

due in part to the advantages of vaulted mortared rubble construction. Altogether, Roman baths appear to have allowed more place for social interaction than their Greek counterparts, while the communal pools suggest a different attitude to body-consciousness between Greek and Roman society. The social implication of bathing clearly taxed Roman moral sensibilities, however, and women were often given the possibility of avoiding mixed bathing by having a separate, and usually smaller, suite of bathing rooms in the same complex. The men had the larger section, and the one most directly connected to an exercise court (often called the *palaestra* in modern literature) where this was included in the plan.

From Republic to Empire

The turbulent half-century that culminated in the new regime of the Augustan era was mirrored by dramatic changes to the physical environment of the city of Rome in the provision of new public spaces. Two buildings from the middle of the first century in particular stand out: the Theatre of Pompey, dedicated in 55 but not finished until 52 BCE, and the Forum of Caesar, completed less than ten years later.

Pompey's theatre was an extravagant statement, the first permanent theatre building in the city and at c. 160 metres in diameter the largest Roman theatre ever built, with a vast porticus erected behind it laid out with groves of plane trees in the manner of a Greek gymnasium; at roughly 34,000 m² it outdid all of the previous porticoes in the Campus Martius.[42] Although Plutarch, writing in the second century CE, says that it was inspired by the theatre at Mytilene (Lesbos)[43] leading modern scholars to argue for a strong Hellenistic influence, what remains displays all the basic elements developed in the theatres of late Republican central Italy, but with further refinements which were to dominate future theatre design. Structurally, the raked *cavea* was entirely supported on a sophisticated network of vaulted substructures in mortared rubble, with intersecting radial and annular passages and stairs giving rapid access and egress to well-defined areas of seating, a system which became standard for all buildings for spectacles irrespective of overall form. Symbolically, the *cavea* had an arcaded façade in travertine ashlar articulated with Tuscan pilasters, a motif which became the hallmark of all Roman buildings for spectacles and has been dubbed by scholars the 'Theatre-motif', but had already been employed from at least the second century BCE, especially in the substructures of sanctuaries like Praeneste and the Capitoline façade on the Forum Romanum (the so-called 'Tabularium').[44] The use of this motif is in keeping with Pompey's supposed arguments that the theatre was merely the steps leading to the temple to Venus, Pompey's tutelary deity, aligning it with the great sanctuaries of Latium. While this is said to have been his main argument to the Senate for overturning the earlier ban, the paramount position he held at the time must have acted very much in his favour. In its original form, it is also likely that the Theatre of Pompey had an elaborate *scaenae frons*, three storeys high, rich in marble and decorated with sculpture. This gives us a context for the *scaenae frons* of Aemilius Scaurus in the very personal politics of the late Republic, as it was erected while Pompey's theatre was being built. Scaurus, immensely rich and well connected, a member of one of the most powerful families in Rome, had spent time in the East on Pompey's staff and about the time he built his theatre had married Pompey's ex-wife; subsequently he was exiled by Pompey. In this case at least, personal animus as well as political one-upmanship may have had a part to play in these exceptional constructions.

Political rivalry also lay behind Julius Caesar's decision to put his own monumental stamp on the city of Rome. While few of his buildings survived later restorations, we are exceptionally well informed about them through the correspondence of his contemporary Cicero. The year after the dedication of Pompey's theatre,[45] Caesar was already planning to rebuild the nearby voting enclosure of the Roman people (the *Saepta*) in marble, and surround it by a mile-long porticus, outshining Pompey's monument. At the same time, he was at work in the Forum Romanum, the political heart of the Roman state, rebuilding on a grand scale the Basilica Sempronia as the Basilica Julia, most likely in direct and visual competition with the Basilica Aemilia, being rebuilt with exceptional magnificence by an adversary of Caesar, Aemilius Paullus.[46] Most crucial of all, Caesar was buying up land from private individuals to extend the Forum Romanum itself. This ultimately became a separate additional public space, the Forum of Caesar, a bounded court with colonnades on three sides with the Temple to Venus Genetrix, Caesar's divine ancestress, set axially at the rear of the enclosure [90].[47] Architecturally, this is the most significant of Caesar's monuments,

Fig. 90

Forum of Caesar, Rome, c. 54–46 BCE. This is the original plan, with entrances on the main street leading from the densely inhabited region of the Subura (the Argiletum) to the old Forum Romanum, before the Augustan alterations.

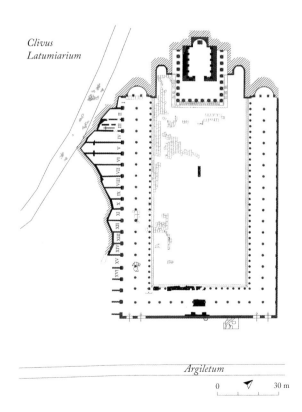

Clivus Latumiarium

Argiletum

0　　　　　30 m

creating a new and influential model for the forum as an architectural entity in its own right, rather than just a loose collection of individual buildings around an open space like the old Forum Romanum, while sharing much of its architectural language with the sacred enclosures and porticoes of the Campus Martius. Although the rectangular shape fits with Vitruvius recommendations for the fora of Italian cities, the long colonnades, of double width and with close-set exterior columns, rather reflect the Greek *agorai* of the Hellenistic period. This complex was a monument to Caesar, destined specifically for state business, where the wide colonnades of Italian fora, designed to facilitate watching gladiatorial games, were not only unnecessary but unwanted.

This is not to say that Caesar was not interested in making or improving the provision for gladiatorial games or other displays, many of which he gave in connection with his quadruple triumph of 46 BCE. Most significantly, the Circus Maximus was given a permanent structure for the first time, using similar technology for its substructures as Pompey had used for his theatre but on quite a different scale, seating perhaps 100,000–150,000 spectators compared with the roughly 20,000 that the theatre may have sat.[48] Other projects included temporary venues—a stadium for athletics and a basin for mock naval battles—and a giant theatre planned to outdo that of Pompey. Between Pompey and Caesar, venues for such activities moved from being simply places equipped—admittedly in an increasingly lavish fashion—for large audiences on a temporary basis to being the largest permanent public structures of their day.

Pompey and Caesar between them set new standards of architectural patronage which were adopted and enhanced by Augustus and later emperors. In an astute political move, Augustus completed or rebuilt structures begun or planned by Caesar, including the Basilica Julia and the *Saepta*, and extended Caesar's forum with the addition of a new Curia, while restoring several other buildings, including the Circus Maximus and the Theatre of Pompey, which had suffered damage in serious fires. The completion of Caesar's work could be presented as an act of piety due to his adoptive father, in good Republican tradition; the restoration of Pompey's theatre, 'at great expense' but left in Pompey's name rather than in his own,[49] cleverly honoured Caesar's defeated rival in an ostensibly even-handed show of generosity. The two major civic buildings which Augustus built from new mirrored his restorations exactly: the theatre he dedicated in the name of his son-in-law and nephew Marcellus [91], and his own forum with its temple to Mars Ultor (the Avenger) adjacent to that of Caesar [12, 63]. While the basic model for the Forum, a long rectangle flanked with porticoes and with the imposing Temple of Mars Ultor at the rear, came from the Forum of Caesar, the pair of semi-circular exedrae which opened off each side of the porticoes were an original addition to the design.[50] The colonnades themselves were an interesting combination of Italian/Roman layout in the wide-spaced single row of columns, with classical Greek detail in the architectural ornament and the caryatids alternating with *tondi* of Jupiter Ammon and barbarians decorating the attic zone [13]. These together represented both the specific defeat of Antony and Cleopatra and the general military success of Rome, continued in statues of Republican heroes set in

Fig. 91

Theatre of Marcellus, Rome, in use by 17 BCE, inaugurated 13 or 11 BCE. The lower two storeys of the façade have Greek Doric (below) and Ionic (above) orders flanking the arched openings in the so-called 'Theatre-motif'.

the shallow rectangular niches framed by half-columns which articulated the walls behind.

The empire message of the Forum of Augustus, that of Rome's glorious past, present, and future, can also be seen in the extensive use of coloured marbles for column shafts, paving, and veneer from the eastern Mediterranean, but with the Italian white marble from Luna for the remaining architectural ornament and sculpture, and some white marble veneer painted in imitation of rich cloth hangings [92]. All this made the forum an appropriate setting for the declaration of war and the award of triumphs by the Senate, as well as the formal starting and return points for military governors going to their provinces.[51] Augustus had also extended the Forum of Caesar to incorporate a new *curia* so that the Senate, passing from there to the Forum of Augustus, was constantly reminded of Rome's recent history and one of the sources of Augustus' power. Augustus also decreed that public prosecutions and the casting of lots for jury service took place only in his Forum, despite the absence of a basilica, presumably leaving the Basilica Aemilia in the old Forum Romanum for private cases. Given that Pliny the Elder named the Basilica Aemilia and the Forum of Augustus as two of the three most beautiful buildings the world had ever seen,[52] this may be another snub to the once all-powerful family of the Aemilii to which Paullus belonged. Nor did Augustus ignore commerce as part of his reorganization of the area, building a new *macellum* in the name

of his wife Livia far away on the Esquiline Hill, finally removing the noise and smells of the meat and fish market from the grandeur of Rome's political heart.

The Theatre of Marcellus **[91]**, on the other hand, reflects Augustus' religious and social reforms, and his dynastic aspirations. Ultimately dedicated in memory of Claudius Marcellus, whom Augustus had seen as a potential heir but who had died in 23 BCE, it was sufficiently complete to be used as one of the seats of the *Ludi Saeculares* of 17 BCE, a traditional three-day festival to honour the guardian deities of the city, which Augustus reformed as part of his revival of traditional religion. Between these two dates Augustus was involved in a programme of social legislation which included regulating behaviour at the games, assigning specific seats to different orders of society as part of his hierarchic vision of a rebuilt Roman society after the disruptions of the civil war.[53] Mirroring the ordering of society within, the façade provides the first surviving theatre in Rome with the 'canonical' hierarchy of the architectural orders framing the arched entrances: Greek Doric at the bottom, followed by Ionic, and most likely Corinthian in the now missing third storey. In all this Augustus, or at least his architect, was working overtly within the constraints of *decor*, either that provided by the precedent of established buildings or, with newly established building types, where the authority of the original builder had established the rightfulness of the new form. Even the choice of the Greek Doric in place of the Roman Tuscan order for the façade was entirely appropriate for a theatre which served predominantly for the games dedicated to the Greek god Apollo. Augustus left it to his great lieutenants, his infantry commander Statilius Taurus and his admiral and son-in-law Agrippa, to introduce two novel but specifically Roman forms of public building which had no precedent at Rome: the permanent amphitheatre and the luxury baths, the *thermae*.

Creating the Imperial City

These three categories of buildings—fora, venues for spectacles, and luxury baths—remained, with temples, the main focus of architectural benefaction by emperors in the city for the next three centuries.

The architectural model established by the fora of Caesar and Augustus was taken up by later emperors [93]. Domitian carved an elongated space out of the busy Argiletum, forming a monumental forecourt to the Temple of Peace while retaining the old connection between the residential area of the Subura and the Forum Romanum [81]. The use of mock porticoes on the long sides, with the columns tied to the precinct walls by short sections of entablature (*ressauts*), in place of full colonnades, emphasizes the importance of the visual precedent of the earlier fora.

The Forum of Augustus was also the reference point for the last and by far the largest of the imperial fora: the Forum of Trajan [94], one of the wonders of Rome. This too was a victory monument, paid for out of the booty from Trajan's military campaigns against Dacia in 101–102 and 105–106, and for once we know the architect, Apollodorus of Damascus. Linked to the Forum of Augustus indirectly via a complex corridor and atrium structure at the south end, the paved forum square with its colossal equestrian statue of Trajan was flanked by single porticoes with semi-circular exedrae clearly imitating the Forum of Augustus, and even the architectural ornament was closer to the Augustan forms than to the more florid Flavian style which preceded it. In the porticoes, however, statues of captured Dacians replaced the caryatids, and portraits of Roman generals of the imperial period the heads of Jupiter Ammon in the *tondi*, serving as a permanent reminder of the power and almost superhuman achievements of the emperor who had taken the empire to its greatest extent.

Where the Forum of Trajan differs most from that of Augustus is in having the dominant Basilica Ulpia, the largest Roman basilica known to us, rather than the more usual temple at its head. This was indeed a covered forum, its footprint roughly equal to that of the open space of the Forum

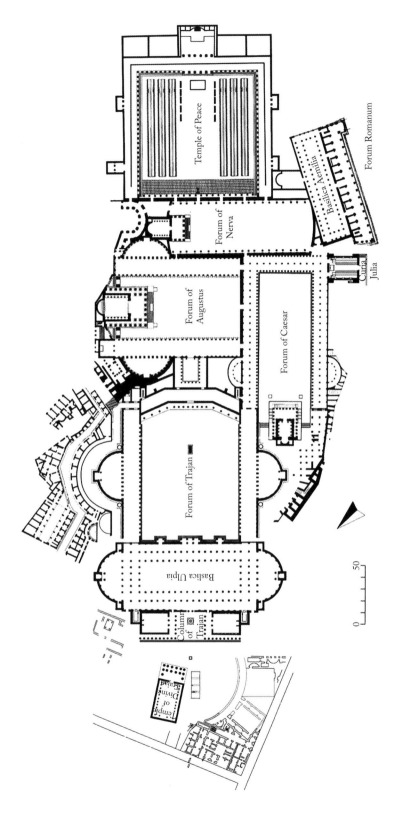

Fig. 93

Reconstructed plan of the imperial fora (Forum of Caesar, Forum of Augustus, Forum of Nerva, and Forum of Trajan), the Temple of Peace, the Markets of Trajan, the Temple of Divine Trajan, and the Augustan Basilica Aemilia on the Forum Romanum.

Temple of Peace

Basilica Aemilia

Forum Romanum

Forum of Nerva

Forum of Augustus

Curia Julia

Forum of Caesar

Forum of Trajan

Basilica Ulpia

Column of Trajan

Temple of Divine Trajan

50

0

Romanum, and about the combined space of the two great civic basilicas, the Aemilia and the Julia. This can hardly be coincidental, given the great efforts that had to be made in order to create a level space of this size, celebrated in the famous column erected by the Senate to mark the height of the spur cut away to make space for Trajan's Forum. The spur itself was buttressed by a vast complex of commercial and administrative spaces known as the Markets of Trajan [30], on five levels curled around one of the semicircular exedrae of the Forum and including a magnificent cross-vaulted hall, flanked by two storeys of *tabernae* like a modern shopping mall.[54] This separation of the utilitarian from the monumental prestige space of the Forum was defined by a solid ashlar wall, in keeping with a trend which goes back to the creation of the *macellum* in the mid-Republic and also used to great effect in the Forum of Augustus.

In Rome, the emperors also transformed buildings for spectacles and performances into permanent symbols of their power. Vespasian commissioned the largest amphitheatre in the Roman world [1, 4], estimated to have seated about 65,000 people, paid for with booty from the Jewish Wars. At the same time, the amphitheatre was raised to the status of the theatre by using the 'Theatre-motif' of hierarchically stacked half-columns in the Tuscan, Ionic, and Corinthian orders in its arcaded façade, with extra height gained from a tall attic with Corinthian pilasters. Like Augustus' theatre and perhaps Nero's temporary amphitheatre, this was a place where the Roman people were on show according to their place in society [95]; calculating the average number of spectators who could fit in the rows assigned to senators, knights, male citizens, and others makes it clear that, while most

Fig. 95

Projected distribution of
seats in the Flavian
Amphitheatre.

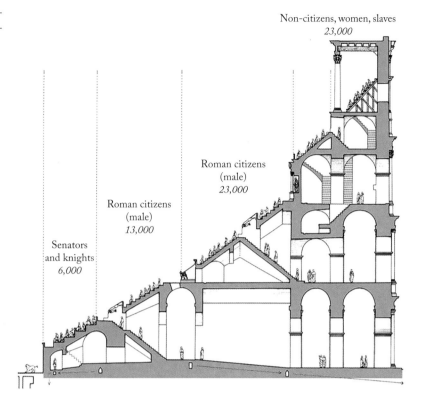

Non-citizens, women, slaves
23,000

Roman citizens
(male)
23,000

Roman citizens
(male)
13,000

Senators
and knights
6,000

of the first two groups, their families, and visiting dignitaries could fit in the Flavian Amphitheatre on any occasion, only a small proportion of the rest of the citizen body could do so. Competition for seats must have been great.[55]

For those lucky enough to attend, the amphitheatre was organized to enhance the experience of the spectators and the quality of the performances. The internal arrangement followed the established pattern of annular corridors and radial passages and stairs, so that from each of the eighty numbered entrances, spectators were led rapidly to a discrete section of the *cavea*, reinforcing the separation of the classes. The *cavea* was arguably the largest that could be built while still allowing those at the back to view the arena,[56] while the heavy cornice helped to support an awning (the *velarium*) which shaded spectators in the upper tiers from the weather. The complex array of structures below the arena floor included twenty platforms in the centre for scenery and human participants, including gladiators, and twenty-eight lifts around the perimeter for animals such as big cats and bears, needing over 200 men to raise them simultaneously. The splendour and excitement of a day at the amphitheatre when the emperor was putting on games is vividly captured in the written sources.[57]

Not to be outdone, Trajan showed his superiority to the discredited Flavian regime by rebuilding and enlarging the Circus Maximus, easily the largest building for spectacles in Rome or indeed anywhere in the Roman world. The impact of this rebuilding is clear from Pliny the Younger's fulsome account in his *Panegyric*, a speech to the emperor in thanks for attaining the consulship. He praises:

the vast façade of the circus [which] rivals the beauty of the temples, a fitting place for a nation which has conquered the world, a sight to be seen on its own account as well as for the spectacles there to be displayed, to be seen indeed for its beauty.[58]

The importance of these buildings in the self-presentation of the emperors can be seen in their appearance on major coin issues, starting with the Flavian Amphitheatre of Vespasian and including Trajan's rebuilding of the Circus Maximus [96]. Later restorations of the amphitheatre and circus under the Severans were marked by issues of almost identical coins, with only the emperor's portrait and name on the obverse changed.[59]

A different approach to providing venues for the benefit of the wider populace came with the construction of lavish public baths, the imperial *thermae*, one of the high points of Roman architecture.[60] Much larger and more luxurious than the public baths of the late Republic, the *thermae* of Agrippa were originally part of his suburban villa in the Campus Martius, left to the Roman people on his death. The *thermae* of Trajan marked a step-change by setting a symmetrical bathing block within a colonnaded precinct roughly 1,000 by 1,000 Roman feet square, the same size as the whole of Trajan's colony of Timgad [97]. The central bathing block alone covered an area more than twenty times larger than the late Republican Forum Baths at Pompeii, which would fit easily into the *natatio*. Small wonder that in the fourth century CE the imperial *thermae* were described as 'built like whole provinces', listed ahead of the Flavian Amphitheatre and Pantheon among the wonders of Rome.[61]

Fig. 96

Bronze coin (*sestertius*) of Trajan showing the Circus Maximus, from the imperial mint at Rome, 103 CE. The bird's-eye view is from the direction of the imperial palace on the Palatine Hill, and shows many of the distinctive elements of the circus: at the left-hand end the Arch of Titus, complete with four-horse chariot (*quadriga*); the central barrier (the *euripus*) with the obelisk erected by Augustus in the centre, the tall cones of the turning posts (*metae*), and a statue of the goddess Cybele with her lion; the Temple of the Sun in the seating on the opposite side; and the starting gates at the right-hand end.

Fig. 97

Plan of the Baths of Trajan,
Rome, c. 104–109 CE, laid
over the plan of the Trajanic
colony of Thamugadi (now
Timgad, Algeria) to the
same scale.

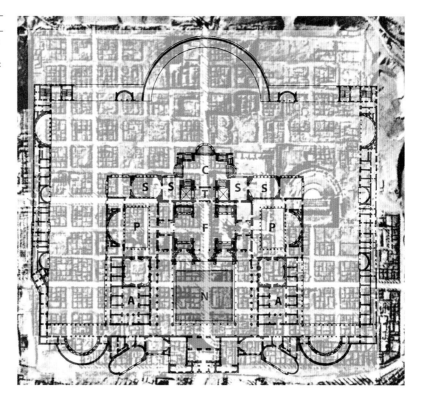

There is much that is city-like in these and the similarly sized *thermae* of
Caracalla [20] and Diocletian, and from the outside the enclosed precincts
must have looked like walled cities. They have also been seen as microcosms
of Rome itself, the precincts recreating the cultural milieu of the Campus
Martius with their libraries and displays of sculpture, and their areas of
tiered seating for the display of athletics. The central bathing block had at
its heart the *frigidarium*, occupying a privileged place at the intersection of
the design axes, recalling the placement of the fora in many Roman cities.
Like fora, they were also gathering places for large crowds, with almost 80
per cent of the total area of the bathing block given over to non-essential
bathing space compared to only 40 per cent in the Forum Baths at Pompeii.
At the same time, they were also palaces for the people, on the scale of the
imperial audience halls, the central vaults of the *frigidarium* soaring to around
130 Roman feet (c. 38.5 metres) [16]. The shining surfaces of marble and glass
mosaic reflected light from large glazed windows onto the many pools, while
the numerous columns of exotic marble and the often theatrical displays of
sculpture provided the urban populace with the illusion of being emperor for
a day, or with a taste of the life of *otium* enjoyed by the rich and powerful. And
not only the general populace; the *thermae* were places for the elite to be seen,
displaying their wealth through the number of their attendants and hangers-
on, and through the refinement of their accoutrements.[62]

The imperial *thermae* were the ultimate acts of euergetism, by far the
largest and most expensive of the public buildings donated by the emperors,

dwarfing the imperial fora and perhaps costing more than enough to pro-vide the corn dole for the city of Rome for nearly two years.[63] The import-ance attached to them by the emperors went beyond simply providing luxury spaces for the urban populace to get clean. The internal courts of the *thermae* of Caracalla were decorated with reliefs representing military cam-paigns, in the manner of the Forum of Trajan, while copies of some official imperial responses to petitions from the provinces were posted in the *thermae* of Trajan, rather than in any of the traditional public places. These were the new urban foci to rival, if not outstrip, the imperial fora.

Rome in the Provinces

By the end of the reign of Augustus, all of the definitively Roman major public building types supplying the major political and social needs of the people could be found in the city of Rome: the forum as a coherent unit and its adjunct, the basilica; the buildings for spectacles; and the baths. Since the activities associated with these buildings were all integral to urban Roman culture and lifestyle, the buildings designed to house them became the hall-marks of Roman civilization and the source of much inter-city rivalry, as well as competition between members of the elites of individual communi-ties.[64] Their importance in defining the Roman way of life can be seen in the extraordinary urban building boom across the length and breadth of the empire which came with the Augustan peace and continued throughout the next two centuries.

None of this was instantaneous nor uniform across the empire. The vet-eran colony of Augusta Emerita in Spain is instructive. Founded by Augustus in 25 BCE, and intended from the start as the capital of the new province of Lusitania, it has long been seen as a typical Augustan city, with a theatre, funded by Augustus' right-hand man Agrippa in 16 BCE, and an adjoining amphitheatre dedicated to Augustus in 8 BCE [98], a forum and '*forum adiectum*' (added forum) with some of its decorative detail copied

Fig. 98

Theatre and amphitheatre at Augusta Emerita (modern Mérida, Spain), end first century BCE for the theatre, and first century CE for the amphitheatre. The theatre was the gift of Agrippa, Augustus' right-hand man and son-in-law.

closely from the Forum of Augustus in Rome [99], and, at the end of the Augustan period, even a circus, built outside the walls.[65] Augusta Emerita was a completely new foundation in an area with a relatively limited pre-existing tradition of urbanism on the Mediterranean model, so that imported versions of Roman building forms were thought to be expected, while the use of the intractable local granite for the theatre and amphitheatre was argued to be representative of this early phase. Here we seem to have a clear case of the kind of top-down Roman influence in architecture, a pattern assumed to be a norm of Roman cultural imperialism, with only the local building materials imposing a degree of adaptation.

Fig. 99

Forum complex at Augusta Emerita (modern Mérida, Spain), Flavian phase. Reconstructed portico of the '*forum adiectum*'. The 'caryatids' derive from the Forum of Augustus (cf. 13) but are carved in relief (a cheaper option which may also have had structural advantages), rather than being free-standing.

Recent investigations have, however, pieced together a rather different story.[66] The marble *scaenae frons* of the theatre is a later replacement, while the amphitheatre is a complete rebuilding of what was probably an original in earth and timber construction, a type more often associated with military camps, while the circus dates to the reign of Tiberius.[67] Likewise, although provision was made for a large forum in the initial phase of the colony, the arrangement as we have it dates only to the Flavian period **[100]**, as does adjacent sanctuary with its fine marble decoration.[68] Augusta Emerita is in fact a typical example, not of some supposed common Augustan urban model, but of the piecemeal development reflecting local conditions and circumstances which was the norm. Architectural forms in the provinces were not always direct imitations of the grand buildings of the capital, or even always close adaptations.[69] Distinctive regional types with different origins existed, but variations can be found even between nearby cities because of their diverse histories, status, wealth, and patronage, and in relation to the type of building concerned. Different architectural solutions to Roman and local public needs were invented, and the direct linear development from Rome to the provinces that is sometimes assumed is very much an over-simplification.[70]

Fora

While the fora in some cities of the empire, like that at Lepcis Magna, continued to be loosely structured spaces flanked by independent structures added over time, renovations and additions often reflected trends at Rome. In the Augustan and early Julio-Claudian periods paving the forum was a popular benefaction both in Italy and elsewhere, the name of the donor advertised in large bronze letters set into the paving itself. Basilicas were another feature, with three added to the *agora* of the colony of Corinth in this period using two different layouts, while Lepcis had to wait until the Flavian period before it acquired its basilica, set alongside, but not opening onto, the old forum. As in Rome, in many cities throughout the empire the monumentalization of the *forum* was helped by the building of separate market buildings (*macella*), the earliest of which is that at Lepcis Magna, part of the city's building boom in the Augustan period. Its peristyle court and colonnaded central pavilions made of the *macellum* a temple of commerce.

Two distinctive developments in the architecture of fora appeared in the northwestern provinces and in the wealthy cities of Asia Minor, reflecting two very different sets of political and social circumstances. The Hellenistic East already had an architectural model for its main civic space, the *agora*.[71] As Vitruvius notes, these tended to be more square than rectangular, with double colonnades and close-set columns facing the open spaces—in other words, lined with stoas.[72] From the early Augustan period onwards, however, a new type of building, somewhat wider than a stoa and with its length divided into a central nave and two aisles, began to be incorporated into some of them. The first known building of its type is in the so-called 'civic' or 'upper' *agora* at Ephesus **[101, 148]**.[73] For once we have a dedicatory inscription which gives the date—II CE—and also identifies this as a '*stoa*' in Greek, but as a '*stoa basilica*' ('royal stoa') in Latin. Ephesus had had mixed

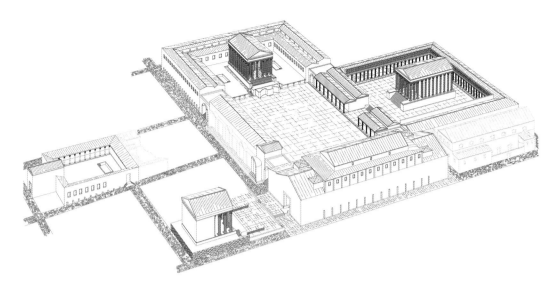

Fig. 100

Forum complex at Augusta
Emerita (modern Mérida,
Spain), Flavian phase. The
main temple is raised above
the open space of the
forum, and faces the forum
basilica across it. To the
right is the additional
sanctuary (the '*forum
adiectum*'), also on a higher
level.

relations with Rome over the first century BCE, but Augustus made it the
provincial capital of Asia Minor, and the *stoa basilica* was financed by
Sextilius Pollio, a wealthy Italian resident and businessman who was
Ephesus' major benefactor at the time. The building raises many questions.
What were the models for this hybrid form, and what was its function? The
conjunction of a long basilical building open to a quadriporticus with a
central temple is known albeit probably from a somewhat later date at
Cyrene, a Greek city in North Africa; there it was added to a complex dedicated to the cult of Julius Caesar (the Caesareum), an idea which had its
origins in Alexandria.[74] The influences on its design might therefore be not
only Greek and Roman but also Hellenized Egyptian—an intriguing
example of architectural synthesis which is typical of this fervid period
of innovation in Roman architecture, when new functions required new
solutions.

This possibility brings into question the identification of the complex at
Ephesus as a forum at all, despite the fact that a series of Greek-style
municipal buildings (*prytaneion* and *bouleuterion*) can be reached through
doors in the rear long wall of the *stoa basilica*. As with the Caesareum at
Cyrene, here too there was a Roman-style temple in the centre of the porticoed space, probably that to Deified Julius Caesar and the Goddess Roma
sponsored by Augustus in 29 BCE for the Roman community, and there were
no *tabernae* within the complex to suggest a commercial function. Later
examples suggest that, like the Roman basilica, the *stoa basilica* was a multi-
purpose hall which functioned differently in different situations, but always set
in the most prestigious positions.[75] The Hadrianic example at Hierapolis in
Phrygia certainly seems to have functioned more like a traditional Roman
basilica, in that it was the place for paying tribute and other economic transactions; in another—by then anachronistic—echo of the function of the old
basilicas in the Roman Forum; however, the entrance steps may have been
used as a seating area to watch games in the *agora* below, which had a beaten
earth floor suited to such activities rather than the formal paving generally
to be found in fora. In contrast, that at nearby Aphrodisias was set

Fig. 101

Reconstruction drawing of
the stoa basilica at
Ephesus, dedicated 11 CE to
Artemis (Diana) of the
Ephesians, Augustus,
Tiberius, and the city of
Ephesus, by C. Sextilius
Pollio.

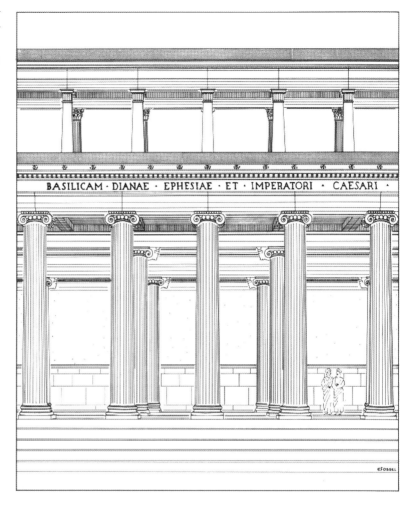

BASILICAM · DIANAE · EPHESIAE · ET · IMPERATORI · CAESARI ·

perpendicular to a ceremonial palm court centred on a monumental pool,
and not connected to its *agora* at all.[76]

A more specifically Roman set of variations can be found in the western
provinces.[77] While many pre-existing fora developed piecemeal with the
addition of porticoes, stone paving, and individual buildings like basilicas,
new fora with dominant temples were frequently built as integrated complexes, but rarely directly on the model of the fora of Caesar or Augustus.
Rather, in terms of layout, the temples were set within a U-shaped portico,
often raised on a vaulted substructure (*cryptoporticus*), elements which go
back to the sanctuaries of late Republican Latium, for example at Gabii and
Tivoli. The earliest, in the Roman settlement of Ampurias in northeastern
Spain, in fact pre-dates the Augustan boom, dating to the start of the first
century BCE, and so is contemporary with the sanctuary at Tivoli. The other
development has the basilica as an integral part of a colonnaded forum, usually on axis across one short side. This too is a layout which already existed
by the early Augustan period, developed probably in northern Italy and
rapidly disseminated through the recently conquered area of Cisalpine Gaul

into Provence. It became an established western form, from Baelo Claudia in southern Spain to London, and may have influenced the arrangement in Trajan's Forum; even the pair of apses at the short ends of the Trajanic Basilica Ulpia can be found in the Flavian phase of the forum at Silchester in Britain [102].[78] While there are arguments for this layout having its origins in the headquarters building (*principia*) of military camps, the reverse is just as likely. In a few places, the temple-forum replaced a more multi-functional arrangement with basilica and *tabernae*. This happened at Conimbriga (Portugal) towards the end of the first century CE, the new complex being given a monumental entrance.[79] It is likely that this rebuilding was a response to the elevation of the status of the town to a *municipium* under the Flavians, and that the temple is to their imperial cult. Here, the monumental has replaced the utilitarian, and prestige has won out over practicality.

In some cities both versions appear together, in what has often been called the 'tripartite forum' model, with a basilica across one short end and an axial temple at the other. While in some of the examples the forum-basilica and temple sections are contemporary, it is by no means always certain that the space enclosed by porticoes and basilica, and the space around the temple, were intended to form a unified whole as a forum. Often the two architectural spaces were treated differently and separated either by a change in level, as at Augusta Emerita [100], or by a road, as at Augusta Raurica (Augst). In Lugdunum Convenarum (Saint-Bertrand-de-Comminges, France), the temple even faces away from, and not towards, the basilica, a solid wall and a difference in level emphasizing that these are two distinct spaces. One aspect which unites these different developments is the

Fig. 102

Artist's impression of the Forum Basilica at Silchester (England), fourth-century CE phase.

notable ambiguity of some of the spaces. In many cases, without any inscriptional evidence it is impossible to tell from the remains whether a complex is to be understood as a civil forum or a religious sanctuary. This ambiguity should not be surprising as it existed already in the Forum Romanum from an early date; for us it becomes an issue only when we try to define architectural forms and assign fixed labels. Many of the examples of this combination in Gaul come from secondary sites, especially thermal spas and sanctuaries, which would not have had fora, as these belong to Roman cities with specific civic and administrative functions. As so often under the empire, urban architectural forms, in their regional guises, were adopted for prestige value by local benefactors and did not necessarily relate to their original functions.

A rare case where at least some direct influence from Rome is clear is the temple-forum-basilica complex of Lepcis Magna, built by the first North African emperor Septimius Severus for his hometown [103].[80] It combined

Fig. 103

Severan Forum at Lepcis Magna (Libya), early third century CE: (a) plan; (b) capitals and arched entablatures of the forum portico.

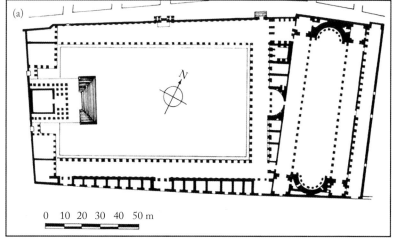

the temple-dominated porticoed space of the Forum of Augustus with flanking rooms in the manner of the Temple of Peace and the transverse twin-apsed basilica of the Forum of Trajan [93], to create a unique complex, the equivalent of an imperial forum in a provincial setting. Although the basilica only had single aisles, the columns were of granite and the apsidal ends were treated almost like part of a *scaenae frons*, with a central giant order rising through two storeys of niches and smaller columns. Even the way that the basilica was reached from the forum through just three doors set within a series of rooms open to the piazza reflects an arrangement which goes back to the Basilica Aemilia in the Forum Romanum [83, 85].

At the same time, many of the details were strongly influenced by the architecture of the eastern empire together with local traditions, starting with the use of Attic and Proconnesian marbles from Greece and Asia Minor together with local limestone, while the columns shafts were predominantly in red Aswan granite from Egypt, a very long-standing trading partner of Lepcis. The portico colonnades had Asiatic lotus and acanthus capitals rather than the conventional Corinthian, a design in use at Lepcis since the Augustan period, but here in Attic marble with Greek masons' marks, identifying the origins of the workmen. These capitals supported arcuated rather than traditional lintels, with heads of Medusa in the spandrels [103b], a motif in use in Asia Minor at least from the Hadrianic period, where they are found on the façade of the *stoa basilica* of Hierapolis. The complex was astonishingly lavish, a real show-piece of imperial power. The octastyle temple, probably dedicated to the emperors, had solid marble walls, with red granite columns on tall decorated plinths which again have parallels in Asia Minor, supported by a massive podium reached by an unusual wedge-shaped staircase which owes more rather to the Levant. Overall, like many imperial-sponsored buildings, this is a unique design which introduces novelties in plan and ornament while working within a recognizable imperial template.

Housing Spectacles

In the relative peace and prosperity of the Roman empire, occasions for community celebrations multiplied. Festivals and games in honour of the emperors, living or deified, and of their families abounded, and were added to those for the traditional gods or related to political office; in Asia Minor the games (*agones*) were widely publicized and bountifully commemorated through coins and inscriptions. These did not necessarily require a permanent monumental structure; in the suburbs of Pollentia in northern Italy, an unknown benefactor founded yearly games to celebrate the dedication of a statue of the emperor Antoninus Pius, which were held in a temporary wooden structure.[81] Where permanent structures were built, their size could make them a drain on resources. In his letters to the emperor Trajan, Pliny the Younger, acting as governor of the rich eastern province of Bithynia, relates the problem of the theatre being built for the city of Nicaea, which, only half-finished, had already cost more than ten times the minimum property requirement for a senator, but was already showing huge cracks and was in danger of collapse.[82]

The pattern of erecting monumental buildings for spectacles therefore varied with time and place, and not all types are found across the whole empire. Only very large or important cities, such as the provincial capitals of Carthage and Augusta Emerita, could afford the complete set of theatre, amphitheatre, and circus. Monumental circuses in particular are only found at the largest and most important sites, mostly in Roman Spain and North Africa which provided many of the horses for the races.[83] Generally dated to the second century CE or later, they are nearly all styled on the rebuilt Circus Maximus at Rome. This is the case even in the eastern provinces, despite the existence of the famous Greek hippodrome at Olympia which might otherwise have seemed the obvious model. The frequency in which chariot races in the Circus Maximus, identifiable by the monuments on the central *spina* [96], appear all over the Roman world in a wide variety of decorative media, from glass cups to mosaics, speaks volumes about the significance of this specific monument as representative of the city of Rome.

Imperial constructions in Rome had a direct impact on the provinces in other ways as well. More Roman-type theatres were built in the western provinces under Augustus than at any other time, reflecting the role of the theatre in Augustus' programme of social renewal.[84] Most Greek and Hellenistic cities in the eastern empire already had theatres, but even there this period saw new Greek-style theatres being built, notably at Ephesus presumably in response to the city being made the provincial capital, and at Hierapolis as late as the end of the first century CE. In the Levant, in contrast, where theatres were previously almost unknown, Roman-style theatres were the norm. The distinctions extend to the design of the *scaenae frons*. In Roman-style theatres these elaborate columnar facades were articulated with projecting and receding rectangular and apsidal recesses to emphasize the three rear doors onto the stage which derive from earlier Roman practice; in the Greek-style theatres, although no less elaborate, they tended to be linear with five entrances, reflecting a continuous tradition of classical Greek performances.

Over time, the reconstruction of the *scaenae frons* of a theatre in the new fashion became a focus of benefactors' attention when a new-build theatre was not needed or not feasible. The most extravagant were extremely expensive; that at Lepcis Magna, added to the existing theatre in 146–147 CE [10], cost half the minimum property qualification for a senator at Rome, and a third as much again as the whole of the small theatre at Madauros (Tunisia), yet was paid for by two local benefactors.[85] A detailed study of the best-preserved stage backdrops of the second century establishes the columns as the most expensive element of these designs, and the easiest to identify; counting columns, therefore, gives a possible way of establishing relative costs of stage backdrops and thus of evaluating the economic choices being made by benefactors. Compared to other examples which are sufficiently well preserved to be reconstructable at least on paper, Lepcis turns out to have had one of the highest number of columns in its *scaenae frons*, using the greatest volume of marble, and taking the most labour to produce, even though neither the theatre nor the stage backdrop are by any means the largest known. We can use the same strategy to compare the very different examples of similar date from two small theatres in two minor cities.[86] That at Teanum Sidicinum [104] in central Italy has an only marginally larger *scaenae frons* than that of Nysa in Asia Minor [105] while using the same number of columns, but the columns have three and a half times the volume and needed nearly three times the amount of labour to produce, as well as being of a variety of imported marbles and granites rather than in the relatively local marble. Although we have no direct evidence, we can assume that the *scaenae frons* at Teanum Sidicinum would have cost at least three or four times as much as that at Nysa, and possibly far more. Given the materials used, it also seems likely that its benefactor came from the imperial circle, as was the case at nearby Suessa Aurunca.

If theatres were expensive, monumental amphitheatres required an even larger investment. Their widespread construction in Italy and the western European provinces also began in the Augustan period, but was given a particular boost by the Flavian Amphitheatre, which by introducing the hierarchy of orders [1] elevated the amphitheatre to the cultural equivalent of the Greek-inspired theatre.[87] Exceptionally, a few cities such as Puteoli on the Bay of Naples had a second amphitheatre, built on imperial lines with the full panoply of seating, *velarium*, and subterranean structures for enhancing spectacles, alongside a surviving earlier one. The last known monumental amphitheatre to be built, in Thysdrus (modern El Djem) in Tunisia [106], was also an addition, arguably under the patronage of the early third-century emperor Gordian III. While its derivation from the Flavian Amphitheatre is readily apparent (it is sometimes called the African Colosseum), it is an altogether heavier-looking structure, with the supporting piers wider than the arched openings, reflecting perhaps a concern about the stability of the structure in the absence of the strong mortars of Rome.[88] Nevertheless, even a rich city like Lepcis Magna did not build a free-standing amphitheatre but installed it in what appears to be a former quarry, entered through a tunnel in the hillside.

Fig. 104

Computer reconstruction of the *scaenae frons* of the theatre of Teanum Sidicinum (modern Teano, Italy), Severan. The *cavea* is 85 metres in diameter, while the *scaenae frons* has an area of 978 metres² using thirty-six columns. The column shafts required 64 metres³ of marble and granite, and would have taken over 10,000 days of labour to produce. The materials of the column shafts include red Aswan granite and purple porphyry from Egypt, purple-veined Phrygian marble from Turkey, and yellow Numidian marble from Tunisia.

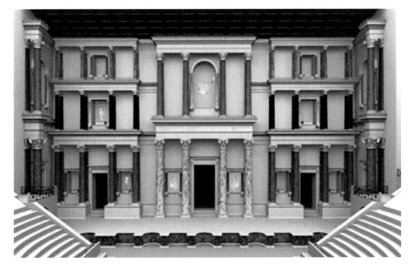

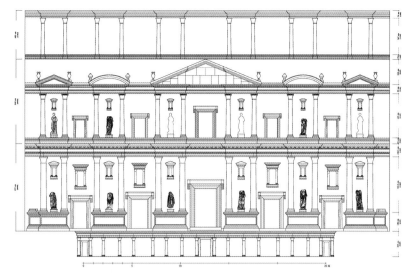

Fig. 105

Reconstruction drawing of the *scaenae frons* of the theatre of Nysa, Asia Minor (modern Sultanhisar, Turkey), Severan. The *cavea* is 115 metres in diameter, while the *scaenae frons* has an area of 831 metres^2 using thirty-six columns. The column shafts required 18 metres^3 of marble, and would have taken over 3,500 days of labour to produce.

Overall, building amphitheatres was very much a western phenomenon. In the Greek East, they are only found in Roman colonies, provincial capitals, or Greek cities with very strong ties to Rome, and few of them were of the free-standing type established in the west. That at Corinth, possibly the earliest of all eastern amphitheatres, was rock cut and described by a Greek orator of the late first century CE as a 'squalid ravine'.[89] Gladiatorial games, however, were not unknown in the Greek east even under the Republic, the earliest reputedly put on by the Hellenistic monarch Antiochus IV of Syria in 166 BCE, initially to the bewilderment of his Greek audience;[90] otherwise, they were put on through the initiative of Roman communities and individuals. This changed very much with the widespread introduction of festivals in honour of the imperial family which were celebrated with the most Roman forms of spectacle, gladiatorial games. Rather than build amphitheatres, however, many Greek cities either used their *stadia* or converted their existing theatres by introducing a parapet wall at the edge of the orchestra in order to protect the spectators from the activity.[91] The earliest known example is in the venerable Theatre of Dionysos in Athens, carried out at the instigation of Tiberius Claudius Novius, a Roman citizen possibly of Italian origin and important in the imperial cult at Athens. Although there are many indications in the ancient sources that this particular usage was met with dismay by the conservative Greek elite—one complained about the front seats being spattered with blood[92]—by the mid-second century such conversions were common, and, as with the circus, gladiators appear so widely in decorative media in the east to suggest that the practice had become thoroughly embedded at least among the lower levels of Greek society.

Other regions had their own responses to providing venues for the spectacles that were an essential part of Roman culture. In the northwestern

Fig. 106

Thysdrus (modern El Djem, Tunisia), large amphitheatre, early third century CE. Possibly built for the emperor Gordian III, this is the second largest known Roman amphitheatre after the Flavian Amphitheatre in Rome.

provinces from the mid-first to the end of the second centuries CE, particularly in northern Gaul, striking new forms developed which were neither quite theatres nor quite amphitheatres but could have housed both theatrical performances and gladiatorial games.[93] The key feature was a *cavea* which was usually larger than that of a theatre but less than that of an amphitheatre [107]. If there was a stage building at all, it had no permanent *scaenae frons* and was small compared to that of the Roman theatre. Unlike the Greek theatres adapted for gladiatorial games, these were a new invention in an area which did not have the Mediterranean familiarity with standard Greek or Roman theatres. Like some of the western fora types,

Fig. 107

Theatre-amphitheatre, Verulamium (modern St Albans, UK), mid-second century CE.

many are found at monumental sanctuaries and thermal spas as well as in cities, some co-existing with traditional theatres and amphitheatres. Unlike in the Greek east, we have very little in the way of inscriptions which might help us understand the context in which these forms were developed and used. Their association with sanctuaries is reminiscent of the situation with the so-called 'theatre-temples' of central Italy in the late Republic, where the marked differences between arrangements suggested rather different cultic usages; the same might also lie behind this particular development.

None of these monumental structures for spectacles of any kind were, however, in any sense necessary for the putting on of games. Simple, often temporary, structures of timber and earth construction continued to be built for chariot racing, wild beast hunts, and gladiatorial games throughout the empire. The erection of imperial-style masonry structures was above all an issue of civic competition and conspicuous benefaction, encouraged by the attention paid to these structures by the emperors in Rome.

Baths

As we have seen with other building types, the impact of the prestige values of Augustan Rome can be seen in the wave of new bath buildings which rapidly sprung up in Italy and the provinces, no longer simply a necessary amenity but increasingly the focus of major benefaction. As early as the mid-Augustan period, the important city of Aquinum, along the Via Latina between Rome and Capua, acquired a new set of baths.[94] In an impressive mosaic inscription from the *frigidarium*, nearly 10 metres long, a local magistrate announces that they were built at his own expense, and proudly enumerates the highlights, including the decoration. Baths clearly had become much more important as objects of individual benefaction than they were in the Republic, and from this time on they take their place with other major public buildings as monuments of conspicuous display. Several inscriptions from Italy explicitly mention baths being rebuilt on a larger scale, in one case together with a change of name from *balnea* to *thermae*, after the imperial *thermae* of Rome;[95] it is quite in keeping that the baths at Aquinum are roughly three and a half times the size of the Forum Baths at Pompeii, built some 80 years' earlier.

Unlike fora or buildings for spectacles, cities of any size all over the empire generally had several sets of public baths, ranging from large and lavish show-piece establishments to small and simple neighbourhood baths serving everyday needs. Free from the moral imperatives which constrained the design of temples and the close relation between form and function that conditioned the layout of buildings for spectacles, baths could be highly original and innovative buildings, employing sophisticated interlocking plans with varied rooms shapes including curvilinear elements [24], and inventive solutions to complex vaulting problems [47], often in the absence of the pozzolanic mortar which allowed the soaring vaults of the imperial *thermae*. The majority, however, followed the typical late Republican pattern, comprising a single row of increasingly heated rooms, culminating in the *caldarium* [89, 108], which required the bather to return by the same route. The simplicity of the design, and its essentially practical nature, meant that it could be scaled up or down depending on circumstances, and, except perhaps for the largest examples, it would be fairly easy to construct

Fig. 108

Caldarium of the Forum Baths, Pompeii. The apse with its marble *labrum* (cold water basin) was added in the early first century CE. According to the inscription made in bronze letters set into its brim, the basin cost 5,250 *sesterces*.

irrespective of the restrictions imposed by local materials and techniques. The only real change came about in the first half of the first century CE with the introduction of window glass, including glass skylights and double glazing, which resolved many lighting problems and enhanced the heating capabilities by capturing solar radiation.[96] Not surprisingly, this simple type of baths is found throughout the empire, including in permanent military camps.

At the opposite end of the scale were those with a symmetrical plan strongly influenced by the imperial *thermae*, with a central *frigidarium* and sweating rooms flanking a projecting *caldarium* with multiple hot pools along the southern façade; all are large in size and lavish in decoration, although only the Antonine Baths in Carthage approach anywhere near the scale and complexity of the *thermae* of Rome. In this type the layout created a circular route for bathers, which, with the symmetrical design, allowed for both a more efficient throughput and a more varied experience for the bather, with ample ancillary space for activities beyond the strict require-ments of getting clean. These were big civic showpieces, found only in the largest and wealthiest of cities like Lepcis Magna and Trier **[9]**, but with considerable variety between the individual examples. In between was an ingenious combination of a symmetrical cold sector with central *frigidar-ium* and a single row of connected hot rooms, allowing a circular route with alternative paths for the bather, with examples from cities as diverse as Rome's port city of Ostia, Bulla Regia in Tunisia, and Paris **[109]**, all of similar size and with similarly proportionate distribution of spaces, suggest-ing a common approach to their design.

Provincial bath buildings on the whole show less inter-regional variation than variation within regions, and often within individual towns, depending on the patronage and specific function. There are, however, some general preferences for one type or another, for example for the simple linear type in Spain and small versions of the symmetrical type in North Africa, which seem to relate in part to the date of introduction of Roman baths into the area, or to the main period of urban expansion, or to the general wealth of the communities. There are also regional preferences for particular features, often within baths of different basic types, for example covered basilical halls for exercise in the northwestern provinces and in North Africa, both arguably responding to different extremes of climate. The only really notable regional variant, typified by the Baths of Vedius at Ephesus **[110]**, belongs to the Greek cities of Asia Minor, where the large colonnaded court of the Hellenistic gymnasium was juxtaposed to a bathing block notable for its rectilinear and symmetrical composition, conditioned at least in part by the continued used of ashlar construction which was less suited to curves than mortared rubble. While the influence of the imperial *thermae* can still be seen, not least in the scale and richness of the buildings, some baths incorp-orated basilical halls similar to those found in North African baths or wrapped around three sides of the cold sector, and some a rectangular hall open to the gymnasium (now often called a 'Marmorsaal') with walls elab-orated like a *scaenae frons* with tiers of marble columns framing statue niches.[97] These were clearly prestige buildings which occupied significant positions in the urban layout.

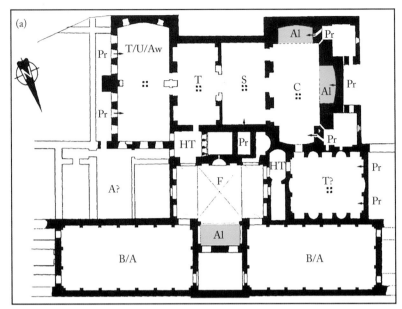

Increased size and splendour meant increased expense. It has been suggested that in North Africa, where the evidence is strongest, it might have taken an ordinary town council thirty years to pay for a reasonably elaborate set of baths out of its disposable income, so financial problems might be expected.[98] Pliny the Younger complained to Trajan about the suspected waste of public funds in the building of baths at Nicaea,[99] while a thirty-year gap between the laying of the foundations and the completion of the superstructure at the bath complex at Wroxeter has been attributed to the local town council running out of money and having to wait until further funds accumulated before continuing.[100] This must have been a relatively common problem, especially away from the main centres of the empire, as must have been that of rebuilding, a particular concern for bath buildings

Fig. 110

Model of the Baths of
Vedius, Ephesus (Turkey),
mid-second century CE.

which were subject to the damaging effects of fire and water. An inscription
from Fano in northeastern Italy tells a tale of woe: the town had rebuilt a set
of baths at public expense, only to have them burn down (presumably
shortly afterwards), leaving the town council without the funds to start
again; a local benefactor, a Roman knight and former chief magistrate of the
town, stepped into the breach and paid for the rebuilding of a larger complex.[101] Communities were therefore extremely grateful when individual
benefactors, who could be wealthy members of purely local elites or have
influence and standing on a wider provincial level or even at Rome, were
willing to endow or even just adorn grand civic baths, as Pliny the Younger
did at his ancestral town of Como.[102] That we know so much about the
life stories of many of these buildings is largely due to the dedicatory
inscriptions of the honorific statues set up by such town councils to their
benefactors.

Housing the Individual

6

> What is more sacred, what more protected by every religious scruple, than the house of every single citizen?
>
> Cicero, *de domo sua*, 41.109

Among the portents of disaster recorded at the death of Agrippa, Augustus' trusted second-in-command and son-in-law, one of the two huts associated with Rome's legendary founder Romulus—either that on the Palatine or that on the Capitoline—burnt down.[1] The maintenance of the huts, thatched with straw and with walls of wattle and daub, was a sacred trust of the chief priests (*pontifices*) who renewed it in the original form and materials only when necessary [26]. Their perpetuation was intimately connected with the survival of the city, invoked when the threat of moving the physical location of Rome was strongest, in the wake of the fourth-century BCE Gallic sack and when Mark Antony and Cleopatra mooted Egypt as the capital of empire. Preserved at least into the fourth century CE, the huts of Romulus were a potent symbol, connecting Rome with its primitive and humble beginnings and with its ancient virtues, but also a tangible affirmation of the city's pre-eminence in an increasingly far-flung empire.

Housing the Republican Elite

This powerful sense of place, of residence as authentication and assurance of continuity and of religious sanctity, resided also in the ancestral homes of the Republican elite. The house (*domus*) lay at the core of Republican society, the focus of individual citizens' connection to the sacred soil of their native land and symbol of their right to belong there. The *lares* and *penates*, household gods of the thresholds and store-rooms, were embedded in the physical structure of the house, overseeing all family rituals from birth to death and linking the living head of the household, the *paterfamilias*, to the spirits of his ancestors. According to the later written tradition, as many as three generations lived under the same roof their ancestors had built, thus providing their clearest possible claim to patrician status, the original aristocracy of the new Republic.[2] Not surprisingly, the earliest identifiable aristocratic houses of the Republic on the lower slopes of the Palatine near the Roman Forum appear to have remained virtually unchanged for several centuries following their establishment in the fifth century.[3]

By the second century BCE, proofs of political success and continuity—sometimes involving more than a little creative invention—were on public display in the *domus*. Records of the achievements of distinguished family members were kept alongside their portrait masks (*imagines*), while the family tree adorned the walls.[4] These were not merely for the gratification

Fig. 111

Tuscan *atrium* of the Samnite House, Herculaneum, second century BCE, showing the roof structure forming the open *compluvium*, and the basin of the *impluvium* in the floor beneath.

of the household, but were designed to impress a far wider audience. Election to public office and continued success in public life at Rome during the Republic depended on the number and quality of personal contacts, ranging from the lowly freed slaves and other dependents (*clientes*) bound by law or debts of gratitude, to social equals of similar or greater standing with whom favours could be exchanged. The *domus* was the focus of these transactions, through which the social and political status of the patron was sustained and enhanced. So important did the house become that crimes against the state could be manifested in the physical destruction of a man's house, as happened to Cicero after his banishment. In a speech just after his return, he conjured up a vivid picture of the war of hatred waged against the physical structure of his house, ending with an impassioned plea for its physical restoration:

My house stands in full view of nearly the whole city; if it remains there not as a monument but as a tomb for the city, inscribed with the name of an enemy, then I must migrate elsewhere.[5]

Such destruction was more than just a symbolic gesture. The full restoration of Cicero's political position, of his standing in the community, and of his very existence as a Roman citizen—that is, of his identity in the fullest sense—depended on the full restoration of his house.[6]

   The old families had extensive networks of dependents and allies, but the changing political structure of the later Republic saw the rise to power of new families, often, like that of Cicero himself, from provincial towns in Italy whose ancestral property was not in Rome. The *domus* then became associated more with the individual and his achievements rather than the family; Cicero relates how Gnaeus Octavius, a newcomer to Roman politics, built a fine house on the Palatine which was thought to have gained him the consulship in 165 BCE.[7] Houses took and kept the names of their builders or of their most illustrious owners in the way that temples or other public buildings were named after their founders. Likewise, they could be adorned with tokens of individual success, such as the prows of captured ships (*rostra*) hung as triumphal spoils in the house of Pompey the Great,[8] insistently recalling the prows that decorated the speaker's platform in the Roman Forum. Urban property in the late Republic changed hands frequently among members of the elite, often for exorbitant sums, and many of the political alliances and rivalries of the time were made visible to all through these transactions. The name and the symbols of greatness remained, however, even when the *domus* passed to others, a reproach to the new owner if he failed to live up to its history, like Mark Antony in the house of Pompey. It says much of the outstanding pre-eminence of Augustus that the name of the house he initially chose to live in on the Palatine, which may once have belonged to the great Republican orator, lawyer, politician, historian, and *bon viveur* Q. Hortensius Hortalus or to a member of his family, passed from being the House of Hortensius to the House of Augustus.

The Shape of the Republican *Domus*

While the *domus* was clearly an integral part of the public identity of the power-brokers in Roman Republican society, its form is less easy to pin

Fig. 112

Plan of the House of Pansa, Pompeii, second century BCE to first century CE. In the nineteenth century scholars produced plans of the 'ideal' atrium house, based on Pompeian examples thought to be early in date. The rooms were given labels taken largely from ancient sources including Vitruvius and, as here, these are still commonly applied to excavated examples of Roman houses, sometimes with little justification. The plan is notable for its bilateral symmetry about the longitudinal axis of the *fauces*/*atrium*/*tablinum*, and for the sideways extensions at the far end of the atrium, the *alae*. The grey-shaded areas are independent residential units.

(1), vestibulum (vestibule);
(2), *fauces* (entrance passage); (3), *taberna* (shop); (4), Tuscan *atrium*;
(5), *impluvium*;
(6), *cubiculum* ('bedroom');
(7), *ala* (literally, 'wing');
(8), *tablinum*;
(9), *triclinium*;
(10), peristyle; (11), *exedra* or *oecus* (reception room);
(12), *coenatio* (dining/ reception room);
(13), *porticus* (portico);
(14), *hortus* (garden).

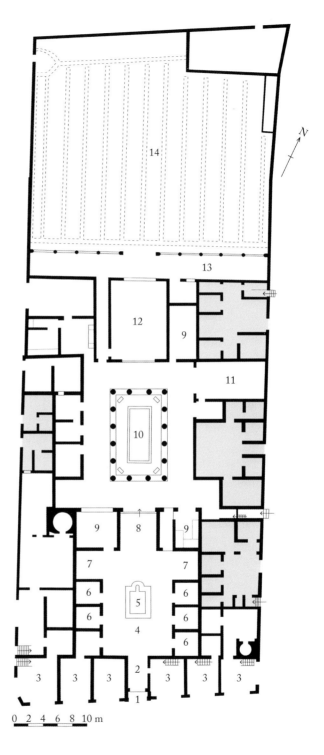

down [112].[9] Literary sources agree that there was a central space, the *atrium*, where the busts of ancestors and triumphal spoils were located, which was common to all members of the household and around which all the other rooms of the house were arranged, but only Vitruvius provides anything like an architectural description,[10] and he speaks not of an '*atrium*' but of a '*cavum aedium*' (the 'hollow of the house') as the central space. Vitruvius seems here to be deliberately archaizing, but the term does suggest that in origin the *atrium* was a courtyard like those found in domestic architecture throughout the ancient Mediterranean, including both the Greek and Punic worlds.[11] Vitruvius describes three main variants: the space was either completely covered (testudinate); with an outward sloping roof open in the centre (displuviate); or—the most common form—the roof could slope inwards with the rain falling down into a basin in the floor (the *impluvium*). By the early Republic, one particular form had developed as the focus of a specific and characteristic arrangement peculiar to Rome and central Italy. This is the Tuscan *atrium*, which, according to Varro, the Romans borrowed from the Etruscans,[12] and to which Vitruvius gives first place [111]. In the Tuscan system, the beams which form the central inward-sloping opening (the *compluvium*) are supported only on the outer walls of the *atrium* itself, while his two other variations on the compluviate *atrium* have the beams supported on four (tetrastyle) or more (Corinthian) columns. Given the dearth of well-preserved examples from Rome, we must rely on Pompeii for most of our evidence; at the time of its destruction in 79 CE, just over 90 per cent of all the compluviate *atria*—many dating to the second and first centuries BCE—were Tuscan, while less than 2 per cent were Corinthian. This seems to confirm our reading of the sources that, if there was a main type of Roman house in the Republic, it was one with a Tuscan *atrium*, or at least that this was the form most prized by the Romans. That we find it in the houses of Pompeii even before it became a Roman colony suggests that it had also become standard in areas of Roman influence in central Italy by the second century BCE.

As part of his rules for designing the *atrium*, Vitruvius identifies two other particular types of room which are usually associated in modern literature with the standard Roman *atrium* house: the *alae* ('wings'), lying to the right and left of the *atrium*, making a T-shape; and the *tablinum*, assumed by modern scholars to be the large, open-fronted room commonly found on axis with the entrance and *impluvium* in Pompeian houses, although Vitruvius does not specifically locate it there. In literature the *tablinum* is associated with the master of the house, as bedroom and then 'office' or personal reception space. While the evidence from Rome is too fragmentary to give a clear date for its earliest use in the city,[13] this type of plan occurs in pre-Roman Etruria as early as the fifth century,[14] and was in vogue in the Roman colony of Fregellae by the first half of the second century BCE.[15] These three elements together form a unique plan with a fundamentally axial and symmetrical arrangement, not found in any other type of housing in the ancient Mediterranean, one that we immediately recognize as Roman.

All the early *atrium* houses tend to be organized as a series of potentially open (*tablinum*, *alae*) and closed (*cubicula*, *triclinia*) rooms around the collective—and distributive—space of the *atrium*. This originally had a dual function, depending on the time of day. The *atrium* and open spaces were the customary setting for the early morning ritual of the *salutatio*, when the massed clients gathered to greet their patron on rising and to receive in return their daily dole, amid the ancestral masks and family records which formed the tangible reminders of the inherited power of the family. Since the *atrium* provided the only protected area with good lighting, it was also the focus of daily tasks in the hours when the house was empty of visitors, as there is no mention in the written sources and no obvious candidates in the physical remains of separate apartments for women, while slave quarters are almost impossible to identify outside a few exceptional later houses in Pompeii and Rome.[16]

In Pompeii, which gives us the most comprehensive domestic landscape of the late Republic and early empire, houses with compluviate *atria* were not, however, the most common form of dwellings but merely the most common type for larger houses, and the *alae/ tablinum* arrangement is found in only 15 per cent of all the houses with compluviate *atria*, most of the rest lacking *alae* altogether.[17] Studies of the electoral inscriptions on their façades suggest that most of these large *atrium* houses in Pompeii, with a footprint of over 1,000 square metres, belonged to the senior magistrates of the town. These are also the houses in which are found the more 'modern' and more obviously ostentatious elements of Vitruvius' Roman house, which bear distinctly Greek-type names and appear again in his description of the Greek house: the *peristylia* (colonnaded courts), *triclinia* (dining rooms), *exedrae* (large open recesses), *pinacothecae* (picture galleries), and *oeci* (columned halls).

Vitruvius, then, is not describing how to design some kind of standard Roman house, but the ideal form of housing his elite audience would be interested in as appropriate to their status.[18] This is in keeping with his use of terms not elsewhere applied to houses or found only in antiquarian literature, such as *ala* borrowed from temple architecture, or *fauces*, more normally used for the jaws of Hell rather than the entrance to a house; even *tablinum* is rare in Latin literature.[19] In addition, some of the Greek words which Vitruvius uses, such as *peristylia* and *triclinia*, were no more normal in Greek than was 'basilica'. That other Latin names once existed for some of these spaces is clear at least for the *triclinium* which, Varro says, used to be called *cenaculum* (from the Latin '*cena*', a meal), a term which had come by his day to be used for all upper-floor rooms from the Republican habit of dining in upstairs rooms.[20] Overall, however, it was the traditional *atrium* which set these elite houses apart as identifiably Roman; as Vitruvius succinctly puts it: 'because the Greeks do not use *atria*, they do not build them'.[21]

These may seem merely semantic quibbles, but they highlight what is patent from the physical evidence: that the Roman houses of the later Republic were an amalgam of earlier Roman, Etruscan, and Greek elements, which had fused together in a variety of ways to make the Roman *domus*. In elite housing, much of the Greek influence ultimately came from the palatial architecture of the Hellenistic kingdoms, developed to suit the needs of the Hellenistic rulers, which in turn borrowed greatly from the language of religious and civic buildings like gymnasia, as well as drawing on the residences of the Pharaohs of Egypt and the Great Kings of Achaemenid Persia.[22] Set like temples in commanding positions above the city, on natural high ground or on artificial terraces as a demonstration of

Fig. 113

The House of the Faun,
Pompeii, second century BCE
to 79 CE. View from the first
peristyle through the
Corinthian exedra, once
floored with the famous
Alexander mosaic, to the
rear *ambulatio* with its Doric
columns, installed in the
former *hortus*.

power over nature, these Hellenistic palaces were arranged around colonnaded courtyards furnished with large reception halls and multiple dining rooms to receive and entertain official guests, while the largest included parks able to host state banquets for thousands of diners, housed in tents and temporary pavilions. Everywhere the emphasis was on grand scale and lavish materials, whether marble, gold, and precious stones, works of art, or exotic flora and fauna.

All of this would have made a profound impression on the Roman aristocracy who visited the palaces as ambassadors or victorious generals, and ultimately stayed as governors. Indeed, by the time of Augustus it had become rather a truism for Roman moralists to blame the decline in Roman virtue on the evil influence of luxury brought home with the victorious general Marcellus from the sack of the rich kingdom of Syracuse in 211 BCE, tempting modern scholars to see the arrival of the peristyle and the decline of the *atrium* as the triumph of Greek taste over old-fashioned Republic traditions.[23] Yet in Pompeii at least, peristyle and *atrium* were already integrated at a relatively early date to produce the greatest examples of domestic architecture known from the city, houses which retained their layout through into the imperial period.[24] The early second-century BCE House of the Faun, the largest in Pompeii, had twin Roman *atria*, one Tuscan and one tetrastyle, and was built from the outset with a peristyle, to which a second was added at the end of the century **[113]**.[25] Similar in size to many of the contemporary palatial houses of Macedonian Pella and Attalid Pergamon, but much smaller than the great palaces of the Hellenistic kings, it also proclaims its debt to the world of Alexandria with its moulded plaster wall decoration in imitation of ashlar masonry, and a fine mosaic depicting the battle of Alexander the Great with the Persian King Darius, paving a graceful

Fig. 114

Doric peristyle of the House
of the Menander, Pompeii,
second to first century BCE.
The extra-wide opening
between two of the
columns, created in the first
century CE, allows a view to
the garden from the main
reception/dining room.

exedra opening off its peristyle through Corinthian columns.[26] Another
likely adoption from Hellenistic culture was its own small bath suite, next to
the kitchen. Even the use of the Hellenistic Doric order for the peristyles,
ubiquitous in the peristyles of second- to first-century BCE houses in
Pompeii [114], employs the language of Hellenistic palaces, while at the
same time referencing the public porticoes of Rome. Other of Vitruvius'
Greek-style spaces can also be identified at Pompeii, such as the Tetrastyle
oecus in the early first-century BCE House of the Silver Wedding [115], or
the 'Egyptian'—presumably Alexandrian—*oecus* of the House of the Mosaic
Atrium at Herculaneum, a form which Vitruvius likens to a basilica, again
in parallel with public buildings.[27]

The second peristyle of the House of the Faun, however, was a much
more Roman formulation. The space had once been the *hortus*, a productive
kitchen garden which connected the Romans to the countryside and to the
simple rustic life which was part of their shared history.[28] Its transformation
into a colonnaded *ambulatio* for gentle exercise and contemplation enclosing a planted garden speaks more of the Greek *gymnasium*, and particularly
the *gymnasium* of the Athenian philosopher Epicurus, than of any
Hellenistic domestic or palatial setting with their paved courts. Nevertheless,
the domestic peristyle garden as such does not seem to have existed in the
Greek east, and even under the empire remained a rarity, while developing
into the central feature of high-status Roman houses in the west. In late
Republican Rome, the aristocratic houses on the lower slopes of the Palatine
near the Roman Forum were rebuilt on palatial lines, raised up on imposing
platforms, one of them incorporating a large formal garden embellished

Fig. 115

Pompeii, House of the
Silver Wedding, tetrastyle
oecus, first century BCE.

with water features including a *nymphaeum* elaborated with statuary niches.[29] From a domestic necessity the garden had become a place for display, and the literary sources mention houses embellished with peristyle gardens full of exotic plants and water features, where the presence of several large trees could substantially raise the asking price even of a very luxurious townhouse.[30]

The addition of the peristyle to the *atrium* house vastly increased the possibilities for establishing highly refined patterns of social differentiation both within the household and between the master of the house and visitors. Vitruvius says explicitly that both *atria* and peristyles were freely open to the general public, contrasting them with the closed spaces which no one had a right to enter without an invitation, specifically *cubicula* ('bedrooms'), *triclinia*, and baths.[31] Yet the physical arrangements suggest that access even to public areas could be strongly controlled.[32] Many *atria* had doors at the inner end of the *fauces*, while peristyles were often accessible only by a narrow passage, allowing a high degree of control by physical or human barriers:[33] 'public' was a relative term. Where windows were inserted into the rear of the *tablinum*, as happened from the early imperial period, the throngs in the *atrium* could have glimpsed the privileged area of the peristyle, but even this was under the control of the master of the house, who could close off just the window or the whole *tablinum* with screens and shutters at will **[116]**.[34] Relatively few of those at the *salutatio* could expect an invitation to dine, while only the patron's close friends and family would be invited to the intimacy of the *cubiculum* for business meetings or philosophical discussion, or to share the baths.[35] The peristyle did, however, allow for the multiplication of dining spaces, some differentiated by size and decoration, others, as Vitruvius

Fig. 116

House of the Wooden
Partition, Herculaneum,
first century CE. View
through the entrance *fauces*
across the *atrium* to the
tablinum, with sliding
wooden partition half-
closed. Slight marks at the
inner end of the *fauces* indicate that this could also be
closed off from the *atrium*.

notes, by orientation and aspect, following the seasons.[36] Increased choice in
this essential area of self-presentation was an important claim to status.

While the peristyle provided an alternative space for communal living,
the impluviate *atrium* crystallized its function as a formal area for social
display, and one related to the particular requirements of the Roman socio-
political system which had no place in the Greek world. The *atrium* of the
domus of Aemilius Scaurus, the largest of the houses on the lower slopes of
the Palatine, could have held a crowd of 1,000–1,500, creating virtually a

public square within a private ambit,[37] a type of forum open not just to those who had some claims of dependency on the house but also, if we can accept Vitruvius' statement, to any of the people of Rome. Both service to the state in the holding of magistracies, and the exercise of personal power over a mass of *clientes* required a suitable setting, as Vitruvius makes clear. His words are worth quoting at length:

> men of common fortune have no need of magnificent vestibules, or archive rooms, or *atria*, because they pay their respects by waiting on others, and others do not visit them…but for the nobles who are required to serve the state by holding offices and magistracies, they need high and regal vestibules, vast *atria* and peristyles, as well as groves and wide ambulatories finished with a suitable majesty; and since in their houses public consultations and private trials and judgements are often heard, they also need libraries and basilicas to compare in magnificence with public buildings.[38]

Here not only the general description but also the choice of language (regal, majestic) connect the houses of Roman magistrates with the palaces of the Hellenistic rulers; even the term 'peristyle' is used elsewhere in Roman literature more for public than domestic buildings.[39]

Really great houses such as the House of the Faun are rare at Pompeii, and were presumably also not very common in relative terms at Rome either. While we do not know how far down the socio-economic ladder the practice of *salutatio* went, the influence of the large houses on the architectural aspirations of the less prominent members of society is one explanation for the fashion for compluviate *atria* even in very small houses, although Wallace-Hadrill argues that this was just the normal way of building houses in this period.[40] There were other models for smaller houses found at Pompeii and in Roman colonies in Republican Italy such as Cosa, with central unroofed courts or with no central opening; some of these were rebuilt in the Augustan period to create a compluviate *atrium*.[41] This may represent an implicit claim to an established family, especially on the part of wealthier freed slaves, in the same way that, at about the same time, there was a notable development of their funerary monuments which stressed family connections. The allure of the peristyle was just as great; even where space was a serious constraint, small gardens were often given colonnades on two or three sides, but with the blank walls painted to represent columns framing illusionistic views or luxurious gardens. These houses may thus reflect a strong desire on the part of the middle levels of society both to reinforce the Roman elements of their houses and to enhance their dignity. Both these phenomena seem to start in the Augustan period, noted for its marked upward social mobility but also one in which Augustus encouraged traditional Republican ideals and forms, living reputedly in a modest house 'with only short porticoes with columns of Alban stone'.[42] Indeed, given the number of *atrium* and *atrium*-peristyle houses which first appear outside of central Italy in this period, the Augustan age arguably marks the heyday of the *atrium* as the distinguishing feature of Roman houses well down the social ladder.

The fashion did not last. Evidence for compluviate *atrium* houses in Rome is hard to find beyond the first century CE, with only one small group appearing on all the surviving fragments of the Marble Plan of Rome **[22]**. It also had a short life under the empire, never gaining a wide foothold outside of Rome and central Italy,[43] despite the fact that scholars have tended to treat it as the standard against which all provincial housing could be tested for degrees of Roman influence. While 'standard' *atrium* houses (often without peristyles) occur in Roman Republican colonies in central Italy, they are rare elsewhere until the mid-first century BCE. Then they become fairly common in northern Italy,[44] and are also found in colonies in the northeast of Spain and southwestern France, with an exceptional example as far north as Cologne in the mid-first century CE.[45] No examples have been identified in North Africa, however, while the supposed examples of compluviate *atria* from the east, even in colonies such as Corinth, refounded in the middle of the first century BCE, generally do not form part of the 'standard' axial pattern.[46] Given that they lacked *alae* and '*tablina*', and were often without the clear distributive function of the Vitruvian *atrium*, these should be considered just as small colonnaded courts of the kind which appear frequently in later Roman houses all over the Mediterranean. Their evolution can possibly be traced to developments in Hellenistic southern Italy and Sicily from the second century BCE, as a hybrid form (now labelled as houses with tetrastyle courts) developed under the influence of the Roman *atrium*, which spread under the empire to the eastern Mediterranean.[47]

Domestic Architecture in the Empire

The disappearance of the *atrium* has been linked to changes in the structure of society under the emperors, when access to real political power has been thought to be so limited that the *salutatio* lost its meaning. Even for Rome, however, this argument is hard to sustain, given the continued importance of the Senate at a local level and of jurists in the legal system. Competition for power and prestige in provincial cities certainly remained strong throughout the empire, election notices on the street façades of Pompeii from the last years before the eruption showing lively canvassing in action. Rather, this is a case where the alternative Mediterranean model ultimately proved more flexible, attractive, and long-lasting than the traditional architecture of Republican Rome.

   In place of the *atrium* house, elite housing throughout the empire followed the peristyle plus dining room/reception hall model which originated in the Hellenistic Mediterranean. In Pompeii it is possible to see how some originally quite modest *atrium* houses expanded over time, absorbing adjoining properties to produce irregular plans which often defy formal classification. One thing that most have in common, however, is that the new space is given over entirely to the peristyle rather than enlarging or doubling the *atrium*. The House of the Gilded Cupids is a typical example [117].[48] Its main *triclinium*, like many others, was very large (roughly the same area as the *atrium*) and designed to make the most of views out over the peristyle garden, embellished with the sculpture and water features which had become *de rigueur* for any claims to social standing. In the House of the Stags at Herculaneum [118] this is taken one step further by all but suppressing the *atrium*, while concentrating on adding a large peristyle, giant dining/reception room, and a terrace with summer houses (*diaeta*) built out over the original city wall, providing sea views. In both cases extra

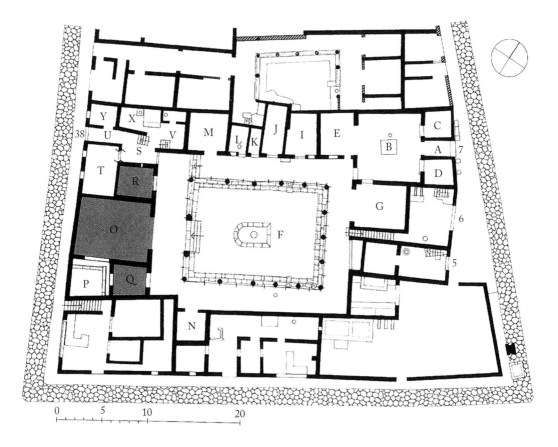

0   5   10   20

Fig. 117

Plan of the House of the Gilded Cupids, Pompeii. Only the lettered rooms belong to the house. The original atrium B now acts as little more than an entrance hall to the main part of the house around the garden peristyle F, onto which open two large reception rooms O and G with views across to the central water feature.

private living and storage space was relegated to upper floors, leaving the ground floor more open for display.

While there are several possible reasons for these changes, some of them at least may have been environmental. The design of the compluviate *atrium*, particularly when open to a garden or peristyle beyond, would have encouraged a cooling airflow in summer, but especially in its common forms would have been draughty, damp, and difficult to heat in the winter.[49] It also did not provide much light relative to its overall space, making the closed rooms opening off the *atrium* notably dark, particularly in winter. Multiple peristyles, especially when of different sizes and with different attributes such as paved floors or vegetation, also created temperature differentials which provided airflow, the cooling effects aided by the introduction of fountains, but were equally difficult to heat. The introduction of glazed windows in the first half of the first century CE dramatically widened the range of possibilities.[50] Peristyles such as that of the House of the Stags could be glassed in, as could the large windows overlooking the garden in *tablina* and *triclinia*, while upstairs windows could be glazed rather than relying just on shutters for closure. In some houses at Pompeii, there is even evidence for glazed windows being installed in the upper walls of *atria*,[51] and for winter suites of rooms looking out onto a garden through glazed porticoes. Light and

Fig. 118

House of the Stags (right) and House of the Mosaic Atrium (left), Herculaneum, first century CE. The terraces above the old city walls are in the middle ground of the image, with the pavilion of the House of the Stags in the centre. The grass in the lower right indicates the original ancient shoreline.

winter temperature control became key elements in the design of domestic architecture, which the *atrium* was particularly ill-suited to provide.

The empire produced many variations on the peristyle model, but common to all—and often the culmination of the design—was a grandiose reception room marked off by its large size, lavish decoration, and articulation of space. A wide open or columnar entrance allowed views through the portico to the open space beyond, with the peristyle columns and water features and/or sculpture arranged to privilege the view of the guest of honour in the traditional formal dining arrangement on three separate couches (*triclinium*), or expanded versions of this [114]. The same interest can be seen in the growing use of semi-circular or segmental apses at the rear of the reception room, designed to house the semi-circular couch (*stibadium*) which gradually came to replace the old arrangement of the *triclinium*. In the houses of the North African and Spanish provinces, the peristyle and this main reception room were often axial with the entrance, arguably influenced by Roman traditions but without the *atrium*, as in the House of the Ephebe at Volubilis (Morocco) [119].[52] In other houses, such as the House of the Mosaic of Venus, also at Volubilis, large vestibules or halls replaced the *atrium* and *fauces* combination as the location for the *salutatio*, while its smaller garden court flanking the main reception room and the suites of private rooms are also typical.[53] In other houses the axial entrance was avoided, a dog-leg approach being preferred which concealed as much of the interior as possible from any casual glance from the street when the door was open. This plan had deep cultural precedents, being a predominant pattern in pre-Roman Punic houses in North Africa,[54] but

Fig. 119

House of the Ephebe,
Volubilis (Morocco), second
to fourth century CE. The
roughly axial arrangement of
the main entrance, central
peristyle with water basin,
and large reception room is
typical of North African
houses of the imperial
period.

also familiar from the houses of classical Greece and often maintained
throughout the Hellenistic and into the Roman period in the Greek east.
Likewise, the pre-existing difference between the colonnaded gardens of
Italy and the west and the paved courts of the Greek east was maintained.
Once inside, however, the layout and organization were little different; the
lives of the residents were laid out on very similar lines, reflecting a shared
set of social customs: vestibules, halls, and courts for the formal reception of
clients; one very large dining hall and several smaller ones for the entertainment of invited guests; and an imposing *cubiculum*, sometimes making a
suite of rooms, for the master to gather for business or pleasure with his
intimates.[55]

As is usual with Roman architecture, these elite houses show a great deal
of individual variety but within a common underlying pattern and the social
structures it represents. The houses occupying a single *insula* terraced down
the slope of the Bülbüldağ at Ephesus [120],[56] identifiable as belonging to
the wealthier inhabitants of this large and important city by their rich decoration, give us a rare opportunity to see how universal this social structure
was. House 6, the largest in the block, was inhabited in the early second
century by C. Flavius Furius Aptus, a man from an important Ephesian
family originally of local Greek origin, a high-ranking holder of municipal
office and a priest of Dionysos, while the smaller House 2 was probably
occupied at roughly the same time by C. Vibius Salutaris, a Roman knight
from Italy who made major contributions to the life of Ephesus. While
their ancestry could not have been more different, their houses are both
centred on a colonnaded and paved court enhanced with water features,
expressing a common set of values through a common architectural

language which must have been recognizable to and understood by their clients and the wider local community.

As with religious architecture, housing of the Roman period on the peripheries of the empire generally continued local formats which went with continuing local patterns of daily life, with an added stratum of Mediterranean-style housing in particular elite contexts. In many places in Roman Britain, long, narrow strip-houses, with a large room for manufacture or other businesses at the front and smaller living rooms behind, made up much of the urban housing stock, using mainly wood and wattle-and-daub construction with stone only gradually coming into use in the second century CE.[57] At the other end of the empire, in contrast, the mud-brick houses with flat roofs of Dura Europos on the Euphrates were closer to early Mediterranean and Near Eastern models, with limited and indirect access, open central courtyards, and a main living room.[58] In some, interconnected courts, each with a principal room with dependent rooms off, or several principal rooms off a single courtyard, catered for extended families. Roman elite forms of housing come only with the army; the one peristyle house in Dura was the so-called 'Palace of the Dux Ripae', which housed the military commander of the Roman legion in the early third century. A thoroughly Roman design, laid out using the Roman foot measure, its apsed main reception room off the smaller of two peristyles looked out over the Euphrates, and it had its own baths and latrine. Likewise, the 'Commandant's House' at the fort of Arbeia (South Shields) on the river Tyne, about a century later, provides a rare example of a peristyle arrangement in Roman Britain, but with some differences due in part to climate;

the peristyle had dwarf columns supported on a waist-high wall, presumably to limit the impact of rain and snow, while several rooms, including one of the dining rooms, were heated.[59]

High-Density Urban Housing

While the peristyle became the hallmark of high-status houses under the empire, it did require space, something that was at a premium in the larger cities of the empire and unavailable for those at lower socio-economic levels. One possible factor contributing to the decline of the *atrium* is that it may simply have been too impractical for the pressures of urban Roman life under the empire. In the traditional compluviate forms the *atrium* used the full height of the building, but in the later phases at Pompeii and Herculaneum, presumably under population pressure, various strategies were used to insert upper floors into the space above the flanking rooms. The Tuscan *atrium*, however, required large timbers set into the flanking walls to form the *compluvium*, restricting the possibilities for the transformation of this space.

In Rome, this was not a new problem, as the exceptional population growth had brought pressure on accommodation from the mid-Republic. The response was the multi-storey apartment block (usually called an *insula*), containing multiple individual dwellings, generally for rent, within a single structure.[60] Already in the late third century BCE a cow is recorded as having found its way up to the third storey of a building,[61] and the *insula* eventually came to dominate the city of Rome. For Vitruvius, the need for building tall structures to accommodate the city's population was a fact of life.[62] The *insulae* of Rome have generally been identified as 'lower-class' housing and portrayed as ramshackle and in danger of collapse or fire by Roman authors, but the widespread use of brick-faced concrete after the fire of 64 CE produced solid yet adaptable structures, up to five storeys high or possibly more, of great longevity, which show a rather different picture. The best-preserved example is the early second-century *insula* built into the side of the Capitoline Hill **[121]**.[63] Fronted by an arcaded portico, the tall ground floor was occupied by *tabernae* with integral mezzanine floors, which would also have provided living accommodation. Above this is an apartment comprising a row of sequentially connected rooms with large windows onto the street, and ending in a corner room taking light from two sides; this would make a reasonably spacious residence for a single family, for rental on a long-term basis by a respectable household. The final surviving floor is very different; while it keeps the well-lit corner room, the rest is divided into rows of small cells, the inner ones scarcely large enough for more than a bed and very poorly lit. Each cell could be rented individually on a short-term basis, particularly by the kind of transient or seasonal populations we would expect in large cities, forming a type of boarding house or *pensione*, with all occupants sharing the corner room for cooking and eating.

Such vertical zoning, with mixed use and status in the same building, was normal in these *insulae*, as it had been, if to a lesser extent, in the *domus* of Pompeii and Herculaneum. There, self-contained rental units can be identified by their independent stairs from the street, and at Herculaneum it has

Fig. 121

Axonometric reconstruction drawing of the multi-storey *insula* on the slopes of the Capitoline Hill (the Aracoeli *insula*), Rome, second century CE.

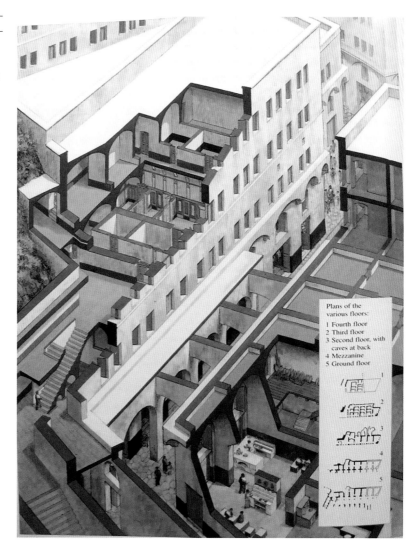

Plans of the various floors:

1 Fourth floor
2 Third floor
3 Second floor, with caves at back
4 Mezzanine
5 Ground floor

been calculated that 15 per cent of all residences were on upper floors.[64] A rare rental notice from Pompeii for the *Insula Arriana Polliana* **[112]** advertised *cenacula equestria*, presumably high-class upstairs apartments, alongside *tabernae* with mezzanine floors and a number of small *domus*, presumably also on the ground floor, while the greater part of the property was occupied by the great house, the so-called 'House of Pansa'. What is different in the multi-storey apartments of Rome and Ostia is that they seem to be conceived from the beginning as purely rental properties, but aimed at a socially and economically varied clientele within the same building, including high-status dwellings, the equivalent of many of the *atrium* houses of Pompeii.

An outstanding example of high-rise living is the so-called 'Garden Houses' at Ostia, the port of Rome **[122]**.[65] This was a single building project comprising one large *domus*, seventeen apartments, and fifty-six *tabernae* (shops/workshops) on the ground floor, all arranged around a large communal

Fig. 122

The Garden Houses at
Ostia, c. 125 CE.

garden served by six fountains, with up to four storeys of upper-floor apartments reached from twenty-one independent staircases. The complex had limited entrances to the communal space which could be closed off as required in the manner of a modern condominium. The single *domus* (the 'Insula of the Muses') was organized around an arcaded central court paved in mosaic, in a manner similar to many Mediterranean upper-class houses. At roughly 750 m², the footprint compares easily with those of many substantial *atrium* houses at Pompeii such as that of Julius Polybius (c. 740 m²), without even taking into account its extensive upper floors, and was equally designed for self-presentation and social differentiation. The main entrance from the street, framed by pilasters in fine brickwork, was carefully sited for visibility and impact from the outside. It allowed a view through to the entrance to a suite of rooms interpreted as the private quarters of the *dominus* (the 'master's suite'), providing for the same kind of formal reception usually associated with *salutationes* and the *tablinum* of an *atrium* house. The ground-floor rooms included a variety of reception rooms, the largest of which at 56 m² was larger than most of the grandest at Pompeii, while the very high quality of the decoration is a further indication of high status. This house is therefore a 'modern' version of the *atrium* houses of the preceding centuries, possibly for a member of Ostia's elite who had country estates elsewhere in the area, or made his money from large-scale commerce.

The characteristic feature of the remaining apartments is a long rectangular central living space (the so-called '*medianum*') from which all other rooms were accessed. Two large reception rooms of different sizes lay at either end of the '*medianum*', while two or more private rooms opened off one long side with an upper floor above them, the whole serviced with a kitchen, latrine, and piped water.[66] These apartments tend to have fewer, but larger, rooms than their Pompeian counterparts, which suggests a different attitude to the use of space, made possible perhaps by the strong natural light from the street coming from large glazed windows.

This also made it easy to apply the design to upper floors, especially in long narrow blocks above rows of *tabernae*, thus maximizing rental income. While the apartments lacked the axial entrance of the *atrium* house, suggesting that they were not designed to accommodate the formal reception of the *salutatio*, the entrances to both the ground-floor apartments and some of the external staircases to the upper floors are often distinguished by decorative pilasters crowned by pediments **[123]** in the same way as some of the richer *domus*.

One of the most striking features of the Garden Houses complex is the sheer range of variation within this '*medianum*' scheme, yet found in a single building project as part of the architect's original plan. In some cases this approaches the modern concept of modular design employed in flexible housing developments, for example with one apartment simply having one more *cubiculum* than another, producing a longer '*medianum*'. Whether this reflects the owners or developers adapting to the needs of particular prospective tenants or anticipating a market which was interested in these specific variants, the 'Garden Houses' complex was clearly designed for long-term rentals to an economically comfortable clientele with some pretensions to status. At the upper end of the range at least, these are large, well-appointed, and even luxurious apartments which could be classed with the smaller *domus* at Pompeii, inhabited by wealthy merchants and the more prosperous members of the many *collegia* (associations) which serviced the city and its commerce, many of whom might have been resident only on a seasonal basis. The overall impression, which must have applied to Rome and a few other very large cities in Italy including Neapolis and Puteoli on the Bay of Naples, is of an exceptionally well-developed housing stock designed for an active and variable rental market.

Worlds Apart? The Town in the Country and the Country in the Town

Town houses were not the only residential properties owned by the Roman elite. While the *domus* was the focus of much political and social interaction in the city, the productive countryside was the source of their wealth and status. Under the empire, as well as a minimum level of assets, senators also had to own land in Italy, and by the first century BCE it was common for wealthy members of the Roman elite to own multiple estates (*praedia* or *fundi*) in different parts of Italy (and later of the empire), run by managers, usually freedmen; Cicero is thought to have had ten such estates. The residential centre of most estates was the villa, which might be a simple farmhouse (*villa rustica*) or include, and sometimes privilege, luxurious accommodation for the owner and his (or her) friends (*villa urbana*).[67]

Villas were ambiguous places. In the Roman historical imagination, true nobility lay with the citizen-farmer, in stories like that of Cincinnatus, called from the plough to take charge of the army and defeat the enemy, only to lay down power and return to his farm the next day;[68] both moral probity and military ability were honed by the sweat of the industrious citizen in his fields. The appeal of this vision of rural life still affected later debates on the right way to live the rural life, with the emphasis on maximizing production, even if by the second century BCE the sweat was that of the chattel slaves who had come with conquest.[69] The same applied to the farmstead; the ancient sources on agriculture as well as Vitruvius, all written from the second century BCE to the first century CE, describe an architecture of production and storage—from cowsheds to granaries, and press-rooms to wine cellars—which defined the *villa rustica*.[70] Yet over this same period, for the elite the countryside also became the place for *otium*, the life lived away from the gaze of the wider public and devoted to private concerns, the most respectable of which were philosophy, learned discourse, and writing; ancient references to such villas are full of Greek terms suitably recalling the *gymnasium* and philosophical schools of Athens. As *villae urbanae*, they were also kitted out with all the luxury of townhouses, but with particular prominence given to peristyles, porticoes, and gardens. There were also fewer restrictions on physical space and on the moral constraints of *decor*, which had functioned to some extent to curb the building ambitions of the wealthy and powerful within the city. Architectural experimentation, conceits, and follies were the norm. The extreme case of the *villa urbana* was the *horti*, opulent residences and pleasure grounds which owed much to the pleasure parks of Hellenistic royal palaces, with walks, pavilions, and lavish water features set out in artificial landscapes, but located just outside the city walls on the urban periphery of Rome, often on the high ground both visible from and overlooking city or countryside.[71] Some of the most famous, and the most extravagant, are associated with the wealthiest Romans of the first century BCE such as Lucullus and Maecenas, who had decided to withdraw from—or not to become involved in—the political life of the forum, but nevertheless made a display of their detachment which was in itself a form of power.

The greatest of the *villae urbanae* drew more than their name from the city: in many ways they *were* cities, with all the facilities like shrines, porticoes, and baths. Pliny the Younger, writing about 100 CE, makes the connection: seen from his estate just south of Ostia, he says, the villas lining the coast appeared like cities.[72] The impact of a substantial villa from its main approach, whether road, river, sea, or lake, was enhanced by it being sited in an elevated position, terraced out on vaulted substructures using the technology and design principles seen elsewhere in suburban sanctuaries like Praeneste [62], and usually crowned by a colonnaded portico. In the late Republican Villa of Settefinestre, a few kilometres from the walled colony of Cosa, a garden wall below the arcaded terrace was decorated with miniature towers, so that from a distance the villa appeared even more like a walled town [124].[73] Vaulted podia (*basis villae*) went with the extensive use of porticoes on an urban scale. Four-sided porticoes enclosed gardens and pools like urban domestic peristyles [125], but on the scale of public buildings like Pompey's porticus behind his theatre, while linear *ambulationes* connecting different parts of the villa recalled the colonnaded streets of the city. Villa estates could even house markets and commemorative or funerary games held in temporary wooden amphitheatres, and had their own cemeteries and monumental tombs, advertising the importance of the owner.[74]

Pliny the Younger's vivid accounts of his various villas make it clear how the architecture of terraces and promenades, with their towers and belvederes forming landmarks and viewing platforms, manipulated the natural setting, enhancing the environmental aspect for physical comfort, providing sun, shade, breeze, and shelter as the season demanded, but equally—if not more importantly—to create appealing views.[75] Views out across large bodies of water, especially the sea but also large lakes like Como, were especially prized, but inland villas had their attractions; Pliny particularly praises the view from his Tuscan villa which seemed to be 'a painted scene of unusual beauty rather than a real landscape'. The elements of Pliny's inland views start with the formal garden within the peristyle, and extend out over the

Fig. 124

Artist's impression of the Roman villa at Settefinestre, near Cosa (Italy), first century BCE to first century CE, with the turreted garden wall below the arcaded *basis villae*.

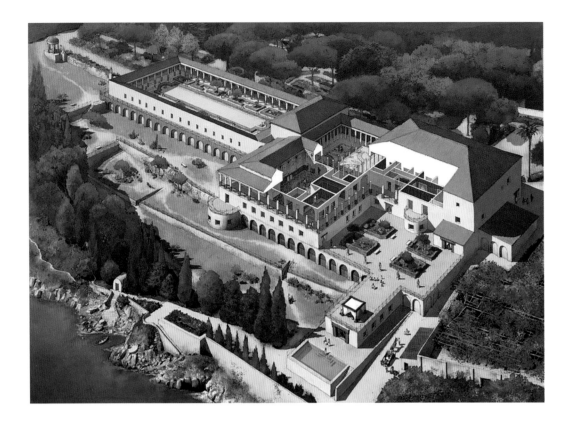

cultivated environment of the estate, then to the woods and mountains beyond. Weather was no hindrance as a development peculiar to the villa was the walled porticus, where the columns were replaced by walls with large glazed windows. Water was also manipulated, to form large pools for swimming or raising fish, and in a wide variety of basins, fountains, and rills. The sounds it made added to the sensory ambience that was part of the villa experience, alongside the scent of flowers and vegetation, and different qualities of light and of air.

At the same time, the idea of the villa as a productive environment remained strong, but often in relation to production which could be put on display and which contributed to the overall opulence of the villa environment. Partly this was carried out by the production of luxury foodstuffs which had a ready market in Rome, requiring specialized structures like aviaries and fishponds, some of considerable architectural and technological sophistication.[76] More common agricultural production, especially of wine and olive oil, was given a theatrical make-over, with press-rooms and storage areas which belonged to the *villa rustica* integrated into the architecture of the *villa urbana*. At Villa Magna, an imperial estate known from the letters of Marcus Aurelius to his tutor Fronto, a colonnaded street led to a semi-circular dining room, where diners looked out onto a wine store paved not in utilitarian herringbone brick but in its imitation in precious marble.[77]

The *villa urbana* was, like the *atrium-peristyle* house, a particularly Roman formulation. It is impossible to unravel the connection between the

House of D. Octavius Quartio, Pompeii, first century CE. View from the porticoed terrace down over miniature villa garden. In front of the four-columned pavilion was once a small fountain in a shallow marble pool, the water from which cascaded into a nymphaeum under the pavilion and fed a 50-metre-long channel below, interspersed with further fountains and flanked by planting beds. The water feature could be enjoyed from vine-shaded walks on either side, beyond which the garden was planted with trees and shrubs. Both terrace and water channel were originally richly decorated with small-scale sculpture and wall paintings.

development of villa architecture and that of elite town houses in the formative years of the later second and first centuries BCE, but the importance of the villa for the town can be seen in later Pompeian houses.[78] One aspect is in the creation of miniaturized villa gardens, like that in the House of Octavius Quartio [126], where nearly 75 per cent of the plot was given over to a garden with trees and shady walks and a central rill with fountains and small-scale statuary, attached to a tiny *atrium* house with a miniscule peristyle. A transverse terrace with a long pool and fountain, on axis with a pair of summer dining couches facing another pool, gave a long view down over the garden.

Vignettes of villas, easily identifiable from their long porticoes, appear in a number of decorative wall painting schemes in Pompeii [127], marking a reification of the villa as structure to be set alongside the still-lifes of villa products showing fish, fowl, game, and fruits.[79] This became the dominant Mediterranean model,[80] and elements are also found in the northwestern

Fig. 127

Roman painting of a portico
villa, from the House of
Lucretius Fronto, Pompeii,
mid-first century CE.

Fig. 128

Main block of the Roman
villa at Nennig (Germany),
third century CE.

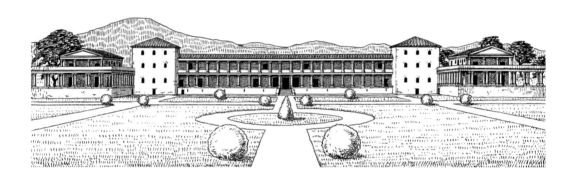

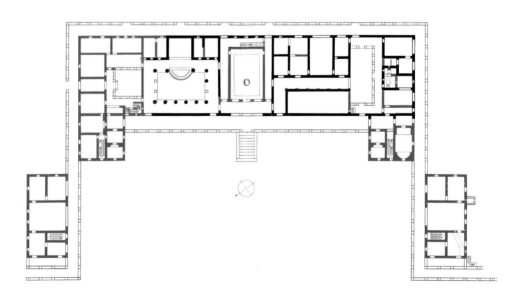

provinces. There, however, the central residential core tended to follow a local pattern, based on a rectangular hall set lengthwise and fronted by a corridor or portico linking symmetrical projecting wings, sometimes developed as towers.[81] In the villa at Nennig (Rhineland) **[128]** the influence of Mediterranean forms can be seen within this regional framework, while its associated long promenade looking out over the river and leading to the baths would not have been out of place in central Italy.

The Dwellings of the Roman Emperors

From Augustus onwards, the Roman emperors developed a residential portfolio which was not very different from that of their peers except in degree—of scale, extent, display, and decoration. Indeed, they acted exactly like late Republican senators, acquiring residential property from others—sometimes by purchase, often through inheritance and bequest, not infrequently under compulsion (including death)—then set about enlarging, amalgamating, embellishing, and, where required, rebuilding. The process was cumulative: by the end of his life, Augustus owned extensive property on the Palatine, the *horti* of Maecenas on the Esquiline, and several villas, including a number on the island of Capri. Tiberius, Caligula, and Claudius all acquired more of the grand *horti* of Rome, by fair means or foul, and all developed luxury villas often based on family property, although even in the later second century forced appropriations of desirable estates were not unknown. Not all emperors actively used all the properties that belonged to them, often privileging either those that had belonged to their own families, something that had particular resonance as dynasties changed, or those that had close ties with Augustus, a frequent source of legitimization for later regimes.

The core of the imperial residences was the house of Augustus, the *Domus Augustana*, with its focal point on the summit of the Palatine.[82] Over time its doorway and entrance hall were distinguished by the marks of respect awarded to Augustus by the Senate of Rome, including an inscription honouring him as Father of his Country (*pater patriae*) and the civic crown for saving the life of citizens, which came to symbolize the emperor's care for the state and his people. Beside it Augustus built a magnificent temple complex dedicated to Apollo, his patron deity, together with a grand porticoed precinct (the 'Portico of the Danaids') including libraries, where the Senate sometimes met and Augustus held audiences. It is often argued that the power of place invested in the Palatine by the 'Hut of Romulus' and other places related to Rome's legendary past were exploited by Augustus, and enhanced by gathering to it the political and religious activities symbolic of the continuity of the state, although scholars are increasingly downplaying this connection.[83] What does seem to be the case is the importance for Augustus of the choice of the Palatine Hill, with its close general association with Romulus. At the same time, this was subordinated to his house which, in good Republican tradition, was a tangible manifestation of the outstanding achievements and political power of the individual.

The rapid accumulation of property by the Julio-Claudian emperors culminated in the most notorious imperial residence, the Domus Aurea or Golden House of Nero, which arose from the ashes of the great fire of Rome in 64 CE **[129]**. In its simplest terms, the Golden House was an amalgamation of all the imperial residences in the city, uniting Palatine and *horti*

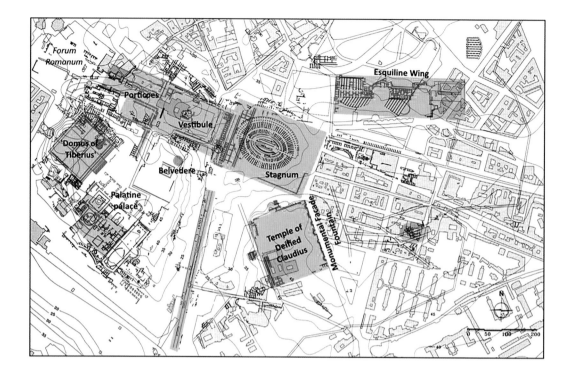

Fig. 129

Plan of the Domus Aurea, Rome, c. 64–68 CE, with known elements in red superimposed over the later Roman (in black) and modern (in brown) topography.

while locating the main state rooms on the Palatine, including a circular space 100 Roman feet in diameter, possibly the famous dining room which revolved day and night. The Roman historian Tacitus, who would have seen what remained of the Golden House when in Rome as a young man in the early 70s, dismissed its gold and jewels as commonplaces; its wonders rather lay in the creation of an artificial landscape, outdoing nature, complete with buildings imitating cities, farmland, and woods full of wild animals—all the things that Pliny later admired in the views from his villas. It included a lake in the low-lying area where the Flavian Amphitheatre now stands, which modern architectural historians had always imagined as something Capability Brown might have designed for a grand eighteenth-century country house, until modern excavations uncovered a formal rectangular pool lined with marble in the tradition of the *villa urbana* or the *horti* of Rome.[84] What made the Domus Aurea notorious was not so much the individual elements or the 'bling' but the sheer scale and the bringing into the heart of the city of *negotium* the trappings of rural—or at least suburban—*otium*, where, according to Suetonius, Nero felt he could 'at last begin to live like a human being'.[85]

A substantial pavilion, the so-called 'Esquiline Wing', gives some sense of the villa aspects of the Domus Aurea, even when stripped of much of its original decoration. It survives as a long narrow terracing structure encompassing at least 300 rooms devoted to reception and entertainment; originally this supported an extensive upper floor, very little of which remains, but which would have given impressive views south across the lake and the invented landscape below to the Caelian and Palatine Hills. The colonnaded façade of the lower level was divided symmetrically by two pentagonal courts, with each section having its own character. The western section centred on a west-facing dining pavilion opening onto an enclosed court with a central water feature, while behind lay a grotto-like nymphaeum with a cascade pouring down from the rear wall and a fountain in the middle. A cascade fed from the hill behind was also the central feature of the famous Octagonal suite, designed around an octagonal space covered with a low dome and lit by a large central oculus; even without the reflective properties of the water or the marble and mosaic decoration, the lighting effects are still impressive [44]. Because the basement of the Esquiline Wing survives, the Domus Aurea has often been seen as a turning point in the development of Roman architecture, both technically and in terms of an architecture of interiors, but if we think of it as villa architecture there is little here that would have seemed particularly novel to Nero's contemporaries other than the scale and location, as is clear from Tacitus' remarks.

Despite the importance to us of the Esquiline Wing of the Domus Aurea, the core of the imperial residence remained the Palatine. While the steep-sided Palatine Hill formed a natural podium increasing the visibility of all that was built upon it, it limited access to the palace. Following the precedent of Hellenistic palaces, the emperors were concerned to create an impressive entrance which might suitably accord with what was to come. Both the original entrance from the river harbour, sanctified by the Lupercal shrine and the Temples of Magna Mater and Victory, and the Via Appia approach, adorned 200 years later by the Severan emperors with the monumental nymphaeum of the Septizodium, looked towards those arriving at the heart of empire from afar. On the other side of the Palatine, facing the city and its inhabitants, the Temple of Apollo dominated the approach to the original house of Augustus.[86] Caligula's entrance from the Roman Forum was through the triumphal Arch of Augustus, flanked by the temples of Castor and Pollux and of Deified Julius Caesar, already decorated with *rostra* like the vestibule to Pompey's house. Even this pales beside Nero's grandiose vestibule to his Golden House, a triple portico a mile long focused on a colossal gilded statue of the emperor 120 Roman feet high.

The new Flavian palace [130] which replaced the Domus Aurea on the Palatine, begun under Vespasian and largely complete by the end of Domitian's reign but with substantial alterations into the late third century, was carefully designed with these approaches in mind in order to regulate the degree of public access to the emperor on different state occasions.[87] While this was something new in residential architecture, the complex could otherwise almost have used Vitruvius' prescription for the elite *domus* as a checklist: lofty halls, spacious porticoes, gardens, ambulatories (the so-called 'stadium'), libraries, and basilicas, as well as a monumental dining room. The design, usually associated with the architect Rabirius, created, however, a unique complex which cleverly compressed the standard tropes of *domus*, *horti*, and *villa* into a small compass by reforming the natural topography, playing with scale, and enhancing the language of public architecture to an unprecedented degree.

The two audience halls (the 'Aula Regia' and the so-called 'Basilica') faced north, and the ceremonial public approach was from Nero's vestibule and up the north slope of the Palatine between the Temple of Jupiter the Stayer and a colossal equestrian statue of Domitian. The state banqueting hall, on the other hand, faced onto a vast colonnaded garden peristyle

Fig. 130

The imperial palaces on the
Palatine Hill in Rome.
Hypothetical reconstruction
of the Flavian phase of the
palace.

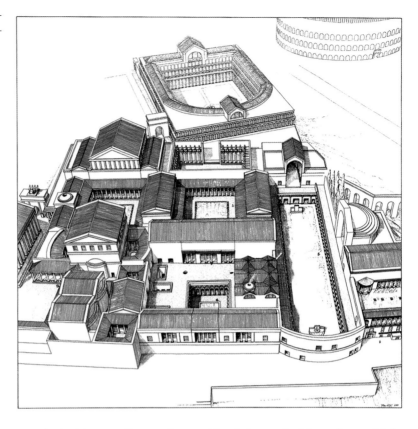

enriched with water features, but could only be reached from the outside by
a suite of entrance rooms opening off the area in front of Augustus' Temple
of Apollo. While one could petition for an audience with the emperor, one
could only be invited to a state banquet; in the tradition of the late Republic,
the physical setting made the distinction clear. The distinction was also
notable in their scale. The 'Aula Regia' was three times the size of the *atrium*
of the late Republican *domus* of Aemilius Scaurus, likened above to a private
forum, but rather than an *atrium* it was a rectangular hall more like the
Curia in the Forum Romanum which housed the Senate, only twice the
size. The whole was reminiscent of a temple interior, with a shallow apse
for the imperial throne at the rear as if for a cult statue, and its walls broken
into bays by projecting piers decorated with tall columns of Phrygian
marble framing large aedicules for colossal statues of major state deities.
Temple-like, too, was the imperial banqueting hall; contemporary sources
stressed its astonishing height, vastness, and rich decoration, fit for Jupiter
himself.[88] Here the lavish columnar decoration of the side walls, on at least
two storeys and framing large windows and doors, echoed the language of
the *scaenae frons*, but gave out onto elaborate fountain courts. The 'Aula
Regia' and banqueting hall also both had timber-trussed roofs, the traditional
form for temples. These huge rooms, with their axial apses where the
emperor could appear in state, emphasized the power of the emperor and
the distance between him and his guests, another feature which distinguished the residence of the emperors from other aristocratic houses. Trajan

Fig. 131

The sunken peristyle of the imperial palace (the *Domus Augustana*), Rome, in the Hadrianic phase with central water garden, once surrounded by a vaulted porticus carrying a terrace.

or Hadrian added a curved façade overlooking the Circus Maximus, physically connecting the Flavian palace to the imperial box of Trajan's rebuilt Circus, allowing the emperor to manifest himself to the populace from the safety of his own house.

Beyond the state rooms and their connecting peristyles, the architecture moved to a more domestic scale but with increased complexity, which even in its present state reveals a master architect at work in the cleverly interlocking spaces of varied shapes. The most complete are those at a lower level around a sunken peristyle with central pool, which, like the surviving part of the Esquiline Wing of the Domus Aurea, are both major reception spaces in themselves and form the substructures of the rooms above [131]. These are clearly more private spaces potentially used by the emperor himself, as access is severely limited by a single easily guarded staircase. Even further removed is the sunken *ambulatio*, shaped like a stadium, and the private

Fig. 132
Site plan of Hadrian's Villa,
Tibur (Tivoli) 118–138 CE.

Key to plan:
1. North ('Greek') theatre
2. Iseum ('Palaestra')
3. Temple of Cnidian Venus
4. *ambulation* ('Stoa Poikile')
5. Peristyle garden with pool
6. Island villa ('Teatro
Marittimo')
7. Heliocaminus baths
8. Republican core
9. Fountain garden
10. Residential block
('Hospitalia')
11. Imperial residence
12. 'Hall of the Doric
Pilasters'
13. 'Piazza d'Oro'
14. 'Gladiators' arena'
15. Houses
16. Apartment houses
17. sacro-idyllic landscape
18. Barracks of the imperial
guard
19. Peristyle with fishpond
and cryptoporticus
20. 'Stadium'-nymphaeum
21. Tri-lobed dining hall
22. Small baths
23. Shrine of Antinoös
24. Vestibule
25. Large baths
26. 'Canopus'
27. Water dining pavilion
('Serapeum')
28. West belvedere ('Torre
di Roccabruna')
29. 'Accademia'
30. 'Small palace'
31. Odeon
32. Garden pavilion
('Ploutonion')
33. East belvedere.

apartments beyond set out on a high terrace around a large colonnaded pool, with fine views of the Circus Maximus and beyond over a suburban landscape of villas, tombs, and market-gardens flanking one of Rome's oldest highways, the Via Appia, and framed by the slopes of the little Aventine. Here Rabirius created a miniature villa in the heart of the palace.

Augustus had chosen to live on the Palatine, taking advantage of the power inherent in the association with Romulus and the Palatine hut of the founder of Rome. Through all its subsequent expansions and rebuildings, the residence of the emperors on the Palatine retained the name of its founder and the founder of the empire, the House of Augustus, although from the time of Nero 'palatium' also came to refer to the imperial residence.[89] When emperors became more peripatetic and the Palatine eventually ceased to be the main official residence of the emperor, it was the toponym 'Palatium' (hence 'palace') which was used to indicate the place where the emperor was residing.[90] The 'House of Augustus', like the huts of Romulus, was inextricably bound with a specific place and a particular type of identity which was both of an individual and of Rome itself. With the foundation of Constantinople as the new Rome, and the shift of power to the eastern Mediterranean, both the huts of Romulus and the House of Augustus remained as potent reminders of the 'real' heart of the empire.

Imperial Villas: Rome in the Countryside

Like their aristocratic predecessors in the Republic, emperors also had real villas, situated on the coast or in the hills within half to a day's travel from Rome, or on the Bay of Naples. Unlike the imperial *horti*, which were just a short stroll from the Palatine, these were places of sojourn, and had to be not only places of *otium* but also of *negotium*. There is ample evidence in the ancient sources of emperors conducting public business from their villas, from receiving foreign embassies to conducting trials or holding fairs and games. All these activities assume an audience, some of whom would have been resident for the time span of the event, in addition to the court and household which attended the emperor or maintained the residence. Imperial villas therefore needed not just audience halls and dining pavilions but also extensive accommodation and facilities like baths for visitors, and places for putting on spectacles: in other words, even more than the villas of the senatorial aristocracy, they were essentially urban spaces, the essence of Rome imposed on the countryside. Some also had close ties to, or even incorporated, significant religious spaces, something which had been an important element of Hellenistic royal palaces as well.

All these things can be seen in Hadrian's Villa below Tibur (modern Tivoli), the best preserved of all the imperial villas [132].[91] It was on a truly urban scale, at over 70 hectares covering an area larger than Pompeii. As well as a theatre, an odeon and a possible amphitheatre, it had at least three baths, the scale and decoration of which were very much those of urban public buildings; the Large Baths are in fact similar in size and layout to the Forum Baths at Ostia. There was a variety of residential accommodation, some of it barracks-like for slaves or guards, but including recently discovered '*medianum*' and courtyard apartments which would not be out of place in second-century Ostia.[92] For a traveller approaching along the Via Tiburtina, the many

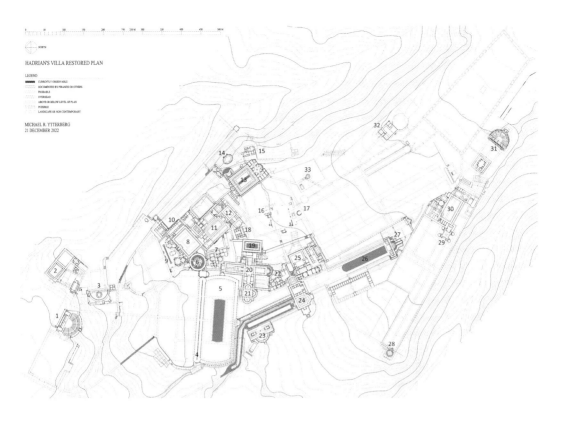

monumental terraces and large buildings of Hadrian's Villa could easily have been mistaken for Tibur itself, an imperial counterpart to the actual city.

In other ways, however, Hadrian's Villa was not as exceptional as is sometimes suggested. As with other aristocratic villas, the emphasis was on landscape and lavish dining pavilions. While the limitless imperial purse provided the wherewithal for exceptional decoration and bold experiments in architectural form, these were not in themselves beyond what was normal for luxury villas. Groups of buildings, notable for their variety and most based around peristyles and water features, were set out on different axes to take advantage of the natural lie of the land and unified by gardens and promenades including a belvedere with distant views to Rome. Some of what was thought to be an empty space is now known to have been dotted with small shrines and pavilions, creating the type of sacro-idyllic landscape which had parallels in the *horti* and derived ultimately from Hellenistic palaces.[93] Architectural follies, sculpture, and other works of art turned some parts into mythological landscapes, while others were designed to recall, but not replicate, celebrated landmarks of Alexandria and Athens, a Republican tradition which goes back at least to Cicero.[94] The Palatine palace in Rome was another source of inspiration, especially in the majestic trilobed reception/dining hall, linked to a stadium-shaped garden with nymphaeum and pavilions, and the private quarters arranged around a high-level pool. The villa even had its own internal circulation system, designed to control the movement of visitors and to ensure the separation of the public

Fig. 133

'Canopus' and 'Serapeum' at Hadrian's Villa, Tibur (Tivoli), 130s CE. In the dining pavilion (the 'Serapeum') the diners reclined on a semi-circular *stibadium*, looking out along the long boating pool (the 'Canopus') which was lined with columns and statues. A water channel on which small dishes for food floated followed the curve of the *stibadium* in front of the diners, while behind them were fountains and a cascade, reminiscent of that in the Octagonal Room of the Domus Aurea.

function of the villa from its private one, a motif which goes back to the late Republican *domus*, but was a particular feature of Domitian's palace.

The most notable—and most discussed—features are the groups of buildings known for their curvilinear designs and experimental roofing solutions, where some scholars would wish to see the hand of Hadrian himself as architect; we can at least imagine that they had his approval. The 'Island Villa' is an elegant retreat based on a plan of concentric circles, with the vestibule, bedroom suite, dining room, and bathing suite all defined by four sweeping curves, around a central courtyard with four concave sides [45]. The semi-circular water *stibadium* (dining room) of the 'Serapeum' has a water cascade behind reminiscent of the Octagonal suite in the Domus Aurea, but roofed with a complex semi-dome of alternate flat and concave segments [133]; the open colonnaded front gave the diners a view down a long canal flanked by colonnades, statuary, and garden planting, traditionally called the 'Canopus' but which also has a predecessor in the great pool of the Domus Aurea. The central area of the 'Piazza d'Oro' pavilion [23], 10.35 metres in diameter with alternate convex and concave sides composed entirely of columns, is so complex that scholars are still not agreed as to whether, or how, it was roofed.[95] Despite the architectural novelties in some of these structures, the basic elements of dining pavilion, cascade, and view over an extensive water feature amid porticoed gardens had already been a part of villa life for well over a century.

Palatium

When the emperors began to build residences outside of Rome under the Tetrarchy, the Palatine palace and the imperial villas of Italy provided the models but were adapted to the new conditions of life in an empire increasingly under threat.[96] The palaces founded in 293 CE at the existing cities of Trier (Germany) and Thessalonike (Greece) both included colonnaded courts and

Fig. 134
Diocletian's villa/palace,
Split (Croatia), c. 305 CE,
artist's reconstruction.

large apsidal audience halls, and were set alongside a circus, while the villas of the emperors Galerius at Gamzigrad (Serbia) and Diocletian at Split (Croatia) (305) were more like walled cities. Diocletian's retirement villa **[134]**, some twenty times smaller than Hadrian's sprawling villa, was bounded on three sides with defensive walls strengthened with square and octagonal towers, and served by three elaborate gates leading to colonnaded streets. Suitably for this soldier-emperor, it has often been likened to a military camp, reflecting the long-standing interaction of civil and military architecture. The villa provides almost a compendium of later Roman imperial and provincial urban architecture. The fourth side faced the sea, presenting a continuous façade topped by an arcaded gallery using the 'Theatre-motif', behind which substantial cross-vaulted substructures once supported the reception rooms and state apartments, now lost. They were reached via a formal entrance court flanked by colonnades bearing arcuated lintels, with a 'Syrian' pediment announcing the entrance itself. On one side of the court was Diocletian's mausoleum, externally octagonal with a projecting pedimented porch, but circular within and articulated with alternately rectangular and apsidal recesses reminiscent of the Pantheon; facing it were three temples of traditional Roman form, one dedicated to Jupiter, the presiding deity of the Roman state and the tutelary deity of the emperor himself, just as the house of Augustus on the Palatine was guarded by the temple of his tutelary deity, Apollo. Even after three centuries of imperial residences, the essentials had not changed.

Housing the Dead

The inclusion of Diocletian's mausoleum within the bounds of his retirement villa reflects the importance of funerary monuments in the Roman architectural tradition. In accordance with an ancient law going back to the

Twelve Tables of the early Republic, it was forbidden to bury the dead within the boundary of a city, so that monumental tombs lining the roads leading into Roman cities, or extending outside the walls in cities of the dead (*necropoleis*) with their own streets and hierarchies, were a normal feature of the peri-urban landscape. These streets of the dead would have often been thronged with crowds of the living, attending the tombs of their ancestors or patrons on the occasion of the Roman festival of the Parentalia, and celebrating them on other more personal feast days such as birthdays.

Roman funerary monuments appear in an extraordinary range and variety of shapes, with considerable variety within those forms, while sharing some common elements. An inscription from a sarcophagus found in Provence shows some of the basic priorities:

You, Proculus, husband of me, Rufina, lie here by the will of the fates abandoning your life and your widow. I built a great tomb in a prominent site, a wonder to all. I added to it gleaming doors. I put in it a statue closely resembling you, dressed to reflect your distinction among the Italian orators.[97]

Tombs were thus a celebration of the life of the individual, identified by portrait, dress, and inscription, placed in a visual context which through its architecture and location attracted the eye of the passer-by and reflected well on the family of the deceased. Not surprisingly, most were raised on high podia to lift the image and text above the heads of the passing traffic, or to create landmarks visible from further afield [135].

Size mattered. Augustus followed Hellenistic precedent for very large royal tombs, resulting in a giant tumulus above a drum clad in white marble. At 300 Roman feet (c. 90 metres) in diameter and perhaps 150 feet (c. 44 metres) high, it was the largest ever made, and only equalled by the next imperial mausoleum, that of Hadrian on the other bank of the Tiber **[136]**.[98] There were plenty of possible models. For size and richness there were the royal tombs of the East, from the fourth-century BCE Mausoleum of Halicarnassus, 150 feet (c. 44 metres) tall and one of the Seven Wonders of the Hellenistic world, to that of Alexander the Great, which Augustus visited in Alexandria. There were also royal tumulus tombs from Macedon to Numidia, the earliest surviving of which ('La Medracen', third century BCE) was about 200 feet (c. 59 metres) in diameter and about 60 feet (18.5 metres) high.[99] Arguably more important were the early tumulus tombs of the Etruscans and that at Lanuvium, associated with Augustus' legendary ancestor Aeneas, providing a semblance of ancient Italian precedent according to the dictates of *decor*. Fitted into the narrow space at the north of the Campus Martius between the Tiber and the Via Flaminia, the Mausoleum of Augustus dominated the skyline for anyone arriving from the north or along the river, its crowning bronze statue rising above the height of the surrounding hills. As a statement of personal power dressed in the manner of Etruscan kings and Hellenistic monarchs, the message could have not been clearer, despite all Augustus' protestations about restoring the Roman Republic.

The Mausoleum of Augustus appears to have started a short-lived fashion among the senatorial order. Smaller tombs comprising a tall circular drum faced in ashlar, but often above a square podium, are found around Rome and in the Italian countryside during the Augustan period, but are relatively rare elsewhere. A curious exception is that built by Q. Lollius Urbicus in the middle of the second century CE, just outside the small town of Tiddis in Algeria. Urbicus, the son of a local landowner of native Berber extraction, had held the important post of urban praetor in Rome in the middle of the second century, before which he had been responsible for the re-conquest of Lowland Scotland and the building of the Antonine Wall; the tomb was for his parents and family, while he himself was honoured by the local town council as their patron.[100] This monument was a display of his elevated status and closeness to the imperial house, deliberately designed to recall the Augustan tombs of Rome, and to confer a distinction that his family could not otherwise have ever achieved.

Other basic monumental tomb types had a much wider geographical and chronological range, although particular local variations were common. We can see this in the popular tower tombs, which gained maximum visibility from a small footprint. The distinctive family tombs at Palmyra on the eastern fringes of the empire were up to six storeys high, with very plain exteriors but elaborate interiors with multiple niches bearing portraits of the deceased, while in the northwestern provinces it was the exteriors which were highly decorated, with a multitude of relief sculpture including family portraits, representations of daily life focusing on commerce, and mythological scenes—in short, a visual representation of identity and place in local society [137].[101] The reliefs in these monuments were set within an architectural framework of pilasters and pediments which, as in other contexts, alluded to sacred architecture. This is more obvious in aedicular tombs, where a series of stacked solids carried an open columnar shrine, usually rectangular or circular, within which were set the portrait statues of the deceased; these are often the most inventive and elaborate, many with tall roofs in a wide variety of forms from simple pyramids to concave-sided cones, with decorative finials to further increase the height [138]. Temple-tombs, where a tall podium carried a temple-like structure, and altar tombs made the most direct statement of the sacrality of the funerary realm. This should not be surprising; Roman funerary monuments were in a sense shrines. The inscriptions often start with the phrase *dis manibus*, to the spirits of the departed, and the form of many monuments, the content of the inscriptions, and the way some of the deceased were portrayed were designed to represent the dead as heroes.

In origin many of these monumental tombs, including that of Augustus, were set in funerary precincts, which could be marked simply by a series of boundary stones but also by low walls which gave the tomb itself greater definition. Over time the precinct itself became the monument, acquiring sometimes doors or false doors, and increasingly under the empire with highly decorated interiors but leaving the exterior relatively plain. There are some exceptions, including the extraordinary elaborate aedicular façade of a tomb at Caesaraugusta (Zaragoza in Spain) which would not have looked out of place on the Embolos of Ephesus [148].[102] These precincts are often without the inscriptional evidence which would allow us to locate them

within the structure of Roman society, but it is sometimes argued that they
belonged to freed slaves and their families, some of whom could be wealthy
but were debarred from public office because of their legal status. The same
group are often associated, but on better evidence, with the so-called 'house
tombs' of Rome, Ostia, and Portus [139], where the entrance led either to a
courtyard with a structure beyond or straight into an often elaborate covered
interior, while the façade was given a formal door, real or fake windows, and
a pediment; some were two-storeyed, and many had masonry dining

Fig. 138

Mausoleum of the Julii, just outside Glanum (Provence), c. 40–20 BCE. It was dedicated by three brothers to their parents, and may have been a cenotaph rather than an actual burial place. The three tiers take the form of a high sarcophagus-like podium on a stepped base, a quadrifrons arch, and a circular tholos with a conical roof containing statues.

couches in front or on the upper level.[103] While there are differences, the overall effect is much more uniform than the aggressively competing forms and rich decoration of the individual monumental tombs, suggestive more of urban back streets than grand processional ways or important city streets lined with the houses of the rich and famous.

Fig. 139

Street of house tombs, necropolis of Portus (Isola Sacra), at the mouth of the Tiber, second century CE.

The Language of
Ornament

7

The whole civilized world lays down the arms which were once its ancient
burden and has turned to adornment…this one contention holds them all,
how each city may appear more beautiful.

Aelius Aristides, *Orationes* 23.13–14

While many of the temples, civic buildings, and monumental tombs served
as memorials to the acts of the public benefactors who bore their names, the
cities of the late Republic and empire were also adorned with commemorative
monuments which had little or no practical function other than to celebrate
in a decorative manner. The idea of adorning the city, while particularly
prevalent in ancient writing about Augustus' buildings in Rome,[1] goes back
at least to the fourth-century BCE Greek world and was still key in civic
panegyrics like those of Aelius Aristides in the second century CE.[2] Urban
ornament stood not only as a symbol of peace but also of civic virtue;
together, the physical structure and appearance of a city were thought to
reflect the virtues—and the flaws—of the society it housed.

Walls—The Symbol of the City

Nothing illustrates the conditions identified in Aristides' oration better
than the transformation of city walls. Originally erected for military defensive reasons, walls became the universal shorthand for the city in visual culture, and the act of building them a shorthand for its foundation [141].[3]
According to Plutarch, writing in the second century CE about the foundation of the city of Rome, Romulus ceremoniously ploughed a deep furrow
round the boundary of the city, marking out the course of the walls and
lifting the plough to leave a space where the gates were going to be; because
of this, he says, 'the Romans regard all the walls as sacred except the gates'.[4]
While this was clearly an invented tradition, the ritual itself had at least
symbolic value. Several coins celebrating the foundation of Augusta Emerita
(modern Mérida, Spain) show a magistrate, head covered in his role as
priest, ploughing the furrow which defined the protective ritual boundary of
the city, while others show the walls with a prominent double-arched gate
[142] to symbolize the new city as a bastion of Rome, protecting the edge
of empire.[5] The image of the city wall with its arched gates and towers,
ashlar construction, and crenellations became a powerfully symbolic motif
in other media from mosaics to reliefs to manuscript illustrations and paintings, and was enough on its own to say 'city'. For a brief period in the late
Republic it was even used for a series of funerary enclosures, protecting the
dead in the way that the city walls protected the living.[6]

Fig. 140

Reconstructed quadrifons
arch at Lepcis Magna,
probably erected to
celebrate the visit by
Septimius Severus to his
hometown in 203 CE.

Fig. 141

Relief sculpture from the Basilica Aemilia, Rome, Augustan. Part of an architectural frieze showing ashlar city walls with an arched gateway flanked by towers being built under the watchful eye of a female divinity.

Fig. 142

Silver *denarius* of Augusta Emerita (modern Mérida, western Spain), reverse showing city walls and double gate, Augustan.

Ritually and defensively gates were weak points in the walls, but also what connected the city to the world outside. The arched main gates, their keystones sometimes carved as heads of deities as a way of ensuring divine protection [143], were often heavily fortified with projecting towers, making a strong architectural statement which went beyond any purely defensive function, increasing their visibility for travellers approaching the city. Such architectural elaboration beyond the functional had become part of the Roman city's self-presentation at least by the later second century BCE, as it had in the Hellenistic East.[7] Under the settled conditions of the early empire, where defence was no longer a consideration, the building of city walls gained even more potency as a symbolic statement of *urbanitas* and *dignitas*, and the civilized standing of a community. Walls were among the most expensive of all public building works, requiring substantial investment from the town council or from individuals, who might include the imperial family or their close associates. In the old Punic and Roman city of Carthago Nova in southern Spain, when the city walls were rebuilt as part of a widespread programme of urban renewal following the city being made a regional capital under Augustus, members of the local elite individually financed sections of walls, gates, and towers in a spirit of competitive cooperation.[8]

The entrances to the city could be enhanced by rebuilding or elaborating the gates, often appropriating the language of temple façades, arguably in

reference—conscious or otherwise—to their continued ritual significance. The external façade of the Porta Iovia (now the Porta dei Borsari) in Verona [144], where the main highway, the Via Postumia, entered the city, is indicative of a widespread phenomenon. In the middle of the first century CE it was given a facelift, with each arched opening framed by Corinthian columns and pediments, and the whole crowned by an elaborate two-storey scheme of arched windows within small aedicules in a surprisingly synco-pated rhythm. This was not just a western phenomenon; in the second cen-tury, a local high-class woman called Plancia Magna bestowed on the city of Perge in Turkey an elaborate addition to the severe Hellenistic gateway, in the form of a richly articulated internal court, embellished with columned niches and statues.[9]

In time the arched gate alone, extracted from its functional setting and used as a free-standing monument, could stand as symbol of the city

Fig. 144

City gate (the Porta Iovia, now Porta dei Borsari) at Verona (Italy), mid-first century CE aedicular façade with multiple 'baroque' elements in a syncopated rhythm. The main arches are framed by an engaged Corinthian order; the middle zone has aedicules with spirally fluted columns framing smaller aedicules with triangular and segmental pediments; and in the top level, free-standing columns once stood on acanthus-leaf brackets, forming two pairs with a single 'orphan' column in the centre.

boundary. In cases like that of Timgad **[8]**, a Trajanic colony in North Africa, arches stood over the main roads marking the boundaries of cities which had no walls; but they could also be set along the main roads in advance of the walls, as an announcement of the city to come, like the Arch of Augustus at Augusta Praetoria (Aosta). Arches could be even further removed from cities, marking regional boundaries like that at Berà 20 kilometres from the provincial capital of Tarraco in Spain. The ultimate city boundary is Hadrian's Wall at the edge of the empire **[5]**, decorated in imitation ashlar which was the standard motif for city walls and with monumental gates signalling Rome to the barbarian territory beyond.

Arches and Columns: Triumph and Commemoration

Free-standing arches not only stood as a shorthand for city walls but were also commemorative monuments in their own right. Their origins lie in the Roman triumph, and may have originated in temporary structures built over the triumphal route as part of its decoration by successful generals. By the start of the second century BCE monumental free-standing arches began to be erected as well, as a permanent reminder of military achievements. From Augustus onwards, when only emperors could celebrate a triumph, they became the gift of a grateful Senate, as is clear from the inscriptions on all three of the surviving triumphal arches in Rome, those dedicated to Titus, Septimius Severus [7], and Constantine. The standard design, of one single arched opening or a central opening flanked by a pair of smaller ones, framed by engaged or free-standing columns, on a high base and supporting a tall attic, is one of the most iconic motifs in the whole of Roman architecture, with many post-antique imitations, from Paris and London to Moscow and Pyongyang.

What is sometimes forgotten is that these arches were from the start intended as monumental statue bases, highly visible against the crowded monumental backdrop of Rome, and bearing statues or busts of the honorands together with inscriptions recording their achievements. The arch provided height and hence visibility for the inscription, set out in large letters on the attic, with the main portrait statue(s) above; the piers of some also supported relief sculpture with narrative and/or symbolic content. Pliny the Elder, writing in the middle of the first century CE, makes this clear: like statues of men placed on columns, he says, their purpose was 'to elevate them above all other mortals'.[10] There is evidence for a continuing tradition of erecting honorific columns in Rome from the later fifth and through the third and second centuries BCE, but not all celebrated military victories—the earliest was for help in supplying grain at a time of famine. The importance of these columnar monuments is clear from their appearance on coins issued by later officials, designed to borrow lustre from the activities of their ancestors.[11] The practice continued with Augustus and into the empire, culminating in the greatest of all these monuments, the Columns of Trajan [94] and Marcus Aurelius; only the scale, and the enhanced potential for sculptural decoration, makes them seem so extraordinary.

We are fortunate to have an inscription which lets us see the process of designing an honorific arch for Germanicus, the emperor Tiberius' nephew and designated successor, following his untimely death in Antioch.[12] First the Senate gathered suggestions, from which the emperor and Germanicus' family selected what they thought appropriate: a marble arch; a series of gilded reliefs showing the nations he had conquered; an inscription listing his public achievements as general and governor; and above the archway a statue of him in a triumphal chariot, flanked by statues of his family, including his parents, siblings, and children. It also called for arches to be erected in Syria where Germanicus had been governor, and on the Rhine where he had enjoyed his greatest military successes.

These arches to Germanicus were not strictly speaking triumphal arches, but rather honorific and commemorative. While true triumphal arches were tied to the route of the triumphal procession in Rome, the form was also used for victory arches outside of Rome. The Arch of Augustus at Aosta was one of the earliest, dedicated to Augustus by degree of the Senate for his victory over the mountain tribe of the Salassi. Pliny specifically identified this as a new phenomenon, which was reflected in the rapid increase of such monuments under the changed circumstances of the new regime.[13] Under the empire the free-standing arch as signifier of city and empire acquired the celebratory and honorific connotations of the triumphal arch. Many were erected in Rome and Italy over the first century CE, some the gift of the Senate and people of Rome like that dedicated to Trajan at Beneventum (modern Benevento), others gifts of provincial administrators or town councils, most frequently recording imperial visits or benefactions. Arches set on road bridges over rivers deep in the countryside commemorated a different kind of conquest, that over nature, while also serving as a reminder of the long reach of the city. While the single or triple one-way arch was the norm, retaining the impression of its origin as a gate in a city wall, the freeing of the monumental arch from its functional constraints also had a liberating effect on its design, resulting in two-way arches (*quadrifrons*) set over crossroads [140]. At the same time, some actual city gates were designed as commemorative arches, one of the earliest being the Arch of Augustus at Ariminum (modern Rimini), dedicated to Augustus by degree of the Senate for his completion of the Via Flaminia and his repair of many other famous roads of Italy.[14]

Honorific arches were also used to mark different kinds of boundaries.[15] As well as being connected with through movement at nodal points along thoroughfares, free-standing arches were erected at entrances to fora, starting with the Forum Romanum, but also at places like Pompeii, as part of the gradual monumentalization of the forum space. The arches defined the main accesses to the forum, blurring the distinction between city gate and commemorative monument. This is very clear where they are added to integrated forum structures. The arched entrance to the rebuilt commercial *agora* at Ephesus was the gift of two freedmen of Augustus, bringing a completely new and very Roman language to a traditional porticoed space, emphasized by the bilingual inscription which privileged the Latin of the new regime over the local Greek [145].[16] The developing Roman practice intersects with a long-standing Greek tradition of monumental entrances (*propylaea*) to sacred spaces. By the second century, the 'triumphal arch' entrance to the walled forum complex at Sufetula (Tunisia) [146], dedicated to the emperor Antoninus Pius and his heirs,[17] contributes to the ambivalence of the space: forum with triumphal entrance, or *temenos* for its three temples with sacred propylon? Like many other sanctuaries and fora under the empire, these are bounded spaces like miniature cities with their entrance gates.

The city effect is even more notable in complexes like the Temple of Peace in Rome [69, 93], the Temple of Deified Trajan in Italica [73], and the Library of Hadrian in Athens [14], where the projections of the recesses which articulated the internal porticoes were expressed on the external face of the boundary walls, appearing as if towers on a city wall.[18] Used in series, the arched gate with flanking columnar orders, which forms the fundamental motif for the façades of monumental theatres [91] and amphitheatres [1, 106], acts at one and the same time as boundary to, and triumphal entrances for, public spaces in which the body politic was put on display, as a microcosm of the city itself. That the keystones of the arched entrances to some amphitheatres were carved as heads of protective deities in the same way as the keystones to some city gates suggests that the connection is more than just coincidental.

Fig. 145

The triple-arched gateway to the commercial *agora* of Ephesus (right), dedicated by Mazeus and Mithridates, freedmen of Augustus; on the left, the early second century CE façade of the Library of Celsus.

Monumental Streets and Streets of Monuments

The chief urban context of these monumental arches and city-gate entrances was the main city thoroughfare, as part of what William MacDonald has labelled 'urban armatures'.[19] As the setting for ritual and celebratory processions in honour of the gods and the emperors, these thoroughfares became a key focus for urban embellishment, most notably in the 'colonnaded street', a broad avenue lined with porticoes, giving dignity and prestige to the city. Especially in the second and third centuries CE, these were a feature of the major cities of the empire, especially in Asia Minor and the Levant where the ready availability of marble and the overall wealth of the communities led to a lavish architecture sometimes called the 'marble style'. Palmyra provides an exceptional but not unique example [147]. Developed over two centuries and never completed, eventually both sides of the 2-kilometre main thoroughfare were flanked by colonnaded porticoes, their continuous rhythm interrupted by the arched gateway to the theatre and the projecting columnar façades of other public buildings. The projecting brackets two-thirds up the shafts of the Corinthian columns originally housed statues of the members of the local mercantile elite who funded the project piecemeal, turning the whole street into a commemorative monument. In the west the columns were more likely to be made of local stone, while in several places, including Ostia and Volubilis in Morocco, street porticoes took the form of a continuous arcade articulated with engaged columns or pilasters, using the 'Theatre-motif' usually associated with the façades of theatres and amphitheatres, some of the most prestigious of public buildings in the west.[20]

Fig. 146

The 'triumphal arch' entrance to the walled forum, Sufetula (modern Sbeitla, Tunisia), mid-second century CE. The entrance is axially aligned with the central of its three temples.

The elaboration of major streets was not a new Roman concept, but a natural development of the importance of processional ways in Mediterranean civic life, and of their function as reminders of the glorious past, written in terms of individuals and events. Such routes had already begun to attract all kinds of small shrines and commemorative monuments by the Hellenistic period, a practice which was multiplied under Rome with ever-increasing elaboration. Ephesus provides a useful example.[21] The processional way from

Fig. 147

Colonnaded street at Palmyra, second to third century CE, drawing by G.B. Borra (1713–86). View of central section looking towards the triangular arch, with arched entrance to the theatre on the right, the projecting columnar porch of the Baths of Diocletian on the left, and the wedge-shaped arch over the street in the background.

the venerable Temple of Artemis, one of the Seven Wonders of the ancient world, wound its way into the city through the Magnesian Gate and down to the theatre by the harbour through a narrow valley, the Embolos, where it was treated as a colonnaded street [148]. As well as the major public buildings, by the middle of the second century CE the route within the city hosted: a Hellenistic heröon celebrating the legendary founder Androkles; the honorific tomb monument of Arsinoë IV (Cleopatra's half-sister) assassinated in 41 BCE;[22] a monument to C. Memmius, grandson of Sulla who had brought Ephesus back into Roman control; the monument of Sextilius Pollio, a major Ephesian benefactor responsible for the *stoa basilica* and other large projects; the early second century CE tomb and library of Iulius Celsus Polemaeanus, once governor of Asia; a monumental gate in honour of Hadrian;[23] the so-called 'Temple of Hadrian', a shrine to an unknown deity dedicated by Quinctilius Varius Varens, a major benefactor also responsible for the baths behind the shrine;[24] several other altars and shrines; and eleven fountains. That we know the names and designations of so many of these monuments is due to the rich collections of inscriptions which were part of their design and decoration, many identifying the statuary, which included the benefactors, the imperial family, the hero founder, and deities associated with the city. These are the monumental billboards of the ancient city, advertising the largesse of the benefactors and honouring the recipients, both of whose names appear in the largest letters and in the most prominent places following a very Roman fashion, even where the text is in Greek. The monumental tombs lining the roads leading into the city functioned in a similar manner and used a similar language [cf. 137, 138], so that often the

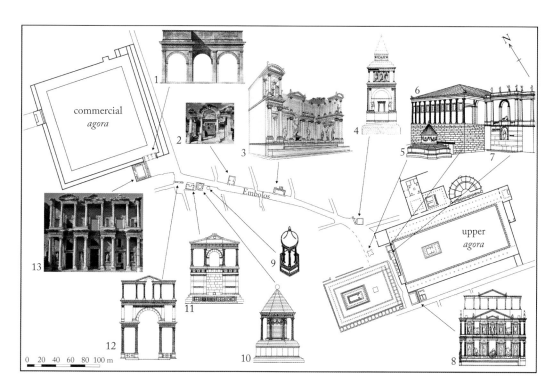

distinction between heröon, honorific monument, and tomb would be impossible to make on purely architectural grounds.

The elaborate fountains, often called *nymphaea*, had a long history as prestige markers for the city, but the Hellenistic examples were relatively simple affairs compared to the lavish displays of the Roman period.[25] The two most spectacular *nymphaea* at Ephesus, one dedicated by Calvisius Ruso, governor of Asia, to the emperor Domitian [148: 7], the other to the emperor Trajan by Claudius Aristion, a major Ephesian benefactor and high priest of the imperial cult [148: 3], were thoroughly urban monuments, stage sets where water played the starring role against a backdrop of columns and statuary, although architecturally they belong to two different traditions.[26] The earlier, that of Ruso, was thoroughly Roman in design, a monumental semi-circular domed niche, framed by Corinthian pilasters and pediment, giving almost the effect of an honorific arch or an aedicular statue niche. That of Ariston, only a couple of decades later, belonged to the same tradition as the façade of the near contemporary Library of Celsus [148: 13], the universal language of the imperial *scaenae frons*. The interchangeability of this type of decoration is shown nowhere better than here; around the fourth century CE, when the actual library had gone out of use, the hall was filled with rubble and the façade became the backdrop to a new monumental fountain built in front of it. The new benefactor added a verse inscription about his financing of the project to the old façade, appropriating the earlier act of euergetism for his own prestige.

The monuments of Ruso and Aristion, however, were not simply new fountain houses but celebrated the addition of new aqueducts to the city's existing water supply. Aqueducts were probably the most expensive of all urban benefactions, often gifts of the emperors, more rarely by private benefactors. Only the wealthiest could afford them, like the father of Herodes Atticus who added sixteen times the minimum assets of a senator to the twelve that Hadrian had donated for an aqueduct at Alexandria Troas.[27] For much of their length aqueducts were largely invisible, except where they crossed rivers and valleys on arched substructures [6]. Where they crossed major roads, the arcades might carry monumental inscriptions, as where the Aqua Claudia and Anio Novus crossed the Via Praenestina and the Via Labicana at the Porta Maggiore just outside Rome [149]. The elaborated aqueduct arches here act both as triumphal arch, celebrating the conquest of nature, and a symbol of the city to come, in the same way that free-standing arches marked urban territories.

The Language of *Magnificentia*

In very few of these commemorative monuments, urban or funerary, did the display elements have any practical or structural function. The most lavish, designed as two- or three-storey screens fronting a wall and framing statue displays, borrowed the language of the *scaenae frons* to great scenographic effect.[28] In these spectacular displays, architects experimented with colour, variety, and movement freed from any consideration of structural necessities. Pairs of columns or pilasters, often topped by pediments to form aedicules, were used to frame important entranceways and highlight sculpture niches [144], sometimes with giant orders rising to the height of two superimposed

Fig. 149

Rome, Porta Maggiore, monumentalized arches of the Aqua Claudia and Anio Novus aqueducts over the Via Praenestina and the Via Labicana, completed 52 CE. It uses unfinished blocks for the columns and heavily rusticated masonry in travertine, suggestive of considerable antiquity and typical of Claudian construction.

smaller orders to emphasize central features **[104]**. The use of *ressauts* to provide stability meant that sections of entablature supporting pediments no longer had to respect the arrangement below, creating syncopated rhythms which often left single columns orphaned at the ends **[145; 148: 8, 13]**. The pediments themselves could be fully triangular, or broken, or segmental or volute, often in alternating patterns, again without any concern for structural rationale **[145; 148: 3, 13]**; in some cases the pediment was so reduced in size it did little more than suggest the concept of 'pediment' **[140]**. In other types of buildings entablatures too were no longer necessarily flat but could be arcuated, or mixed, as in the so-called 'Syrian' pediment with an arch replacing the central lintel **[148: 2]**. All of these features have been called 'baroque',[29] given the obvious similarities with the way post-Renaissance architects played with the orders in very different contexts. Thanks to Judith McKenzie's careful re-examination of the tombs of Petra, which has redated tomb façades like 'El-Khasneh' **[150]** from the second century CE back to the first century BCE, the origin of the style is now recognized as Hellenistic Alexandria, and has been related to the style of wall painting typical of Rome and Italy in the first century BCE **[151]**.[30] Often commemorative monuments stacked up a number of elements to gain enhanced visibility **[148: 4]**, in a manner perhaps derived from the Mausoleum of Halicarnassus, one of the Seven Wonders of the ancient world, an arrangement also much used in funerary architecture **[137, 138]**.

Even within the columnar orders themselves, the possibilities for exercising choice and conveying a particular message were almost endless. There were several forms of column base, the mouldings of which could be left

Fig. 150

'El-Khasneh', monumental tomb façade, Petra (Jordan), c. first century BCE. As the façade is carved from solid rock, there were no structural constraints, as indicated by the upper storey where the central section of the pediment has been removed to insert an unrelated tholos.

plain or elaborately ornamented, and the bases could sit on independent pedestals, which could be decorated with relief sculpture [7]. Column shafts could be in a variety of white and coloured imported marbles or local stones [104], smooth and polished, normal for the hard granites and porphyries but common in all other stones, or fluted [140]. There were several varieties of fluting, straight and of equal width or alternating wide and narrow, sometimes with the lower third filled in, or flutes could be carved in a spiral [144]. The whole shaft could spiral—the so-called 'barley-sugar' columns—and these, the ordinary unfluted shafts, and the pilasters which reflected them on the walls behind could be richly carved with vegetal scrolls often peopled with small birds, animals, insects, and *erotes* (cupids). More variety could be introduced by the choice of capitals, with Corinthian predominating, but including other variations such as the Composite, which combined Ionic and Corinthian, or figured capitals incorporating divinities, animals, or

symbolic elements as the outer volutes [67] or in place of the central element [152]. A rare survival in *opus sectile* [153] reminds us of the colour which
once enlivened architectural ornament and surface treatments, a key element in Roman architectural aesthetics from the time of the early temples but
most recognizable in painted representations of architecture, especially
from the late second to first centuries BCE [151].

All this came at a price. The only source we have for the relative cost of
marble comes from the late third-century Prices Edict of the emperor
Diocletian. While there is considerable controversy over what the unit of
measurement was and whether it refers to new or second-hand material,
nevertheless it is clear that some of the highly prized coloured marbles and
porphyries were priced at five to six times as much as some of the plain
white marbles.[31] The expensive ones all came from quarries which were in
imperial possession, while one of them—the marble from Skyros—is a
good imitation of the imperial Phrygian but is listed at only a fifth of the
price. There were local substitutes for several of the other imperial marbles,
for example from the Pyrenees, but not all of these quarries could provide
especially the larger column shafts or very large numbers of them. The variety
shown in some monuments, especially for the *scaenae frons*, is arguably as
much to do with sourcing material at relatively short notice as an interest in
variety per se; in some cases, using a single type of high-quality decorative
stone might have been more impressive than a mix-and-match approach.

Common to all the monuments which were erected to adorn the city
and commemorate its inhabitants was a shared architectural language
comprising a few easily recognizable motifs, based on the columnar orders

Fig. 152

Baths of Caracalla, Rome,
figured Composite capital,
c. 211–217 CE.

Fig. 153

Corinthianizing *intarsia*
pilaster capital from the
Horti Lamiani (Rome). The
background is formed from
a slab of red marble from
Cape Taenaros (southern
Greece), with inlays of
yellow Numidian marble,
white palombino, and green
limestone.

and/or the arch: pediment, aedicule, and columnar display; gateway, triumphal arch, and 'Theatre-motif'; and tower. While each motif had its
origin in the fundamental architectural forms of temple, *scaenae frons*, and
city wall, the choice of motif (or motifs) for any particular monument
appears to have been largely personal rather than necessarily related to any
specific function or ideological message. Thus the highly visible monument

Fig. 154

The trophy of the Alps at La
Turbie (France), erected
c. 6 BCE to celebrate and
record Augustus' victory
over forty-five Alpine tribes.

at La Turbie [154] celebrating Augustus' victory over the tribes of the
Maritime Alps takes the form of a tomb-as tower arguably based on
the Mausoleum of Halicarnassus, but functions as a triumphal arch and
boundary marker at the edge of the city-empire.[32] Scale, location, and
inscribed text carried the overt political message; form and ornament had
more elusive connotations.

Roman Architecture and Society

In a well-known section of *On architecture*, Vitruvius gives a definition of the parts of architecture.[33] He divides building into public and private, and public further into three functional categories: defence, including walls, towers, and gates; religion, covering shrines and temples to the gods; and public convenience, including fora, porticoes, baths, and theatres. All these, he says, should have *firmitas* (strength), *utilitas* (usefulness), and *venustas* (beauty). Although this was written at the start of the Augustan age, one of the defining moments of Roman architecture, it could in fact have been written at almost any time before or after, as we have seen. What Vitruvius gives us, then, is a sense of the common concepts which explain the functional and experiential similarities within and between building types and monuments and enable us to identify a Roman architecture, or better still a family of Roman architectures. These are also the aspects which would have been recognizable and familiar to many of the varied inhabitants of the far-flung empire. Based largely on function, they did not change fundamentally over time, reflecting the conservative aspect of Roman architecture which provided a sense of familiarity and belonging to the participants in this urban culture.

Vitruvius is less helpful with the other side of the story, that is the infinite variety which is equally the hallmark of Roman architecture. If the common values reflect the collective sensibilities of the Roman peoples, the variety mainly marks the impact of individual choices, driven by the inherently competitive nature of Roman politics and society, and by the histories and aesthetics of local communities. By using a basic repertoire of forms—wall, gate, arch, column, and pediment—buildings and monuments remained familiar and recognizable, but the varied ways those forms were deployed was what made them individually memorable.

Over the long years of Rome and its empire things did change, but not necessarily in an evolutionary or incremental way. There were important periods of invention and innovation, always at times of rapid societal change: the sixth century BCE with the introduction of stone construction; the second century BCE when many of the defining building types crystallized; and the Augustan period, when the change in regime brought new wealth and a new ideology to fuel a period of intense building to reflect it. Different parts of the Roman empire had different histories, and were absorbed into the state at different times in different circumstances, creating different patterns of urbanization and hence of architectural forms. Some reflected changing fashions in the heart of the empire, others more local traditions and conditions, while frequently there was an inventive interplay between the two, something particularly apparent in the fertile years of the first century CE. Rich cities posed a particular problem; once a city had its full panoply of public buildings, major benefactors looking to erect permanent monuments to their largesse had to find other ways to enhance their cities. While this might result in a new set of baths—the only type of public building where multiples were common—most often it took the form of pure embellishment, using the most prestigious of materials and forms, the columnar orders in marble.

Over the course of the first to third centuries CE, communities throughout the empire, but particularly in the areas around the Mediterranean which had had a long history of urbanism, were faced with the need not just to construct but also maintain their public buildings. Even in the richest cities, natural disasters, especially earthquakes, fires, and the occasional volcanic eruption, could devastate the urban fabric, requiring intervention at the highest level including the emperor, as Titus did for Naples after the eruption of Vesuvius and Marcus Aurelius for Smyrna in Asia Minor following a catastrophic earthquake. Poorer towns might struggle to maintain key buildings ('collapsed from old age' is a common motif in building inscriptions),[34] or find funds from the town coffers to replace them, so that many building and rebuilding projects relied on individual benefactors whose wealth and influence went beyond the purely local. Such acts were essential to the well-being of the community, as the success, if not the very existence, of the city was tied closely to the health of its urban fabric.[35] The Republican laws against the unnecessary demolition of buildings strengthened over the course of the empire, with Antoninus Pius in the mid-second century ordering that those who wanted to spend money on building should undertake the restoration of old buildings rather than the construction of new ones; how often 'restoration' meant a completely new build is a moot point. Even among the buildings that Augustus proudly listed in his *Res Gestae*, the account of his achievements which was inscribed in bronze in front of his Mausoleum, many were not in fact new creations but reconstructions or restorations, in new materials and the new fashions of the day. The efforts made to maintain at least an outward appearance of monumentality in the visual environment of the city in the late empire, despite the changed and difficult conditions of the times, reflect more than anything the continuing importance of architecture in Roman society.

Notes

Introduction

1. Quintilian, *Institutio oratoria* 11.6.18–21.
2. Dionysius of Halicarnassus, *Antiquites Romanae* 3.67.5.
3. In this book I have deliberately avoided the term 'Romanization' in any of its forms as being too tied up with modern debates, and meaning too many different things to different scholars, to be useful without the kind of long discussion that has no place in this study.

Chapter 1

1. Ammianus Marcellinus 16.10.14.
2. Aelius Aristides, *Orations*, 26.
3. P. Bidwell, 'The exterior decoration of Roman buildings in Britain', in P. Johnson and I. Haynes (eds.) *Architecture in Roman Britain* (York, 1996), 19–29.
4. Jerome, *Commentary on Ezekiel*, preface, bk 3.
5. For the development of Roman Italy and the whole question of the transformation of Roman culture, see A. Wallace-Hadrill, *Rome's Cultural Revolution* (Cambridge, 2008).
6. Tacitus, *Germania*, 16.
7. Tacitus, *Agricola*, 21.
8. A. Wilson, 'Neo-Punic and Latin inscriptions in Roman North Africa: function and display', in A. Mullen and P. James (eds.) *Multilingualism in the Graeco-Roman Worlds* (Cambridge, 2012), 265–316.
9. E.g. Cato the Elder, as presented by Livy 34.1–8.
10. For the Library of Hadrian, see M.C. Monaco et al., 'Significato e funzioni della cosidetta biblioteca di Adriano ad Atene', in E. Calandro and B. Adembri (eds.) *Adriano e la Grecia* (Milan, 2014), 49–60.

Chapter 2

1. For the attribution of the Pantheon to Trajan rather than Hadrian, see L. Hetland, 'New perspectives on the dating of the Pantheon', in T.A. Marder and M. Wilson Jones, *The Pantheon: From Antiquity to the Present* (Cambridge, 2015), 79–98.
2. Vitruvius 1.3.
3. For the history of attitudes to and scholarship on Vitruvius, see I.D. Rowland, 'From Vitruvian scholarship to Vitruvian practice', *MAAR*, 50 (2005), 15–40.
4. Vitruvius 1.preface.3.
5. Vitruvius 7.preface.10–14; 8.3.26–7; 9.8.1–2; 10.13.3–8.
6. Cf. A. Wallace-Hadrill, *Rome's Cultural Revolution* (Cambridge, 2008), chapter 3.
7. Vitruvius 6.preface.6.
8. Vitruvius 5.preface.2–3.
9. Sidonius Apollonaris, *Epistulae* 4.3.5, 8.6.10.
10. See, for example, L.T. Pearcy Jr, 'Horace's architectural imagery', *Latomus*, 36 (1977), 772–81.
11. See M. Wilson Jones, *Principles of Roman Architecture* (New Haven, CT, 2000), chapter 2.
12. Vitruvius 1.1.3.
13. Cicero, *Epistulae ad Atticum* 2.3.2.
14. *Codex Theodosianus* 13.4.1.
15. Vitruvius 6.preface.6.
16. Cicero, *de officinis* 1.151.
17. J. Anderson Jr, *Roman Architecture and Society* (Baltimore, MD, 1997), chapter 1.
18. See the story in Vitruvius 2.preface.
19. See Velleius Paterculus 1.11.2–5 and Vitruvius 3.2.5.
20. E. Rawson, 'Architecture and sculpture: the activities of the Cossutii', *PBSR*, 43 (1975), 36–47.
21. *CIL* I.².2961, and see Anderson, *Roman Architecture*, 26–34.
22. See Anderson, *Roman Architecture*, 52–64, and W.L. MacDonald, *The Architecture of the Roman Empire*, *1. An Introductory Study* (New Haven, CT, 1982), 122–37 for a discussion of the major practitioners.
23. Pliny the Younger, *Epistulae* 10.40.
24. See M. Donderer, *Die Architekten der späten römischen Republik und der Kaiserzeit. Epigraphische Zeugnisse* (Erlangen, 1996).

25. T.F.C. Blagg, 'An examination of the connexions between military and civilian architecture in Roman Britain', in T.F.C. Blagg and A. King (eds.) *Military and Civilian in Roman Britain: Cultural Relationships in a Frontier Province* (Oxford, 1984), 249–63.

26. Anderson, *Roman Architecture*, 44–7.

27. Vitruvius 6.8–9.

28. Wilson Jones, *Principles*, 40–5. See also E. Thomas, 'On the sublime', in J. Elsner and M. Meyer, *Art and Rhetoric in Roman Culture* (Cambridge, 2014), 37–88.

29. See Vitruvius 3.1.1–4, 9; 5.preface.2, 10.preface.12–4.

30. Vitruvius 6.2.1.

31. M. Wilson Jones, 'Designing the Roman Corinthian order', *JRA*, 2 (1989), 35–69.

32. Cicero, *de officinis* 1.139.

33. Lucian, *Hippias, or the bath*. See E. Thomas, *Monumentality and the Roman Empire: Architecture in the Antonine Age* (Oxford, 2007), 221–9.

34. M. Wilson Jones, 'Designing amphitheatres', *RM*, 100 (1993), 391–442.

35. Vitruvius 6.3.1–8.

36. See J. DeLaine, 'The imperial thermae', in A. Claridge and C. Holleran (eds.) *A Companion to the City of Rome* (Chichester, 2017), 325–42.

37. For the Baths of Caracalla, see J. DeLaine, *The Baths of Caracalla: A Study in the Design, Construction and Economics of Large-Scale Building Projects in Imperial Rome* (Portsmouth, RI, 1997), chapter 2.

38. L. C. Lancaster, *Concrete Vaulted Construction in Imperial Rome* (Cambridge, 2005), 60–5, 116–18, 124.

39. Vitruvius 10.11.2.

40. Vitruvius 6.3.7.

41. Pliny, *Epistulae*, 9.39, 3–6, and cf. C. Siwicki, *Architectural Restoration and Heritage in Imperial Rome* (Oxford, 2019), 50–2.

42. E.g. Cicero *Epistulae ad Quintum Fratrem* 3.1, *Epistulae ad Atticum* 2.3.

43. Aulus Gellius, *Noctes Atticae* 19.10.2–3.

44. Vitruvius 6.8.10.

45. Cicero *Epistulae ad Quintum Fratrem* 2.6(5)3.

46. Literary references to architect's plans and models: Vitruvius 1.2.2; Cicero *Epistulae ad Quintum Fratrem*, 2.2.1 and 2.6(5).3, *Epistulae ad Atticum* 2.3.2 and 12.18.1; Plutarch, *Moralia* 498E.3, *Pompeius* 42.4; Aulus Gellius, *Noctes Atticae*, 19.10, 2–4.

47. For examples, see H. von Hesberg, 'Römische Grundrißpläne auf Marmor', in *Bauplanung und Bautheorie der Antike* (Berlin, 1984), 120–33, and L. Haselberger, 'Architectural likenesses: models and plans of architecture in classical antiquity', *JRA*, 10 (1997), 77–94.

48. Granius Licinianus, 28.10.

49. For the Marble Plan of Rome, see the website of the Stanford project (https://formaurbis.stanford.edu).

50. Varro, *de re rustica*. 3.5.8–17. For the design of the Herodium, see D.M. Jacobson, 'The design of the fortress of Herodium', *Zeitschrift des deutschen Palästina Vereins*, 100 (1984), 127–36, and for recent plans and views, R. Porat, R. Chachy, and Y. Kalman, eds., *Herod's Tomb Precinct. Herodium: Final Reports of the 1972–2010 Excavations Directed by Ehud Netzer, Vol. 1* (Jerusalem, 2015), xi, xiv, xv.

51. See B. Adembri, S. Di Tondo, and F. Fantini, 'Architecture with concave and convex rhythms and its decoration in Hadrian age: the Maritime Theatre and the southern pavilion of Piazza d'Oro in Hadrian's Villa', in P. Pensabene and E. Gasparini (eds.) *Proceedings of the Tenth International Conference Interdisciplinary Studies on Ancient Stone, ASMOSIA, 10* (Rome, 2015), 3–12, W.L. MacDonald and B. Boyle, 'The small baths at Hadrian's villa', *JSAH*, 39 (1980), 5–27 and B. Marzuoli and F. Mollo, 'Le Piccole Terme di Villa Adriana tra innovazione e funzionalità', in R. Hidalgo, G. E. Cinque, A. Pizzo and A. Viscogliosi (eds.) *Adventus Hadriani. Investigaciones sobre Arquitectura Adrianea* (Rome, 2020), 525–49.

Chapter 3

1. Vitruvius 2.preface.5.

2. Vitruvius 2.4.1.

3. Vitruvius 1.2.9.

4. Vitruvius 2.1.1–3.

5. Cf. Seneca, *Epistulae* 90.7–18.

6. Vitruvius 2.1.5–8.

7. Livy 1.33.6–7; Dionysius of Halicarnassus 3.45.2.

8. For the religious aspect to these rebuildings, see C. Siwicki, *Architectural Restoration and Heritage in Imperial Rome* (Oxford, 2019), chapter 4.

9. See, for example, T. Cornell, *The Beginnings of Rome: Italy and Rome from the Bronze Age to the Punic Wars (c. 1000–264 BC)* (London, 1995), chapter 8.

10. For the use of stone in the Archaic period of Rome, see G. Cifani, *Architettura romana arcaica. Edilizia e societá tra Monarchia e*

Repubblica (Rome, 2008), and for a summary, J.N. Hopkins, *The Genesis of Roman Architecture* (New Haven , CT, 2016), 92–7.

11. M. Jackson and F. Marra, 'Roman stone masonry: volcanic foundations of the ancient city', *AJA*, 110 (2006), 403–36.

12. Strabo, *Geography* 5.3.11.

13. Vitruvius 2.4.2.

14. M.F. Jackson, F. Marra, D. Deocampo, et al., 'Geological observations of excavated sand (*harenae fossiciae*) used as fine aggregate in Roman pozzolanic mortars', *JRA*, 20 (2007), 25–53.

15. M. Mogetta, 'A new date for concrete in Rome', *JRS*, 105 (2015), 1–40.

16. Vitruvius 2.8.1.

17. Vitruvius 2.8.1.

18. For a Roman foot of 29.5 centimetres, these are 19.7, 44.3, and 59 centimetres, and c. 3.5–3.7 centimetres thick.

19. On the origin and functionality of these sizes, see E. Bukowiecki, 'La taille des briques de parement dans l'opus testaceum à Rome', in S. Camporeale, H. Dessales, and A. Pizzo (eds.) *Arqueología de la construcción II: los procesos constructivos en el mundo romano: Italia y provincias orientales* (Madrid, 2010), 143–51.

20. For the *opus* sectile, see G. Becatti, 'Edificio con opus sectile fuori Porta Marina', *Scavi di Ostia* 6 (Rome, 1969).

21. Vitruvius 3.3.4–5.

22. As noted by A. Mau, *Pompeii, Its Life and Art* (translated F.W. Kelsey, London, 1902), 50–1.

23. R.B. Ulrich, *Roman Woodworking* (New Haven, CT, 2007), 138–482.

24. J.M. Turfa and A.G. Steinmayer Jr, 'The comparative structure of Greek and Etruscan monumental buildings', *PBSR*, 64 (1996), 1–40.

25. Cassius Dio 55.8; Pliny, *Naturalis Historiae* 16.76.201, 36.24.102.

26. The function, precise identification, and exact date of this building are the subject of debate; see L. Cozza and P. L. Tucci, 'Navalia', *ArchCl*, 57 (2006), 175–201 and F.P. Arata and E. Felici, 'Porticus Aemilia, navalia o horrea? Ancora sui Frammenti 23 e 24 b-d della Forma Urbis', *ArchCl*, 62 (2011), 127–53.

27. Polybius 6.13.3.

28. S.G. Bernard, 'Pentelic marble in architecture at Rome and the Republican marble trade', *JRA*, 23 (2010), 35–54.

29. L.C. Lancaster, *Concrete Vaulted Construction in Imperial Rome: Innovations in Context* (Cambridge, 2005), 134–8.

30. Vitruvius 5.10.5.

31. See the analysis in Lancaster, *Concrete Vaulted Construction*, 142 and 156–8.

32. J. DeLaine, 'Bricks and mortar: exploring the economics of building techniques at Rome and Ostia', in D.J. Mattingly and J. Salmon (eds.) *Economies beyond Agriculture in the Classical World* (London, 2000), 230–68.

33. See R. Volpe, 'Un antico giornale di cantiere delle terme di Traiano', *RM*, 109 (2002), 377–94, and R. Volpe and F.M. Rossi, 'Nuovi dati sull'esedra sud-ovest delle Terme di Traiano sul Colle Oppio. Percorsi, iscrizioni dipinte e tempi di costruzione', in S. Camporeale, H. Dessales, and A. Pizzo, *Arqueología de la construcción III. Los procesos constructivos en el mundo romano: la economía de las obras* (Madrid, 2012), 69–81.

34. F. Coarelli, 'Public building in Rome between the Second Punic War and Sulla', *PBSR*, 45 (1977), 1–23; M. Torelli, 'Innovations in Roman construction techniques between the 1st century BC and the 1st century AD', in M. Torelli, *Studies in the Romanization of Italy* (Edmonton, 1995), 212–45.

35. M. Serlorenzi, 'La costruzione di un complesso horreario a Testaccio. Primi indizi per delineare l'organizzazione del cantiere edilizio', in *Arqueología de la construcción II*, 105–26.

36. Lancaster, *Concrete Vaulted Construction*, 68–85.

37. For an overview, see J. DeLaine, 'The production, supply and distribution of brick', in E. Bukowiecki, R. Volpe, and U. Wulf-Rheidt, *Il laterizo nei cantieri imperiali. Roma e il Mediterraneo, Archeologia dell'Architettura*, 20 (2016), 226–30, and the rest of the volume for case studies.

38. J.B. Ward-Perkins, *Roman Imperial Architecture* (Harmondsworth, 1981), 97–101; cf. W.L. MacDonald, *The Archaeology of the Roman Empire I: Introduction* (New Haven, CT, 1982), 41.

39. See Ulrich, *Roman Woodworking*, 150–7 for a discussion of the Palatine halls.

40. D. and M. Heinzelmann, 'The bronze truss of the portico of the Pantheon in Rome', in J. DeLaine, S. Camporeale, and A. Pizzo (eds.) *Arqueología de la construcción V. Man-made materials, engineering and infrastructure* (Madrid, 2016), 59–73.

41. For one interpretation of Agrippa's Pantheon, see E. La Rocca, 'Agrippa's Pantheon and its origin', in T.A. Marder and M. Wilson Jones (eds.) *The Pantheon from Antiquity to the Present* (Cambridge, 2015), 49–78.

42. The classic study is H. Lavagne, *Operosa antra: Recherches sur la grotte à Rome de Sylla a Hadrien* (Rome, 1988), and see F.B. Sear, *Roman Wall and Vault Mosaics* (Heidelberg, 1977) for the decoration.

43. For Sperlonga and its sculptures, see A.F. Stewart, 'To entertain an emperor: Sperlonga, Laokoon and Tiberius at the dinner-table', *JRS* 67 (1977), 76–90.

44. J. DeLaine, *The Baths of Caracalla: A Study in the Design, Construction, and Economics of Large-Scale Building Projects in Imperial Rome* (Portsmouth, RI, 1997), 69–70.

45. Mosaic—Sear, *Mosaics*, 92; silk—D. Hemsoll, 'Reconstructing the Octagonal Dining Room of Nero's Golden House', *Architectural History*, 32 (1989), 1–17.

46. Athenaeus, *Deipnosophistae* 5.196, and E. Calandra, *The Ephemeral and the Eternal: The Pavilion of Ptolemy Philadelphos in the Court of Alexandria* (Athens, 2011) for a reconstruction.

47. See Lancaster, *Concrete vaulted Construction*, chapter 6, and cf. C.M. Amici, *Architettura romana dal cantiere all'architetto: soluzioni concrete per idee progettuali* (Rome, 2016), chapter 3.

48. See U. Quatember, 'Natural resources and the formation of a regional architectural identity in Roman Asia', in T. Ismaelli and G. Scardozzi (eds.) *Ancient Quarries and Building Sites in Asia Minor* (Bari, 2016), 725–90.

49. Pliny, *Naturalis historia* 36.5.46.

50. S. Camporeale, 'Merging technologies in North African ancient architecture: *opus quadratum* and *opus africanum* from the Phoenicians to the Romans', in N. Mugnai, J. Nikolaus, and N. Ray, *De Africa Romaque: Merging Cultures across North Africa* (London, 2016), 57–71.

51. Vitruvius 2.1.4–6.

52. S. Camporale, 'Materiali e tecniche delle costruzioni', in A. Akerraz and E. Papi (eds.) *Sidi Ali Ben Ahmed. Thamusida, 1. I contesti* (Rome, 2008), 62–178.

53. On early uses and forms of brick, see the collected studies in J. Bonetto, E. Bukowiecki, and R. Volpe, *Alle origini del laterizio romano. Nascita e diffusione del mattone cotto nel Mediterraneo tra IV e I secolo* (Rome, 2019).

54. M. Vitti and P. Vitti, 'Trasmissione ed adattamento delle techniche costruttive romane in Peloponneso. Il caso di Trezene', in. A.D. Rizakis and C.E. Lepenioti (eds.) *Roman Peloponnese, 3. Society, Economy and Culture under the Roman Empire: Continuity and Innovation* (Athens, 2010), 267–89.

55. M. Spanu, M. 'Tecniche costruttive nella Cilicia di età imperial. Lineamenti generali', in *Arqueología de la construcción II*, 397–409.

56. See R. Tomber, 'Evidence for long-distance commerce: imported bricks and tiles at Carthage', *Rei Cretariae Romanae Fautores*, 25/26 (1987), 161–74, and B. Russell, 'Imported building materials in North Africa: brick, stone and the role of return cargoes', in Mugnai, Nikolaus, and Ray, *De Africa Romaque*, 171–81.

57. See M. Medri, 'La diffusione dell'opera reticolata: considerazioni a partire dal caso di Olimpia', in J.-Y. Marc and J.-C. Moretti, *Constructions publiques et programmes édilitaires en Grèce entre le IIe siècle av. J.-C. et le Ier siècle ap. J.-C.* (Athens and Paris, 2001), 15–40, and M. Spanu, 'L'opus reticulatum e mixtum nelle province asiatiche', in M. Khanoussi, P. Ruggeri, and C. Vismara, *L'Africa romana XI* (Ozieri, 1996), 923–39.

58. C. Brandon, R.L. Hohlfelder, M.D. Jackson, and J.P. Oleson, *Building for Eternity: The History and Technology of Roman Concrete Engineering in the Sea* (Oxford, 2014), 73–81.

59. L. C. Lancaster, *Innovative Vaulting in the Architecture of the Roman Empire* (Cambridge, 2015), especially chapters 3 and 4.

60. Lancaster, *Innovative Vaulting*, chapter 5, with earlier bibliography.

61. Lancaster, *Innovative Vaulting*, chapters 6 and 7, and for Argos, P. Vitti, *Building Roman Greece: Innovation in Vaulted Construction in the Peloponnese* (Rome, 2016), 84–109.

62. See P. Warry, 'Legionary tile production in Britain', *Britannia*, 41 (2010), 127–47 for Britain and Camporeale, 'Materiali', for Mauritania Tingitana, and for Cilicia see Spanu, 'Tecniche costruttive'.

63. S. Bernard, *Building Mid-Republican Rome* (Oxford, 2018), 153–7.

64. J. Anderson, Jr, *Roman Architecture and Society* (Baltimore, MD, 1997), 68–107; J. DeLaine, 'The construction industry', in C. Holleran and A. Claridge (eds.) *A Companion to the City of Rome* (New York, 2018), 473–90.

65. Strabo 5.3.7–8.

66. *CIL* I.698 = *ILS* 5317.

67. M. Steinby, 'L'edilizia come industria pubblica e privata', in K. de Fine Licht (ed.) *Città e architettura nella Roma imperiale* (Odense, 1983), 219–21.

68. *CIL* VI 9034.

69. P. Ducret, 'The restoration of the columns of the *templum* Castoris during Verres' praetorship: the *machina* and the organisation of the building site', *Arqueología de la construcción*, 5 (2016), 201–6.

70. Horace, *Letters*, 2.2.72–3.

71. F. Sinn and K.S. Freyberger, *Die Grabdenkmaeler II: Die Ausstattung des Hateriergraben* (Mainz 1996) and J. Trimble, 'Figure and ornament, death and transformation in the Tomb of the Haterii', in N. Dietrich and M. Squire (eds), *Ornament and Figure in Greco-Roman Art: Rethinking Visual Ontologies in Classical Antiquity* (Berlin 2018), 327–52.

72. Livy 1.43; Dionysius of Halicarnassus 7.59.

73. S. Panciera, '*Fasti fabrum tignariorum urbis Romae*', *ZPE*, 43 (1981), 271–80.

74. *CIL* VI 9405.

75. Plutarch, *Crassus*, 2.4.

76. *CIL* VI 9412-15.

77. *Digest* 17.1.26.8.

78. *Digest* 45.1.137.3.

79. J. DeLaine, 'The Pantheon builders—a preliminary estimate of manpower for construction', in Marder and Wilson Jones, *Pantheon*, 160–92; DeLaine, *Baths of Caracalla*, 191–3.

80. L.C. Lancaster, 'Building Trajan's markets', *AJA*, 102 (1998), 283–308 and 'Building Trajan's markets, 2. The construction process', *AJA*, 104 (2000), 755–85.

81. J. Magness et al., 'The Huqoq Excavation Project: 2014–2017 Interim Report', *Bulletin of the American Schools of Oriental Research*, 380 (2018), 61–131.

82. Varro, *On Agriculture* 1.2.22–3.

83. L. Camilli and F. Taglietti, 'Osservazioni sulla produzione laterizia della tarda età repubblicana e della prima età imperiale', in *Epigrafia della produzione e della distribuzione* (Rome, 1994), 307–33.

84. Steinby, 'L'edilizia', 220–1.

85. E. Lo Cascio, 'La concentrazione delle figlinae nella proprietà imperiale (II–IV secolo)', in C. Bruun and F. Chausson (eds.) *Interpretare i bolli laterizi di Roma e della valle del Tevere. Produzione, storia economica e topografia* (Rome, 2005), 95–102.

86. For different views on how this operated, see M. Steinby, 'L'organizzazione produttiva dei laterizi. Un modello interpretativo per l'instrumentum in genere?', in W.V. Harris (ed.) *The Inscribed Economy: Production and Distribution in the Roman Empire in the Light of Instrumentum Domesticum* (Ann Arbor, MI, 1993), 139–43, and J.J. Aubert, 'L'estampillage des briques et des tuiles. Une explication juridique fondée sur une approche globale', in Bruun and Chausson, *Interpretare*, 53–9.

87. Lancaster, *Concrete Vaulted Construction*, 59–63.

88. R. Meiggs, *Trees and Timber in the Ancient Mediterranean World* (Oxford, 1982), 326.

89. Cf. Juvenal, *Satires* 3.254–9.

90. DeLaine, *Baths of Caracalla*, 197–205.

91. The main collection of material is J.P. Waltzing, *Étude historique sur les corporations professionnelles chez les Romains: depuis les origines jusqu'à la chute de l'Empire d'Occident* (Louvain, 1895–1900), vol. 3, *passim*.

92. *CIL* XIII 1734; *CIL* XIII 1034.

93. *AGRW* 332 = *CIL* XI 2702 = *ILS* 7217, cf. *CIL* XI 970 = *ILS* 7216.

94. *CIL* V 4216; *CIL* XII 722.

95. E. Borgia, 'Attestazioni epigrafiche di mestieri legati alla costruzione dell'Asia Minore romana e proto-bizantina. Specializzazione e ruolo sociale', in *Arqueología de la construcción III*, 53–68.

96. *AGRW* 179 = *GRA* 133 = *IMilet* 935 = *PHI* 252569, see also W.H. Buckler, 'Labour disputes in the province of Asia', in W.H. Buckler and W.M. Calder (eds.) *Anatolian Studies Presented to Sir William Mitchell Ramsey* (London, 1923), 27–50.

97. J. Bingen, and H. Cuvigny, *Mons Claudianus. Ostraca Graeca et Latina I* (Cairo, 1992) and *II* (Cairo, 1997); A. Bülow-Jacobsen, *Mons Claudianus: Ostraca Graeca et Latina IV—The Quarry Texts: o. Claud. 632–89* (Cairo, 2009).

98. See B. Reitz, *Building in Words: Representations of the Process of Construction in Latin Literature* (Leiden, 2013).

Chapter 4

1. See, for example, Livy, 2.8 and 7.3.8; Polybius 3.22; Tacitus, *Historiae* 3.72; Plutarch, *Publicola* 14. On the temple, see J.N. Hopkins, *The Genesis of Roman Architecture* (New Haven, CT, 2016), 97–124.

2. E.g. Vitruvius 4.preface.1.

3. C.R. Potts, 'Vitruvius and Etruscan design', *Accordia Research Papers*, 14 (2014–15) [2016], 87–101.

4. For a good critical summary of the debate, see C. Siwicki, *Architectural Restoration and Heritage in Imperial Rome* (Oxford, 2019), 86–102.

5. Cicero, *In Catilinam* 3.9; Dionysius of Halicarnassus 4.61; Pliny, *Naturalis Historia* 33.18.

6. Cf. Livy 34.4.4; Seneca, *De consolatione ad Helviam* 11.12.3.

7. See F.E. Brown, E. Richardson, and L. Richardson, Jr, *Cosa II: The Temples of the Arx* (Rome, 1960), 49–108. The original identification of this temple as a Capitolium has been called into question by J. Crawley Quinn and A. Wilson, 'Capitolia', *JRS*, 103 (2013), 117–73.

8. G. Tagliamonte, 'Considerazioni sull'architettura santuariale di età tardo-repubblicana tra Campania e Sannio', in L. Quilici and S. Quilici Gigli (eds.) *Architettura pubblica e privata nell'Italia antica* (Rome, 2007), 53–68.

9. C. Aranegui Gascó, 'Un temple republican en el centro cívico saguntino', *CuadArquitRom*, 1 (1992), 67–82.

10. Livy 4.25.3.

11. For stone entablatures, see P.J.E. Davies, 'On the introduction of stone entablatures in Republican temples in Rome', in M. Thomas and G.E. Meyers (eds.) *Monumentality in Etruscan and Early Roman Architecture: Ideology and Innovation* (Austin, TX, 2012), 139–65.

12. For the temple, see I. Ruggiero, 'Ricerche sul tempio di Portuno nel Foro Boario: per una rilettura del monument', *BullCom* 94 (1991–2), 253–86, with earlier bibliography.

13. Vitruvius 3.3.8–9; 4.3.1. For Hermogenes, see R.A. Tomlinson, 'Vitruvius and Hermogenes', in H. Geertman and J.J. De Jong, *Munus Non Ingratum* (Leiden, 1989), 71–5.

14. For this kind of capital in Sicily, see R.J.A. Wilson, 'Roman architecture in a Greek World', in M. Henig (ed.) *Architecture and Architectural Sculpture in the Roman Empire* (Oxford, 1990), 72–3.

15. For the Corinthian order in the later Republic, see H. von Hesberg, 'Lo sviluppo dell'ordine corinzio in età repubblicana', in X. Lafon and G. Sauron (eds.) *L'art decoratif à Rome* (Rome, 1981), 19–53.

16. This is the so-called 'Italic-Republican capital'; see H. Lauter-Bufe, *Die Geschichte des sikeliotisch-korinthischen Kapitells: der sogenannte italisch-republikanische Typus* (Mainz am Rhein, 1987).

17. A. Villa, *I capitelli di Solunto* (Rome, 1988), 36–60, especially 41–7.

18. See D. Theodorescu, 'Le forum et le temple "doric-corinthien" de Paestum: une experience pré-Vitruvienne', in *Munus non ingratum*, 114–25.

19. On the use of marble in mid- to late-Republican Rome, see S.G. Bernard, 'Pentelic marble in architecture at Rome and the Republican marble trade', *JRA*, 23 (2010), 35–54, and P. Pensabene, 'Il fenomeno del marmo nella Roma tardo-repubblicana e imperiale', in P. Pensabene (ed.) *Marmi antichi II* (Rome, 1998), 333–90.

20. Vitruvius 3.2.5; Velleius Paterculus 1.11. 2–5, and see P. Gros, 'Hermodorus et Vitruve', *MEFRA*, 85 (1973), 137–61.

21. The essential study in English remains D. Strong and J.B. Ward-Perkins, 'The Round Temple in the Forum Boarium', *PBSR*, 28 (1960), 6–32. The ongoing debates about the identification of the temple are summarized by J.W. Stamper, *The Architecture of Roman Temples: The Republic to the Middle Empire* (Cambridge, 2005), 68–70.

22. For the Porticus of Metellus, see A. Viscogliosi, 'Porticus Metelli', *LTUR*, 4 (1999), 130–2 with previous bibliography.

23. J.J. Coulton, *The Architectural Development of the Greek Stoa* (Oxford, 1976), 22–5.

24. Coulton, *Architectural Development of the Greek Stoa*, 234, 275–6.

25. Pliny, *Naturalis historia* 34.7.13.

26. E.g. by Velleius Paterculus 2.1.2.

27. For the central Italian sanctuaries, see F. Coarelli, *I santuari del Lazio in età repubblicana* (Rome, 1987). The fundamental publication of the Sanctuary of Fortuna Primigenia remains F. Fasolo and G. Gullini, *Il Santuario della Fortuna Primigenia a Palestrina* (Rome, 1953).

28. A. D'Alessio, 'Santuari terrazzati e sostruiti italici di età tardo-repubblicana. Spazi, funzioni, paesaggi', *Bollettino di archeologia online*, 1 (2011), F.11.3, 17–33.

29. See D. Maschek, 'Der Tempel neue Kleider? Rezeptionsästhetische und semantische Aspekte von Bauornamentik im spätrepublikanischen Mittelitalien', in J. Lipps and D. Maschek (eds.) *Antike Bauornamentik. Grenzen und Möglichkeiten ihrer Erforschung* (Wiesbaden, 2014), 181–202.

30. For detailed descriptions of the temples in Rome discussed in this and the next section, see the respective entries in M. Steinby (ed.) *Lexicon Topographicum Urbis Romae* (Rome, 1993–2000). Many are also discussed in Stamper, *Roman Temples*.

31. For the final publication, see I. Nielsen and B. Poulsen (eds.) *The Temple of Castor and Pollux I* (Rome, 1992).

32. Vitruvius 1.2.5.

33. For Republican coins showing the Capitoline temple, see N.T. Elkins, *Monuments in Miniature: Architecture on*

Roman Coinage (New York, 2015), 26–7 and 35–6. Dionysius of Halicarnassus 4.61.4 and other ancient sources indicate that the temple was rebuilt in its original form but with finer materials, but there is no agreement among scholars as to whether this included changing the order from Tuscan to Corinthian, using columns (or just capitals) brought by Sulla from the unfinished Temple of Zeus at Athens, an idea based on an ambiguous passage in Pliny the Elder, *Naturalis Historia* 36.5.45. Elkins and Stamper, *Roman Temples*, 81–3, argue that the coins are not a true reflection of the actual architecture, but see R. Tolle-Kastenbein, *Das Olympieion in Athen* (Cologne, 1994) for the counter-arguments.

34. Vitruvius 3.3.5.

35. For the Temple of Apollo on the Palatine, see S. Zink, 'Reconstructing the Palatine Temple of Apollo: a case study in early Augustan temple design', *JRA*, 21 (2008), 47–63.

36. For the Temple of Mars Ultor, see J. Ganzert and P. Herz, *Der Mars-Ultor-Tempel auf dem Augustusforum in Rom* (Mainz am Rhein, 1996).

37. Vitruvius 7.preface.15.

38. Suetonius, *Augustus* 60.

39. Vitruvius 1.2.6.

40. For the Corinthian cornice, see Wilson Jones, *Principles of Roman Architecture* (New Haven, CT, 2000), 141–2, and the detailed discussion in D.E. Strong, 'Some observations on early Roman Corinthian', *JRS*, 53 (1963), 73–84.

41. For the Temple of Apollo Medicus, see A. Viscogliosi, *Il tempio di Apollo 'in Circo' e la formazione del linguaggio architettonico augusteo* (Rome, 1996).

42. I owe this observation to Amanda Sharp.

43. Vitruvius 6.8.9. For the significance of *magnificentia* in Augustan architecture, see H. Von Hesberg, '*Publica magnificentia*: Eine antiklassizistische Intention der frühen augusteischen Baukunst', *JDAI*, 107 (1992), 123–47.

44. Vitruvius 7.preface.17.

45. S. Zink with H. Piening, '*Haec aurea templa*: the Palatine temple of Apollo and its polychromy', *JRA*, 22 (2009), 109–22.

46. For coloured marble, see J.C. Fant, 'Ideology, gift, trade: a distribution model for the Roman imperial marbles', in W.V. Harris (ed.) *The Inscribed Economy: Production and Distribution in the Roman Empire in the Light of Instrumentum Domesticum* (Ann Arbor, MI, 1993), 145–70.

47. See especially Pliny, *Naturalis historia* 36.7.48–8.50.

48. Suetonius, *Augustus* 29.2.

49. Cassius Dio 55 10.3–5.

50. Plutarch, *Publicola* 15.3–4.

51. See Siwicki, *Architectural Restoration*, 103–18, for the various rebuildings and the religious aspect to maintaining the ground plan.

52. Pliny the Elder, *Historia Naturalis* 36.14.102. For the building, see P.L. Tucci, *The Temple of Peace in Rome* (Cambridge, 2018), especially chapters 1–3 and 7 for the original Flavian temple.

53. Ammianus Marcellinus 16.10.14.

54. For the temple, see C. Del Monti, *Il tempio di Venere e Roma nella storia* (Milan, 2010).

55. Cassius Dio 69.4. Dio was writing a century after the events and the whole anecdote may be apocryphal.

56. E. La Rocca, 'Agrippa's Pantheon and its origin', in Marder and Wilson Jones, *Pantheon*, 49–78.

57. Pliny, *Historia naturalis* 34.7.13; 36.4.38.

58. Cassius Dio 69.7.1.

59. M. Wilson Jones, 'The Pantheon and problems with its construction', in Marder and Wilson Jones, *Pantheon*, 193–230.

60. See the discussion in J. DeLaine, 'The Pantheon builders: estimating manpower for construction', in Marder and Wilson Jones, *Pantheon*, 160–92, and for the Temple of Divine Trajan, A. Claridge, 'Hadrian's lost temple of Trajan', *JRA*, 20 (2007), 54–94. For a different reading see P. Baldassarri, 'Templum Divi Traiani et Divae Plotinae: Nuovi dati dalle indagini archeologiche a Palazzo Valentini', *Rendiconti della Pontificia Accademia Romana*, 89 (2016–17), 599–698, and P. Balsassare, 'Gli scavi di Palazzo Valentini e il *Templum divi Traiani et divae Plotinae*: omaggio di Adriano *divis parentibus*', in R. Hidalgo, G. E. Cinque, A. Pizzo and A. Viscogliosi (eds.) *Adventus Hadriani. Investigaciones sobre Arquitectura Adrianea* (Rome, 2020), 37–62.

61. Ammianus Marcellinus 16.10.14.

62. Based on the data in H. Jouffroy, *La Construction Publique en Italie et dans l'Afrique Romaine* (Strasbourg, 1986).

63. S.R.F. Price, *Rituals and Power: The Roman Imperial Cult in Asia Minor* (Cambridge, 1984), 40–7.

64. Cassius Dio 51.20.6; Tacitus, *Annales* 4.37.

65. Tacitus, *Annales* 4.55.

66. Tacitus, *Annales* 1.78.

67. R. Mar and P. Pensabene, 'Finanziamento dell'edilizia pubblica a

calcolo dei costi dei materiali lapidei. Il caso del Foro superiore di Tarraco', *Arqueología de la construcción*, 2 (2010), 509–37.

68. For the temple in Athens, see P. Baldassarri, *Sebastoi sotéri: edilizia monumentale ad Atene durante il saeculum Augustum* (Rome, 1998), 45–63, and for Ankara, U. Peschlow and W. Brandes, *Ankara: Die Bauarchäologischen Hinterlassenschaften aus römischer und byzantinischer Zeit* (Vienna, 2015).

69. The building is no longer extant, but see R. Pococke, *A Description of the East, and Some Other Countries*, vol. 2.2 (London, 1745), 61–2 for an early description and drawing.

70. See P. Leòn, 'Nuevas consideraciones sobre el *Traianeum* de Italica', in R. Hidalgo, G. E. Cinque, A. Pizzo, and A. Viscogliosi (eds), *Adventus Hadriani. Investigaciones sobre Arquitectura Adrianea* (Rome, 2020), 297–308.

71. Aelius Aristides, *Orationes* 27, 16–22.

72. J. DeLaine, 'The Temple of Hadrian at Cyzicus, and Roman attitudes to exceptional construction', *PBSR*, 70 (2002), 205–30.

73. See D. Laroche, '4. Le temple de Zeus Lepsynos', in A. Kızıl, T. Doğan, D. Laroche, E. Le Quéré, V. Lungu, F. Prost, and B. Vergnaud, 'Eurômos: Rapport préliminaire sur les travaux réalisés en 2017', *Anatolia Antiqua*, 26 (2018), 165–208.

74. Pliny, *Epistulae* 9.39.

75. M. Minas-Nerpel, 'Egyptian temples', in C. Riggs (ed.) *The Oxford Handbook of Roman Egypt* (Oxford, 2012), 363–74; J. McKenzie, *The Architecture of Alexandria and Egypt. C. 300 B.C. to A.D. 700* (New Haven, CT, 2007), 136–46.

76. McKenzie, *Alexandria*, 90, 166–8.

77. D.M. Bailey, 'Classical architecture in Roman Egypt', in Henig, *Architecture and Architectural Sculpture*, 121–37 for classical-type temples.

78. For the early second-century BCE transformation of the sanctuary of Ba'al Hammon at El-Hofra, outside of Cirta (modern Constantine, Algeria), see A. Berthierand and R. Charlier, *Le sanctuaire punique d'El-Hofra à Constantine* (Paris, 1952–5), 231–2.

79. See M. Le Glay, *Saturne africain: histoire* (Paris, 1966), 265–95, and S. Saint-Amans, *Topographie religieuse de Thugga: ville romaine d'Afrique proconsulaire (Tunisie)* (Pessac, 2004), 213–37, especially 222–7, with the useful observations of M. Miatto, 'Modelli del contatto culturale nell'Africa ronana: per una reflessione sulle "teologie" africane',

Sacrum facere. Atti del II Seminario di archeologia del sacro. Contaminazioni. Forme di contatto, traduzione e mediazione nei sacra del mondo greco e romano (Trieste, 2014), 231–41. Also useful is V. Brouquier-Reddé, *Temples et cultes de Tripolitaine* (Paris, 1992).

80. Especially M. Euzennat and G. Hallier, 'Les forums de Tingitane: observations sur l'influence de l'architecture militaire sur les constructions civiles de l'Occident romain', *AntAfr*, 22 (1986), 73–103.

81. The examples discussed in what follows are collected in A. Segal, *Temples and Sanctuaries in the Roman East: Religious Architecture in Syria, Iudaea/Palaestina and Provincia Arabia* (Oxford, 2013), with useful bibliographies, but note that most examples with internal staircases are reconstructed (wrongly in my estimation) with full pitched roofs.

82. For the Temple of Jupiter, see D. Lohmann, *Das Heiligtum des Jupiter Heliopolitanus in Baalbek: Die Planungs- und Baugeschichte* (Rahden, 2017), and for the dates of the temples in Baalbek, see H. Wienholz, 'The relative chronology of the Roman buildings in Baalbek in view of their architectural decoration', in M. Van Ess (ed.) *Baalbek/Heliopolis: Results of the Archaeological and Architectural Research, 2002–2005* (Beirut, 2008), 271–85.

83. The main publication is H. Seyrig, R. Amy, and E. Will, *Le temple de Bêl à Palmyre* (Paris, 1975), but note that the evidence for the merlons and their location is tenuous.

84. T. Derks, *Gods, Temples and Ritual Practices: The Transformation of Religious Ideas and Values in Roman Gaul* (Amsterdam, 1998), chapter 4 and 170–6, 18–183 for Hayling Island; generally see V. Brouquier-Reddé and K. Gruel, 'Variations autour d'un plan type de sanctuaire', in V. Brouquier-Reddé et al., *Mars en Occident* (Rennes, 2006), 135–53.

85. For the Martberg temple, see M. Thoma and R. Gogräfe, *Der gallorömische Tempelbezirk auf dem Martberg bei Pommern an der Mosel* (Koblenz, 2006).

86. For Mars Mullo, see K. Gruel and V. Brouquier-Reddé, *Le sanctuaire de Mars Mullo: Allonnes (Sarthe)* (Le Mans, 2003). Other examples include the Temple of Lenus-Mars, Altbachtal sanctuary, Trier. See T. Derks, 'Le grand sanctuaire de Lenus Mars à Trèves et ses dédicaces privées. Une réinterprétation', in M. Dondin-Payre and M.T. Raepsaet-Charlier (eds.) *Sanctuaires,*

pratiques culturelles et territoires civiques dans l'Occident romain (Brussels, 2006), 239–70.

Chapter 5

1. E. La Rocca, 'L'affresco con veduta di città dal colle Oppio', in E. Fentress (ed.) *Romanization and the City: Creation, Transformations and Failures* (Portsmouth, RI, 2000), 53–71.
2. Vitruvius 1.3.1, cf. 1.7.1.
3. Virgil, *Aeneid* 4.421–38.
4. Livy 40.46.15–6.
5. Confusingly, this basilica is known by three names depending on the building phase: Fulvia (or Fulvia and Aemilia) after the first pair of censors; Aemilia after the member of the family responsible for the first rebuilding; and Paulli, after Aemilius Paullus, responsible for the last rebuilding. To avoid confusion, 'Basilica Aemilia' will be used for all.
6. Pliny, *Naturalis Historia* 36.24.121–3.
7. On this, see H. Von Hesberg, '*Publica magnificentia*: Eine antiklassizistische Intention der frühen augusteischen Baukunst', *JDAI*, 107 (1992), 123–47.
8. For the development of the Forum in the Republican period, with the ancient sources, see N. Purcell, 'Forum Romanum (the Republican Period)', in *LTUR II* (Rome, 1995), 325–36, and for the latest theories P.E. Davies, *Architecture and Politics in Republican Rome* (Cambridge, 2017).
9. J.N. Hopkins, *The Genesis of Roman Architecture* (New Haven, CT, 2016), 29–37, with previous bibliography.
10. For a summary of the standard account, see F. Coarelli, 'Comitium', in *LTUR I* (Rome, 1993), 309–14, and for the new reading P. Carafa, *Il comizio di Roma dalle origini all'età di Augusto* (Rome, 1998), especially chapters 5 and 6.
11. For the *macellum*, see the overview by G. Pisani Sartorio, 'Macellum', in *LTUR III* (Rome, 1996), 201–3, and C. De Ruyt, *Macellum. Marché alimentaire des romains* (Louvain-la-Neuve, 1983), 236–52 for an architectural assessment.
12. For specific examples, see the comprehensive study by A. Nunnerich-Asmus, *Basilika und Portikus: Die Architektur der Säulenhallen als ausdruck gewandelter Urbanität in Später Republik und Früher Kaiserzeit* (Cologne, 1994).
13. For the suggestion and earlier theories, see K. Welch, 'A new view of the origins of the Basilica: the Atrium Regium, Graecostasis, and Roman diplomacy', *JRA*, 16 (2003), 5–34.

14. For the context of the basilicas of the Roman Forum, see Davies, *Architecture and Politics*, 133–7.
15. For an outline, see G. Mousourakis, *A Legal History of Rome* (London, 2007), chapters 2 and 5, esp. 59–60.
16. Cf. A. Russell, 'Domestic and civic basilicas: between public and private space', in K. Tuori and L. Nissin (eds.) *Public and Private in the Roman House and Society* (Portsmouth, RI, 2015), 49–61, especially 55–60.
17. For the history of the Circus Maximus, see J.H. Humphrey, *Roman Circuses: Arenas for Chariot Racing* (London, 1986), chapter 3.
18. Livy 1.35.8.
19. Tacitus *Annales* 14.21.
20. K. Welch, *The Roman Amphitheatre from Its Origins to the Colosseum* (Cambridge, 2007), 11–14.
21. Cf. Livy 1.35.8 (Circus Maximus); Livy 40.51.3 (by Temple of Apollo); Cicero, *Pro Sestio*, 124–6 and Plutarch, *Life of C. Gracchus*, 12.3 (Forum Romanum).
22. Livy 8.20.2.
23. Livy 40.51.3.
24. See K. Mitens, *Teatri greci e teatri ispirati all'architettura greca in Sicilia e nell'Italia meridionale, c. 350–50 a.C.* (Rome, 1988).
25. Livy *Periochae* 48.
26. Valerius Maximus 2.4.6; Pliny, *Naturalis historia* 36.24.116–20.
27. Pliny, *Naturalis Historia* 36.24.113–16.
28. On Scaurus, see D. Potter, 'Holding court in Republican Rome (105–44)', *AJPh* 132 (2011), 64–9.
29. On the early Roman theatre, see R.C. Beacham, *The Roman Theatre and Its Audience* (Cambridge, MA, 1991), chapters 1 and 3.
30. Vitruvius 5.1.1–2.
31. Livy 23.30.15.
32. For this theory, see K. Welch, 'The Roman arena in Late-Republican Italy: a new interpretation', *JRA*, 7 (1994), 59–80, with bibliography.
33. On designing theatres see Vitruvius 5.6.1–6 and 5.7.
34. Pliny, *Naturalis historia* 36.24.116–20.
35. M. Wilson Jones, 'Designing amphitheatres', *RM*, 100 (1993), 391–442.
36. F. Sear, *Roman Theatres: An Architectural Study* (Oxford, 2006), chapter 5, especially 50–2.
37. J. Ortalli, *Il teatro romano di Bologna* (Bologna, 1986).
38. Seneca, *Epistulae* 86.10.
39. V. Tsilolis, 'The baths at Fregellae and the transition from balaneion to balneum', in

S.K. Lucore and M. Trümper, *Greek Baths and Bathing Culture: New Discoveries and Approaches* (Leuven, 2013), 89–111.
40. G.G. Fagan, 'The genesis of the Roman public bath: recent approaches and future directions', *AJA*, 105 (2001), 403–26.
41. M. Trümper, C. Brünenberg, J.-A. Dickmann, D. Esposito, A.F. Ferrandes, G. Pardini, A. Pegurri, M. Robinson, and C. Rummel, 'Stabian baths in Pompeii: new research on the development of ancient bathing culture', *RM*, 125 (2019), 103–59.
42. For Pompey's theatre, see http://www.pompey.cch.kcl.ac.uk, and A. Monterroso Checa, *Theatrum Pompei. Forma y arquitectura de la genesis del model teatral de Roma* (Madrid, 2010), for an alternative view on the Temple of Venus Victrix.
43. Plutarch, *Pompeius* 42.4. For a summary of scholarly interpretations see Sear, *Roman Theatres*, 57.
44. E.M. Steinby, 'The arch meets the orders', *Atlante tematico di topographia antica*, 21 (2011), 7–13.
45. Cicero, *Epistulae ad Atticum* 4.17.7.
46. For the Basilica Aemilia, see K.S. Freyberger and C. Ertel, *Die Basilica Aemilia auf dem Forum Romanum in Rom. Bauphasen, Rekonstruktion, Funktion und Bedeutung* (Wiesbaden, 2016). Cicero (*Epistulae ad Atticum* 4.16.14) says nothing was more to Paullus' glory.
47. For the latest on the Forum of Caesar, see A. Delfino, *Forum Iulium: L'area del Foro di Cesare alla luce delle campagne di scavo 2005–2008: Le fasi arcaica, repubblicana e cesariano-augustea* (Oxford, 2014), with previous bibliography.
48. For the Circus of Caesar, see Humphrey, *Roman Circuses*, 73–7; for seating capacities, see P. Rose, 'Spectators and spectator comfort in Roman entertainment buildings', *PBSR*, 73 (2005), 99–128. The capacity would have been less than the Circus as rebuilt by Trajan, but it is unclear by how much.
49. Augustus, *Res Gestae* 20.9.
50. For the Forum of Augustus prior to the latest finds, see J. Ganzert, *Im Allerheiligsten des Augustusforums: Fokus 'Oikoumenischer Akkulturation'* (Mayence, 2000), with R. Meneghini and R. Santangeli Valenzani (eds.) *I Fori Imperiali. Gli scavi del Comune di Roma (1991–2007)* (Rome, 2007), 43–60.
51. Suetonius, *Augustus* 29.1–2.
52. Pliny, *Naturalis historia* 36.24.102.
53. E. Rawson, '*Discrimina ordinum*: the Lex Julia Theatralis', *PBSR*, 55 (1987), 83–114.
54. For a comprehensive study of the Markets of Trajan, see M. Bianchini and M. Vitti, *Mercati di Traiano* (Rome, 2017).
55. See J.C. Edmondson, 'Dynamic arenas: gladiatorial presentations in the city of Rome and the construction of Roman society during the early empire', in W.J. Slater (ed.) *Roman Theater and Society. E. Togo Salmon Papers I* (Ann Arbor, MI, 1996), 69–112, especially pp. 91–5. The distribution is based partly on Calpurnius Siculus, *Eclogues*, 7.23–34, probably relating to Nero's temporary amphitheatre.
56. On this and other aspects of designing for spectators, see Rose, 'Spectators', 99–128.
57. K.M. Coleman, *Martial: Liber Spectaculorum* (Oxford, 2006).
58. Pliny, *Panegyricus*, 51.3–4.
59. For these coins, see N.T. Elkins, *Monuments in Miniature: Architecture on Roman Coinage* (New York, 2015), 80–1, 86–7, 103–4, and for the context 105–18.
60. J. DeLaine, 'The imperial thermae', in A. Claridge and C. Holleran (eds.) *A Companion to the City of Rome* (Chichester, 2017), 325–42, with further bibliography.
61. Ammianus Marcellinus 16.10.14.
62. Ammianus Marcellinus 28.4.8–9.
63. J. DeLaine, *The Baths of Caracalla: A Study in the Design, Construction and Economics of Large-Scale Building Projects in Imperial Rome* (Portsmouth, RI, 1997), chapter 9, especially 220–4 for the implications of the cost of the Baths of Caracalla.
64. See P. Zanker, 'The city as symbol: Rome and the creation of an urban image', in Fentress (ed.) *Romanization and the City*, 25–41, and M. Reddé, 'Les capitales des cités gauloises, *simulacra Romae*?', in M. Reddé and W. Van Andringa (eds.) *La naissance des capitales de cités en Gaule Chevelue*, *Gallia* 72.1 (2015), 1–17 for the west. For the east, see A. Zuiderhoek, *The Politics of Munificence in the Roman Empire: Citizens, Elites and Benefactors in Asia Minor* (Cambridge, 2009), chapter 5 on benefactions in Asia Minor and T. Bekker-Nielsen, *Urban Life and Local Politics in Roman Bithynia: The Small World of Dion Chrysostomos* (Aarhus, 2008).
65. For the original formulation of this idea, see the influential article by I.A. Richmond, 'The first years of Emerita Augusta', *The Archaeological Journal*, 87 (1930), 98–116.

66. For revised interpretations of the urban development of Emerita Augusta, see P. Mateos Cruz and A. Pizzo, 'L'architecture monumentale d'*Augusta Emerita*. De Nouvelles perspectives', *MEFRA* 123.2 (2011), 581–95, and T. Nogales Basarrate and J.M. Álvarez Martínez, 'Colonia Augusta Emerita. Creación de una cuidad en tiempos de Augusto', *Studia Historica. Historica Antigua*, 32 (2014), 209–47.

67. For the theatre and amphitheatre, see R.-M. Durán Cabello, *El teatro y el anfiteatro de Augusta Emerita: Contribución al conocimiento histórico de la capital de Lusitania* (Oxford, 2004).

68. For the forum, see R. Ayerbe Vélez, T. Barrientos Vera, and F. Palma García (eds.) *El foro de Augusta Emerita. Génesis y evolución de sus recintos monumentales* (Merida, 2009).

69. For example, the generally supposed direct influence of the Forum of Augustus outside of Italy has been challenged by V. Goldbeck, *Fora augusta: das Augustusforums und seine Rezeption im Westen des Imperium Romanum* (Regensburg, 2015).

70. For the whole question of the adoption and adaptation of Roman architectural forms in the provinces, see L. Revell, 'Romanization', in R.B. Ulrich and C.K. Quenemoen, *A Companion to Roman Architecture* (Chichester, 2014), chapter 20.

71. See C.P. Dickenson, *On the Agora: The Evolution of a Public Space in Hellenistic and Roman Greece (c. 323 BC–267 AD)* (Leiden, 2017).

72. Vitruvius 5.1.1.

73. P. Stinson, 'Imitation and adaptation in architectural design: two Roman *basilicae* at Ephesus and Aphrodisias', in M. Meyer (ed.) *Neue Zeiten—Neue Sitten. Zu Rezeption und Integration römischen und italischen Kulturguts in Kleinasien* (Vienna, 2007), 91–100.

74. J.B. Ward-Perkins, M.H. Ballance, and J.M. Reynolds, 'The Caesareum at Cyrene and the *basilica* at Cremna, with a note on the inscriptions of the Caesareum by J. M. Reynolds', *PBSR*, 26 (1958), 137–94.

75. For the multi-functional nature of basilicas, see P. Gros, 'Basilica sous le Haut-Empire: ambiguïtés du mot, du type et de la function', *BABesch*, 78 (2003), 191–204.

76. For Hierapolis, see F. d'Andria, 'Hierapolis of Phrygia: its evolution in Hellenistic and Roman times', in D. Parrish (ed.) *Urbanism in Western Asia Minor* (Portsmouth, RI, 2001), 97–115, especially 104–8. For Aphrodisias, P.T. Stinson, *Aphrodisias VII: Results of the Excavations at Aphrodisias in Caria Conducted by New York University—The Civil Basilica* (Wiesbaden, 2016).

77. The classic study is J.B. Ward-Perkins, 'From Republic to Empire: reflections on the early provincial architecture of the Roman west', *JRS*, 60 (1970), 1–19, to be read with R. Sablayrolles, 'Les fora tripartites de Gaule romaine: norme ou normalisation?' *Pallas*, 46.1 (1997), 51–66. For subsequent material, see the papers in *Los foros romanos de las provincias occidentales* (Madrid, 1987), and A. Bouet (ed.) *Le Forum en Gaule et dans les régions voisines* (Bordeaux, 2012).

78. See M. Fulford and J. Timby, *Late Iron Age and Roman Silchester: Excavations on the Site of the Forum-Basilica 1977, 1980–86* (London, 2000).

79. J. de Alarcão, *Fouilles de Conimbriga: Vol. 1. L'architecture* (Paris, 1977).

80. J.B. Ward-Perkins, *The Severan Buildings of Lepcis Magna* (London, 1993), 7–66.

81. G.L. Gregori, *Epigrafia anfiteatrale dell'occidente romano. II. Regiones Italiae VI–XI* (Rome, 1989), no. 8, 27–8.

82. Pliny, *Epistulae* 10.39.

83. Humphrey, *Roman Circuses*, chapters 6–9.

84. See the catalogue in Sear, *Roman Theatres*.

85. Lepcis: J.M. Reynolds and J.B. Ward-Perkins, *The Inscriptions of Roman Tripolitania* (Rome, 1952), no. 372; Madauros, S. Gsell, *Inscriptions Latine de l'Algérie*, I (Paris, 1922), no. 2121.

86. For Nysa, see M. Kadıoğlu, *Die scaenae frons des Theaters von Nysa am Mäander* (Mainz, 2006); for Teanum Sidicinum, see H.-J. Beste, 'Il teatro di Teano (Italia) e la sua scaenae frons in età severiana', in S.F. Ramallo Asencio and N. Röring (eds.) *La scaenae frons en la arquitectura teatral romana* (Murcia, 2010), 119–35.

87. J.-Cl. Golvin, *L'amphithéâtre romain. Essai sur la théorisation de sa forme et de ses fonctions* (Paris, 1988).

88. Wilson Jones, 'Designing amphitheatres', 391–444.

89. Dio Chrysostom, *Orationes* 31.121.

90. Livy 41.20 10–11.

91. Welch, *Roman Amphitheatre*, chapter 6.

92. Dio Chrysostom, *Orationes*, 31.121.

93. For a summary, see P. Gros, *L'architecture romaine. 1. Les monuments publics* (Paris, 1996), 294–8, 343–4; Sear, *Roman Theatres*, 96–101 and 196–294 for discussion and catalogue.

94. G. Ceraudo, 'Aquinum (Castrocielo, FR). Le Terme Centrali o Vecciane', in M. Medri and A. Pizzo (eds.) *Terme pubbliche in Italia romana (II secolo a.C.–fine IV d.C.): Architettura, tecnologia e società* (Rome, 2019), 66–79.

95. See J. DeLaine, 'Benefactions and urban renewal: bath buildings in Roman Italy', in J. DeLaine and D. Johnson (eds.) *Roman Baths and Bathing. Part 1: Bathing and Society* (Portsmouth, RI, 1999), 67–74. For a detailed analysis, see G.G. Fagan, *Bathing in Public in the Roman World* (Ann Arbor, MI, 1999), especially chapters 5 and 6, and the epigraphic sample.

96. See J. DeLaine, 'Strategies and technologies of environmental manipulation in the Roman world: the thermal economy of baths', in C. Schliephake, N. Sojc, and G. Weber (eds.) *Nachhaltigkeit in der Antike: Diskurse, Praktiken, Perspektiven* (Stuttgart, 2020), 75–93.

97. B. Burrell, 'False fronts: separating the imperial cult from the aedicular facade in Roman Asia Minor', *AJA*, 110 (2006), 437–69.

98. R.P. Duncan-Jones, *Structure and Scale in the Roman Economy* (Cambridge, 1990), 177–8.

99. Pliny, *Epistulae* 10.39–40.

100. R.H. White, 'The evolution of the baths complex at Wroxeter, Shropshire', in J. DeLaine and D. Johnson (eds.) *Roman Baths and Bathing. Part 2: Design and Context* (Portsmouth, RI, 1999), 278–91.

101. *CIL* XI 6225 = *ILS* 5679. See Fagan, *Bathing in Public*, no. 73/74.

102. For Pliny the Younger's benefactions to Como, see *CIL* V 5262 = *ILS* 2927. For aspects of the relation between benefactors and architecture see F. des Boscs (ed.), *Évergétisme et architectures dans le monde romain (ii⁴ s. av. J.-C. – v⁴ s. ap. J.-C)* (Pau 2020).

Chapter 6

1. Cassius Dio 54.29.7–8. One hut was on the Palatine, the other on the Capitoline Hill. For the hut(s) of Romulus and its implications, see C. Siwicki, *Architectural Restoration and Heritage in Imperial Rome* (Oxford, 2019), chapter 4, with emphasis on this as a sacred edifice.

2. See, for example, Cicero *De Senectute* 11.37; Valerius Maximus 8.13.

3. For these houses, see A. Carandini and P. Carafa (eds.) *Palatium e Sacra Via I: Prima delle mura, l'età delle mura, e l'età case archaiche, BollArch*, 31–3 (1995) [2000], 215–84.

4. See H.I. Flower, *Ancestor Masks and Aristocratic Power in Roman Culture* (Oxford, 1996).

5. Cicero, *de domo sua* 37.100.

6. S. Treggiari, 'The upper-class house as symbol and focus of emotion in Cicero', *JRA*, 12 (1999), 33–56.

7. Cicero, *de officiis* 1.39.138.

8. Cicero, *Orationes Philippicae* 2.27.67–8.

9. For the origin and development of the traditional Roman atrium house, see V. Jolivet, *Tristes Portiques: sur le plan canonique de la Maison étrusque et romaine des origines au principat d'Auguste (VIe–Ier siècles av. J.-C.)* (Rome, 2011).

10. Vitruvius 6.1–2.

11. See P. Gros, 'La maison romaine selon Vitruve: statut du texte et stratification de l'exposé', *Scholion: Bulletin*, 10 (2016), 65–90.

12. Varro, *De lingua Latina* v.33.161.

13. A. Carandini, D. Bruno, and F. Fraioli, *Le case del potere nell'antica* (Rome, 2010), 78–111.

14. For an overview, see E. de Albentis, *La casa dei Romani* (Milan, 1990), 64–72.

15. F. Coarelli, *Fregellae. La storia e gli scavi* (Rome, 1981).

16. R. Laurence, *Roman Pompeii: Space and Society* (London, 1994), 122–32, and 'Space and text', in R. Laurence and A. Wallace-Hadrill (eds.) *Domestic Space in the Roman World: Pompeii and Beyond* (Portsmouth, RI, 1997), 7–14.

17. A. Wallace-Hadrill, *Houses and Society in Pompeii and Herculaneum* (Princeton, NJ, 1994), chapter 4.

18. Cf. A. Wallace-Hadrill, 'What makes a Roman house a "Roman house"?', in K. Tuori and L. Nissin (eds.) *Public and Private in the Roman House and Society* (Portsmouth, RI, 2015), 177–86.

19. E.W. Leach, 'Oecus on Ibycus: investigating the vocabulary of the Roman house', in S.E. Bon and J. Jones (eds.) *Sequence and Space in Pompeii* (Oxford, 1997), 50–72, especially 52–4.

20. Varro, *De lingua Latina* v. 162.

21. Vitruvius 6.7.1.

22. J.-A. Dickmann, 'The peristyle and the transformation of domestic space in Hellenistic Pompeii', in Laurence and Wallace-Hadrill, *Domestic Space*, 121–36, and S. Simelius, 'Activities in Pompeii's private peristyles: the place of the peristyle in the public/private dichotomy', in Tuori and Nissin, *Public and Private*, 119–31.

23. E. Gruen, *Culture and National Identity in Republican Rome* (Ithaca, NY, 1992), 94–8.

24. See the important study of J.-A. Dickmann, *Domus Frequentata: Anspruchsvolles Wohnen im pompejanischen Stadthaus* (Munich, 1999).

25. For a brief description, see
L. Richardson, Jr, *Pompeii: An Architectural
History* (Baltimore, MD, 1989), 115–17 and
124–6, and cf. E. Dwyer, 'The unified plan
of the House of the Faun', *JSAH*, 60.3
(2001), 328–43.

26. For this interpretation of the House of
the Faun, see A. Hoffman, 'Die Casa del
Fauno in Pompeji. Ein Haus wie ein Palast',
in W. Hoepner and G. Brands (eds.) *Basileia.
Die Paläste der hellenistischen Könige* (Mainz,
1996), 258–9.

27. For the House of the Silver Wedding,
see W. Ehrhardt, *Casa delle Nozze d'Argento
(V 2, i)* (Munich, 2004), and for the House of
the Mosaic Atrium, see A. Maiuri, *Ercolano.
I nuovi scavi (1927–1958)* I (Rome, 1958),
280–302.

28. For an overview, see E. Morvillez, 'The
garden in the *domus*', in W.F. Jashemski,
K.L. Gleason, K.J. Hartswick, and
A.-A. Malek (eds.) *Gardens of the Roman
Empire* (Cambridge, 2018), 17–71.

29. See A. Carandini and E. Papi (eds.)
*Palatium e Sacra Via II: l'età tardo-
repubblicana e la prima età imperiale (fine III
secolo a.C.–64 d.C.), BollArch*, 59–60 (1999)
[2005], 17–118.

30. Pliny, *Naturalis historia* 17.1.3–5; Valerius
Maximus 9.1.4.

31. Vitruvius 6.5.1.

32. Cf. J. Berry, 'Boundaries and control in
the Roman house', *JRA*, 29 (2016), 125–41,
and M.T. Lauritsen, 'The form and function
of boundaries in the Campanian house', in
A. Anguissola (ed.) *Privata Luxuria: Towards
an Archaeology of Intimacy, Pompeii and Beyond*
(Munich, 2012), 95–114.

33. E. Proudfoot, 'Secondary doors in
entranceways at Pompeii: reconsidering
access and the view from the street', in
A. Bokern, M. Bolder-Boos, et al., *TRAC
2012: Proceedings of the Twenty-Second Annual
Theoretical Roman Archaeology Conference*
(Oxford, 2013), 91–115.

34. See S. Speksnijder, 'Beyond "public"
and "private": accessibility and visibility
during *salutationes*', in K. Tuori and L. Nissin
(eds.) *Public and Private in the Roman House
and Society* (Portsmouth, RI, 2015), 87–99.

35. Cf. Seneca, *de beneficiis* 6.34.1–5, on the
three-tiered hierarchy of receiving visitors
privately, in company with a select group,
and en masse. For the *cubiculum*, see
A.M. Riggsby, 'Public and private in Roman
culture: the case of the *cubiculum*', *JRA*,
10 (1997), 36–56.

36. Vitruvius 6.4.2.

37. F. Coarelli, 'La casa dell'aristocrazia
romana secondo Vitruvio', in H. Geertman
and J.J. de Jong, *Munus non ingratum*
(Leiden, 1989), 178–87, but his figure of
2,500 for an area of 430 metres^2 would
produce a 'high-risk' density of nearly six
persons/metre^2. An upper limit of 3.5
persons/metre^2 giving 1,500 in total would
be more realistic.

38. Vitruvius 6.5.1–2.

39. For the relation between domestic and
public architecture, see A. Russell,
'Domestic and civic basilicas: between
public and private space', in Tuori and
Nissin, *Public and Private*, 49–61.

40. See note 18.

41. E.g. the House of the Birds at Cosa,
V.J. Bruno and R.T. Scott, 'Cosa IV: the
houses', *MAAR*, 38 (1993), 161–73. For early
courtyard houses at Pompeii, see S. Nappo,
'The urban transformation at Pompeii in the
late third and early second centuries B.C.', in
Laurence and Wallace-Hadrill, *Domestic
Space*, 91–120.

42. Suetonius, *Augustus* 72.1–2.

43. For a late example in central Italy, see
C. Pavolini, 'Una *domus* ad atrio di Ferento
come esempio della persistenza di tipologie
architettoniche e di tecniche edilizie
repubblicane nella prima età imperiale',
in M. Bentz and C. Reusser (eds.)
*Etruskisch-italische und römisch-republikanische
Häuser* (Wiesbaden, 2010), 197–206.

44. For northern Italy, see the examples
collected in F. Ghedini, M. Annibaletto,
and I. Cerato, *Atria longa patescunt: le forme
dell'abitare nella Cisalpina romana*
(Rome, 2012).

45. For the atrium house of Cologne, see
P. Gros, *L'architecture romaine 2. Maisons,
palais, villas et tombeaux* (Paris, 2006),
193, fig. 210.

46. See M. Papaioannou, 'The Roman
domus in the Greek world', in R. Westgate,
N.R.E. Fisher, and J. Whitley (eds.) *Building
Communities: House, Settlement and Society in
the Aegean and Beyond* (London, 2007),
351–61.

47. See the collected papers of the
Tetrastylon project in A. Cortés Vincente
and L. Migliorati, *Roman Influence on the
Greek House of Magna Graecia and Sicily*
(Rome, 2020).

48. For the House of the Gilded Cupids,
see F. Seiler et al., *Casa degli Amorini dorati:
(VI 16,7.38)* (Tübingen, 1992).

49. The environmental aspects of Roman
houses, particularly cooling, are relatively

understudied. For parallels with later systems, see B. Ford, R. Schiano-Phan, and J.A. Vallejo, *The Architecture of Natural Cooling* (London, 2020), chapters 1–2.

50. See P. Vipard, 'L'usage du verre á vitre dans l'architecture romaine du Haut Empire', in S. Lagabrielle and M. Philippe (eds.) *Verre et Fenêtre de l'Antiquité au XVIIIe siècle* (Paris, 2009), 3–10; Vipard, 'Un aménagement méconnu: les portiques fenêtres dans les *domus* du Haut-Empire', in R. Bedon and N. Dupré (eds.) *Amoenitas Urbium. Les agréments de la vie urbaine en Gaule romaine et dans les regions voisines, Caesarodunum*, 35–6 (2001–2), 39–56.

51. See V. Spinazzola, *Pompei alla luce degli Scavi Nuovi di via Dell'Abbondanza (anni 1910–1923)* (Rome, 1953), 70–1 and fig. 76.

52. For the House of the Ephebe, see R. Thouvenot, 'La maison à l'Éphèbe', *Publications du Service des Antiquités du Maroc*, 7 (1945), 114–31.

53. For the house, see R. Thouvenot, *Maisons de Volubilis: le Palais dit de Gordien et la Maison à la Mosaïque de Vénus* (Rabat, 1958), and for a revised dating, see S. Walker, 'La Maison de Vénus à Volubilis', in E. Fentress and H. Limane, *Volubilis après Rome* (Leiden, 2019), 38–50.

54. R. Daniels, 'Punic influence in the domestic architecture of Roman Volubilis (Morocco)', *Oxford Journal of Archaeology*, 14.1 (1995), 79–95.

55. For the common Roman elements of elite housing in the empire, see Wallace-Hadrill, 'What makes a Roman house a "Roman house"?', in Tuori and Nissin, *Public and Private*, 177–86.

56. For House 2, see F. Krinzinger and A. Hofeneder, *Hanghaus 2 in Ephesos: Die Wohneinheiten 1 und 2: Baubefund, Ausstattung, Funde* (Vienna, 2010), and for House 6, see *Hanghaus 2 in Ephesos: Die Wohneinheit 6: Baubefund, Ausstattung, Funde* (Vienna, 2014) and H. Thür and E. Rathmayr, *Hanghaus 2 in Ephesos. Die Wohneinheit 6* (Vienna, 2014).

57. D. Perring, *The Roman House in Britain* (London, 2002), chapter 4.

58. J.A. Baird, *The Inner Lives of Ancient Houses: An Archaeology of Dura-Europos* (Oxford, 2012), chapters 2 and 3.

59. N. Hodgson, 'A late Roman courtyard house at South Shields and its parallels', in P. Johnson and I. Haynes (eds.) *Architecture in Roman Britain* (York, 1996), 135–51.

60. For 'insula', see G.R. Storey, 'The meaning of "insula" in Roman residential terminology', *MAAR*, 49 (2004), 47–84, and

J. DeLaine, 'Insulae', in C. Holleran and A. Claridge (eds.) *A Companion to the City of Rome* (Oxford, 2018), 317–23.

61. Livy 21.62.3

62. Vitruvius 2.8.17.

63. J. Packer, 'La casa di via Giulio Romano', *BullCom*, 81 (1968–9), 127–48; S. Priester, *Ad summas tegulas. Untersuchungen zu vielgeschossigen Gebäudeblöcken mit Wohneinheiten und Insulae im kaiserzeitlichen Rom* (Rome, 2002), especially 47–114.

64. For Pompeii, see F. Pirson, *Mietwohnungen in Pompeji und Herkulaneum* (Munich, 1999), and for Herculaneum, J.N. Andrews, 'Onwards and upwards: the development of upper floors in housing at Herculaneum', in J. Berry and R. Benefiel (eds.) *The Oxford Handbook of Pompeii and Environs* (Oxford, forthcoming), and 'Rooms with a view: status, spatial hierarchy, and seasonality in the upper floors of houses at Herculaneum', in A. Dardenay and N. Laubry (eds.) *Anthropology of Roman Housing* (Turnhout, 2020), 87–114.

65. For the Garden Houses, see R. Cervi, 'Evoluzione architettonica delle cosidette "case a giardino" ad Ostia', in L. Quilici and S. Quilici Gigli (eds.) *Città e monumenti nell'Italia antica. Atlante tematico di topografia antica* 7 (Rome, 1999), 141–56, and A. Gering, 'Die Case a Giardino als unerfüllter Architektentraum. Planung und gewandelte Nutzung einer Luxuswohnanlage im antiken Ostia', *RM*, 109 (2002), 109–40.

66. J. DeLaine, 'Housing Roman Ostia', in D.L. Balch and A. Weissenrieder (eds.) *Contested Spaces: Houses and Temples in Roman Antiquity and the New Testament* (Tübingen, 2012), 335–40 with earlier bibliography.

67. For the origins of the villa, see N. Terrenato, 'The auditorium site in Rome and the origins of the villa', *JRA*, 14 (2001), 5–32, and the review article by E. Fentress, 'Stately homes: recent work on villas in Italy', *JRA*, 16.2 (2003), 545–56.

68. Livy 3.26.8–9, cf. Cicero, *De senectute* 56, with different details.

69. N. Purcell, 'The Roman *villa* and the landscape of production', in T.J. Cornell and K. Lomas (eds.) *Urban Society in Roman Italy* (London, 1995), 151–79.

70. Cf. Cato, *De agricultura*, 3-4, second century BCE; Varro, *De re rustica*, 1.11–13, later first century BCE; and Columella, *De re rustica*, 1.6, mid-first century CE. For the *villa rustica*, see G.P.R. Metraux, '*Villa rustica alimentaria et annonaria*', in A. Frazer (ed.)

The Roman Villa: Villa Urbana (Philadelphia, PA, 1998), 1–19.

71. For the *horti*, see M. Cima and E. la Rocca (eds.) *Horti Romani* (Rome, 1998).

72. Pliny, *Epistulae* 2.17.27.

73. A. Carandini and R.M. Filippi, *Settefinestre: Una villa schiavistica nell'Etruria romana* (Modena, 1985).

74. See J. Bodel, 'Villa monuments and monumental villas', *JRA*, 10 (1997), 5–35.

75. Pliny *Epistulae* 2.17 (Laurentum); 5.6 (Tuscan); 9.7 (two villas on Lake Como).

76. A. Marzano, *Roman Villas in Central Italy: A Social and Economic History* (Leiden, 2007), chapters 1–2.

77. E. Fentress, C. Goodson, and M. Maiuro, *Villa Magna: An Imperial Estate and Its Legacies—Excavations 2006–10* (London, 2016), 89–119, especially 97 for the floor.

78. P. Zanker, translated by D. Schneider, *Pompeii: Public and Private Life* (Cambridge, 1998), chapter 5.

79. B. Bergmann, 'Painted perspectives of a villa visit: landscape as status and metaphor', in E.K. Gazda, *Roman Art in the Private Sphere* (Ann Arbor, MI, 1991), chapter 2.

80. See, for example, M. Rind, *Römische Villen in Nordafrika: Untersuchungen zu Architektur und Wirtschaftsweise* (Oxford, 2009).

81. For a selection of these villa types, see J.T. Smith, *Roman Villas: A Study in Social Structure* (London, 1997), chapters 3–10, and A. Ferdière et al., 'Les grandes villae "à pavillons multiples alignés" dans les provinces des Gaules et des Germanies: Répartition, origine et fonctions', *RevArchAEst*, 59 (2010), 357–446.

82. On the Palatine residences of the emperors in general, see M. Royo, *Domus imperatoriae: topographie, formation et imaginaire des palais impériaux du Palatin, IIe siècle av. J.-C.–Ier siècle ap. J.-C* (Rome, 1999), and for the house(s) of Augustus M. Tomei, 'Le case di Augusto sul Palatino', *RM*, 107 (2000), 7–36, I. Iacopi and G. Tedone, 'Bibliotheca e Porticus ad Apollinis', *RM*, 112 (2005–6), 351–78, and T.P. Wiseman, *The House of Augustus: a historical detective story* (Princeton, 2019).

83. Cf. A. Wallace-Hadrill, 'Casa: the poets and the peasant's hut', in M. Citroni, M. Labate, and G. Rosati (eds.) *Luoghi dell'abitare, immaginazione letteraria e identità romana da Augusto ai Flavi* (Pisa, 2019), 19–16, and Siwicki, *Architectural Restoration*, 151–4.

84. M. Medri, 'Suet., Nero, 31.1: Elementi e proposte per la ricostruzione del Progetto

della Domus Aurea', in *Meta Sudans I* (Rome, 1996), 165–88.

85. Tacitus, *Annales* 15.41; Suetonius *Nero* 31.

86. For the argument that the Temple of Apollo faced the Roman Forum see A. Claridge, 'Reconstructing the temple of Apollo on the Palatine hill in Rome', in C. Häuber, F.-X. Schütz, and G. M. Winder, G. M. (eds.) *Reconstruction and the Historic City: Rome and Abroad*, Beiträge zur Wirtschaftsgeographie München 6, (Munich 2014), 128–52.

87. For the new work on the Flavian palace and its evolution, see U. Wulf-Rheidt and N. Sojc, 'Evoluzione strutturale del Palatino sud-orientale in epoca Flavia', in F. Coarelli (ed.) *Divus Vespasianus. Il bimillenario dei Flavi* (Milan, 2009), 268–79, N. Sojc (ed.) *Domus Augustana: neue Forschungen zum 'Versenkten Peristyl' auf dem Palatin* (Leiden, 2012), J. Pflug, 'Die bauliche Entwicklung der Domus Augustana im Kontext des südöstlichen Palatin bis in severische Zeit', and U. Wulf-Rheidt, 'Die Bedeutung der severischen Paläste auf dem Palatin für spätere Residenzbauten', in N. Sojc, A. Winterling, and U. Wulf-Rheidt (eds.) *Palast und Stadt im severischen Rom* (Stuttgart, 2013), 181–211 with plates 9–16, and 287–306.

88. For the dining room, see S. Gibson, J. DeLaine, and A. Claridge, 'The Triclinium of the Domus Flavia: a new reconstruction', *PBSR*, 62 (1994), 67–97.

89. See M. Citroni, 'La rappresentanza del palazzo imperiale, e la sua designazione come *palatium* nei testi letterari latini da Augusto ai Flavi', in Citroni et al., *Luoghi di abitare*, 105–59.

90. Cassius Dio 53.16.5–6.

91. W.L. MacDonald and J.A. Pinto, *Hadrian's Villa and Its Legacy* (New Haven, CT, 1995).

92. For these apartments, see the brief indications in M. Carrive, F. de Angelis, S. Falzone, M. Maiuro, F. Monier, and P. Tomassini, 'Dalla didattica alla ricomposizione. Primi risultati del workshop sulle pitture frammentarie dal Macchiozzo di Villa Adriana', in *Pareti dipinte. Dallo scavo alla valorizzazione. Atti del XIV Colloquio AIPMA (Napoli-Ercolano 9–13 settembre 2019)*, forthcoming.

93. P. Pensabene, A. Ottati, and P. Fileri, 'Nuovi scavi e prospettive di ricerca nella parte orientale della Villa Adriana', *ScA*, 17 (2011), 687–714.

94. *Historia Augusta, Hadrian* 26.5, cf. Cicero, *Tusculanae disputationes* 2.9 and *De legibus* 2.2.

95. See the investigations by J. Nielsen, T. Jespersen, and J. Asserbo, 'Investigazioni statiche sull'edificio romano della "Piazza d'Oro" a Villa Adriana', *ARID*, 35–6 (2010–11), 101–17.

96. The topic is treated in detail by E. Mayer, *Rom ist dort, wo der Kaiser ist: Untersuchungen zu den Staatsdenkmälern des dezentralisierten Reiches von Diocletian bis zu Theodosius II* (Mainz, 2002).

97. British Museum 1867, 0508.74. Despite the Roman names, the inscription is in Greek; see S. Walker, *Memorials to the Roman Dead* (London, 1985), 17, fig. 7.

98. For tumulus tombs in general and the Mausoleum of Augustus, see H. von Hesberg, *Monumenta. I sepolcri romani e la loro architettura* (Milan, 1994), 112–34. For the Mausoleum of Hadrian, see L. Abbondanza, F. Coarelli, and E. Lo Sardo (eds.) *Apoteosi da uomini a dei: il Mausoleo di Adriano* (Rome, 2013), especially P. Vitti, 'Il Mausoleo di Adriano, costruzione e architettura', 244–67.

99. D.W. Roller, *The World of Juba II and Kleopatra Selene: Royal Scholarship on Rome's African Frontier* (London, 2004), 128–30.

100. A. Gibb, 'Q. Lollius Urbicus. Builder of the wall between the Forth and the Clyde', *The Scottish Antiquary*, 55 (1900), 140–6.

101. N. Laubry, 'Aspects de la romanisation en Gaule et en Germanie: les monuments et les inscriptions funéraires sous le Haut Empire', *Pallas*, 80 (2009), 281–305.

102. von Hesberg, *Monumenta*, 73–89 and fig. 25.

103. For Isola Sacra, see I. Baldassarre, I. Bragantini, and C. Morselli, *Necropoli di Porto: Isola Sacra* (Rome, 1996).

Chapter 7

1. See L. Haselberger, *Urbem adornare. Stadt Rom und ihre Gestaltumwandlung unter Augustus = Rome's Urban Metamorphosis under Augustus* (Portsmouth, RI, 2007).

2. Cf. A.-V. Pont, *Orner la cité: enjeux culturels et politiques du paysage urbain dans l'Asie gréco-romaine* (Pessac, 2010).

3. As well as the relief from the Basilica Aemilia shown here (K.S. Freyberger and C. Ertel, *Die Basilica Aemilia auf dem Forum Romanum in Rom. Bauphasen, Rekonstruktion, Funktion und Bedeutung* (Wiesbaden, 2016), Taf. 47, Fig. c), there are similar scenes in wall paintings from the first-century CE Tomb of the Statilii in Rome (P.J. Holliday, 'The rhetoric of "Romanitas": the "Tomb of the Statilii" frescoes reconsidered', *MAAR*, 50 (2005), 89–129), and in mosaic from fourth-century CE Apamea in Syria (M.T. Olszewski and H. Saad, 'Pella-Apamée sur l'Oronte et ses héros fondateurs à la lumière d'une source historique inconnu: une mosaïque d'Apamée', in M.P. Castiglioni, R. Carboni, M. Giuman, and H. Bernier-Farella (eds.) *Héros fondateurs et identités communautaires dans l'Antiquité entre mythe, rite et politique, Quaderni di Otium*, 3 (2018), 365–408).

4. Plutarch, *Romulus* 11.3.

5. For these coins, see M.A. Cebrián Sánchez, 'Emerita Augusta y sus imágenes monetales I', *Omni*, 4 (2012), 31–42, especially 38–38, and Cebrián Sánchez, 'Emerita Augusta y sus imágenes monetales II', *Omni*, 6 (2013), 78–84.

6. H. von Hesberg, *Monumenta. I sepolcri romani e la loro architettura* (Milan, 1994), 79–81, fig. 20.

7. For the east, see L.M. Caliò, 'Dalla *polis* alla città murata. L'immagine delle fortificazioni nella sociatà ellenistica', *ArchCl*, 63 (2012), 169–221.

8. J.M. Abascal and S.F. Ramallo, *La ciudad romana de Carthago Nova: la documentación epigráfica* (Murcia, 1997), 86–94, and J.M. Noguera Celdrán and M.J. Madrid Balanza, 'Carthago Nova: fases e hitos de monumentalización urbana y arquitectónica (siglos iii a.C.–iii d.C.)', *Espacio, tiempo y forma. Serie I Prehistoria y Arqueología*, 7 (2014), 13–60. Livy 26.47.6 calls it one of the richest cities in Spain.

9. M.T. Boatwright, 'The city gate of Plancia Magna in Perge', in E. D'Ambra (ed.) *Roman Art in Context* (Englewood Cliffs, NJ, 1993), 189–207.

10. Pliny, *Naturalis Historia* 34.12.27.

11. N. Elkins, *Monuments in Miniature: Architecture on Roman Coinage* (New York, 2015), 21–2, 24–5.

12. *Tabula Siarensis*, in R.K. Sherk, *The Roman Empire: Augustus to Hadrian (Translated Documents of Greece and Rome 6)* (Cambridge, 1988), no. 36.

13. Pliny, *Naturalis Historia* 34.12.27.

14. For the Arch at Rimini, see S. De Maria, 'La porta augustea di Rimini nel quadro degli archi commemorative coevi. Dati strutturali', in *Studi sull'arco onorario romano* (Rome, 1979), 73–91.

15. See D. Scagliarini Corlàita, 'La situazione urbanistica degli archi onorari

nella prima età imperiale', in *Studi sull'arco onorario romano* (Rome, 1979), 29–72.

16. Cf. A.S. Russell, 'The word is not enough: a new approach to assessing monumental inscriptions. A case study from Roman Ephesos', *AJA*, 117 (2013), 383–412.

17. *CIL* VIII 11319.

18. Cf. E. La Rocca, 'Il Traianeo di Italica e la biblioteca di Adriano a Atene', in E. Calandro and B. Adembri (eds.) *Adriano e la Grecia* (Milan, 2014), 61–70.

19. W.L. MacDonald, *The Architecture of the Roman Empire II: An Urban Appraisal* (New Haven, CT, 1986), chapter 2.

20. See J. Frakes, *Framing Public Life: The Portico in Roman Gaul* (Vienna, 2009), chapters 3 and 5 for a detailed regional study.

21. See H. Thür, 'Zur Kuretenstrasse von Ephesos: eine Bestandsaufnahme der Ergebnisse aus der Bauforschung' in S. Ladstätter, J. Auinger, and I. Kowalleck (eds.) *Neue Forschungen zur Kuretenstrasse von Ephesos* (Vienna, 2009), 9–28.

22. A. Waldner, 'Heroon und Oktogon. Zur Datierung zweier Ehrenbauten am unteren Embolos von Ephesos anhand des keramischen Fundmaterials aus den Grabungen von 1989 und 1999', in S. Ladstätter, J. Auinger, and I. Kowalleck (eds.) *Neue Forschungen zur Kuretenstrasse von Ephesos* (Vienna, 2009), 283–316.

23. H. Thür, *Das Hadrianstor in Ephesos* (Vienna, 1989).

24. U. Quatember, *Der Sogenannte Hadrianstempel an der Kuretenstrasse* (Vienna, 2017).

25. For the early history of monumental fountains, see B. Longfellow, *Roman Imperialism and Civic Patronage: Form, Meaning and Ideology in Monumental Fountain Complexes* (Cambridge, 2011), chapter 1.

26. For these fountains, see Longfellow, *Roman Imperialism*, 64–8, 77–95, and for Ariston's fountain U. Quatember, *Das Nymphaeum Traiani in Ephesos* (Vienna, 2011). For the other major ornamental fountain on the Embolos, see K. Jung, 'Das Hydrekdocheion des Gaius Laecanius Bassus in Ephesos', in G. Wiplinger (ed.) *Cura Aquarum in Ephesus* (Leuven, 2006), 79–86.

27. Philostratus, *Vitae Sophistarum* 548.

28. On this type of architecture and its range of uses, see C. Berns, 'Frühkaiserzeitliche Tabernakelfassaden. Zum Beginn eines Leitmotivs urbaner Architektur in Kleinasien', in C. Berns, H. von Hesberg, L. Vandeput, and M. Waelkens (eds.) *Patris und Imperium. Kulturelle und politische Identität in den Städten der römischen Provinzen Kleinasiens in der frühen Kaiserzeit* (Leuven, 2002), 159–74.

29. The classic study is M. Lyttelton, *Baroque Architecture in Classical Antiquity* (London, 1974).

30. J. McKenzie, *The Architecture of Petra* (Oxford, 1990), chapter 5, and *The Architecture of Alexandria and Egypt 300 BC and AD 700* (New Haven, CT, 2007), chapter 5.

31. See B. Russell, *The Economics of the Roman Stone Trade* (Oxford, 2013), 33–6 for the text and a discussion.

32. The basic study remains J. Formigé, *Le Trophée Des Alpes (La Turbie)* (Paris, 1949).

33. Vitruvius 1.3.

34. For this and other aspects of rebuilding inscriptions, see E. Thomas and Ch. Witschel, 'Constructing reconstruction: claim and reality of Roman rebuilding inscriptions from the Latin West', *PBSR*, 60 (1992), 135–77.

35. See E. Thomas, *Monumentality and the Roman Empire* (Oxford, 2007), chapter 9.

List of Figures

The publisher would like to thank the following individuals and institutions who have kindly given permission to reproduce the illustrations listed below.

Huqoq, Israel, c. early fifth century CE. Copyright 2018 American Schools of Oriental Research.

52. Capitolium, Dougga (Tunisia), 167–169 CE. Photo Niccolò Mugnai.

53. Temple of Jupiter Optimus Maximus, Juno and Minerva (Capitoline temple), Capitoline Hill, Rome, said to have been dedicated c. 509 BCE. Copyright: John N. Hopkins. Printed in *The Genesis of Roman Architecture* 2016, Fig. 87 and Fig. 89.

54. Reconstruction of the terracotta pediment decoration of an unknown Etrusco-Italic temple, c. 530 BCE. From Nancy A. Winter, *Symbols of Wealth and Power*, University of Michigan Press, Copyright © 2009, Drawing by Renate Sponer Za.

55. Plan and computer reconstruction of the Republican victory temples in Largo Argentina, Rome. Courtesy of Penelope J. E. Davies.

56. The Roman orders. Credit: Luka Pajovic.

57. Temple of Portunus, Rome, c. 100 BCE. From J.W. Stamper, *The architecture of Roman temples. The Republic to the middle Empire*, CUP 2005, Fig. 44. Reproduced with permission of Cambridge University Press through PLSclear.

58. Second to early first century BCE Corinthian capitals.
a) 'Temple of Vesta', Tibur (Tivoli), Italic Corinthian G. Taylor and E. Cresy, *The Architectural Antiquities of Rome*, plate 70, Temple of Vesta at Tivoli, 1821.
b) 'Capitolium' or 'Temple of Peace', Paestum, Italic figured Corinthian; Adapted from F. Krauss and R. Herbig, *Der korinthisch-dorische Tempel am Forum von Paestum*, © 1939.
c) Round Temple by the Tiber, Rome, standard Hellenistic Corinthian (so-called 'Normal' Corinthian). Photo Niccolò Mugnai.

59. Round temple by the Tiber (also known as the Temple of Hercules Olivarius), Rome, late second century BCE. Photo Niccolò Mugnai.

60. Restored original plan of the Porticus of Metellus in the Campus Martius, Rome, post-146 BCE. Courtesy of Penelope J. E. Davies.

61. Terracotta Campana plaque, first century CE. Photo © Louvre Museum, Dist. RMN-Grand Palais / Anne Chauvet.

62. Sanctuary of Fortuna Primigenia, Palestrina (modern Praeneste), near Rome, c. 120 BCE. Courtesy Angelo Pinci.

63. Forum of Augustus and Temple of Mars Ultor, Rome, dedicated 2 BCE. Photo Niccolò Mugnai.

64. Temple of Mars Ultor, Forum of Augustus, Rome, dedicated 2 BCE. Photo Niccolò Mugnai.

65. Distribution map of the main sources of marble used in the Roman empire. Map credit: Konogan Beaufay.

66. Computer reconstruction of the interior of the Temple of Mars Ultor, Rome, dedicated 2 BCE. © Altair4 Multimedia.it.

67. Figured pilaster capital with Pegasus volutes from the interior decoration of the Temple of Mars Ultor, Rome, dedicated 2 BCE. Photo Janet DeLaine.

68. Temple of Castor, Rome, rebuilt and rededicated c. 6 CE. Photo Janet DeLaine. By concession of the Ministero della Cultura - Parco archeologico del Colosseo.

69. Artist's reconstruction of the Temple of Peace, Rome, dedicated 75 CE, paid for by the spoils of the Jewish War (70–71 CE). Copyright Ministero per i Beni e le Attività Culturali, Soprintendenza speciale per i beni archeologici di Roma.

70. Temple of Roma Aeterna and Venus Felix, Rome, vowed by Hadrian in 121 CE and not finished before 135 CE. a) Credit Konogan Beaufay b) daryl_mitchell / Wikimedia Commons / CC BY-SA 2.0.

71. Pergamon, *cistophorus* of Augustus, silver, 20–18 BCE. © The Trustees of the British Museum.

72. Temple of Roma and Augustus, Mylasa (Asia Minor), c. 11 BCE – 2 CE. From: Richard Pococke. *A Description of the East, and some other Countries*, London, W. Bowyer, MDCCXLV (1743–1745).

73. Reconstructed plan of the Temple of Deified Trajan, Italica (Spain), early Hadrianic. Copyright: Pilar Leon.

74. Egyptian-style Temple of Hathor at Dendara, Egypt, dedicated by Augustus 30 BCE. Juergen Ritterbach / Alamy Stock Photo.

75. Temple of Jupiter Heliopolitanus, Baalbek, begun in the early first century CE. Copyright: Mark Wilson Jones.

76. Interior of the 'Temple of Bacchus', Baalbek, Lebanon, mid-second century CE. Bernardo Ricci Armani / Getty Images.

77. Temple of Bel, Palmyra, Syria, completed around 32 CE. a) James Gordon / Wikimedia Commons / CC BY 2.0 b) H. Sayrig, R. Amy, and E. Will, *Le Temple de Bel a Palmyre, Vol. 2. Album* (Paris 1975) plate 4.

Helissa Grundemann / Shutterstock.com. By concession of the Ministero della Cultura - Parco archeologico del Colosseo.

132. Site plan of Hadrian's Villa, Tibur (Tivoli), 118–138 CE. Courtesy Michael Ytterberg, M Y Architecture.

133. 'Canopus' and 'Serapeum' at Hadrian's Villa, Tibur (Tivoli), 130s CE. Photo Janet DeLaine.

134. Diocletian's villa/palace, Split (Croatia), c. 305 CE, artist's reconstruction. Credit Ernest Hébrard / Wikimedia Commons.

135. Historic photograph of the Tomb of Caecilia Metella on the Via Appia outside of Rome, 20s BCE. Credit: Historical Views / agefotostock.

136. The Mausoleum of Hadrian, begun in the 120s and completed in 139 CE after Hadrian's death, with the contemporary Pons Aelius over the Tiber. Credit: Boris Stroujko / Shutterstock.com.

137. Painted replica of the Monument of the Secundinii in the Rheinisches Landesmuseum, Trier (Germany). Credit: imageBROKER / Alamy Stock Photo.

138. Mausoleum of the Julii, just outside Glanum (Provence), c. 20–20 BCE. Credit: Danita Delimont / Alamy Stock Photo.

139. Street of house tombs, necropolis of Portus (Isola Sacra), at the mouth of the Tiber, second century CE. Credit: DEA / S. VANNINI / Getty Images.

140. Reconstructed quadrifons arch at Lepcis Magna. © Andrew Lane.

141. Relief sculpture from the Basilica Aemilia, Rome, Augustan. Credit: Marie-Lan Nguyen / Wikimedia Commons / CC BY 2.5.

142. Silver *denarius* of Emerita Augusta (modern Mérida, western Spain), reverse showing city walls and double gate, Augustan. Courtesy American Numismatics Society. Gift of P. K. Anderson.

143. The 'Porta di Giove', one of the nine city gates of Falerii Novi (Italy), mid third century CE. Credit: Howardhudson / Wikimedia Commons / CC BY-SA 3.0.

144. City gate (the Porta Iovia, now Porta dei Borsari) at Verona (Italy). Photo Janet DeLaine.

145. The triple arched gateway to the Commercial Agora of Ephesus (right), dedicated by Mazeus and Mithridates, freedmen of Augustus; on the left, the façade of the Library of Celsus. Credit: OeAI-OeAW.

146. The 'triumphal arch' entrance to the walled forum, Sufetula (modern Sbeitla, Tunisia), mid second century CE. Credit: Keren Su/China Span / Alamy Stock Photo.

147. Colonnaded street at Palmyra, second to third centuries CE. From: Robert Wood, *The Ruins of Palmyra, Otherwise Tedmor, in the Desart.* (London, 1753), Plate 35.

148. Commemorative monuments along the Embolos, Ephesus, representing an accumulation from the second century BCE to the third century CE. Photos by Janet DeLaine; Reconstruction drawing Pollio Monument and Fountain of Domitian, Ephesos, A-W-OAI-PLN-00910 ©OeAI-OeAW/ F. Eichler; Reconstruction drawing Memmius Monument, Ephesos, A-W-OAI-PLN-01894 © OeAI-OeAW/ U. Outschar; Reconstruction drawing Embolos, Ephesos, A-W-OAI-PLN-12136 © OeAI-OeAW/H. Thür; Reconstruction drawing Embolos, Ephesos, A-W-OAI-PLN-15172 © OeAI-OeAW; Reconstruction drawing Nymphaeum of Trajan, Ephesos, A-W-OAI-PLN-19114 © OeAI-OeAW/ H. Pellionis; Reconstruction drawing Gate of Mazaeus and Mithridates, Ephesos, A-W-OAI-PLN-19152 © OeAI-OeAW/ W. Wilberg. Photo composition credit: Konogan Beaufay.

149. Rome, Porta Maggiore, monumentalised arches of the Aqua Claudia and Anio Novus aqueducts over the via Praenestina and the via Labicana, completed 52 CE. Credit: adam eastland / Alamy Stock Photo.

150. 'El-Khasneh', monumental tomb façade, Petra (Jordan), c. 1st c BCE. Credit: Armando Oliveira / Shutterstock.com.

151. Villa of the Mysteries at Pompeii, Second 'Architectural' Style Wall painting in Cubiculum 16, first century BCE. Credit: Mentnafunangann / Wikimedia Commons / CC BY-SA 4.0.

152. Baths of Caracalla, Rome, figured Composite capital, c. 211–217 CE. Credit: Konogan Beaufay.

153. Corinthianizing *intarsia* pilaster capital from the Horti Lamiani. Rome. Credit: Collezione dei Musei Capitolini / Creative Commons Attribution 3.0.

154. The trophy of the Alps at La Turbie (France), erected c. 6 BCE to celebrate and record Augustus' victory over Alpine 45 tribes. Credit: CMN dist. Scala, Florence. Image from Scala Archives.

Glossary

abacus: a flat slab forming the upper element of a column capital.

acanthus: a common Mediterranean plant, with divided leaves forming soft (*acanthus mollis*) or spiky (*acanthus spinosus*) lobes, the basis of much of the ornament of the Corinthian order.

adyton (or *adytum*): inner shrine of a temple, typically used in Syrian temples.

aedes, *-is*: literally 'a building for habitation' in Latin, used both for a dwelling of the gods and hence a shrine or temple, or more commonly a dwelling for men and hence a house.

aedicule (Latin: *aedicula*, *-ae*): a small decorative structure like a miniature temple front, comprising two columns supporting a pediment, usually triangular but also segmental.

agora, *ai*: a Greek term for an open market and meeting place of a town, roughly the same as the Roman Forum.

ala, *-ae*: literally 'wings', used for the side projections of temples, or in houses for the deep alcoves at the rear of the atrium in a Roman house.

ambulatio, *-ones*: literally 'a place for walking', hence paths, colonnades, or corridors, particularly associated with gardens in domestic architecture or baths.

amphitheatre: an elliptical or oval theatre-like structure for viewing entertainment from all sides.

amphora, *-ae*: a terracotta transport and storage container, two-handled and usually with a pointed base.

apodyterium, *-a*: the changing room of a bath, sometimes with niches for the storage of garments and benches.

aqueduct: a water-supply system with water carried from a distant source in conduits buried in the ground or raised on a series of piers and arches to cross low-lying land and valleys.

architrave: a stone beam or lintel; the lowest horizontal element of the classical entablature spanning the interval between two columns.

arcuated lintel: an arched lintel springing directly from columns, replacing the normal flat lintel, sometimes called a 'Syrian arch'.

areostyle: column spacing of more than three times the lower diameter of the column shaft.

artifices tectorum: literally, roof-makers.

ashlar masonry: masonry of large squared blocks in horizontal courses, usually arranged lengthwise (stretchers) or alternatingly lengthwise and crosswise (headers).

Aswan granite: a coarse red granite from Aswan on the Nile, much used in Roman imperial building projects.

atrium, *-a*/*cavum*, *-a aedium*: the main space of an Italic or Roman house, usually partly roofed. See also *compluvium*, *impluvium*, compluviate, displuviate.

attic: a section of wall with its own cornice above the entablature of a columnar order, common in porticoes, monumental arches and gateways, and amphitheatres.

auctoritas: literally, 'authority', one of the desirable attributes of public building.

balneum, *-a* (*balaneion* in Greek): the original term for baths in Latin, later used for small and/or simple baths, usually privately owned, in contrast to major public baths (*thermae*).

'barley-sugar' column: a column where the shaft is twisted along its length like a stick of barley-sugar.

barrel-vault: a vault with a semicircular or segmental cross-section.

basalt: a general term for the stone produced by solidified lava, used around Rome for paving roads and in foundations.

basilica: in the Roman form, a large rectangular hall comprising a tall central nave with upper galleries and clerestory windows, usually with aisles on all four sides.

basilical hall (in baths), also *basilica thermarum*: a multi-purpose large hall in a bath building arranged like a civic *basilica*, used primarily for exercise or social intercourse.

basis villae: large foundation terraces, predominantly of vaulted concrete, supporting extensive villa constructions on sloping terrain.

belvedere: a lookout designed for enjoying the view.

bessalis, -es: a square brick measuring two-thirds of a Roman foot each side.

bipedalis, -es: a square brick measuring two Roman feet each side.

bonding course: a horizontal course, usually of brick, that runs the whole length and thickness of a wall.

bouleuterion: a public building for the meeting of the town council in Greek cities.

brick facing: a common form of facing for Roman concrete walls.

brick stamp: a stamp impressed into the wet clay of a brick, particularly one containing a text. The most basic form, in use also in the Hellenistic world, comprises a name in the possessive, i.e. of x, usually a person but also an entity like a city. At Rome in the imperial period, especially from the late first to early third centuries CE, the texts were further developed and can indicate the name of the landowner, the name of the brick-field, the name of the workshop owner, and occasionally the name of the actual worker; at particular times, they can also include the names of the consuls, which provide a specific date.

buttress: a structure built up against a wall for support or reinforcement.

caldarium, -a: the main hot room in a Roman bath, containing heated pool(s).

capital: the upper member of a classical column and a distinguishing feature of the columnar orders (Tuscan, Doric, Ionic, Corinthian).

caryatid: sculpted female figure used in place of a column or pillar to support an entablature.

cavea, -ae: the raked seating area in a theatre, amphitheatre, or circus.

cella, -ae: the inner main chamber of a temple containing the cult image of the deity.

cenaculum, -a: originally a term for a dining room, but later used for an upper-floor apartment.

cenotaph: a monument commemorating a dead person (or persons) who is buried elsewhere.

centering: a temporary framework, usually wooden, built to support an arch or vault during its construction and intended to be removed. See also formwork.

circus: an arena for chariot or horse racing, usually curved at one end with the starting gates at the other.

clerestory: a row of windows in the upper part of a wall above an aisle, usually to light the central nave of a basilica.

collegium, -a: an association or corporation of individuals with a common interest, usually connected with religion, trade, or occupation, with a predominantly social and funerary function.

colonia, -ae: originally a military colony of Roman or Latin citizens; later a privileged municipal status.

colonnade: a row of evenly spaced columns, usually supporting a roof or terrace, and generally opening onto an exterior space.

columbarium, -a: a tomb chamber with many small niches or recesses resembling a dovecote used to hold the cremation urns of the dead.

comitium: a building for civic assembly, usually located at or near the forum.

compluviate: of an *atrium*, with the roof sloping inwards to the *compluvium*.

compluvium, -a: the opening in the roof of an *atrium* in a Roman house which directs rainwater into the *impluvium* below.

Composite capital: a hybrid capital combining the bell and acanthus leaves of the Corinthian capital with the four-sided Italic Ionic capital in places of the Corinthian volutes.

Corinthian *atrium*: an atrium in which the edge of the *compluvium* is supported on columns arranged around the *impluvium*.

Corinthian order: the most decorative of the Greek and Roman orders. The normal Roman form has fluted or unfluted columns on bases, tall capitals decorated with one or more usually two rows of acanthus leaves with vertical volutes supporting the corners of the abacus, and an Ionic cornice usually comprising a three-step architrave, a continuous plain or sculpted frieze, and a projecting cornice supported on modillions.

cornice: the uppermost element of the classical entablature or the crowning element of a roof, which projects away from the vertical surface of the wall

crenellation: by a regular pattern of uniform rectangular openings dividing the top of a parapet wall, normally associated with fortifications.

crepis: low platform of a Greek temple with steps all round.

cross vault: a vault formed by the intersection of two semi-circular barrel vaults.

crow-stepped merlon: a triangular merlon where the sloping sides are cut into square steps.

crown (of vault/dome): the highest point of a vault or dome.

cryptoporticus: usually a slightly sunken arcade or a fully underground barrel-vaulted gallery or storage area, usually lit by openings or windows cut into the upper part of the vault.

cubiculum, -a: a multi-functional private chamber in a Roman house, sometimes but not invariably used as a bedroom.

curatores operum publicorum: the high-ranking officials in charge of public works in Rome.

decastyle: describes a temple with ten columns across the front.

decor, decorum: a key concept used by Vitruvius meaning both visual grace or beauty, and appropriateness or suitability.

decuria, -e: a division, group or company, literally consisting of ten, but also used more generally for groups of other sizes.

decurio, -ones: a member of a town council.

diaeta, -ae: a summer-house or pavilion.

dignitas: dignity

dipteral: a temple surrounded by two rows of columns instead of the usual one.

displuviate: of an *atrium*, with the roof sloping away from the *compluvium*.

dispositio: literally, a regular arrangement of something, one of the elements of architecture according to Vitruvius, in relation to the working out of the details of a design.

distributio: literally, a distribution, one of the elements of architecture according to Vitruvius, in relation to the economic aspects of a building project.

domus: strictly speaking in Roman terms a citizen household, and by extension a house, in modern scholarship usually used for a single-family dwelling, and generally one of some standing.

Doric order: one of the three main Greek orders, comprising a fluted shaft without a base, a simple capital of a circular *echinus* and square *abacus*, a plain architrave with a distinctive triglyph and metope frieze, and a cornice with mutules and *guttae*.

double shell vault: a vault with an inner and outer shell, separated at least in part by voids.

drum: a cylindrical element, either the supporting structure of a dome, or section of a column shaft.

dry-stone wall: a wall built without the use of mortar.

echinus: a circular, rounded, cushion-shaped element forming the lower part of a Doric or Tuscan capital.

Egyptian *oecus*: an *oecus* of basilical form with clerestory windows and two stories of columns.

engaged order: a decorative order projecting from but forming an integral part of a wall, typically in the form of half-columns or pilasters.

entablature: the horizontal elements carried by a colonnade, or over a wall, consisting of architrave (lintel), frieze, and cornice.

ergepistatos, -oi: a builder.

ergolabos, -oi: contractor, equivalent to *redemptor* in the Greek East.

euergetism: the voluntary gift-giving of individual members of the wealthy élite classes to the benefit of the wider urban community.

eurythmia: a Greek term meaning visual harmony, one of the elements of architecture according to Vitruvius.

exedra: a recess, rectangular or apsidal, with a wide front opening, often divided by columns.

ex manubiis: paid for from war booty.

faber tignuarius, fabri tignuarii: literally a worker in wood, but also the general term for a builder.

fauces: the entry passage in a Roman *atrium* house.

figured capital: a capital of any type incorporating a figured element, human or animal, or a symbolic motif, either replacing some part of the capital or added to it.

firmitas: strength, one of Vitruvius' key aspects of good architecture.

flat arch: an arch with horizontal upper and lower surfaces, also called a lintel arch.

formwork: supporting structure, usually of wood, to give shape to earth or mortared rubble construction, including foundations, walls, and vaults.

forum, -a: originally a market-place, but in general the centre of a Roman city, with one or more of political, juridical, religious, social, and commercial functions.

frieze: the intermediary element of an entablature between the architrave and the cornice, in the Ionic and Corinthian orders often decorated in relief or used for an inscription.

frigidarium, -a: a cold room with cold plunge pool(s) in a Roman bath.

gymnasium, -a: the primary educational and athletic training institution of the Greek-speaking world, which was eventually combined with the Roman bath as the bath-gymnasium.

harena, -ae fossicia, -ae: literally 'pit-sand', the volcanic ash from around Rome, the key ingredient in Roman mortar.

haunch: the lower part of a vault or arch just above its springing point.

hexastyle: describes a temple with six columns across the front.

hippodrome: the Greek word for a circus.

hollow voussoir: a type of voussoir generally used in baths, comprising a terracotta box which allowed heated gases to pass through.

hortus: a garden, originally the productive garden of a house.

horti: literally gardens, used specifically for the suburban villas and pleasure gardens of the rich on the outskirts of Rome.

hypocaust: the standard Roman heating system, used mainly for baths but also sometimes in houses, where a floor raised on short piers (*pilae*) is heated by the circulation of hot gases from one or more furnaces stoked from outside.

impluvium, -a: a shallow pool in the *atrium* of a Roman house, designed to collect the rainwater from the *compluvium*, often to store in an underground cistern.

impost: the point or element from which an arch or vault arch springs.

impost block: a trapezoidal element set directly above a column or pier to accept the end of an arch.

incertum: a facing for mortared rubble construction made of small irregular pieces of stone with one flat face.

insula, -ae: literally meaning an island, in Roman legal terms it referred to accommodation which was rented out and brought in an income. The term could also mean a city block, a single structure comprising several different types of accommodation, an apartment block, or a single apartment in a block. In modern usage it is most often used for a multi-storey apartment block.

Ionic order: one of the three main Greek and Roman orders, in the Roman period comprising a base on a plinth, a fluted column shaft, and a capital with horizontal scrolling volutes, and an entablature with a usually three-stepped architrave, a plain or decorated frieze, and a complex cornice with a varied series of mouldings but normally including dentils.

keystone: the central element of a voussoir arch, which locks the other stones into place.

laconicum, -a: a dry sweating room in Roman baths.

lapidarius, -i: a worker in stone.

levelling course: through course of brick in a mortared rubble wall, the functions of which are debated but relate mainly to the construction process.

lime: produced by burning limestone, which removes the carbon dioxide leaving calcium oxide, known as quicklime, which is mixed with excess water to produce slaked lime, the key component of mortar.

Luna marble: a fine grey-white marble from the quarries of Cararra in northwestern Italy, in the Apuan Alps above the Roman colony of Luna (modern Luni).

lunette: the semi-circular space below an arch.

macellum, -a: a market building, especially for meat, fish, and other foodstuffs.

magistri quinquennales: chief magistrates of an association, elected for a five-year term.

magnificentia: grandeur, magnificence or splendour, one of Vitruvius' aspects of good architecture.

manubial: see *ex manubiis*.

marmorsaal: a modern term used to describe a richly decorated hall in a bath-gymnasium, sometimes thought to be associated with the imperial cult (also called a Kaisersaal).

mausoleum: originally a large and lavish tomb at Halicarnassus (modern Bodrum, Turkey), named after the tomb of Mausolus, fourth-century BCE ruler of Caria, and one of the Seven Wonders of the Hellenistic world, then used to denote any large tomb.

medianum: the central shared living space of a rented apartment in multiple occupancy, often used (erroneously) to designate an apartment with a wide hall acting as the central access space.

merlon: the solid upright section of a crenellated parapet.

modillion: a horizontal bracket, ostensibly supporting the cornice of the Roman Corinthian order, most commonly scroll-shaped with an acanthus leaf underneath but can also be S-shaped or rectangular.

mortared rubble construction: a construction technique where usually fist-sized pieces of rubble are laid in roughly horizontal courses in strong mortar, usually made of a pozzolanic substance mixed with slaked lime, often but erroneously called concrete; outer surfaces of vertical walls are usually faced with brick or with small stone blocks.

municipium, -a: originally a free town in Roman Italy with its own laws but also some rights of Roman citizenship, later a native city in the empire with Roman citizenship (as opposed to a Roman *colonia*).

natatio: cold swimming pool in Roman baths.

necropolis, -eis: a cemetery.

niche: a rectangular or curved recess in a wall set above ground level.

Numidian marble: a hard, dense limestone from the quarries at Simitthus (modern Chemtou, Tunisia), valued primarily for its tawny yellow colour, often shading through to pink.

nymphaeum, -a: originally, a cave or grotto with running water source sacred to the nymphs, then generally an elaborate or monumental fountain structure.

octastyle: with eight columns across the front.

oculus: a round opening in the crown of a dome.

oecus, -i: a room in a house, especially a large one with interior columns on three sides.

oikodomoi: builders, particularly master-builders in the Greek East.

opus africanum: a wall construction technique using a framework of vertical and horizontal stone blocks, with a filling in a different technique.

opus sectile: a wall or floor decoration consisting of pieces of cut marble or other coloured material to make a pattern, which could be geometrical or figured.

orchestra: the flat area between the *cavea* and the stage of a theatre, circular in Greek but semi-circular in Roman theatres.

ordinatio: literally, an orderly arrangement, one of the elements of architecture according to Vitruvius, in relation to the numerical dimensions and proportions of a design.

ostracon, -a: a piece of broken pottery used for writing temporary documents, the ancient equivalent of scrap paper.

otium: leisure, in the sense of freedom from business, but also inactivity or idleness.

palaestra, -ae: a colonnaded enclosure for exercise in Greek gymnasia and Roman baths.

palombino: a dense creamy-white limestone, much used in *opus sectile*.

paraskenion, -a: one of the two wings either side of the stage in a Greek or Roman theatre.

pediment: the triangular end of a gabled roof as in a temple.

Pentelic marble: a fine, creamy-white marble from near Athens.

peripteral *sine postico*: describes a temple with a colonnade on three sides, but not on the rear.

peripteral: describes a temple with a continuous external colonnade on all four sides

peristasis: the colonnade of a peripteral building.

peristyle/*peristylium, -a*: a court with a colonnade on at least two sides, but often on all four.

Phrygian marble: a fine, translucent white marble with deep purple veins, much prized in the Roman period.

pietas: dutiful conduct towards the gods, relatives, the state, etc.

pila, -ae: a small, pier or column supporting a hypocaust floor.

pilaster: a rectangular strip like a flat column, projecting slightly from a wall.

pinacotheca, -ae: a picture gallery.

pit-sand: see *harenae fossiciae*.

pozzolan (also pozzolana): a volcanic ash rich in silica and alumina used with lime to make a very strong hydraulic mortar.

pulvis Puteolanis: a naturally occurring pozzolan from the Bay of Naples.

polis: the Greek word for a city, especially a city-state.

polygonal masonry: masonry made out of large irregular shaped blocks closely fitted together, typical of city walls in the limestone areas of central Italy in the Republican period.

porphyry: a hard igneous stone related to granite, in particular the purple porphyry of the eastern desert of Egypt, much prized for the association of its colour with royalty and the gods, and the green porphyry of Sparta.

portico: a passageway defined by columns or piers on one side and a wall on the other, also a colonnade.

porticus: a building composed of porticoes, see also *quadriporticus*.

praedium, -a: a landed estate.

principia: the headquarters building in a Roman legionary fortress where the standard of the Legion was kept.

Proconnesian marble: coarse-grained grey-white marble from the island of Proconnesus (modern Marmara, Turkey).

pronaos: the entrance porch in front of the *cella* (or "naos") of a temple.

propylaeum, -a: an entrance structure or gateway to a sanctuary or other large building (also propylon).

prostyle: describes a temple with columns on the façade only.

prytaneion: a civic building where the magistrates of a Greek city met.

pseudo-dipteral: describes a temple with a dipteral arrangement but with the inner row of columns removed resulting in wide space between the outer colonnade and the *cella*.

pseudo-peripteral: describes a prostyle temple with engaged columns on the sides and back of the *cella* as if in a peripteral arrangement.

pumice: a lightweight volcanic material, full of holes created by expanding gases during an eruption.

pycnostyle: describes a temple with a column spacing of one-and-a half column diameters.

quadrifrons: a four-way arch with two intersecting passages and four façades, usually placed over a crossroads.

quadriporticus: a four-sided portico enclosing an open space.

quicklime: see lime.

quinquennalis, -es: a chief magistrate holding office for a period of five years.

redemptor, -es: someone who contracts to provide goods or services, especially a building contractor.

relieving arch: an arch built into a wall usually to relieve the pressure on an opening below.

ressaut: a free-standing column placed in front of a wall and linked to it by a short section of projecting entablature.

reticulatum: a facing for mortared rubble construction made of small square blocks of stone set on the diagonal in a net-like pattern.

rostra: a speakers' platform or tribunal in a forum, named after the metal 'beaks' of captured ships which were put on display in the Forum Romanum.

roundel: a circular decorative feature with a central head or figure, also called a *tondo* (pl. *tondi*).

scaenae frons: the permanent decorative rear wall of the stage of a Roman theatre.

scoria: a lightweight volcanic material similar to pumice but denser.

sesquipedalis, -es: a square brick measuring one and a half Roman feet each side.

slaked lime: the result of mixing quicklime with copious mortar, and a principal component of mortar.

spandrel: the roughly triangular area between the haunch of an arch and a wall or another arch.

spectaculum, -a: a show or spectacle, in the Republican period used in the plural for a theatre or especially an amphitheatre.

spina: the central strip or divider running down the middle of a circus, more correctly called *euripus*.

springing: the starting point of an arch or vault.

stadium: a race course 600 feet long for foot-races.

stibadium: a semi-circular dining couch.

stoa (pl. *stoai* or stoas): a continuous linear portico in Greek and Hellenistic architecture.

structor, -es: a builder.

stucco: a fine plaster surface treatment and decoration, sometimes worked in relief.

symmetria: the abstract mathematical harmony of a design, one of the elements of architecture according to Vitruvius.

syncopated rhythm: an arrangement of columns and columnar aedicules on two or three levels where the spaces between column pairs alternates from one level to another.

Syrian pediment: a triangular pediment where the lintel of the central intercolumniation is arched rather than straight.

taberna, *-ae*: a one- or two-roomed commercial unit (shop or workshop) with a wide opening to the street.

tablinum: the central room at the rear of the *atrium* of a Roman house, originally used as master bedroom and records room, later a formal and public reception space.

temenos: a sacred area surrounding a temple, sometimes but not necessarily enclosed by a wall.

templum, *-i*: a ritually defined sacred space or sanctuary, not necessarily containing an *aedes*, or building.

tepidarium, *-a*: a warm room in a Roman bath.

testudinate *atrium*: an *atrium* with no opening in the roof.

tetrapylon: a free-standing structure on four piers, often erected at the intersection of two streets.

tetrastyle: with four columns, used equally for a temple façade and for a type of domestic *atrium* where the *compluvium* is supported on four columns set at the corners of the *impluvium*.

theatre motif: a series of arched openings in a wall flanked by engaged columns or pilasters.

thermae: baths, particularly the exceptionally large and lavish baths built by the emperors in Rome, and increasingly used for any large and/or luxurious baths in the imperial period.

tholos: a circular building, particularly a circular temple, but also used for the circular room with tubs in Greek-style baths.

tondo (pl. *tondi*): a circular decorative sculptural element usually with a head of a deity or a portrait head in the centre in high relief.

trabeated: refers to a structure with horizontal lintels and beams.

travertine: a form of limestone, resistant to weathering, relatively easy to work and commonly used in Rome. The main quarry of travertine supplying Rome was near Tibur, modern Tivoli.

tribunal: a raised platform found in some basilicas, used by the presiding magistrate.

triclinium, *-a*: a dining room, literally one containing three couches (*klinai*).

trilobe [trilobed]: with three apses.

tripartite forum: a modern term for a forum, usually in the western empire, with a temple precinct, an open porticoed space, and a basilica, usually at the opposite end to the temple.

truss: a closed triangular support for a roof, usually in wood.

tuff (also tufa; It. tufo): a lightweight sedimentary stone, used particularly for the consolidated volcanic ash which forms the basic geology of the city of Rome and in the Bay of Naples.

tumulus: a burial mound.

Tuscan *atrium*: an *atrium* in a Roman *domus* where the *compluvium* is supported on large beams fixed into the side walls.

Tuscan order: an Italic and Roman order with a plain circular capital, an unfluted shaft, and a base.

Tuscan temple: a temple built in the Tuscan order and with a hollow pediment.

Umbrella vault or dome: a domical vault where the inner surface is divided from springing to crown into a series of concave sections, or with concave sections alternating with flat ones.

urbanitas: city life, living in an urban fashion.

utilitas: utility, usefulness, one of the key virtues of good architecture according to Vitruvius.

vaulting tubes: terracotta tubes with interlocking ends made specifically to form the intrados of a vault, acting as permanent centering.

velarium, *-a* (also *vela*): the awning over the seating area of a theatre or amphitheatre to protect spectators from the sun.

veneer: wall cladding, usually in marble.

venustas: beauty, gracefulness, one of the key virtues of good architecture according to Vitruvius.

villa rustica: a working farm, or that part of a country estate devoted to farming.

villa urbana: the residential part of a country estate devoted to leisure pursuits and including the amenities of a *domus*.

volute: a decorative scroll motif, in particular horizontally in Ionic capitals, or in pairs vertically in Corinthian capitals.

voussoir: the wedge-shaped element of a stone arch or vault.

wattle-and-daub: a framework of interwoven branches or twigs (wattlework) plugged with clay or mud (daub).

xylikarios, -oi: a builder, particularly a carpenter working on roofs, in the Greek East.

Timeline

800–700 BCE

a) political	b) social/cultural	c) architecture
753 foundation of Rome (traditional) 753–716: legendary reign of Romulus	First contacts with the Greek and Phoenician worlds Emergence of the Greek *polis* Foundation of Carthage	'Hut of Romulus' on the Palatine

700–600 BCE

a) political	b) social/cultural	c) architecture
616–579: reign of Tarquinius Priscus	Emergence of Rome as an organized city-state Traditional date for the introduction of the *Ludi Romani* with chariot racing in the Circus Maximus	Creation of the Forum Romanum Building of the Cloaca Maxima *Pons Sublicius*, the first known bridge to span the Tiber

600–500 BCE

a) political	b) social/cultural	c) architecture
579–534: reign of Servius Tullius 534–509: reign of Tarquinius Superbus, last king of Rome 509: foundation of the Roman Republic	Greek world Building of colossal temples at Ephesus, Samos, Agrigentum, and Selinus (Sicily) Construction of the first Temple of Olympian Zeus in Athens	First monumental stone buildings in Rome First Tuscan-type temples in Italy First known use of the roof truss in Rome and central Italy 509: dedication of the Temple of Jupiter Optimus Maximus, Juno, and Minerva (Capitoline temple)

500–400 BCE

a) political	b) social/cultural	c) architecture
Establishment of joint Roman and Latin colonies (called Latin colonies) in central Italy as independent but allied communities Greek world 480: Greeks defeat Persians at Battle of Salamis 478: Athens becomes an imperial power	496: alternative date for the introduction of the *Ludi Romani* in honour of Jupiter Optimus Maximus Greek world Public baths become a feature of urban life in the Greek world c. 450–400: First known Corinthian capital in the Temple of Apollo at Bassae (Greece) 447–432: Parthenon, Athens c. 450: Iktinos and Kallikrates, architects of the Parthenon, active 421–406: Erechtheion, Athens	Earliest *atrium*-style houses 495–484: Temple of Castor and Pollux 433–431: First Temple of Apollo Medicus

400–300 BCE

a) political	b) social/cultural	c) architecture
Roman expansion in central Italy Earliest Roman citizen colonies on coastal sites 396: conquest of Veii by Rome 390: Sack of Rome by the Gauls 338: Defeat of Volscian fleet off Antium (modern Anzio) 328: foundation of the colony of Fregellae Greek world 323: death of Alexander the Great, his empire divided among his generals into the kingdoms of Macedonia (Antigonid), Syria (Seleucid), and Egypt (Ptolemaic) Start of the Hellenistic period	363: Inclusion of pantomime in the *Ludi Romani* Greek world c. 366–350: Mausoleum at Halicarnassus (one of the Seven Wonders of the ancient world) 331: foundation of Alexandria by Alexander the Great c. 331: Deinocrates, architect of Alexandria, active	c. 378–350: 'Servian' Walls of Rome c. 338: beaks (*rostra*) of defeated Volscian ships attached to speaker's platform in Forum Romanum 329: introduction of starting gates in the Circus Maximus 312: construction of the Via Appia from Rome to Capua begins

300–200 BCE

a) political	b) social/cultural	c) architecture
275: Rome completes conquest of peninsular Italy with defeat of Pyrrhus of Epirus 273: foundation of the colonies of Cosa and Paestum 264–241: First Punic War with Carthage 218–201: Second Punic War, culminating with the Battle of Zama in 202 218–184: military and political career of P. Cornelius Scipio Africanus (the Elder), defeated Hannibal 211: Sack of Syracuse by M. Claudius Marcellus Hellenistic world 282: establishment of the Attalid dynasty and kingdom of Pergamon 277–274, 272–239: reign of Antigonas Gonatas, king of Macedonia	264: earliest known gladiatorial contests in Rome, as part of funerary games by 240: first literary works in Latin 240: first plays as part of *Ludi Romani* 238: Introduction of the *Ludi Florae* 220: Introduction of the *Ludi Plebei* 216: Funerary games of M. Aemilius Lepidus, first attested gladiatorial contests in the Forum Romanum 212: Introduction of the *Ludi Apollinares* 204: introduction of *Ludi Megalenses* (for Cybele/ Magna Mater) by 202: introduction of the *Ludi Cereales* Hellenistic world Late third–early second: architect Hermogenes of Priene active Late third–early second: Apollonius of Perge wrote the *Conics* Origins of baroque style in Hellenistic Alexandria Vaulting tubes used in Hellenistic baths Royal tumulus tombs of the Numidian kings	Architectural development of the Comitium ?290: construction of the Temple of Feronia in Largo Argentina, Rome 241: Temple of Juturna in Largo Argentina after 241: 'Porta di Giove' at Falerii Novi (Italy) by 216 (rebuilt 209): *Macellum* (market) built off the Forum Romanum c. 204: stands built in Circus Maximus

200–150 BCE

a) political	b) social/cultural	c) architecture
204–after 149: political and military career of M. Porcius Cato the Elder 197: Spain becomes a Roman province 184: M. Porcius Cato the Elder censor 179: M. Aemilius Lepidus and M. Fulvius Nobilior censors c. 177 larger Roman citizen colonies replace Latin colonies 175: conquest of northern Italy complete 169: T. Sempronius Gracchus censor 168: naval victory over Perseus under Cn. Octavius 168–129: military and political career of P. Cornelius Scipio Africanus (the Younger), conqueror of Carthage	c. 200: Plautus, *Curculio*, partly set in the Forum Romanum by 190: Romans given permission to participate in pan-Hellenic games by 186: Greek athletic competitions in the Circus Maximus by 169: wild beast hunts (*venationes*) in the Circus Maximus Hellenistic world c. 190: Sanctuary of Athena at Pergamon, built by Eumenes II c. 168: rebuilding of the Temple of Olympian Zeus at Athens c. 168: Roman architect Cossutius active 166: first gladiatorial games in the Greek East	Corinthian order increasingly used for temple exteriors in Rome and Italy Earliest known Tuscan temple outside of Italy (at Saguntum, Spain) Start of '*opus africanum*' in North Africa and central Mediterranean c. 200: first mention of a *basilica* in Rome 196: earliest monumental free-standing arch 184: Basilica Porcia 179: Senate dedicates all the state income of the year to public building 179: Basilica Fulvia/Aemilia 179: temporary theatre in the Campus Martius for the *Ludis Apollinares*

Hellenistic world
179–169: reign of Perseus, king of
 Macedonia
175–164: reign of Antiochus IV
 Epiphanes, king of the Seleucid empire
159–138: reign of Attalos II, king of
 Pergamon

179: Temple of Juno Regina, Campus
 Martius
174: turning posts (*metae*) and lap
 counters (eggs) added to Circus Maximus
169: Basilica Sempronia
168: Porticus Octavia, the first public
 quadriporticus in Rome
154: first attempt to build a permanent
 theatre in Rome aborted by Senate

150–100 BCE

a) political	b) social/cultural	c) architecture
149–146: Third Punic War, destruction of Carthage and formation of the Roman province of Africa 146: Destruction of Corinth, creation of the province of Achaia 146: Conquest of Macedonia by Q. Caecilius Metellus Macedonicus 133: Asia Minor under Roman control 133: All except northwestern Spain under Roman control 125–121: conquest of southern Gaul and formation of the province of Gallia Narbonensis (modern Provence) 122: first attempt to found a Roman colony outside of Italy (Carthage) 118: first Roman colony outside of Italy established at Narbo Martius (modern Narbonne, Provence)	After 147: Greek architect Hermodorus of Salamis active in Rome After 146: Polybius completes *The Histories* 105: *Lex parieti faciundo Puteolana* at Puteoli (modern Pozzuoli)	Early second century: House of the Faun, Pompeii (restructured late second century) Samnite House, Herculaneum c. 150 First known use of mortared rubble as a building material for free-standing walls c. 150: construction of the main temple and the basilica in the colony of Cosa c. 150: Sanctuary of Juno at Gabii after 146: Porticus of Metellus in the Campus Martius 146–143: construction of the Temple of Jupiter Stator c. 120: Sanctuary of Fortuna Primigenia, Palestrina (modern Praeneste) c. 120: Stabian Baths, Pompeii 117: rebuilding of the Temple of Castor and Pollux in the Forum Romanum Late second century: 'Porticus Aemilia'/*navalia* built using mortared rubble Late second century: Temple ?of the Nymphs in Largo Argentina, Rome Late second century: Samnite sanctuary at Pietrabbondate

100–50 BCE

a) political	b) social/cultural	c) architecture
90: Tibur/Tivoli becomes *municipium* 91–88: Social war between Rome and Italian allies ('*socii*') 88–81 Civil war leading to L. Cornelius Sulla becoming dictator, returning to private status in 79 80: *deductio* of a Roman colony at Pompeii 81–48 Pompey the Great (Gnaeus Pompeius Magnus) in power 63: consulship of M. Tullius Cicero 61: third triumph of Pompey for his victories in Asia 60: first triumvirate (Pompey, Julius Caesar, M. Licinius Crassus) 58: Cicero exiled and his house destroyed 58–50: conquest of Gaul by Caesar	Bathing in public normal part of Roman daily life Second 'Architectural' Style Wall painting in Rome and central Italy c. 70s: birth of Vitruvius	Start of importation of coloured marble to Rome development of *reticulatum* Theatre at Iguvium 'El-Khasneh', monumental tomb façade, Petra (Jordan) c. 100: Temple of Fortuna Huiusce Dei (Fortune of this day), Largo Argentina c. 100: Round temple by the Tiber (earliest surviving marble temple in Rome) c. 100: Temple of Portunus, Forum Boarium c. 100: 'market building' at Ferentinum c. 100: Sanctuary of Hercules Victor, Tibur c. 100: basilica, Ardea (Italy) c. 100: basilica, Pompeii 83: Capitoline temple damaged by fire 80–70: amphitheatre, Pompeii c. 78: Substructures of the Capitoline Hill ('Tabularium') c. 70: Forum Baths of Pompeii c. 60: Temple of Hercules Pompeianus, near Circus Maximus, (re)built by Pompey the Great 58: temporary theatre of Aemilius Scaurus with extravagant *scaenae frons* 55–52: Theatre of Pompey 54–46: Caesar dedicates Forum of Caesar, Temple of Venus Genetrix, and Basilica Julia 52: temporary twin theatres/amphitheatre of tribune C. Scribonius Curio

a) political	b) social/cultural	c) architecture
Extensive colonization outside of Italy becomes regular	c. 44–24 CE: Strabo, Greek geographer, active	Introduction of Luna (Carrara) marble to Rome
45: Quadruple triumph of Caesar	c. 40–8: Horace, Roman poet, active	Major phase in building of *horti* in Rome and *villae urbanae* in Italy
44: murder of Caesar	37: Varro, *De re rustica*	Earliest Romano-Celtic temples
44: refounding of Corinth as a Roman colony	c. 30–9: Dionysius of Halicarnassus, *Roman Antiquities*	c. 50–25: Vitruvius' basilica at Fanum Fortunae (modern Fano), Italy
44–8: G. Maecenas, ally and friend of Augustus, active	c. 25 BCE–17 CE: Livy, *From the Foundation of the City* (history of Rome)	c. 50: Caesar starts work on Circus Maximus, completed by Augustus
43: second triumvirate (Octavian, Mark Antony, Lepidus)	c. 25–19: Virgil, *Aeneid*	49–45: Temple of Quirinus rebuilt in Doric order
37–4 CE: Herod the Great king of Judea	c. 27–25: Vitruvius's *De architectura*, dedicated to Augustus	43–30: rebuilding of the Temple of Saturn in the Forum Romanum in the Ionic order
31: Battle of Actium, Octavian defeats the forces of Mark Antony and Cleopatra	17: *Ludi Saeculares* in the Theatre of Marcellus	42–29: Temple of Deified Julius Caesar, Forum Romanum
29: Foundation of Nikopolis in western Greece by Augustus	7: (re)organization of the *collegium* of the *fabri tignarii*	36–28: Temple of Apollo Palatinus, Portico of the Danaids, on Palatine
29: Ephesus becomes the provincial capital of Asia Minor		c. 34: Reconstruction of the Temple of Apollo Medicus in Rome by Gaius Sosius, as the Temple of Apollo Sosianus
27: Octavian becomes Augustus, first emperor of Rome		30: dedication of the Temple of Hathor at Dendera (Egypt) by Augustus (started under Ptolemy XII)
Beginning of the imperial period		30–20: Tomb of Caecilia Metella on the Via Appia
25: foundation of the veteran colony of Augusta Emerita in Spain by Augustus		29: Augustus completes the enlargement of Forum of Caesar and rebuilding of the Curia (Curia Julia)
23: death of Claudius Marcellus, designated heir of Augustus		29: Temple (probably) to Deified Julius Caesar and the Goddess Roma at Ephesus, sponsored by Augustus
20–18: Pergamon becomes the centre of the cult of Rome and Augustus for the province of Asia		29 (or 19): Arch of Augustus, Forum Romanum
		After 29: Mausoleum/cenotaph of the Julii, Glanum (France)
16: foundation of Colonia Julia Augusta Felix Heliopolitana (Baalbek, Lebanon)		28: Mausoleum of Augustus completed
12: Death of Agrippa		26: Saepta Julia completed
		27: Arch of Augustus, Rimini
		c. 27–12: Agrippa's Pantheon
		25–c. 19: Baths of Agrippa in the Campus Martius
		23–15: Herod's fortress/palace at Herodium, 22–6: Herod's harbour and city at Caesarea
		c. 20–1: Temple of Ba'alshamin and Temple of Dushara in the sanctuary at Seeia (modern Si', Syria)
		20–18: Temple to Rome and Augustus, Pergamon
		16–8: Dedication of theatre and amphitheatre at Augusta Emerita (modern Mérida, Spain)
		after 16: start of the construction of the Temple of Jupiter Heliopolitanus, Baalbek (Lebanon)
		13/12: Temple to Augustus built by the governor of Egypt at Philae
		13/11: Theatre of Marcellus completed, in use by 17 for the *ludi saeculares*
		12: Baths of Agrippa left to the people of Rome
		11–2: Temple of Rome and Augustus at Mylasa (Turkey)
		7: Completion of the Diribitorium by Augustus (started by Agrippa)
		6: Trophy of the Alps, La Turbie (France)
		3/2: gateway to the Commercial Agora of Ephesus, dedicated by Mazeus and Mithridates, freedmen of Augustus
		2: Dedication of the Forum of Augustus and the Temple of Mars Ultor, in Rome (vowed 42 BCE)
		Late first century: 'Temple of Mercury' at Baiae

1–50 CE

a) political	b) social/cultural	c) architecture
14: Death of Augustus, publication of his *Res Gestae* 14–69: Julio-Claudian dynasty 14–37: Tiberius emperor 37–41: Caligula emperor 41–54: Claudius emperor	Cults of Roma and Augustus and to the deified emperors become widespread in the empire After 5: *Lex Julia Theatralis*	Introduction of window glass (incl. skylight and double glazing) 1–2: dedication of the theatre, Lepcis Magna (Libya) 6: reconstruction of the Temple of Castor and Pollux, Forum Romanum 11: dedication of the stoa-basilica at Ephesus 21–3: Camp of the Praetorian Guard, earliest large-scale use of brick in Rome c. 32: Completion of the Temple of Bel, Palmyra (Syria) 38–52: Aqua Claudia and Anio Novus aqueducts, including the Porta Maggiore c. 40–60: Pont du Gard near Nîmes, France

50–100 CE

a) political	b) social/cultural	c) architecture
54–68: Nero emperor 69–96: Flavian dynasty 69–79: Vespasian emperor 70–1: Jewish War 79–81: Titus emperor 81–96: Domitian emperor 96–8: Nerva emperor 98–117: Trajan emperor	c.40–79: Pliny the Elder active 62: earthquake in the Bay of Naples, heavy damage in Pompeii 64: Great Fire of Rome c. 64–8: Severus and Celer, architects of Nero's Domus Aurea, active 79: eruption of Vesuvius 80: Fire in Rome, destroying the Diribitorium and the Pantheon c. 80–120: Plutarch, philosopher and biographer, writing c. 81–96: Rabirius, architect of Flavian Palace, active c. 95–130: Suetonius, imperial biographer and scholar, active 99–109: Pliny the Younger, consul and provincial governor, active 98–120: Tacitus, consul and historian, writing	Earliest known colonnaded streets in eastern empire c. 50–75: refurbishing of the Porta Iovia (now Porta dei Borsari), Verona (Italy) 62–4: Baths of Nero in Campus Martius c. 62–79: *atrium* loses importance in houses at Pompeii and Herculaneum 64–8: Nero's Domus Aurea 70–5: Temple of Peace 70–80/1: Flavian Amphitheatre (Colosseum) ?70–81: Baths of Titus after 70: replacement of the Augustan Forum at Conimbriga with temple-forum complex c. 81: Arch of Titus c. 81–92: Reconstruction of the Pantheon by Domitian 81–9: Capitoline temple rebuilt by Domitian c. 81–96: main phase of the imperial palace on the Palatine c. 89–97 Forum Transitorium and Temple of Minerva, rededicated 97 as the Forum of Nerva Late: South Temple in the sanctuary at Seeia (modern Si', Syria)

100–50 CE

a) political	b) social/cultural	c) architecture
100: foundation of the colony of Timgad/ Thamugadi (Algeria) 101–2, 105–6: Trajan's military campaigns against Dacia 117: greatest extent of the Roman empire 117–38: Hadrian emperor c. 130–60: Q. Lollius Urbicus, soldier, provincial governor and urban prefect of Rome, active 138–61: Antoninus Pius emperor	Start of the 'Second Sophistic' c.104–20s: architect Apollodorus of Damascus active c. 120–66/7: M. Cornelius Fronto, orator and tutor to Marcus Aurelius, active c. 140–77: Herodes Atticus, sophist and consul, active c. 140–80: Aulus Gellius, author of the *Attic Nights*, active	Beginning of use of amphorae in vaults Start of 'marble style' in Asia Minor and the Levant 'Temple of Diana', Nîmes (France) (date disputed) House of the Mosaic if Venus, House of the Ephebe, Volubilis (Morocco) Early second century: Forum and sanctuary at Augusta Raurica (modern Augst, Switzerland) (phase 2 later second century CE) c. 100: Tomb of the Haterii in Rome (relief showing treadmill crane) c. 103: Trajan rebuilds Circus Maximus 103–5: Trajan's bridge over the Danube 104–9: Baths of Trajan 106–13: Forum of Trajan, Basilica Ulpia, Trajan's Column, and Trajan's Markets c. 110: insula ('Aracoeli') on the slopes of the Capitoline Hill c. 110–25: Reconstruction of the Pantheon 110s: Library of Celsus, Ephesus (Turkey) c. 118–38: Hadrian's Villa, Tivoli

a) political	b) social/cultural	c) architecture
		c. 118–30: Temple of Deified Trajan, Italica (Spain) after 118: Temple of Deified Trajan, Tarraco (modern Tarragona) c. 120s: Corinthian temple to Olympian Zeus at Euromos (Turkey) 121–not before 135: Temple of Roma Aeterna and Venus Felix in Rome, vowed by Hadrian c. 121: embellishment of the Hellenistic gateway of Perge (Turkey), by Plancia Magna c. 122–6: Hadrian's Wall (Britain) c. 125: Garden Houses, Ostia c. 130: Insula of the Paintings, Ostia c. 130–60: Colossal Temple of Hadrian, Cyzicus c. 132: Library of Hadrian in Athens; completion of the Temple of Olympian Zeus, Athens c. 136: Tomb to the family of Q. Lollius Urbicus, Tiddis (Algeria) c. 140–50: Theatre-amphitheatre, Verulamium (modern St Albans) 142: start of the construction of the Antonine Wall (Britain) 146/7: new *scaenae frons* for the Theatre of Lepcis Magna (Libya) 147–9: Baths of Vedius, Ephesus (Turkey), inaugurated

150–200 CE

a) political	b) social/cultural	c) architecture
161–80: M. Aurelius emperor, co-ruler with Lucius Verus in 161–9 180–92: Commodus emperor 193–235: Severan dynasty 193–211: Septimius Severus emperor	c. 150–80: Aelius Aristides, sophist and orator, active c. 150: Lucian of Samosata, writer and satirist, active c. 150: Pausanias, travel writer, active	c. 150: 'Temple of Bacchus', Baalbek (Lebanon), begun c. 150: 'triumphal arch' entrance to the forum of Sufetula (Tunisia) c. 160: Forum Baths, Ostia (Italy) 167–9: Capitolium, Dougga (Tunisia) 193: completion of the Column of M. Aurelius 193–211: colossal Temple of Hercules and Bacchus on the Quirinal Severan: Temple of Mars Mullo, Allones (France) Large baths, Thaenae (Tunisia) North ('Cluny') Baths, Paris

200–50 CE

a) political	b) social/cultural	c) architecture
211–17: Caracalla sole emperor 222–35: Severus Alexander emperor 235–85: Third-century crisis 238–44: Gordian III emperor 270–5: Aurelian emperor	203–11: Severan marble plan of Rome (Forma Urbis) 212: Caracalla grants universal Roman citizenship to all free men and women	Beginning of use of vaulting tubes in North Africa Villa at Nennig (Germany) Temple of Venus at Baalbek (Lebanon) c. 200: 'Palace of the Dux Ripae', Dura Europos (Syria) 203: Septizodium and of the Arch of Septimius Severus c. 203: quadrifons arch dedicated to Septimius Severus, Lepcis Magna c. 203–16: Severan Forum-Basilica complex at Lepcis Magna (Libya) 211–17: Baths of Caracalla 222–35: Baths of Nero rebuilt by Severus Alexander 230: Baths of Julia Memmia, Bulla Regia (Tunisia) c. 240: construction of the last known amphitheatre at Thysdrus (modern El Djem, Tunisia), possibly built by Gordian III c. 270–5: Aurelian builds new set of walls for Rome

250–300 CE

a) political	b) social/cultural	c) architecture
284–305: Diocletian emperor 293–313: Tetrarchy		c. 250: Monument of the Secundinii, Igel (Germany) After 283: Curia in the Forum Romanum rebuilt 298–305/6: Baths of Diocletian After 293–316: Imperial baths, Trier (Germany)

300–400 CE

a) political	b) social/cultural	c) architecture
306–37: Constantine emperor (sole emperor 324–37) 324: foundation of Constantinople as the new capital of Roman empire 357: Visit of Constantius II to Rome	301: Diocletian's Edict on Maximum Prices c. 350–c. 391: Ammianus Marcellinus, historian, active	Tomb of Trebius Justus (painting showing construction scene) c. 305: Diocletian's villa/palace, Split (Croatia) 306–13: Basilica of Maxentius/Basilica of Constantine (Basilica Nova) 312: Arch of Constantine

400–500 CE

a) political	b) historical/cultural	c) architecture
410: sack of Rome by Goths under Alaric 476: Odoacer, first barbarian king to rule Rome	416: Rutilius Namatianus, urban prefect in 414, *On His Return* 450–89: Sidonius Apollinaris, politician, writer and bishop, active c. 370–420: Jerome, writer and Christian ascetic, active	

Bibliographic essay

All chapters have notes, which refer the reader to further bibliography on specific buildings or topics and include all the references to the ancient sources. For the bibliography, I have given preference to the most recent works, in English where possible, in which earlier bibliography can be found. Under the Introduction, I have focused on the most important and accessible general works on Roman architecture, and not just the most recent.

Introduction

There are a number of good introductions to Roman architecture in English that cover more ground than has been possible in this short volume, most organized on more strictly chronological and geographical lines than here, and more closely fulfilling the needs of a handbook. The most up-to-date comprehensive treatment is F.K. Yegül and D.G. Favro, *Roman Architecture and Urbanism: From the Origins to Late Antiquity* (Cambridge, 2019). To some extent this supersedes A. Boethius and J.B. Ward-Perkins, *Etruscan and Roman Architecture* (Harmondsworth, 1970) (most easily accessible in two volumes as A. Boethius, *Etruscan and Early Roman Architecture*, 2nd edition revised by R. Ling and T. Rasmussen (Harmondsworth, 1978), and J.B. Ward-Perkins, *Roman Imperial Architecture* (Harmondsworth, 1981)), but these are still invaluable, if out-of-date in some aspects. There are useful introductory essays in R.B. Ulrich and C.K. Quenemoen (eds.) *A Companion to Roman Architecture* (Chichester, 2014), although the coverage is naturally less complete. The two volumes by W.L. MacDonald, *The Architecture of the Roman Empire, I: Introduction*, 2nd edition (New Haven and London, 1982) and *The Architecture of the Roman Empire, II: an Urban Appraisal* (New Haven and London, 1986) continue to be useful, the first for the concrete architecture of imperial Rome, the second on the architecture of Roman cities.

Despite the lack of an English translation, the well-illustrated two-volume compendium by P. Gros, *L'architecture romaine: du début du IIIe siècle av. J.-C. à la fin du Haut-Empire. 1. Les monuments publics, 2. Maisons, palais, villas, et tombeaux*, 3rd edition (Paris, 2017), which is organized by building typology, is immensely valuable.

For broad regional studies of Roman architecture see P. Johnson and I. Haynes (eds.) *Architecture in Roman Britain* (York, 1996); J.C. Anderson, *Roman Architecture in Provence* (Cambridge, 2013); J. McKenzie, *The Architecture of Alexandria and Egypt. C. 300 B.C. to A.D. 700* (New Haven and London, 2007); and S. Macready and F.H. Thompson, *Roman Architecture in the Greek World* (London, 1987).

For an introduction to the visual culture of Rome see J. Elsner and M. Squire, 'Sight and meaning', in M. Squire (ed.) *Sight and the Ancient Senses* (London, 2015), chapter 10. A more detailed study which includes the Greek world is T. Hölscher, *Visual Power in Ancient Greece and Rome: Between Art and Social Reality* (Oakland, 2018), especially chapter 1 on public architecture. For an experiential account of the city of Rome, see R. Jenkyns, *God, Space and City in the Roman Imagination* (Oxford, 2013).

As the bibliographies on most of the four key structures are extensive, I give here just the most recent and/or accessible. For the Pantheon, see T.A. Marder and M. Wilson Jones, *The Pantheon. From Antiquity to the Present* (Cambridge, 2015) with earlier bibliography; for the Flavian Amphitheatre (the Colosseum), see F. Coarelli (ed.) *The Colosseum* (Los Angeles, 2001) and N.T. Elkins, *A Monument to Dynasty and Death: The Story of Rome's Colosseum and the Emperors Who Built It* (Baltimore, 2019). For Hadrian's Wall, see D.J. Breeze and B. Dobson, *Hadrian's Wall* (London, 2000). Most of the bibliography for the Pont du Gard is in French, but see G. Fabre, *The Pont du Gard: Water and the Roman Town* (Paris, 1992), translated by J. Abbott.

The most accessible if somewhat idiosyncratic overview of Rome's history and culture is M. Beard, *SPQR: A History of Ancient Rome* (London, 2015). More detailed essays on specific topics can be found in H.I. Flower (ed.) *The Cambridge Companion to the Roman Republic* (Cambridge, 2014) and D. Potter (ed.) *A Companion to the Roman Empire* (Oxford, 2006), both with further bibliography.

On the problems of defining Roman, see L. Revell, *Roman Imperialism and Local Identities* (Cambridge, 2009), especially the preface and chapter 1. For an introduction to the variety of Roman architectures see N. Mugnai (ed.) *Architectures of the Roman World: Models, Agency, Reception* (Oxford, 2023) For a good overview of the Romanization debate see M.J. Versluys, 'Understanding objects in motion. An archaeological dialogue on Romanization', *Archaeological Dialogues*, 21 (2014), 1–20, and responses by T.D. Stek, 'Roman imperialism, globalization and Romanization in early Roman Italy: research questions in archaeology and ancient history', 31–40, and G. Woolf, 'Romanization 2.0 and its alternatives', 45–50. On Rome as a global culture, see M. Pitts and M.J. Versluys (eds.) *Globalisation and the Roman World: World History, Connectivity and Material Culture* (New York, 2015), especially chapter 1.

For the history of the excavations at Pompeii and changing interpretations, see A. Cooley, *Pompeii* (London, 2003). The best account of the history of the fabric of the city of Rome up until the twentieth century is still R. Lanciani, *The Destruction of Ancient Rome* (New York, 1899), and for the Fascist period R. Ridley, 'Augusti manes volitant per auras: the archaeology of Rome under the Fascists', *Xenia*, 11 (1986), 19–46.

On the need for and problems with reconstructions in Roman architecture, with numerous case studies, see L. Haselberger and J. Humphrey (eds.) *Imaging Ancient Rome. Documentation—Visualization—Imagination* (Portsmouth, RI, 2006), with F. Gabellone, 'The scientific transparency in virtual archaeology: New guidelines proposed by the Seville charter', in F. Chen, F. Gabellone, R. Lasaponara, G. Leucci, N. Masini, and R. Yang (eds.) *Remote Sensing and ICT for Cultural Heritage: from European and Chinese perspectives* (2015), 77–111, while for the broader context see T. Lanjouw, 'Discussing the obvious or defending the contested: why are we still discussing the 'scientific value' of 3D applications in archaeology?', in H. Kamermans, W. de Neef, C. Piccoli, A.G. Posluschny, and R. Scopigno (eds.) *The Three Dimensions of Archaeology* (Oxford, 2016), 1–12.

Chapter 1. An Empire of Cities

Useful short introductions to Rome's political history can be found in E. Bispham and W. Bowden (eds.) *Roman Europe: 1000 BC–AD 400* (Oxford, 2008), particularly G. Bradley, 'The Roman Republic: political history', 32–68, and B. Salway, 'The Roman Empire from Augustus to Diocletian', 69–108, and in A. Barchiesi and W. Scheidel, *The Oxford Handbook of Roman Studies* (Oxford, 2010), especially the essays by N. Terrenato, 508–18, 'Early Rome', H.I. Flower, 519–32, 'The Imperial Republic', and C.F. Noreña, 'The Early Imperial Monarchy', 533–46, all with further bibliographies. For more detailed surveys see the volumes of the Cambridge Ancient History: F.W. Walbank, *The Cambridge Ancient History. Volume 7. Part 2, The Rise of Rome to 220 B.C.* (Cambridge, 1989); A.E. Astin, *The Cambridge Ancient History. Volume 8, Rome and the Mediterranean to 133 B.C.* (Cambridge, 1989); J.A. Crook, A.W. Lintott, and E. Rawson, *The Cambridge Ancient History. Volume 9, The Last Age of the Roman Republic, 146–43 B.C.* (Cambridge, 1994); A.K. Bowman, E. Champlin, and A.W. Lintott, *The Cambridge Ancient History. Volume 10, The Augustan Empire, 43 B.C.–A.D. 69* (Cambridge, 1996); A.K. Bowman, P. Garnsey, and D. Rathbone, *The Cambridge Ancient History. Volume 11, The High Empire, AD 70–192* (Cambridge, 2000); and A.K. Bowman, P. Garnsey, and A. Cameron, *The Cambridge Ancient History. Volume 12, The Crisis of Empire A.D. 193–337* (Cambridge, 2005).

For a good account of the early history of Rome and the city's development into the early Republic, see T. Cornell, *The Beginnings of Rome: Italy and Rome from the Bronze Age to the Punic Wars (c. 1000–264 BC)* (London, 1995), and T.P. Wiseman, *Unwritten Rome* (Exeter, 2008), or T.P. Wiseman, *Remus: A Roman Myth* (Cambridge, 1995) for the problems with the sources for the earliest period.

Useful introductions to Rome as an imperial power are A. Erskine, *Roman Imperialism* (Edinburgh, 2010), and P.J. Burton, *Roman Imperialism* (Leiden, 2019). On the importance of Roman citizenship see E. Dench, *Romulus' Asylum* (Oxford, 2005), especially chapter 2, and K. Berthelot and J. Price (eds.) *In the Crucible of Empire: The Impact of Roman Citizenship upon Greeks,*

Jews and Christians (Leuven, 2019). E. Dench, *Empire and Political Cultures in the Roman World* (Cambridge, 2018) gives a stimulating account of local experiences of the Roman empire. For the Roman triumph, see M. Beard, *The Roman Triumph* (Cambridge, MA and London, 2007).

For recent and changing ideas on Roman colonization in Italy see the collected papers in G. Bradley and J.-P. Wilson, *Greek and Roman Colonization: Origins, Ideologies and Interactions* (Swansea, 2006), and T.D. Stek and J. Pelgrom, *Roman Republican Colonization. New Perspectives from Archaeology and Ancient History* (Rome, 2014), with extensive bibliographies.

On the Hellenistic world in general see G.R. Bugh (ed.) *The Cambridge Companion to the Hellenistic World* (Cambridge, 2006), with J.R.W. Prag and J.C. Quinn (eds.) *The Hellenistic West: Rethinking the Ancient Mediterranean* (Cambridge, 2013) for the often overlooked West. For its relation to Rome see J. Allen, *The Roman Republic and the Hellenistic Mediterranean: From Alexander to Caesar* (New York, 2020), and for the role of the Hellenistic city see R. Boehm, *City and Empire in the Age of the Successors: Urbanization and Social Response in the Making of the Hellenistic Kingdoms* (Oakland, 2018). On the common idea of a city between the Greek and Roman worlds see N. Purcell, 'Urbanism', in A. Barchiesi and W. Scheidel, *The Oxford Handbook of Roman Studies* (Oxford, 2010), 579–92.

For Rome and the West beyond the Mediterranean, see G. Woolf, *Becoming Roman: The Origins of Provincial Civilization in Gaul* (Cambridge, 1998) and his *Tales of the Barbarians: Ethnography and Empire in the Roman West* (Oxford, 2011). For some case studies see S. Keay and N. Terrenato (eds.) *Italy and the West. Comparative Issues in Romanization* (Oxford, 2001).

The fundamental work on euergetism is P. Veyne, abridged with an introduction by O. Murray, translated by B. Pearce, *Bread and Circuses: Historical Sociology and Political Pluralism* (London, 1992), and for the specific case of Roman Italy see K. Lomas and T. Cornell, *Bread and Circuses: Euergetism and Municipal Patronage in Roman Italy* (London, 2003). On the benefits to the donor, and the potential problems of euergetism, see A. Zuiderhoek, 'The Ambiguity of Munificence', *Historia*, 56 (2007), 196–213.

On Lepcis Magna in general, see A. Di Vita, G. di Vita-Evrard, L. Bacchielli, and R. Polidori, *Libya: The Lost Cities of the Roman Empire* (Cologne, 1999), with copious illustrations, and D.J. Mattingly, *Tripolitania* (London, 1995).

The literature on the relations between Greek and Roman culture is extensive. For the Republican period see E. Gruen, *Culture and National Identity in Republican Rome* (Ithaca, 1992), and A. Wallace-Hadrill, *Rome's Cultural Revolution* (Cambridge, 2008), and for the contemporary view from the east see R.M. Errington, 'Aspects of Roman Acculturation in the East under the Republic', in P. Kneissl and V. Losemann (eds.) *Festschrift für Karl Christ zum 65. Geburtstag* (Darmstadt, 1988), 140–57.

For the Augustan period, J. Richardson, *Augustan Rome 44 BC to AD 14: The Restoration of the Republic and the Establishment of the Empire* (Edinburgh, 2012) provides an accessible overview. P. Zanker, *The Power of Images in the Age of Augustus* (Ann Arbor, 1988) remains influential, and see G. Woolf, 'Provincial perspectives', in K. Galinsky (ed.) *The Cambridge Companion to the Age of Augustus* (Cambridge, 2005), 106–29 for the culture of cities under Augustus. For aspects of the empire in the imperial period, see P. Garnsey and R.P. Saller, *The Roman Empire: Economy, Society and Culture* (London, 2014).

For the life and career of Hadrian, see A. Birley, *Hadrian: The Restless Emperor* (London, 1997), and the beautifully illustrated exhibition catalogue edited by T. Opper, *Hadrian: Empire and Conflict* (London, 2008). For his impact on the provinces, see M.T. Boatwright, *Hadrian and the Cities of the Roman Empire* (Princeton, 2000), and T.E. Fraser, *Hadrian as Builder and Benefactor in the Western Provinces* (Oxford, 2006).

On the Second Sophistic, see G. Anderson, *The Second Sophistic: A Cultural Phenomenon in the Roman World* (London, 1993), T. Whitmarsh, *The Second Sophistic* (Oxford, 2005) and the essays in B. Borg (ed.) *Paideia: The World of the Second Sophistic* (Berlin, 2004). For the imperial cult, see the influential study of S.R.F. Price, *Rituals and Power: The Roman Imperial Cult in Asia Minor* (Cambridge, 1984), and J. Madsen, 'Joining the Empire: The imperial cult as a marker of a shared imperial identity', in W. Vanacker and A. Zuiderhoek, *Imperial Identities in the Roman World* (Abingdon and New York, 2016). On the continuation of Greek culture under the empire, see G. Woolf, 'Becoming

Roman, Staying Greek: Culture, Identity and the Civilizing Process of the Roman East', *Proceedings of the Cambridge Philological Society*, 40 (1994), 116–43.

For citizenship and mobility, see N. Purcell, 'Romans in the Roman World', in K. Galinsky (ed.) *The Cambridge Companion to the Age of Augustus* (Cambridge, 2005), 85–105, and on bilingualism, the fundamental study of J.N. Adams, *Bilingualism and the Latin Language* (Cambridge, 2003).

Chapter 2. Architects and Roman Society

The Loeb edition, *Vitruvius On Architecture* (Cambridge and London, 1931), translated by F. Granger provides the Latin text with an English translation, but is not without problems of interpretation. The best modern translation and commentary in English is I.D. Rowland and T.N. Howe, *Vitruvius. Ten Books on Architecture* (Cambridge, 1999), while *Vitruvius. On Architecture* (London, 2009), translated by R. Schofield is also useful. The best modern text is that of the Budé series edited by P. Gros (ed.) *Vitruve, De l'architecture*, 10 volumes (Paris, 1969–2009).

On Vitruvius and his background see A. Wallace-Hadrill, *Rome's Cultural Revolution* (Cambridge, 2008), chapter 4 with previous bibliography, and for other modern analyses and interpretations, I.K. McEwen, *Vitruvius. Writing the Body of Architecture* (Cambridge, MA and London, 2003), and the collection papers in S. Cuomo and M. Formisano, 'Vitruvius: Text, Architecture, Reception', *Arethusa*, 49.2 (2016) with extensive bibliography. M.F. Nichols, *Author and Audience in Vitruvius' De architectura* (Cambridge, 2017) gives one new perspective, and D. Harris-McCoy, 'Making and Defending Claims to Authority in Vitruvius' *De architectura*', in J. König and G. Woolf, *Authority and Expertise in Ancient Scientific Culture* (Cambridge, 2017), 107–28 provides another, while T.N. Howe, 'Vitruvian critical eclecticism and Roman innovation', *MAAR*, 50 (2005), 41–65, is good on Vitruvius' design process. Many essays (all in French) on Vitruvius by P. Gros, the leading authority on the subject, are collected in *Vitruve et la tradition des traités d'architecture: fabrica et ratiocinatio: recueil d'études* (Rome, 2006).

On Roman encyclopaedic and technical writing see J. König and G. Woolf, 'Encyclopaedism in the Roman empire', in J. König and G. Woolf (eds.) *Encyclopaedism from Antiquity to the Renaissance* (Cambridge, 2013), 23–63.

For Roman architects in general see J. Anderson Jr, *Roman Architecture and Society* (Baltimore and London, 1997), and for Greek architects, J. J. Coulton, *Greek Architects at Work: Problems of Structure and Design* (London, 1977).

On architects and the design process, see the fundamental work of M. Wilson Jones, *Principles of Roman Architecture* (New Haven and London, 2000). On the concept of *decor* in ancient art and architecture in general, see T. Hölscher, *Visual Power in Ancient Greece and Rome: Between Art and Social Reality* (Oakland, 2018), chapter 6. For the design analysis of the Baths of Caracalla, see J. DeLaine, *The Baths of Caracalla: A Study in the Design, Construction and Economics of Large-Scale Building Projects in Imperial Rome* (Portsmouth, RI, 1997), chapter 2.

On Roman cartography and the creation of maps see O.A.W. Dilke, 'Maps in the Service of the State: Roman Cartography to the End of the Augustan Era', and 'Roman Large-Scale Mapping in the Early Empire', in J.B. Harley and D. Woodward (eds.) *The History of Cartography, Volume One: Cartography in Prehistoric, Ancient, and Medieval Europe and the Mediterranean* (Chicago, 1987), chapters 12 and 13, and for the cultural and political background to Roman mapping see C. Nicolet, *Space, Geography, and Politics in the Early Roman Empire* (Ann Arbor, 1991), translated by H. Leclerc, and S. Rutledge, *Ancient Rome as a Museum: Power, Identity, and the Culture of Collecting* (Oxford, 2012), chapter 6. For the Marble Plan of Rome see the website of the Stanford project (https://formaurbis.stanford.edu/).

For complex curvilinear designs, see D.M. Jacobson, 'Hadrianic architecture and geometry', *AJA*, 90 (1986), 69–85, D.M. Jacobson and M. Wilson Jones, 'An exercise in Hadrianic geometry: the "Annex" of the Temple of Venus at Baiae', *JRA*, 12 (1999), 57–71, and W.L MacDonald and B. Boyle, 'The Small Baths at Hadrian's Villa', *JSAH*, 39 (1980), 5–27.

Chapter 3. Construction—The Civilizing Art

An excellent introduction to Roman construction is L.C. Lancaster and R.B. Ulrich, 'Materials and Techniques', in R.B. and C.K. Quenemoen (eds.) *A Companion to*

Roman Architecture (Chichester, 2014), 157–92. For a more detailed overview with useful explanations of building materials and techniques and excellent illustrations see J.-P. Adam, *Roman Building. Materials and Techniques* (London, 1994), translated by A. Mathews. J. Anderson Jr, *Roman Architecture and Society* (Baltimore and London, 1997) has useful sections on the organization of building in Rome (chapter 2) and manpower and materials (chapter 3).

Much interesting work on building materials and construction, most not in English, can be found in the five volumes of *Arqueología de la Construcción*: S. Camporeale, H. Dessales, and A. Pizzo (eds.) *Arqueología de la Construcción I. Los procesos constructivos en el mundo romano: Italia y provincias occidentales* (Madrid and Merida, 2008); S. Camporeale, H. Dessales, and A. Pizzo (eds.) *Arqueología de la Construcción II. Los procesos constructivos en el mundo romano: Italia y provincias orientales* (Madrid and Merida, 2010); S. Camporeale, H. Dessales, and A. Pizzo (eds.) *Arqueología de la Construcción III. Los procesos constructivos en el mundo romano: la economía de las obras* (Madrid and Merida, 2012); J. Bonetto, S. Camporeale, and A. Pizzo (eds.) *Arqueología de la Construcción IV. Las canteras en el mundo antiguo: sistemas de explotacíon y procesos productivos* (Madrid and Merida, 2014); and J. DeLaine, S. Camporeale, and A. Pizzo (eds.) *Arqueología de la Construcción V. Man-Made Materials, Engineering and Infrastructure* (Madrid and Merida, 2016), and the complementary volume J. DeLaine, S. Camporeale, and A. Pizzo (eds.) *Materials, Transport and Production. Posters Presented at the 5th International Workshop on the Archaeology of Roman Construction, Arqueología de la Arquitectura* (Madrid and Merida, 2016).

On the geology of Rome and its volcanic building materials, see M. Jackson and F. Marra, 'Roman stone masonry. Volcanic foundations of the ancient city', *AJA*, 110 (2006), 403–36, and M.F. Jackson, F. Marra, D. Deocampo, *et al.*, 'Geological observations of excavated sand (*harenae fossiciae*) used as fine aggregate in Roman pozzolanic mortars', *JRA*, 20 (2007), 25–53. A detailed chronological account of the building materials and techniques of the city of Rome, which focuses on the use of construction for dating, was published in the mid-twentieth century and is still useful, although some of the dating has been revised: M.E. Blake, *Ancient Roman Construction in Italy from the Prehistoric Period to Augustus* (Washington, DC, 1947); *Roman Construction in Italy from Tiberius through the Flavians* (Washington, DC, 1959); and D.T. Bishop (ed.) *Roman Construction from Nerva through the Antonines* (Philadelphia, 1973). For revised datings, especially on the introduction of concrete technology, see M. Mogetta, *The Origins of Concrete Construction in Roman Architecture: Technology and Society in Republican Italy* (Cambridge, 2021). There are also several useful essays on mortared rubble technology in A. Ringbom and R.L. Hohlfelder, *Building Roma aeterna. Current Research on Roman Mortar and Concrete* (Helsinki, 2011). For mud-brick and pisé in Roman architecture see B. Russell and E. Fentress, 'Mud brick and *pisé de terre* between Punic and Roman', in J. DeLaine, S. Camporeale, and A. Pizzo (eds.) *Arqueología de la Construcción V. Man-Made Materials, Engineering and Infrastructure* (Madrid and Merida, 2016), 131–43.

On timber construction and roofing, see R.B. Ulrich, *Roman Woodworking* (New Haven and London, 2007). For an unrivalled account of vaulted construction in Rome, including materials and techniques, see L.C. Lancaster, *Concrete Vaulted Construction in Imperial Rome. Innovations on Context* (Cambridge, 2005). On the lintel arch, see J. DeLaine, 'Structural experimentation: the lintel arch, corbel and tie in western Roman architecture', *WA*, 21.3 (1990), 407–24.

On the general economics of mortared rubble construction see J. DeLaine, 'The cost of creation: technology at the service of construction', in E. Lo Cascio (ed.) *Innovazione tecnica e progresso economico nel mondo romano* (Bari, 2007), 237–52, and 'Bricks and mortar: exploring the economics of building techniques at Rome and Ostia', in D.J. Mattingly and J. Salmon (eds.) *Economies beyond Agriculture in the Classical World* (London, 2000), 230–68. For marble and stone in general, see B. Russell, *The Economics of the Roman Stone Trade* (Oxford, 2013), and on marble H. Dodge and B. Ward-Perkins, *Marble in Antiquity* (London, 1992), and J.C. Fant, 'Ideology, gift, trade: a distribution model for the Roman imperial marbles', in W.V. Harris (ed.) *The Inscribed Economy. Production and Distribution in the Roman Empire in the Light of instrumentum domesticum* (Ann Arbor, 1993).

Further on the construction of the Pantheon can be found in G. Martines, 'The conception and construction of drum and dome', and M. Wilson Jones, 'Building with adversity: the Pantheon and problems with its construction', in T.A. Marder and M. Wilson Jones, *The Pantheon from Antiquity to the Present* (Cambridge, 2015), 99–131 and 193–230. For the Baths of Caracalla, see J. DeLaine, *The Baths of Caracalla in Rome: A Study in the Design, Construction, and Economics of Large-Scale Building Projects in Imperial Rome* (Portsmouth, RI, 1997). On the importance and symbolism of scale in construction see M. Mogetta, 'Monumentality, building techniques, and identity construction in Roman Italy: the remaking of Cosa, post-197 BCE', in F. Buccellati, S. Hageneuer, S. van der Heyden, and F. Levenson (eds.) *Size Matters—Understanding Monumentality across Ancient Civilizations* (Bielefeld, 2019), 241–68, and J. DeLaine, 'The Temple of Hadrian at Cyzicus, and Roman attitudes to exceptional construction', *PBSR*, 70 (2002), 205–30.

On Hellenistic tents and pavilions, see E. Calandra, *The Ephemeral and the Eternal. The Pavilion of Ptolemy Philadelphos in the Court of Alexandria* (Athens, 2011), and on wall and vault mosaics see F.B. Sear, *Roman Wall and Vault Mosaics* (Heidelberg, 1977).

There is no single comprehensive account in English of Roman construction in the provinces. For the Greek East, see the short overviews of M. Waelkens, 'The adoption of Roman building techniques in the architecture of Asia Minor', in S. Macready and F.H. Thompson (eds.) *Roman Architecture in the Greek World* (London, 1987), 94–105, and M. Spanu, '*Opus caementicium* in Asia Minor: its introduction and development', in D. Favro, F.K. Yegül, J. Pinto, and G. Métraux (eds.) *Paradigm and Progeny: Roman Imperial Architecture and its Legacy* (Portsmouth, RI, 2015), 27–36. U. Quatember, 'Natural resources and the formation of a regional architectural identity in Roman Asia', in T. Ismaelli and G. Scardozzi (eds.) *Ancient Quarries and Building Sites in Asia Minor* (Bari, 2016), 725–90 emphasizes the importance of local materials, and for Britain see J.R.L. Allen, 'The "Petit Appareil Masonry Style" in Roman Britain. Geology, builders, scale and proportion', *Britannia*, 41 (2010), 149–74. For the export of volcanic materials for harbour building see C. Brandon, R.L. Hohlfelder, M.D. Jackson, and J.P. Oleson, *Building for Eternity: The History and Technology of Roman Concrete Engineering in the Sea* (Oxford, 2014).

For an overview on the use of brick and tile in the provinces, see P. Mills, 'The social life of tile in the Roman world', in J. DeLaine, S. Camporeale and A. Pizzo (eds.) *Arqueología de la Construcción V. Man-Made Materials, Engineering and Infrastructure* (Madrid and Merida, 2016), 88–97, and for specific areas see H. Dodge, 'Brick construction in Roman Greece and Asia Minor', in S. Macready and F.H. Thompson (eds.) *Roman Architecture in the Greek World* (London, 1987), 106–16, and L. Roldán Gómez and M. Bustamante Álvarez, 'The production, dispersion and use of bricks in Hispania', in E. Bukowiecki, R. Volpe, and U. Wulf-Rheidt, *Il laterizio nei cantieri imperiali: Roma e il Mediterraneo, Archeologia dell'Architettura*, 20 (2015), 135–44.

On vaulted construction across the provinces see the comprehensive study by L.C. Lancaster, *Innovative Vaulting in the Architecture of the Roman Empire* (Cambridge, 2015), with previous bibliography, and for an excellent regional study on Roman Greece see P. Vitti, *Building Roman Greece. Innovation in Vaulted Construction in the Peloponnese* (Rome, 2016).

The construction industry and its relation to society has also seen considerable interest in recent years. For the Republican period see S.G. Bernard, *Building Mid-Republican Rome* (Oxford, 2018), and for the imperial period, J. DeLaine, 'The construction industry', in C. Holleran and A. Claridge (eds.) *A Companion to the City of Rome* (Hoboken and Chichester, 2018), 473–90, and S.G. Bernard, 'Workers in the Roman imperial building industry', in K. Verboven and C. Laes, *Work, Labour, and Professions in the Roman World* (Leiden, 2017), 62–86. For Ostia, see J. DeLaine, 'The builders of Roman Ostia: organisation, status and society', in S. Huerta (ed.) *Proceedings of the First International Congress on Construction History* (Madrid, 2003), 723–32. In general on the legal texts as a source for the Roman building industry see S.D. Martin, *The Roman Jurists and the Organization of Private Building in the Late Republic and Early Empire* (Brussels, 1989). On *collegia*, see J.S. Perry, 'Organised societies: *collegia*', in M. Peachin (ed.) *The Oxford Handbook of Social Relations in the Roman World* (Oxford, 2011), 499–513, and K. Verboven, 'Guilds and the organisation of urban populations during the Principate', in K. Verboven and C. Laes (eds) *Work, Labour, and Professions in the Roman World* (Leiden, 2017), 173–202.

For the supply of building materials for the city of Rome, see the overview by J. DeLaine, 'The supply of building materials to the city of Rome', in N. Christie (ed.) *Settlement and Economy in Italy 1500 BC to AD 1500, Papers of the Fifth Conference of Italian Archaeology* (Oxford, 1995), 555–62. The classic study of the organization of brick production and supply to Rome is T. Helen, *Organization of Roman Brick Production in the First and Second Centuries AD: An Interpretation of Roman Brick Stamps* (Helsinki, 1975), and see also S. Graham, *Ex Figlinis: The Network Dynamics of the Tiber Valley Brick Industry in the Hinterland of Rome* (Oxford, 2006), and for a summary J. DeLaine, 'The production, supply and distribution of brick', in E. Bukowiecki, R. Volpe, and U. Wulf-Rheidt, *Il laterizio nei cantieri imperiali: Roma e il Mediterraneo, Archeologia dell'Architettura*, 20 (2015), 226–30.

Chapter 4. Building for the Gods

Roman religion is a complex subject, and there is a large bibliography. For a good introduction, see V.M. Warrior, *Roman Religion* (Cambridge, 2006), and for a more challenging analysis, with extensive bibliography, see J. Rüpke and D.M.B. Richardson, *Pantheon: A New History of Roman Religion* (Princeton, 2018).

On the evolution of religious architecture in the Archaic period in Rome and central Italy, see C.R. Potts, *Religious Architecture in Latium and Etruria c. 900–500 BC* (Oxford, 2015), part 1, and J.N. Hopkins, *The Genesis of Roman Architecture* (New Haven and London, 2016), especially chapters 2–3.

On the architecture of temples in Rome in general see J.W. Stamper, *The Architecture of Roman Temples. The Republic to the Middle Empire* (Cambridge, 2005), especially for the Republic chapters 4–5, although his views on the Capitoline temple need to be read with J.N. Hopkins, *The Genesis of Roman Architecture* (New Haven and London, 2016). For Republican temple architecture in its political and historical context, see P.J.E. Davies, *Architecture and Politics in Republican Rome* (Cambridge, 2017), while A. Ziolkowski, *The Temples of Mid-Republican Rome and Their Historical and Topographical Context* (Rome, 1992), and E.M. Orlin, *Temples, Religion and Politics in the Roman Republic* (Leiden, 1997) focus more on the historical context.

On Greek stoas in general, see J.J. Coulton, *The Architectural Development of the Greek Stoa* (Oxford, 1976), and on Hellenistic temples and stoas, often in relation to Roman versions, see F.E. Winter, *Studies in Hellenistic Architecture* (Toronto, 2006), chapters 1 and 3, and chapter 11 on the orders. For the Hellenistic predecessors to the central Italian sanctuaries, see I. Nielsen, *Cultic Theatres and Ritual Drama: A Study in Regional Development and Religious Interchange between East and West in Antiquity* (Aarhus, 2002). On the importance of the *quadriporticus*/peristyle in different types of Hellenistic architecture see B. Emme, 'The Emergence and Significance of the Palaestra Type in Greek Architecture', in U. Mania and M. Trümper (eds.) *Development of Gymnasia and Graeco-Roman Cityscapes* (Berlin, 2018), 143–59.

For Augustan temples in general see the still invaluable study by P. Gros, *Aurea Templa: Recherches sur l'architecture religieuse de Rome à l'époque d'Auguste* (Rome, 1976). For the Temple of Castor, see S. Sande and J. Zahle (eds.) *The Temple of Castor and Pollux III: The Augustan Temple* (Rome, 2008). On the development and use of the Roman Corinthian order, see M. Wilson Jones, *Principles of Roman Architecture* (New Haven and London, 2000). For a list of the main marbles used in Rome see H. Dodge and B. Ward-Perkins, *Marble in Antiquity* (London, 1992), appendix 1. Examples of ancient marbles housed in the University Museum, Oxford, can be found at http://www.oum.ox.ac.uk/corsi/stones. On geography as power, see C. Nicolet, *Space, Geography, and Politics in the Early Roman Empire* (Ann Arbor, 1991), translated by H. Leclerc.

For the Pantheon see T.A. Marder and M. Wilson Jones, *The Pantheon. From Antiquity to the Present* (Cambridge, 2015), and the essential study of K. de Fine Licht, *The Rotunda in Rome. A Study of Hadrian's Pantheon* (Copenhagen, 1968).

There is no comprehensive study in English of Roman temples and sanctuaries in the provinces to compare with P. Schollmeyer, *Römische Tempel: Kult und Architektur im Imperium Romanum* (Munich, 2008). Important regional studies include S.R.F. Price, *Rituals and Power: The Roman Imperial Cult in Asia Minor* (Cambridge, 1984); A. Segal, *Temples and Sanctuaries in the Roman East: Religious Architecture in Syria, Iudaea/Palaestina and Provincia Arabia*

(Oxford, 2013), and for the context P. Richardson, *City and Sanctuary: Religion and Architecture in the Roman Near East* (London, 2002) and R. Raja, *Contextualizing the Sacred in the Hellenistic and Roman Near East: Religious Identities in Local, Regional, and Imperial Settings* (Turnhout, 2017); M. Minas-Nerpel, 'Egyptian Temples', in C. Riggs (ed.) *The Oxford Handbook of Roman Egypt* (Oxford, 2012), 362–82, and D. M. Bailey, 'Classical architecture in Roman Egypt', in M. Henig (ed.) *Architecture and Architectural Sculpture in the Roman Empire* (Oxford, 1990), 121–37; W.E. Mierse, *Temples and Towns in Roman Iberia. The Social and Architectural Dynamics of Sanctuary Designs from the Third Century B.C. to the Third Century A.D.* (Berkeley and Los Angeles, 1999), and T. Derks, *Gods, Temples and Ritual Practices. The Transformation of Religious Ideas and Values in Roman Gaul* (Amsterdam, 1998); and M.J.T. Lewis, *Temples in Roman Britain* (Cambridge, 1966). For Baalbek, see S. Paturel, *Baalbek-Heliopolis, the Bekaa, and Berytus from 100 BCE to 400 CE: A Landscape Transformed* (Leiden, 2019), with earlier bibliography.

Chapter 5. The Architecture of Civic Life

For an overview of the formation of Roman cities, especially in the western empire, see the account in R. Laurence, S.E. Cleary, and G. Sears, *The City in the Roman West, c. 250 BC–c. AD 250* (Cambridge, 2011). For the eastern empire see G. Woolf, 'The Roman urbanization of the East', in S.E. Alcock (ed.) *The Early Roman Empire in the East* (Oxford, 1997), 1–14, and for more detailed studies R. Willet, *The Geography of Urbanism in Roman Asia Minor* (Sheffield, 2019), and D. Parrish (ed.) *Urbanism in Western Asia Minor* (Portsmouth, RI, 2001) on Asia Minor.

For broad accounts of urban civic architecture see the relevant sections of F.K. Yegül and D.G. Favro. *Roman Architecture and Urbanism: From the Origins to Late Antiquity* (Cambridge, 2019), R.B. Ulrich and C.K. Quenemoen (eds.) *A Companion to Roman Architecture* (Chichester, 2014), P. Gros, *L'architecture romaine 1: Les monuments publics* (Paris, 1997), and J.-B. Ward-Perkins, *Roman Imperial Architecture* (Harmondsworth, 1981).

For individual monuments in the city of Rome, see A. Claridge, *Rome: An Oxford Archaeological Guide*, 2nd edition (Oxford, 2010), and for details E.M. Steinby (ed.) *Lexicon Topigraphicum Urbis Romae* (Rome,

2000) (mostly in Italian), with more synthetic overviews in C. Holleran and A. Claridge (eds.) *A Companion to the City of Rome* (Hoboken and Chichester, 2018). H. von Hesberg and P. Zanker (eds.) *Storia dell'architettura italiana: Architettura romana: I grandi monumenti di Roma* (Milan, 2009) has useful essays with excellent illustrations.

For the transformation of Rome's monumental landscape in different periods see I. Edlund-Berry, 'Early Rome and the making of "Roman" identity through architecture and city planning', in J.D. Evans (ed.) *A Companion to the Archaeology of the Roman Republic* (Oxford, 2013), 406–25; P.J.E. Davies, *Architecture and Politics in Republican Rome* (Cambridge, 2017); L. Haselberger, '*Urbem adornare*': Rome's Urban Metamorphosis under Augustus* (Portsmouth, RI, 2007); H.-J. Beste and H. von Hesberg, 'Buildings of an emperor—how Nero transformed Rome', in E. Buckley and M. Dinter (eds.) *A Companion to the Neronian Age* (Chichester, 2013), 314–31; A. Gallia, 'Remaking Rome', in A. Zissos (ed.) *A Companion to the Flavian Age of Imperial Rome* (Chichester, 2016), 148–65, and the richly illustrated catalogue edited by F. Coarelli, *Divus Vespasianus: il bimillenario dei Flavi* (Rome, 2009); S.S. Lusnia, *Creating Severan Rome: The Architecture and Self-image of L. Septimius Severus (A.D. 193–211)* (Brussels, 2014).

On the imperial fora of Rome in the light of the most recent excavations, see the well-illustrated account by R. Meneghini and R. Santangeli Valenzani (eds.) *I Fori Imperiali. Gli scavi del Comune di Roma (1991–2007)* (Rome, 2007). There is no comprehensive account of Roman fora/agoras in the provinces, but for the West J.B. Ward-Perkins, 'From Republic to Empire: reflections on the early provincial architecture of the Roman West', *JRS*, 60 (1970), 1–19 is still fundamental. For the Roman *agora* in the East see C.P. Dickenson, *On the Agora: The Evolution of a Public Space in Hellenistic and Roman Greece (c. 323 BC–267 AD)* (Leiden, 2017). For the specific case of Lepcis Magna, see J.B. Ward-Perkins, *The Severan Buildings of Lepcis Magna* (London, 1993).

There are good surveys covering Rome and the empire for all the types of performance spaces. For the circus, see J. Humphrey, *Roman Circuses. Arenas for Chariot Racing* (London, 1986), and K.M. Coleman, 'Spectacles', in A. Barchiesi, and W. Scheidel,

The Oxford Handbook of Roman Studies (Oxford, 2010), 651–70.

For the theatre, see F. Sear, *Roman Theatres. An Architectural Study* (Oxford, 2006) and for the performative background, R.C. Beacham, *The Roman Theatre and Its Audience* (Cambridge, MA, 1991). For the amphitheatre, see the fundamental study of J.-C. Golvin, *L'amphithéâtre romain. Essai sur la théorisation de sa forme et de ses fonctions* (Paris, 1988), and for its origins see K. Welch, *The Roman Amphitheatre from Its Origins to the Colosseum* (Cambridge, 2007). On the architecture of amphitheatres see M. Wilson Jones, 'Designing amphitheatres', *RM*, 100 (1993), 391–442.

On baths in Rome and the empire, see F.K. Yegül, *Baths and Bathing in Classical Antiquity* (Cambridge, MA and London, 1992), and I. Nielsen, *Thermae et Balnea* (Aarhus, 1992), and for the cultural background G. Fagan, *Bathing in Public in the Roman World* (Ann Arbor, 1999). For baths in the Hellenistic world and the early baths in Italy see S.K. Lucore and M. Trümper, *Greek Baths and Bathing Culture: New Discoveries and Approaches* (Leuven, 2013). On the imperial baths in Rome, see J. DeLaine, 'The imperial thermae', in A. Claridge and C. Holleran (eds.) *A Companion to the City of Rome* (Hoboken and Chichester, 2018), 325–42 for an overview, and on the social context A. Hrychuk Kontokosta, 'Building the Thermae Agrippae: Private Life, Public Space, and the Politics of Bathing in Early Imperial Rome', *AJA*, 123.1 (2019), 45–77, and N. Zajak, 'The thermae: a policy of public health or personal legitimation?', in J. DeLaine and D.E. Johnston (eds.) *Roman Baths and Bathing, Vol. 1, Bathing and Society* (Portsmouth, RI, 1999), 99–105.

On Roman civic buildings as essential to the urban image, see P. Zanker, 'The city as symbol: Rome and the creation of an urban image', in E. Fentress (ed.) *Romanization and the City: Creation, Transformations and Failures* (Portsmouth, RI, 2000), 25–41, and as a source of rivalry and competition, see A. Zuiderhoek, *The Politics of Munificence in the Roman Empire: Citizens, Elites and Benefactors in Asia Minor* (Cambridge, 2009), especially chapter 5, and R. Raja, *Urban Development and Regional Identity in the Eastern Roman Provinces, 50 BC–AD 250: Aphrodisias, Ephesos, Athens, Gerasa* (Copenhagen, 2012); for a case study T. Bekker-Nielsen, *Urban Life and Local Politics in Roman Bithynia: The Small World of Dion Chrysostomos* (Aarhus, 2008).

Chapter 6. Housing the Individual

For broad introduction to domestic architecture see F.K. Yegül and D.G. Favro. *Roman Architecture and Urbanism: From the Origins to Late Antiquity* (Cambridge, 2019), chapter 5, and S.P. Ellis, *Roman Housing* (London, 2000). While scholarship has since moved on, A.G. McKay, *Houses, Villas and Palaces in the Roman World* (London, 1977) still forms a useful introduction. The most comprehensive compendium is the monograph by P. Gros, *L'architecture romaine 2: Maisons, palais, villes et tombeaux* (Paris, 2001), while J.-P. Adam and H. Hôte, *La maison romaine* (Arles, 2012) provides a wealth of illustrations. For houses in Roman Italy see also J.R. Clarke, *The Houses of Roman Italy, 100 B.C.–A.D. 250* (Berkeley, 1991), chapter 1. On domestic gardens, see the relevant chapters of W.F. Jashemski, K.L. Gleason, K.J. Hartswick, and A.-A. Malek (eds.) *Gardens of the Roman Empire* (Cambridge, 2018).

Much has been written recently about Roman housing in its social context, based predominantly on the rich data from Pompeii and Herculaneum. The fundamental work is A. Wallace-Hadrill, *Houses and Society in Pompeii and Herculaneum* (Princeton, 1994), with S. Hales, *The Roman House and Social Identity* (Cambridge, 2003) providing a wider perspective including the provinces. For the interpretation of space beyond the information provided by the architecture see P. Allison, *Pompeian Households: An Analysis of Material Culture* (Los Angeles, 2004), and L.C. Nevett, *Domestic Space in Classical Antiquity* (Cambridge, 2010), introduction and chapters 4 and 5. On the temporal distribution of household activities see R. Laurence, *Roman Pompeii: Space and Society*, 2nd edition (London, 2007), chapter 9. On the nature of households see K.J. Holkeskamp, 'Under Roman roofs: family, house, and household', in H.I. Flower (ed.) *The Cambridge Companion to the Roman Republic* (Cambridge, 2014), 113–38. For dining, see K.M. Dunbabin, *The Roman Banquet. Images of Conviviality* (Cambridge, 2003), chapters 1–2.

On the atrium house in general see the works above and E. Dwyer, 'The Pompeian atrium house in theory and practice' in E.K. Gazda and A.E. Haeckl (eds.) *Roman*

Art in the Private Sphere: New Perspectives on the Architecture and Decor of the Domus, Villa, and Insula (Ann Arbor, 2010), 25–48. For the houses of Pompeii and Herculaneum in particular see the introductory essays by P.M. Allison, 'The "atrium-house" type', and A. Wallace-Hadrill, 'The development of the Campanian house', in J.J. Dobbins and P.W. Foss (eds.) *The World of Pompeii* (London, 2008), 269–78 and 279–91. There are important essays in R. Laurence and A. Wallace-Hadrill (eds.) *Domestic Space in the Roman World: Pompeii and Beyond* (Portsmouth, RI, 1997). On their relation to villa architecture see part two of P. Zanker and D. Schneider, *Pompeii: Public and Private Life* (Cambridge and London, 1998).

For domestic architecture in northern Italy and the western empire see M. George, *The Roman Domestic Architecture of Northern Italy* (Oxford, 1997), K.E. Meyer, 'Axial peristyle houses in the western empire', *JRA*, 12 (1999), 101–21, J.-P. Guilhembet, M. Lloris, et al., *La maison urbaine d'époque romaine en Gaule narbonnaise et dans les provinces voisines* (Avignon, 1996), and D. Perring, *The Roman House in Britain* (London, 2002). For North Africa see Y. Thébert, 'Private life and domestic architecture in Roman North Africa', in P. Veyne (ed.) *A History of Private Life from Pagan Rome to Byzantium* (Cambridge and London, 1987), 313–409, and M. Carucci, *The Romano-African domus. Studies in Space, Decoration, and Function* (Oxford, 2007). For the eastern empire, see M. Papaioannou, 'The Roman domus in the world', in R. Westgate, N.R.E Fisher, and J. Whitley (eds.) *Building Communities. House, Settlement and Society in the Aegean and Beyond* (London, 2007), 351–61; H. Thür, 'Art and architecture in Terrace House 2 in Ephesus. An example of domestic architecture in the Roman Imperial Period', in D.L. Balch and A. Weissenrieder (eds.) *Contested Spaces: Houses and Temples in Roman Antiquity and the New Testament* (Tübingen, 2012), 237–59; J.A. Baird, *The Inner Lives of Ancient Houses: An Archaeology of Dura-Europos* (Oxford, 2014).

On rental accommodation, see B.W. Frier, *Landlords and Tenants in Imperial Rome* (Princeton, 1980), and his 'The rental market in early imperial Rome', *JRS*, 67 (1977), 27–37, and F. Pirson, 'Rented accommodation at Pompeii: the evidence of the Insula Arriana Polliana V.i.6', in R. Laurence and A. Wallace-Hadrill (eds.) *Domestic Space in the Roman World: Pompeii and Beyond* (Portsmouth, RI, 1997), 165–81. For Ostia see J.E. Packer, *The Insulae of Imperial Ostia* (Rome, 1971), and the overview in J. DeLaine, 'Housing Roman Ostia', in D.L. Balch and A. Weissenrieder (eds.) *Contested Spaces. Houses and Temples in Roman Antiquity and the New Testament* (Tübingen, 2012), 332–44.

For an introduction to Roman villas see M. Zarmakoupi, 'Private Villas: Italy and the Provinces', in R.B. Ulrich and C.K. Quenemoen (eds.) *A Companion to Roman Architecture* (Oxford, 2014), 363–80, and for the western empire J. Percival, *The Roman Villa* (London, 1976). For a more detailed survey of villas in the Mediterranean see the collected papers in A. Marzano and G.P.R. Métraux (eds.) *The Roman Villa in the Mediterranean Basin. Late Republic to Late Antiquity* (New York, 2018).

For *villae urbanae* see M. Zarmakoupi, *Designing for Luxury on the Bay of Naples: Villas and Landscapes (c.100 BCE–79 CE)* (Oxford, 2014), with E. Gazda and J.R. Clarke (eds.) *Leisure and Luxury in the Age of Nero: The Villas of Oplontis near Pompeii* (Ann Arbor, 2016), while for the social background, see the still valuable study by J.H. D'Arms, *Romans on the Bay of Naples. A Social and Cultural Study of the Villas and Their Owners from 150 B.C. to A.D. 400* (Cambridge, MA, 1970), and A. Wallace-Hadrill, 'The villa as cultural symbol', in A. Frazer (ed.) *The Roman Villa: Villa Urbana* (Philadelphia, 1998), 43–53.

On the *horti* of Rome, see A. Wallace-Hadrill, 'Horti and Hellenization', in M. Cima and E. la Rocca, *Horti Romani* (Rome, 1998), 1–12.

On the productive element of luxury villas see A. Marzano, *Roman Villas in Central Italy: A Social and Economic History* (Leiden, 2007), and N. Purcell, 'The Roman *villa* and the landscape of production', in T.J. Cornell and K. Lomas (eds.) *Urban Society in Roman Italy* (London, 1995), 151–79. On Villa Magna, see E. Fentress, C. Goodson, and M. Maiuro, *Villa Magna: An Imperial Estate and Its Legacies: Excavations 2006–10* (London, 2016).

On villa cemeteries, see J. Bodel, 'Monumental villas and villa monuments', *JRA*, 10 (1997), 5–35. For Pliny's villas see P. de la Ruffinière du Prey, *Villas of Pliny from Antiquity to Posterity* (Chicago, 1994), and on villa gardens in general see K.J. Hartswick, 'The Roman villa garden', and E. Macaulay-Lewis, 'The archaeology of gardens in the Roman villa', in W.F. Jashemski, K.L. Gleason, K.J. Hartswick, and A.-A. Malek (eds.)

Gardens of the Roman Empire (Cambridge, 2018), 72–86 and 87–120.

For villas in the western empire see J.T. Smith, *Roman Villas. A Study in Social Structure* (London, 1997), and N. Roymans and T. Derks, *Villa Landscapes in the Roman North: Economy, Culture and Lifestyles* (Amsterdam, 2012).

For the house of Augustus see T.P. Wiseman, *The House of Augustus: A Historical Detective Story* (Princeton, 2019), and for an up-to-date overview of Nero's Golden House the overview by E. Segala and I. Sciortino, *Domus Aurea* (Milan, 1999), translated by C. Swift. For the Esquiline Wing, see D. Hemsoll, 'The architecture of Nero's Golden House', in M. Henig (ed.) *Architecture and Architectural Sculpture in the Roman Empire* (Oxford, 1990), 10–38. For the context of these see D. Spencer, *Roman Landscape: Culture and Identity* (Cambridge, 2010), chapter 3.

For the Flavian palace, see P. Zanker, 'Domitian's palace on the Palatine and the imperial image', in A.K. Bowman, H.M. Cotton, M. Goodman, and S. Price (eds.) *Representations of Empire: Rome and the Mediterranean World* (London, 2002), 105–30, and for the revolutionary new chronology U. Wulf-Rheidt, 'The palace of the Roman emperors on the Palatine in Rome', in M. Featherstone *et al.* (eds.) *The Emperor's House. Palaces from Augustus to Absolutism* (Berlin, 2015), 3–18.

For Hadrian's Villa see W.L. MacDonald and J.A. Pinto, *Hadrian's Villa and Its legacy* (New Haven and London, 1995). On the villa of Diocletian at Split, see J.J. Wilkes, *Diocletian's Palace, Split: Residence of a Retired Roman Emperor* (Sheffield, 1993).

On Roman ideas about funerary practices and the commemoration of the dead, see M. Carroll, *Spirits of the Dead: Roman Funerary Commemoration in Western Europe* (Oxford, 2006), especially chapter 2.

For funerary architecture, J. Toynbee, *Death and Burial in the Roman World* (London, 1971) is still the most detailed study available in English, but is out-of-date in places. For the most comprehensive study see H. von Hesberg, *Römische Grabbauten* (Darmstadt, 1992) (also available in Italian translation as *Monumenta. I sepolcri romani e la loro architettura* (Milan, 1994)), and P. Gros, *L'architecture romaine 2: Maisons, palais, villes et tombeaux* (Paris, 2001) also gives a very useful coverage. On the commemorative aspects of tombs, see

E.V. Thomas, *Monumentality and the Roman Empire: Architecture in the Antonine Age* (Oxford, 2007), chapter 10.

For the tombs of the emperors in Rome, see P.J.E. Davies, *Death and the Emperor: Roman Imperial Funerary Monuments from Augustus to Marcus Aurelius* (Austin, 2004), and for Rome in general see B. Borg, 'Roman cemeteries and tombs', in C. Holleran and A. Claridge (eds.) *A Companion to the City of Rome* (Hoboken and Chichester, 2018), 403–24, and for more detail, her *Roman Tombs and the Art of Commemoration: Contextual Approaches to Funerary Customs in the Second Century CE* (Cambridge, 2019), especially chapters 1 and 2.

On the dead as deities, see C.W. King, 'The Roman manes: the dead as gods', in M.-C. Poo (ed.) *Rethinking Ghosts in World Religions* (Leiden, 2009), 95–114, and on the social structure see V. Hope, 'A roof over the dead: communal tombs and family structure', in R. Laurence and A. Wallace-Hadrill (eds.) *Domestic Space in the Roman World: Pompeii and Beyond* (Portsmouth, RI, 1997), especially 69–88 on Isola Sacra.

Chapter 7. The Language of Ornament

For the organization, variety, and forms of urban embellishments, see the important study by W.L. MacDonald, *The Architecture of the Roman Empire, II: An Urban Appraisal* (New Haven and London, 1986), and on the symbolic significance of architectural forms see E.V. Thomas, *Monumentality and the Roman Empire: Architecture in the Antonine Age* (Oxford, 2007), especially chapter 3. For a regional study see A. Segal, *From Function to Monument: Urban Landscapes of Roman Palestine, Syria and Provincia Arabia* (Oxford, 1997), especially for gate, arches, and nymphaea, and for a case study on the motives of urban embellishment, see G. Ryan, 'Building order: unified cityscapes and elite collaboration in Roman Asia Minor', *Classical Antiquity*, 37 (2018), 151–85.

On free-standing commemorative arches and their origins in the Roman triumph see M.L. Popkin, *The Architecture of the Roman Triumph* (Cambridge, 2016), and on the triumph itself see the Roman triumph see M. Beard, *The Roman Triumph* (Cambridge, 2007).

On colonnaded streets and street porticoes see J. Frakes, *Framing Public Life: The Portico in Roman Gaul* (Vienna, 2009), and R. Burns, *Origins of the Colonnaded Streets in the Cities of the Roman East* (Oxford, 2017).

For the context of the processional way at Ephesus see G.M. Rogers, *The Sacred Identity of Ephesos: Foundation Myths of a Roman City* (London, 1991), and P. Scherrer, 'The historical topography of Ephesos', in D. Parrish (ed.) *Urbanism in Western Asia Minor* (Portsmouth, RI, 2001), 57–87. For the monuments see H. Thür, 'The Processional Way in Ephesos as a place of cult and burial', in H. Koester (ed.) *Ephesos, Metropolis of Asia: An Interdisciplinary Approach to Its Archaeology, Religion and Culture* (Cambridge, MA, 1995), 157–99. For this example in its broader architectural context see also E. Thomas, 'On the sublime', in J. Elsner and M. Meyer, *Art and Rhetoric in Roman Culture* (Cambridge, 2014), 37–88.

On monumental fountains see B. Longfellow, *Roman Imperialism and Civic Patronage: Form, Meaning, and Ideology in Monumental Fountain Complexes* (Cambridge, 2011), and for decorative aspects see J. Richard, 'In the elites' toolkit. Decoding the initiative and reference system behind the investment in the architecture and decoration of Roman nymphaea', *Facta*, 5 (2011), 65–100. On the monumental aqueduct arches of the Porta Maggiore in Rome see R. Coates-Stephens, *Porta Maggiore: Monument and Landscape* (Rome, 2004).

On the impact of the *scaenae frons* on other architecture, see G. Aristodemou, 'Theatre façades and façade nymphaea. The link between', *BCH*, 135.1 (2011), 163–97.

For the identification and definition of a Roman 'baroque', see the classic study by M. Lyttelton, *Baroque Architecture in Classical Antiquity* (London, 1974), with the revised dating by J. McKenzie, *The Architecture of Petra* (Oxford, 1990), and J. McKenzie, *The Architecture of Alexandria and Egypt 300 BC and AD 700* (New Haven and London, 2007), chapter 5.

Index

Aurelian, Roman emperor 11
axiality 36–7, 91–2, 131, 140, 145–6, 155
    in houses 162, 167*f*, 171

Baalbek, temples 110, 111–2
Baelo Claudia, forum 146
Baia (Baiae), 'Temple of Mercury' 57
'baroque' style 209
basilicas 12, 14, 29, 52, 54, 61 *see also* Rome,
    public buildings: Basilica Aemilia/
    Fulvia, Basilica Julia/Sempronia,
    Basilica Nova, Basilica Porcia,
    Basilica Ulpia
    design 33, 121
    functions 122
    origins and development 121–2
    in provinces 143–8
    stoa-basilica type 143–4, 148
Bath (Aquae Sulis), baths 71
baths 4, 12*f*, 42 *see also* imperial thermae,
    Pompeii
    construction 69, 70, 71, 129
    cost of 156–7
    elements and layout 41, 56–7, 128, 154–5
    Greek 128–30
    in provinces 153–7
    origins and development 129–30
bilingualism 15–6, 21, 36, 143, 204
benefactors 1, 13, 23, 90, 149, 153–4, 214, 215
    imperial 94, 99, 100, 118–9, 132–41,
        147–8, 150
    individuals 105–6, 118, 135, 148, 151,
        156–7, 207, 208
    local elites 15–6, 93, 104–5, 144, 149, 157,
        205, 207–8
    Senate/Roman magistrates 85, 89, 90,
        117–8, 123–4, 130–2, 208
    town councils/local magistrates 104–5,
        127*f*, 153–4, 156–7
Benevento (Beneventum), Arch of
    Trajan 204
Berà, boundary arch 202
Bologna (Bononia), theatre 128
Brescia (Brixia), temples 109
brick, uses of 50, 69
    in vaulting 70–1
    production of 60, 77–8
    types of facing 50–51
brickstamps 60, 77–8
Britain/Britannia 14, 19, 20, 31, 71, 72
    see also Hadrian's Wall, Silchester,
    South Shields, Wroxeter
building contracts 10, 55, 73
building industry 72–80
    fabri tignuarii 74–5, 76, 79
    workforce 32, 54–5, 78–80, 100, 105, 148

building materials, at Rome 45, 46–51,
    77–8, *see also* brick, mortar, stone
    in provinces 68–9, 142
    timber 46, 78
    transport 48–9
Bulla Regia 70, 71*f*

Caesarea Maritima 69, 104
Caligula, Roman emperor 18
Campania 31, 69, 129
Capitoline Temple *see* Temple of Jupiter
    Optimus Maximus Capitolinus,
    Juno and Minerva
Caracalla, Roman emperor 11, 78
Carthage 3, 9, 13, 14, 68, 77, 88, 117
    public buildings 149, 155
Cartagena (Carthago Nova), city
    walls 200
Cato the Elder 122, 128
cemeteries 192, 195–6
Cicero, Marcus Tullius 27–8, 38–9, 41, 68,
    131, 178, 189
    house in Rome 159–60
    on *decor* 35
Circus Maximus 10, 186–7
    as model for provinces 149
    in visual media 139, 149
    origins and development 123, 132, 138–9
circuses 59–60, 142–3, 149 *see also* Circus
    Maximus
cities, Hellenistic 19, 28–9
    nature of 13–16, 117
citizenship, Roman 3, 10, 11, 13, 14–15,
    18, 31
city gates 2, 52, 200–2
city walls 9, 24, 68, 140, 191
    and ritual boundaries 199–200, 201–2
    as symbols of a city 199–201
    in visual media 199
civic processions 206–8
Claudiopolis, baths 30
Claudius, Roman emperor 209*f*
Conimbriga (Coimbra), forum
    complexes 146
Coins, architecture on 115, 148, 200
colonies (*colonia/e*) 12, 15, 18, 39, 103, 104,
    127, 128, 141–3
Colosseum *see* Flavian Amphitheatre
colour in architecture 51, 96, 211
columnar displays 149–50, 155, 211 see also
    scaenae frons
columns *see* columnar displays, orders,
    architectural; streets
columns, as building type 137, 203
commemorative monuments 199, 206–8,
    207*f*, 212–3